RESCUED

Saving the Lost Horses

-A Dimity Horse Mystery-

LEANNE OWENS

ISBN-13: 979-85-18748-99-6

DEDICATION

This book is dedicated to the thousands of great horse people I've been lucky enough to know over the decades: friends, family, competitors, judges, trainers, instructors, Board members, breeders, those who compete nationally and internationally, and those who never leave their paddock. Thanks for the friendship, the laughter, the inspiration, and more laughter. There's a little bit of each of you in Lane and his friends.

CONTENTS

PROLOGUE

We toss the term 'heart horse' around, but what does it mean? You might know or own a hundred horses, but those few heart-horses that cross your path are the ones that add sunshine and color to your life. You love them like family, and when they leave, they take a piece of your heart with them. That is a small price to pay for knowing them because while they were with you, they fed your heart until it grew big enough to give pieces away. If you have known one heart-horse, you are luckier than most. If you have known more than one, then you have more wealth than gold. Your memories of them are treasures that will remain with you until your last breath.

'The Horses I Have Known' by Lane Dimity. Page 3

Windsor, New South Wales

Bands of panic tightened around Mel's chest as she stared at the photo. Emotional acid dripped into her mind, and she couldn't think, couldn't breathe. The pain of grief caused her hands to shake, and the photo dropped to the floor. It landed on the polished wood between her feet, image side up. The faces she loved stared up at her.

She scratched at her chest, trying to make her lungs work. Gasping, she doubled over, desperate to cry, to scream, to breathe.

'It's OK, Mel, it's OK.' A soothing voice came from above, and the bed moved as Carla sat next to her cousin.

Knowing how Mel felt about physical contact, Carla fought the instinct to rub her back and, instead, reached down and picked up the photo. 'They're still alive, Mel, I know they are. You'll find them. He was a rotten mongrel to do what he did, but we always knew he was like that. What's important is that you are alive, and that means you can go on looking for them.'

Carla's soft voice neutralized the acid in her mind and loosened the bands that squeezed her lungs. She gulped in air, sobbed, and breathed again.

'He wanted to hurt you,' continued Carla, knowing that talking was helping to ease the panic attack, 'that's what narcissists do when they lose control of their victim. He's been controlling everything you did for so many years, and we were terrified he'd kill you. But you got away. Leaving the horses behind was hard, but at least you are alive. Life is what matters. You're alive, and you can make sure he stops hurting you. You have to take away his power to hurt you. That is the worst thing that can ever happen to him. Apart from me castrating him with a blunt knife, of course. That might be worse.'

A single cough of laughter came from Mel, and she sat up, wiping her eyes with the back of her hand. Her voice wasn't ready to work, but at least she could make eye contact to show her appreciation. It wasn't the first time since she'd escaped from Connor that Carla helped her through a panic attack.

Carla handed her some tissues. 'And don't think I wouldn't take that blunt knife to him. There'd be six horsewomen there to hold him down and another dozen to provide alibis for us.'

'I don't know what I'd do without you,' sniffed Mel, finding her voice at last.

'You'd do what we all do – get up the morning, survive the day, and go to bed at night. You were the one who found the courage to walk away from Connor - you can do anything. You'll find the horses.'

Mel took the photo and sighed at the two beautiful faces that looked at her. The palomino geldings Dibby and Rev were the loves of her life. They kept her alive when death seemed the only escape from Connor. She had to keep living to look after them. He used them to control her. If she left, he promised to shoot them. If she took them with her, he'd find them and make sure they died slowly. If she wanted to go and visit her family, he'd let them starve while she was away. If she wanted to complain about him, then it meant she didn't care if one of the horses got an ax through his leg.

She stopped going to the riding club. She stopped seeing friends. She stopped visiting family. Bit by bit, he controlled every part of her life - she was something he owned. His words eroded her even though she looked whole. His fists hit her, but makeup covered the bruises. The only beauty that remained in her life lay in the two palominos. Burying her face into their manes and breathing in the essence of horse kept her sane and kept her alive.

Then, on a Sunday morning when the wind blew down from the Snowy Mountains, she sat in their car in the main street of Tumut, thinking about driving into a tree on her way home. Down the road, a magazine blew into pieces, and the pages fluttered past. A page with an advertisement for jeans landed on her windscreen. A bare-chested man rode a palomino horse down the side of a hill in the Arizona desert. His face glowed with life and love. Lane Dimity: the silent horseman who changed the world. She read the words under his image: *Life is your greatest gift. Don't throw it away.*

The wind caught the page, and it joined the others in a tumbled dance along the bitumen. Mel started the car, and instead of heading home, she drove to Windsor outside Sydney, where Carla lived.

With the help and support of her family and friends, she broke free of Connor and took back possession of her life. He didn't shoot her horses as he'd always threatened - he gave them to the horse rescue, Rescuing Equines Everywhere.

'I don't know what to do,' Mel placed her treasured photo on the bed next to her and rubbed her temples. 'He gave them to REE, but they say he didn't. We know they were there as we've spoken to the truck driver who took them there. Why can't they find them?'

Carla thought the situation with the horse charity was odd. 'Why don't you send everything to Lane Dimity and see if he can help? I saw on Instagram that he's coming home to Australia for a few weeks.'

'He's too busy to worry about two missing horses.'

'I think Lane cares about every horse. It can't hurt to try.'

CHAPTER ONE

I stopped speaking on my eighth birthday when my voice wasn't enough to save everything and everyone I loved on that day. It's not that I'm physically unable to speak – there's no damage to my vocal cords – it's more like the connection between my brain thinking the words and commanding my voice to say them stopped working that day. On rare occasions, the link flickers into life, and some words come out, but I haven't consciously made myself speak. To me, at those times, it feels more like the words magically appeared without explanation. The selective mutism doesn't worry me because I choose to be thankful for all that is good in my life, and I find the strengths in my silence. I'm surrounded by friends who can speak for me if someone needs to hear words, I have text-to-speech devices, I'm fast on a keyboard, and I've learned to appreciate the beauty and power of silence. It's also helped me understand the language that horses and other animals use since they don't have speech. It's not a weakness to me.

Lane Dimity's response to the questions, 'Why don't you speak? Does it worry you?' The Horse World United magazine, May 2021

Turbulence

The Boeing 747-400 cargo plane plummeted for two seconds, creating havoc in the freight compartment. Horses in the travel stalls became airborne before smashing back to the floor. Several grooms smacked against the ceiling and landed heavily between the Air Stables. The crashing and banging in more than a dozen stalls signaled the panicked struggles of horses that failed to regain their feet.

The professional grooms employed by the airline picked themselves up and rushed to attend the horses. Several grooms wiped the blood from their faces or arms as they went to the stalls, more concerned with the horses' welfare than their injuries. One young woman lay gasping in pain, and when a co-worker bent to check on her, she ordered her to tend the horses first.

'Sorry about the bump in the road there, folks,' the pilot's calm voice addressed them through the speakers. 'We skirted around a storm system and didn't expect to find clear air turbulence four hundred kilometers from the storms. Let's hope the road up here doesn't have any more like that.'

In the body of the plane, the rows of Air Stables closest to the cockpit contained stallions and some geldings. General freight divided them from the mares, fillies, and other geldings at the rear. Although most stallions raced or competed against mares, it was safer to keep some distance between them in the confines of a plane.

As the twenty airline grooms moved from stall to stall, they spoke soothingly to the horses, stopping to help some that thrashed wildly trying to find their feet. With their halters cross-tied to either side of the stall, some horses lay awkwardly with their heads held in the air, scrabbling to stand. The skilled handlers released the cross-ties, allowed the horses to stand, re-tied them, and moved on.

Lane Dimity and Tom Claw traveled with two stallions destined for Wunya Warmbloods in Queensland. They checked their charges to find the two bay horses standing without signs of injury. They held their heads higher than usual, and their ears flicked back and forth in alarm at the noises around them.

'Aren't you a smart horse?' Tom crooned to Bisente Bajoran, placing a hand on his neck and looking over his legs.

Lane placed one hand on the forehead of Bisente Barabel and the other on his neck. The horse's fear drained away at Lane's touch. He lowered his head and sighed heavily, releasing the tension.

'No injuries here.' Tom nodded at both the Bisente horses before waving at the Air Stables further back. 'There have to be injuries with all that noise.'

Lane's hands left Barabel and signed, *Let's help.*

'Not my circus; not my monkeys,' Tom drawled in dry Arizona tones before shrugging. 'But that's never stopped us before.'

Flashing a grin at him, Lane headed to the next line of stalls where three grooms struggled to help two horses. The noises elsewhere in the plane decreased as workers calmed the horses and moved onto others, but the racket in this pair of stalls increased. Looking over their shoulders, Lane saw two Thoroughbreds jammed together in the one bay, struggling against their predicament.

When the plane dropped, the black horse found enough air to come down in the adjoining stall. With the cross-ties holding firm, his neck and head stretched over the barrier into the empty stall while his body sprawled sideways over the bay horse. The bay's head was held in the air by his cross-ties while the rest of him lay under the weight of the thrashing black horse. Two grooms tried to steady the black as he lunged and kicked, attempting to right himself, while a third, Paige, comforted the terrified bay by holding his head with her strong arms.

'Get the vet!' yelled one of the grooms as he grasped the halter of the black horse and tried to keep him still.

Several rows of stalls away, another voice relayed the message. 'Jacob! You're needed up the front.'

The vet ensured a pregnant mare was steady on her feet before making his way forward. The pilots usually did an excellent job of avoiding clear air turbulence, but it remained one of the risks of flying, and Jacob was relieved the situation wasn't worse. With over one hundred million dollars of horses on board, it was a big responsibility to keep them safe.

A howl of pain rang out as the black horse fastened his teeth on the arm of the groom who held his halter. He bit down savagely. With no understanding of the source of hurt and fear, the black stallion attacked the person closest to his mouth with bone-crunching force. The young man repeatedly punched the horse with his free hand in an attempt to have him release his hold, but the stallion held fast.

The second man at the stallion's head grabbed one of his ears and twisted hard, trying to break the horse's attention. The horse roared, kicked out frantically, and managed to turn his body so that he became jammed upside down on the other side of the bay gelding. He wrenched the arm held between his teeth before releasing, leaving the man staggering backward, cradling his broken limb.

If the bay managed to stand, he risked breaking the neck of the stallion wedged next to him and across his wither, his neck already twisted at a precarious angle.

'We need the bolt gun,' said Paige as she tried to keep the gelding calm while the hooves of the stallion slashed through the air, occasionally connecting with the sides of the Air Stable and drawing blood on his legs as he kicked himself. 'We can't get a needle into his neck. It's too dangerous.'

Lane knew there were several types of tranquilizers on the flight if a horse became fractious, but the fastest acting required delivery to the jugular. Looking at the thrashing stallion, he knew there was no way anyone could accurately place a needle in his neck. The vet used the bolt gun to euthanize horses in flight if they threatened the plane's safety.

Both the black stallion and his stablemate faced death. Lane rubbed a hand over his eyes as he looked at them. There was no safe way to extricate both from the tangle in which they found themselves. He knew the professional grooms were responsible for these horses, and it wasn't his place to interfere. If they wanted help, they would ask for it.

Meeting the eyes of the bay gelding, Lane felt a punch of recognition in his chest. Twenty-five years earlier, on his eighth birthday, his pony Punkin looked at him with the same beseeching expression. Punkin knew death was coming, and he expected Lane to help him. Nothing he did that day saved his pony. This bay gelding with a white question mark on his forehead needed him.

Stepping forward, Lane tapped Paige on the shoulder and indicated he wanted to help.

'If you think you can do something, Lane, please do.' Paige's blue eyes filled with tears as she held the bay's halter with both hands. She cared about the horses she tended, and the thought of having any euthanized upset her. 'We've never had anything like this happen before. They'll have to be put down.'

Lane put his hands above hers on the halter and tilted his chin to let her know that she could stand back. Paige felt the force of his presence as he smiled down at her, and she found herself wishing that her platinum blonde hair was less scruffy and that she'd put makeup on for a change. Like the other grooms, she knew Lane's reputation with horses and was glad to have him on board. She knew that his selective mutism in no way impeded his ability to communicate with horses. They grew calm at his touch, they told him their stories through their body language and behavior, and they understood him.

Although it seemed unlikely that anyone could save these two horses, she was willing to give Lane a chance.

'What do you want me to do?' Tom stood to one side of the Air Stable, unsure of how they could help the Thoroughbreds.

Lane raised a finger asking him to wait. He focussed on the bay gelding, who began to relax under his touch. His fingers gently rubbed the horse around the eyes, easing the fear from his expression. Looking at Paige, he tapped his jugular as though injecting it and raised his eyebrows.

'You want a sedative?' Paige asked.

Lane nodded. He needed the bay to remain relaxed once he moved to the black. Paige took a syringe from one of the other grooms who had come to assist, checked the contents, and passed it to Lane. Holding the syringe in his teeth, he removed the needle and ensured the angle on the point was facing the right way before sliding it gently into the crease in the horse's neck. Dark blood started to drip from the end, indicating it was in the jugular, and Lane injected the sedative.

In seconds, the horse grew sleepy. Lane unclipped the cross-ties so he could lower his head. The stallion continued to flail his hooves. Jammed firmly upside down between the bay and the side of the stall, he struggled in vain to escape. Aware of the vet standing by with the humane killer in his hands, Lane motioned to Tom for a knife.

'He needs a knife,' said Tom.

A first aid kit appeared, and someone handed a blade to Tom, who passed it to Lane. He cut the cross-ties that held the stallion's head over the stall divider and hoped that relieving the pain of having his head twisted at a tortuous angle might calm the stallion.

As soon as the pressure on his halter eased, the stallion groaned, and his struggles lessened. He remained upside-down between the gelding and the wall, preventing the gelding from standing.

'We can't get him out of there.' Jacob, the vet, moved to stand next to Lane, who rubbed a hand around the stallion's ears. Both men remained wary of his front hooves, which could slash forward towards them. 'It's another eight hours to Melbourne, and he can't travel like that.'

Lane removed his hands from the stallion and looked at Tom, signing. *Open the stall door, and we can put straps on him and drag him out. He can get to his feet once he's out there.*

'We can't do that,' Jacob shook his head when Tom passed on Lane's words. 'No horses are allowed outside their stalls. It's a safety risk.'

Can we remove the divider? Lane examined the interior of the stalls. *We can roll him over the gelding, so his feet are under him.*

When Tom relayed that option, the vet looked at the head groom, Brett, who rubbed both hands down the side of his jeans as he weighed up the risks. The stallion, Sucre Noir, was worth twenty million dollars. If there was any chance of saving him without risk to the plane and other horses, they had to try. He was also responsible for his crew's safety, and Sucre Noir's legs posed a considerable risk to anyone trying to get close to the horse. One blow from any of the four legs could kill.

'I want to save this horse,' began Brett before waving a hand at the legs that made a sudden slash through the air, 'but I can't risk anyone getting within range of those weapons. The horse is insured. I want to make sure all our people get home safely.'

Pointing to his chest and the horse, Lane made it known that he was volunteering to put himself in danger.

'Don't do it, man.' Tom placed a hand on his friend's shoulder. He knew Lane put the welfare of horses above his safety, and it worried him that he accepted danger on behalf of a horse he didn't even know. 'Let them do their job. We're just traveling with the Wunya horses. These aren't our problem.'

Lane twitched an eyebrow at him. He knew Tom felt obliged to try and stop him because friends looked out for each other. It must be difficult, he mused, to have the sort of friend who dives into contained spaces with trapped horses, one of which had already broken a man's arm.

Let's remove this divider, Lane's hands spoke. *I'll get in there with them. I need some straps or ropes.*

'We'll take this out,' Tom tapped the metal between the two stalls. 'Lane will roll the stallion back into his stall and on his feet.'

Jacob scowled at the black horse whose eyes rolled with equal amounts of rage and fear at being trapped. 'That horse is too dangerous. We can't sedate him while he keeps throwing his legs around like that, and even if you could get him to his feet, he's going to come up fighting. You can't be in there with him.' He raised the bolt gun. 'This is our best and safest option.'

'Let Lane try,' said Chloe, the youngest groom. 'Sucre Noir was calmer as soon as Lane touched him.'

Chloe grew up on a Thoroughbred stud, and being a handler for horses traveling around the world was her dream job. Describing herself as an obsessed fan of Lane Dimity, she read all his books, articles, and social media posts and learned about his friends. Tom was her favorite, and she nursed a secret crush on the tall, dark-haired Navaho who regarded the world with a fierce expression. She knew the serious exterior covered kindness and warmth. On her bedroom wall, she had a series of photos of him taken from videos, catching him in moments of laughter and smiles.

When she learned they were on her flight, her heart almost flipped out of her chest. For years, she dreamed of meeting her idols, and knowing they were traveling on her flight had her sleepless for two days. She knew that if anyone could save this horse, Lane and Tom could do it. In her year of flying with horses, there was one incident when a horse required the humane killer after it broke a leg during a panic attack. She didn't want to see another horse put down, and she had faith that Lane and Tom could save Sucre Noir.

'Thanks,' Tom flashed a grin at her, unaware it nearly stopped her heart. 'I agree. Once Lane can work his magic, the stallion will calm down.'

Lane rolled his eyes and grimaced at the praise. *Have a mild sedative ready. We don't want him too sleepy to stand, and my magic works better with a bit of science to help it.*

'So you say.' Tom turned his attention to the clips that locked the stall divider in place. 'I've seen your crazy horse magic work without anything to help it.'

A groom brought a carton of straps and ratchet tie-downs used for fastening freight. Lane nodded approval - they were ideal for what he wanted to achieve. He climbed into the empty stall and removed the clips at the far end so they could lift the barrier out. A couple of times, he ducked as Sucre Noir's hind legs cut through the air near his head.

Once the barrier was out, he knelt at the head of the bay horse to check him. The horse sat with his legs under him and his nose resting on the floor of his stall. Soft eyes turned to him as the horse battled the confusion of the sedative. Lane stroked his head to reassure him. There was an indefinable quality to the gelding that pulled at his heartstrings. Not only was he a beautiful-looking racehorse, his eyes held so much intelligence that Lane wished he had the chance to get to know the horse better.

He reached over the bay's neck to put his hands on the stallion's head. Keeping low to avoid the upside-down horse's front legs, he spoke to the animal through his hands, drawing the fear from his mind. For more than a minute, he rubbed the horse around the eyes and forehead, picturing safe places with him guarding the horses. He found that imagining himself watching over a horse on the range helped calm the horse. Not for a moment did he believe the horse could read his mind. It was a case of his thoughts changing his body language, and the horse understood that like humans could comprehend words in books.

When the stallion calmed his movements, Lane motioned for the tranquilizer. He injected the stallion and, as it took effect, he began looping straps around the horse's lower legs, one through the halter, and another around the horse's neck. He passed the straps to the grooms outside the stall.

The vet looked at how far down the stallion was wedged between the bay and the wall. 'We'll damage his legs trying to pull him up and over. It can't be done.'

Lane tapped his forehead to show he had an idea and raised a finger to ask Jacob to be patient. Nodding at the men holding the straps to tell them to apply pressure, he watched the horses closely. As the black began to resist the pull from the straps, Lane took the head and neck of the bay and pulled him over onto his side. As he rolled toward the empty stall, the ropes pulled the body of the black tightly against him, so they moved as one. When the stallion teetered on top of the gelding, the men pulled hard, tipping him over. As he began to slide off, they released his legs, allowing him to fold them underneath his body.

With a scramble of legs and head tossing, the black made it to his feet. He stood, shaking and sweating from his experience, trusting the man who stood next to him in the stall. Lane picked up each leg and removed the straps, running his hands over the horse in reassuring strokes as he checked for injuries.

Jacob attached new cross-ties and watched Lane feel along the horse's spine and down his legs. 'Is there anything more than the superficial cuts?'

Lane shook his head. The bleeding where the horse kicked himself was minor, and there didn't appear to be any sign of pulled muscles, which surprised him. He helped the gelding roll upright and clicked his tongue to encourage him to stand. Although sleepy, the bay rose to his feet, resting his head on Lane, who rubbed his neck affectionately. Once the horse was steady and clipped back in his cross ties, Lane left the stalls so Jacob could enter and treat the stallion's wounds.

'Thanks, Lane,' the vet slapped the tall Australian on the back as they swapped places. 'Brian Farley-Wells is going to be mighty pleased we didn't have to put either of these horses down. The stallion has a full book of mares at Brian's stud in Victoria, and Quest - Putin The Question is his racing name if you want to back him - is supposed to be running at Flemington after he comes out of quarantine.'

'Good name,' said Tom, looking at the perfect question mark on the front of the bay's head. 'I hope he runs fast. I wouldn't like to think of him ending up as pet food.'

'It doesn't happen as much as it used to.' Jacob carefully bandaged a front canon of the stallion. 'The horse rescue, REE, tries to save every slow or retiring racehorse from the pet food trade. Luckily for Quest, I've heard Farley-Wells makes sure all his horses have a home for life, and none end up at knackery. He's as rich as Croesus and can afford to look after them, but not everyone is like that. Some pay a few hundred thousand or even millions for yearlings, spend a fortune getting them to racing age and started, then fifty thousand or more to fly them into the country. If they're slow or injured and they aren't going to be useful for breeding, then it's pot luck where they end up. The pretty ones might become show horses. The good jumpers might head to competitions. And a whole lot of them ended up as pet food until REE came along.'

'Yeah - thank goodness for the charities that look after the racehorses when their career is over.' Paige plumped up Quest's haynets and stroked his face. 'I make a monthly donation to Rescuing Equines Everywhere, and I volunteer at some of the others. Thanks to them, even if a horse like Quest is as slow as a snail, he'll have a home for life.'

'I've done some work for REE,' said Jacob as he exited the stalls. 'As well as Equines In Need Of Funds. There are some great horse charities out there these days. It almost restores my faith in humanity to see them taking care of what the racing industry discards.'

Paige looked at Tom and Lane. 'Have you had anything to do with them?'

Both men shook their heads. They were keen to return to the Warmbloods and didn't want to engage in conversation about horse charities or anything else. With Quest and Sucre Noir on their feet, they had no reason to stay with them.

Seeing they wanted to go back to the Wunya horses, Jacob picked up his veterinary bag and started towards some other stalls. 'I'll make sure Brian knows what you did. He's a good man, and he loves his horses.'

***

Dibby and Rev

'If you don't keep those two together,' the diminutive ex-jockey pointed at the two palominos in the corner of the yard, 'they'll scream the house down.'

'Noted.' The driver who was taking the horses from the quarantine facility to the airport took a small writing pad from his pocket and wrote, *Keep two pallies together.* 'Anything else?'

'Yeah. Watch that big bay clumper over there.' He nodded at a horse standing against the rails, his head high in alarm. 'It might be worth throwing a bit of ace into him. Or a lot. I think they're mad putting that one on a plane, but what do I know?'

'As long as he leads and loads, it's not my problem.'

They moved to the next yard, ignoring Rev's soft call. He hoped the men might talk to him. From the moment Dibby and Rev were born, humans offered friendship, comfort, and guidance, but in the past few months, the people they met showed no interest in providing pats or reassuring words.

If they pushed their noses forward to a passing person, they expected a quick pat or even a look to acknowledge them, but these didn't even look at them. Worse, there were ones who yelled and others who smacked them on the muzzles for reaching out in friendship. It was confusing for horses used to having complete trust in people.

Dibby, at 16.2 hands, was a full hand taller than Rev and the tallest horse in the yard of ten, but he was the most fearful. After being attacked by other horses during quarantine and before, he cringed in corners when the horses began moving around. His friend Rev remained with him, staunchly protecting his tall friend from the sour horses that used teeth and hooves rather than looks and tail swishing to tell others to move.

They had been friends for seven years, and now, as the world turned against them, they clung together. If anyone separated them, they called to each other, desperate to be reunited. The people didn't care for their feelings, but they wanted to reduce the noise, so they remained together.

CHAPTER TWO

Naturally, you should use your head when choosing a horse, but never underestimate the heart when it comes to finding your equine partner. It's a bit like going to a party hoping to find your perfect partner. You don't have to speak to everyone there to know there are some you won't get along with and others who don't interest you, and then you meet the eyes of a person across the room, and you know they are the one. Occasionally, you might be wrong, but people often know from that first glance that there is something special. Since we are likely to spend more years with a horse than many spend in marriages, I think you need that same spark of recognition when you see your horse for the first time. At one level, you fall in love with your horse, and that helps to create the magic in your partnership. Don't ever underestimate the value of heart decisions.

Lane Dimity's answer to Horse and Hound when asked about buying a horse.

Gratitude

After landing at Melbourne, a scissor lift at the back of the aircraft lowered the air stables to the ground and moved them to First Point Animal Services. The horses were inspected in the safe indoor area, given a walk, and moved to horse trucks taking them to the quarantine centers. Most horses had two weeks at the Post Entry Quarantine center at Mickleham. The racehorses went to the Werribee International Horse Center to continue training during quarantine.

An early morning mist wrapped around the airport, dulling the light from the rising sun and lending an air of gloom to the grey day. Grooms, air stables, and vehicles moved around in a complicated dance as the horses were removed from the plane in their travel compartments and taken to a safe unloading area. The clip-clopping of hooves and the occasional snort or whinny seemed out of place at the international airport.

After they loaded the Wunya horses on a truck, Lane and Tom headed indoors to clean themselves. There were strict decontamination procedures to follow, so they didn't carry any viruses into Australia. After Equine Influenza escaped a quarantine facility in 2007, shutting down the Australian horse industry, biosecurity became more stringent to prevent a similar incident.

They were about to enter the building when Jacob called to them. He stood with Quest and Sucre Noir while another vet checked them before putting them on the truck bound for Werribee. Two grooms held the horses while Jacob spoke to a tall man whose intelligent eyes scanned everything as though examining a puzzle and looking for the missing piece.

As Tom and Lane approached, the stranger evaluated them with narrowed eyes. Apart from the silvering at the temples of his dark brown hair, there was little else to indicate his age. His tanned skin and unlined face could have placed him anywhere between thirty and fifty, and his muscular body told of fitness and workouts. The man looked powerful and stood with the authoritative air of someone used to giving orders.

'Lane and Tom,' Jacob smiled at them as they approached, 'I'd like to introduce you to Brian Farley-Wells, the owner of the two horses you saved on the flight. Brian, this is Lane Dimity – I'm sure you've heard of him – and Tom Claw. They were responsible for you having two live horses rather than two bodies.'

Brian's face split into a warm grin, making him look younger than someone with greying temples. He held a hand out for Lane to shake. 'Glad to meet you, Lane. And you, Tom.' He offered Tom his hand. 'Jacob's been telling me what you did to save my horses. I can't thank you enough.'

'It was Lane.' Tom wanted to be clear on that. 'I didn't do anything.'

'You let Lane save my horses,' Brian smiled at him, 'and that's doing something. They're fine horses.' He reached over and rubbed Quest on the face, startling the horse into taking a step back. 'It's not the fact that they're worth a lot of money; it's that they deserve to live. I'm the one who bought them and put them on a plane, so it would have been my fault if they'd died up there. I owe you both.'

Lane signed a reply which Tom spoke. 'Lane and I want to make it clear that you don't owe us anything. We'll always try to help horses where we can, whether they're worth a lot of money or nothing.'

'That's what I like to hear,' declared Brian in admiring tones. 'You're here for the horses - that's my belief, too. They make me a lot of money, mind you, but they cost a whole lot more than they make. Sucre Noir will be one of the few to make more than he costs. He has a full book of mares this year, so he'll earn his keep. Jacob made it clear he was ready to euthanize him.'

'I'm sorry about that,' Jacob apologized, 'but it seemed an impossible situation.'

Brian gave him a friendly mock-punch to the shoulder. 'It's your job, Jake. If that's what had happened, I know it would have been the only option. Don't lose any sleep over it.'

'I'm glad I'm not standing here explaining to you why you don't have any horses walking away from that flight. And they're relatively uninjured. Sucre Noir's cuts are superficial, and I can't see any reason why Quest won't be fine to continue work and race as planned.'

An idea occurred to Brian, and he held out both hands, palms upturned, as though offering something to Lane and Tom. 'Can I interest you in coming to see Quest race? At Flemington, in a bit over two weeks from now. All expenses paid – I'll fly you, your partners, and friends whether you're here or overseas. Make a weekend of it, all on me. He might not be a first-up winner, mind you, but he's standing here because of you, so how about you come and see what you saved?'

Lane was hesitant to commit without knowing what Karen, his partner, had organized for that weekend. He signed his thoughts to Tom.

'We're not sure what plans we have for that weekend.' Tom spoke for them both. 'If we're free, I know Lane would like to see Quest run. He's quite taken by that horse. In fact,' his dark eyes brightened as he thought of something Lane would like, 'since Quest is a gelding and won't have a breeding life after racing, would you consider selling him to Lane at the end of his racing life? He'd be well cared for and won't ever end up as pet food.'

Brian turned his dark brown eyes to Lane. 'Is that what you'd like? To take on a horse when he's no longer racing?'

In reply, Lane nodded and put a hand out to Quest, who leaned into his touch. For a moment, Lane met the horse's eyes and knew in his heart that they belonged together.

'Then, that's an easy fix.' Brian smiled broadly at how the horse enjoyed Lane's touch. 'Clearly, Quest likes you. He didn't want me patting him, but he's eating that up. When he finishes his racing career, he'll be your horse - for free. I'm happy to know any of my horses have a good home when they've finished racing. Mind you, I'm hoping he has a few years of racing in him.'

Lane nodded a thank you. He would enjoy watching Quest's races knowing they had a future together. It wasn't that he needed another horse as there were scores of them on his outback property; it was a more of a niggling feeling that Quest needed him. Over the years, he learned to heed the sense that some called *gut instinct*, and, in this case, it told him that he and Quest had a date with destiny.

'I'd better get back to work.' Jacob looked across at the horses waiting to go to the quarantine centers. 'It's been great meeting both of you. Brian, let me know if there are any problems with your two, but I think they'll be fine.'

'Good vet,' muttered Brian as Jacob went to check on the remaining horses. 'I'm always happy when he's flying with my horses. Of course, if I could convince you two to start traveling with them, I'd be even happier. Any chance you're looking for a job?'

Lane shook his head. The sales of his books and income from his social media profile meant he didn't have to look for work. He did favors for friends, like accompanying the Warmbloods, but he liked to be his own boss. Likewise, Tom's primary income came from his books and work as an influencer. As a climatologist previously employed by NASA, his books about environmental issues were popular enough to fund his time with Lane and their friends.

'Not at the moment,' Tom replied, 'but thanks for the offer.'

'I still feel as though I owe you for what you did to save my horses.' Brian's brow creased as he tried to figure out a way to repay them. 'Giving you Quest isn't enough as you'd be doing me a favor by giving him a good home when he's no longer racing. Are you sure you don't need some money? I'm happy to pay you.'

He doesn't want to be in our debt, Lane signed to Tom. *I can understand that. Tell him to donate some money to a charity, and we'll be even.*

'We don't want money for helping your horses,' Tom assured Brian. 'If you feel you have to repay us, Lane suggested donating some money to a charity.'

'A horse charity?'

Lane had been thinking more along the lines of a children's charity. *Sounds fair,* he signed.

'That would be fine,' Tom confirmed.

'We've donated to Rescuing Equines Everywhere in the past.' Brian tapped a finger against his chin as he considered the various horse charities worth supporting. 'And I've heard good things about them.

I'm not sure what else is out there.'

'Horse Helpers,' suggested the young woman who was holding Quest. 'They're excellent. Grace, who runs it, is fantastic with horses.'

Brian gave her a stern look. He wasn't happy about others jumping in uninvited on his conversations. The woman blushed and apologized for interrupting.

Turning to Tom, Brian's expression became amicable again. 'Have you heard of them?'

'I can't say I'm familiar with Australian horse charities.' Tom was skeptical of charities. When he learned that as little as five cents in every dollar was going to the cause the donor wanted to help, he became suspicious of all charities.

'There have been some troubling reports about how Grace runs her charity,' Brian continued. 'A few of her horses ended up in pet food tins. Not exactly what you expect of a horse rescue charity. I don't think I'll be giving her any money.'

'I don't blame you.' Tom noticed that the woman holding Quest was itching to say something, but she bit her lip and turned away. He was almost curious enough to ask her what was on her mind. Almost. 'So, that first one, Rescuing Equines Everywhere. If you've heard that it's above board, donate something to them, and that will even the score with us. Not that there's anything to even, but if it makes you feel better, go ahead.'

'I'll send them twenty thousand first thing tomorrow,' promised Brian, hoping his generosity impressed the younger men.

They were not impressed. If Sucre Noir cost twenty million dollars, that represented a tenth of one percent of his value. Lane liked the fact that the REE horses would benefit from the donation, but he didn't show the level of astonishment that Brian expected.

'That's very generous of you.' Tom's steady voice lacked enthusiasm. 'It should help quite a few horses.'

Brian wanted these men to admire his generosity. He knew Lane had over seventy million social media followers, and Tom mixed with the political elite because of his environmental knowledge and books. Part of him was drawn to their fame like a moth to twin candles. Wealth was good to have, but what use was it if he didn't also have respect? Lane and Tom were held in high esteem by many, and he wanted what they had.

Growing up, he desired all the things money could buy. Now, with seemingly endless money at his disposal, he wanted the things money couldn't buy – like the admiration of the silent outback horseman and the Navaho climatologist who regarded him with a guarded expression. He was about to tell them that he would double his donation when the vet inspecting Quest and Sucre Noir waved for the grooms to take them to the waiting truck.

'They're right to go, Brian,' the grey-haired equine vet said as he packed up his veterinary bag. 'Nothing serious. Quest will be fine to recommence training tomorrow, and Sucre Noir has two weeks to recover before heading up to the Hunter.'

'Thanks, mate.' Brian addressed him as a friend. The man had worked for his racing stables for several years, and he trusted his opinion when it came to his horses' welfare. 'It could have been a lot worse if Lane and Tom here weren't on board.'

'Absolutely,' the vet agreed. 'Jacob told me about it. You wouldn't have the stallion, and there was a high chance Quest wouldn't have made it, either. Good job, you two.'

Lane was beginning to feel uncomfortable with the praise. He wanted to leave the airport and find Karen. His heart grew warm thinking about her. They hadn't seen each other for over a week, and it was too long - he wanted to hold her in his arms and never let her go. She had a three-week break from Pilatos, though he knew from experience that her *break* involved lots of office time on her phone and laptop. While she continued to run Pilatos remotely, he could sit next to her, writing his next book.

'You're daydreaming,' Tom broke into his thoughts with an elbow to his ribs. 'Brian asked if we wanted a ride anywhere.'

I'm easy, he signed. *If he has a vehicle here, it will save us hiring a car for a day.*

'If you can wait until we go through biosecurity,' Tom nodded towards the building, 'we'd appreciate a lift into Melbourne. We're staying here tonight before flying to Sydney tomorrow, then on to Queensland.'

'No problems,' Brian smiled at them. 'I have to go through all the decontamination procedures since I've been in contact with the horses and people here. I couldn't wait any longer to see my new horses. I hated waiting for Christmas morning to unwrap my presents, and I couldn't sit at home without meeting the horses.'

'I can understand that.' Tom thawed enough to grin at the older man. His love of horses would have had him doing the same. 'They're certainly something special.'

They made their way to the showers, making small talk about weather, flying, and airport facilities. Lane groaned when he saw Jacob approaching with a short, stocky man in a suit whose head seemed to have an excess of hair. The stranger had eyebrows like giant hairy caterpillars, thick black hair that extended onto his face as sideburns, and a dark shadow of hair across his chin. It seemed they faced another delay. He wanted to reach his hotel room and spend some quiet time texting Karen, not talk to more people.

'Brian, just a moment.' Jacob and his companion stepped in front of them.

The glare Brian sent the new arrival did not slip Lane's attention. It seemed he wasn't enjoying the delay, either.

'I wanted to introduce Derek Anderson,' continued Jacob. 'He's the owner of Horse Air Transport Company – HATCO - who flew your horses in. Derek, Brian Farley-Wells, owns the two horses that had the problem onboard – the ones that Lane and Tom saved. I was ready to put them down, but they managed to save them without any risk to the plane.'

'Lane saved them,' corrected Tom as he shook Derek's hand. 'I was just a spectator.'

'I heard otherwise,' Derek pumped everyone's hand in his warm grip. He smiled warmly at the faces above him, his cheeks shining like red apples above his stubble. 'I wanted to offer an official thank you for what you did. And express my regret to Brian that his horses were in danger. The pilot informed me it was an unexpected patch of turbulence hundreds of kilometers from the storms.'

Brian looked down at the shorter man and waved away his apology. 'I've owned horses long enough to know that accidents happen. It was our lucky day to have these two on board to help. I've offered them a job with my horses, but they're not buying it.'

'I was about to make the same offer,' Derek chortled, his Adam's-apple bobbing in and out above his collar like an alien trying to break free. 'We have excellent horse people working at HATCO, but we're always looking for more.'

It only took a fleeting glance for Tom to know what Lane thought. They'd enjoyed so many years working together that Lane didn't always need to sign his meaning. A quirk of an eyebrow, narrowing eyes, or a twitch of his lips communicated hundreds of words. Lane wanted to hurry out of here and get to their hotel.

'We appreciate your offer, but we aren't looking for jobs. Thanks, anyway.'

'I expected as much,' Derek shrugged. Turning to Brian, his rosy cheeks glowed as he smiled broadly at him. 'I'm not sure if you remember, but we met at the races a few months ago. I was part of the syndicate that bought Rasputin's Beard.'

'I thought you looked familiar. He won well that day.'

'He's been a good investment.'

Brian chuckled. 'That's not something you can say very often about racehorses.'

'If you'll excuse us…' Tom began, only to have Derek cut him off in his cheery voice.

'Before you go, I hope you'll accept a gift from me to thank you for helping out with horses that weren't in your care. I know your only responsibilities were the Warmbloods, and by helping out, you saved me a big headache with paperwork and insurance.'

'You and me both,' agreed Brian.

'There's no need for anything.' Tom spoke flatly. He didn't mean to be unfriendly, but, like Lane, he was tired and longed to reach the quiet of a hotel room where he could relax. Speaking to these men was an unwanted delay.

'I couldn't get them to take anything,' Brian told Derek. 'I'm going to donate to REE, the horse rescue, in their names.'

'Fabulous. We support Rescuing Equines Everywhere, too.' Derek nodded enthusiastically. 'Great people. We give them discounted travel whenever possible. Their horse-riding programs in developing countries are amazing – helping kids and horses at the same time. I'll sling them a donation, too,' he raised his hairy caterpillars at Tom and Lane, 'if that suits you.'

'Sounds great.' Tom gave him a tight smile while Lane offered a thumbs-up gesture. 'Now, if you don't mind, we want to clean up so we can head out of here.'

They extricated themselves from the conversation, leaving Brian and Derek to talk horses, business, and charities. After showering and scrubbing with disinfectant, they donned clean clothes and shoes and waited for Brian.

When Tom saw the groom who mentioned Horse Helpers earlier, he wandered over to her. Like them, she had cleaned and changed and was waiting for a lift. She smiled nervously when he stopped in front of her.

'I'm Tom. You were hanging on to Quest when we were talking to his owner.'

The girl held out her hand. 'I know who you are. And Lane, too. I'm a huge fan of you both, and Matthew and Andrea, too. A big fan.'

'I hope it's not too disappointing to see us in the flesh and realize we're just people like you.'

'Not exactly like me,' the girl grinned, 'I'm a Melbourne girl, and you're an Arizona man.'

'Yeah, there is that.'

'I'm Binky Laurie. I get called in to help when a shipment of horses comes in or goes out. You saw it – it's hectic as we change the horses from air stables to horse trucks, and it's the same when it's happening the other way. I only live ten minutes away, so it's great for me. I hope to get a job as one of the flight grooms one day.'

'It looks like a good job.' He looked over at Lane, who was regarding him with a quizzical expression. *I want to ask her something,* he signed to Lane in explanation.

'What do you want to ask?' Binky tilted her head to one side. 'My brother is hearing impaired, so I know sign language.'

'Just as well I didn't sign anything rude, then,' he grinned at her, his eyes glinting with amusement.

Binky laughed a sweet tinkling sound. 'I've read enough about you to know that that you wouldn't be rude to a girl who was standing alone waiting for her mother. And, anyhow, I know you're going out with that reporter, Vicki Marshall, so you're not going to hit on me or anything like that.'

'You really are a fan, aren't you?' Tom wasn't sure whether he should be flattered or scared by how much she knew about him.

'I'm a little obsessed,' she admitted, before rushing to add, 'but not cray-cray obsessed. I won't start sending weird notes or anything like that.'

'What a relief,' he chuckled. 'Back to my question, though. What did you want to say when we were talking about horse charities? You mentioned Horse Helpers.'

'Grace is fantastic,' Binky enthused, her words tumbling out as though tipped from a bucket. 'Don't listen to anything anyone says against her. Those big charities have become enormous, and they don't like the smaller ones like Horse Helpers. I wanted to let you know that they are good. At least, I think they are. I met Grace once at the Horse Expo, and she was genuine. She's been struggling to raise money since the big charities like REE and EINOF have opened up, but she is worth supporting. She started a campaign to find out about the pits of dead horses as soon as she heard of them this week. She cares about horses. Her petition had over five hundred signatures by last night, and...'

'Pits of dead horses?' Tom cut in, pouncing on the phrase that stood out in her flood of words.

'Haven't you heard?' Binky's eyes widened with excitement. Being able to tell one of her idols a snippet of news was thrilling. 'They found fifty dead horses in an unused coal mine up in the Hunter. They'd tried to cover them, but it wasn't a good job, and someone saw the broken gate into the mine and smelled them. A few days later, another fifty turned up in a gully near Mount Royal National Park. Everyone thought some of the Thoroughbred studs in the Hunter were getting rid of excess horses rather than face another public outcry about sending them to the meatworks, but they weren't all Thoroughbreds. Some were. At least, they thought they were. Someone cut their brands off. Some were ponies, and a few looked like heavy breeds, so it wasn't a Thoroughbred stud. Everyone's talking about it.'

'Not us,' Tom nodded towards Lane, who leaned against the building, his eyes closed. 'We've been traveling this past week and haven't tuned in to the Australian news.'

'I don't think it was on the news.'

That surprised Tom. It seemed the sort of story that the media would be keen to follow up. 'How were the horses killed?'

'No one will say.' Binky looked around as though she suspected someone was spying on their conversation. She lowered her voice to a whisper. 'That's one of the things Grace wants to find out. It's all so weird, and the police have gone hush-hush on it. No one knows if it's because they don't care or if someone is telling them to leave the whole thing alone. One hundred horses, and no one knows where they came from or who did it.'

'It seems unusual,' Tom admitted, trying to think of reasons to discard so many horses like rubbish. Maybe the owner couldn't afford to feed them and, rather than face the shame of selling skinny horses through the sales, put them down and tried to hide the bodies. Perhaps a knackery had a contamination problem and couldn't use the meat, so dumped them.

'I keep wondering if there'll be more.' Binky wrinkled her nose as she thought about the mystery. She wanted to do something to prevent another fifty horses turning up dead but had no idea where to start. 'What if there are more out there, only no one has found them yet?'

'Let's hope that's not the case.' Seeing her concern, Tom gave her a supportive smile. 'Lane and I might look into it since we're in Australia for a few weeks.'

'Really?' Binky's face shone with adoration as she looked up at the tall American with the strongly chiseled lines to his face that made him impossibly handsome. 'You should get in contact with Grace. It seems she's the only one who wants to find out what is going on with these horses. I know she's busy with all the horses she has at her rescue, but she's worried about why those horses were dumped.'

'I'll keep that in mind. If you hear anything else, let us know.'

'I'm going up to the Hunter Valley this evening with a truckload of yearlings. I'll see if I can find out anything. What number should I call if I do get some info?'

Tom took out his phone and swapped phone numbers with Binky, who wanted to squeal with joy about having direct access to him. She promised herself not to annoy him but was equally determined to find out more about the dead horses so that she had a reason to contact him.

Returning to Lane, Tom quietly told him about the one hundred horses. He paused to raise a hand in farewell to Binky as a car pulled up for her. Lane opened one eye wide to look from him to the young woman who waved back so frantically that her hand risked flying off her wrist.

I think she likes you, he teased.

'All of us,' returned Tom wryly. 'She may well be a walking encyclopedia on our lives, right down to knowing about Vicki.'

Lane knew that Tom and Vicki Marshall were keeping their relationship quiet in its early stages. As a high-profile journalist, she wanted to avoid the scrutiny of her peers and readers as she negotiated her private life, while Tom was, by nature, so reserved that he would prefer his life to remain unnoticed. He wanted the results of his actions to be seen, not his personal life.

Such is the price of fame. Lane grinned at Tom, who swatted his arm. Returning to Binky's news, his lips twisted to one side as he thought about the mystery. One dumping site was curious; two was almost a habit.

'I wonder if they were tested for disease,' mused Tom, still trying to work out reasons to turn that many horses into landfill.

'*Fifty at each site?* Lane asked, curious if the numbers were exact or approximate. Two precise lots of fifty would be unusual.

'That's what Binky said, but if there isn't much information out there, it could be wrong. Maybe the police are keeping quiet about it because they have a suspect in mind and don't want to damage their chances of catching him.'

Maybe. I have a feeling we'll learn more in the coming days.

'Same here. I might chase up Grace at Horse Helpers. Or get Matthew to do it.'

Both men laughed, amused at the thought of having Matthew chase up anything relating to horse rescues. He was an outspoken critic of horse hoarders posing as rescues so that other people could fund their obsession with collecting horses. The larger charities like REE and EINOF might win his approval since they took horse welfare to a corporate level and were less likely to have individuals gathering horses paid for by donations. A woman called Grace running a smaller facility seemed to fit right in with all he disliked about the equine rescues.

Lane tapped a hand on his leg impatiently. He wanted to get going and wished he hadn't accepted the lift as he couldn't very well start texting Karen if Brian talked to them in the car. Judging from what they saw of him in the few minutes they'd known him, he was going to talk.

When Brian joined them, a limousine glided up to park beside them. The driver came around to hold the door open, and Brian took a front-facing seat while Lane and Tom sat opposite, looking out the back window.

'You're both welcome to stay at my place,' Brian offered as they sped away from the airport. 'I have a house at Toorak, which isn't that far from the city center. I'm serious about being in your debt for saving my horses. The old *mi casu, su casa* holds true at any of my houses – here, Sydney, the stud in the Hunter, up on the Sunshine Coast, or anywhere else. You are always welcome. Those horses mean the world to me.'

'We might take you up on that some time.' Tom had no intention of staying at any of his houses. 'We appreciate your offer.'

'Don't be backward in coming forward.' Brian waved a finger at him to emphasize his statement. 'Having homes in good places doesn't mean much if I can't convince friends to come and stay. So, what are you doing in Australia this time around? Derek said you accompanied some Warmbloods for the Lomond family up in Queensland. I've met them before. Good people.'

Lane nodded and looked to Tom, glad to have his friend there to speak for both of them. He rarely noticed a downside to his selective mutism until communicating with someone who didn't know Auslan or ASL. On the upside, it was interesting to watch the people speaking. A life around horses taught him the importance of observing the language of others because there were far more communications made non-verbally than most realized. Also, having Tom talking on his behalf allowed him to have imaginary conversations with Karen in his head.

As the car swept along the road into the city, Tom's thoughts returned to the horses Binky mentioned. 'Have you heard about the horses that were found at the coal mine in the Hunter and Mount Royal National Park?'

Brian raised his eyebrows quizzically. 'You heard about them? It's a bad business. I'd be interested to hear what you think about it.'

'We don't know enough about it to think anything at this stage.'

Tom lifted his shoulders in a dismissive gesture. 'Hopefully, it's just the two sites and no more.'

'At first, everyone blamed the racing industry.' Brian frowned and rubbed a hand through his hair as he considered what to say about the discoveries. 'I can't blame them. It was my first thought when both places were close to so many Thoroughbred studs, including mine. Plenty of studs breed far too many horses – I accept that – and they keep the best and dump the rest, only they usually do that through sales or send them quietly to the knackery. They don't kill them and dispose of the bodies in coal mines and national parks.'

'They weren't all racehorses, though,' observed Tom.

'No, thank goodness. It took the spotlight off us for a change. I'm guilty of not thinking too much about it once it was clear it wasn't one of my fellow breeders treating their horses with disrespect. I don't know why they ended up there, but I hope they were put down humanely and didn't suffer.'

Why two lots of fifty? Lane asked, knowing that Tom would embellish the question satisfactorily. They had worked together for so long that Tom always guessed at the unspoken words. Lane didn't expect Brian to know; he was more interested in seeing his reactions. It was like offering a horse something new to look at and seeing if he shied away or accepted it. Observing responses was educational.

'We were curious about the numbers,' said Tom. 'Do you know if there were exactly fifty horses at each site, or is that a guesstimate?'

'I couldn't tell you.' Brian appeared bored by the conversation. His love of horses seemed limited to Thoroughbreds, and he had little interest in the plight of the unknown animals. 'To put it in perspective, my three closest neighbors and I have stallions that sire over a thousand foals a year. That represents hundreds of millions of dollars at the breeding stage and much more by the time they make it to the yearling sales and when they are racing. It's unpleasant that someone has killed and dumped those horses, but I won't lose sleep over the deaths of one hundred or even five hundred unwanted non-Thoroughbreds. That's something for the pleasure horse industry to look into.'

'Fair enough.' Tom was happy to leave the subject there.

'Are you going to look into it?'

'I doubt it. It was simply a case of us being mildly interested in a crime involving horses.'

'I'd hardly call it a crime.' Brian frowned across at them, his brown eyes growing a shade darker. 'There are no reports of stolen horses. For all we know, they were knackery horses that died accidentally during transport. It's happened before.'

'Then it would still be a crime,' countered Tom. 'Admittedly, the small crime of littering since they disposed of their rubbish unlawfully. I hope there is no animal cruelty case related to this.'

Brian's expression grew soft as though the fate of those horses affected him more than he let on. 'If those horses suffered, I hope whoever did it is found and punished to the full extent of the law and then placed in a jail cell with someone who loves horses.'

They all agreed, and for the rest of the journey, they discussed cheerier topics and shared laughter over the antics of horse people the world over.

When the car swept to a halt outside their hotel, Brian regretfully bade them farewell. 'It's been a real experience chatting with you. I could go on like this all night - it's not often I enjoy talking to people this much. You remind me of myself at your age: confident and in love with life as well as horses. Are you sure you won't reconsider and continue to Toorak with me?'

For a moment, his face looked as earnest as a child hoping his new friends would come and play with him, and Tom almost felt guilty turning him down. 'Thanks again for the offer, but we're looking forward to getting some sleep. Maybe another time.'

'All good,' Brian smiled and motioned to his driver to open the door. 'Don't be strangers, now. I'll send you the information on Quest's first start,' he patted the phone in his pocket. They had exchanged contact details during the drive. 'I'll organize to get you and your friends there from wherever you are in the world. My treat, remember. It's the least I can do, and I'll make sure that donation goes to REE. If there's anything else you need, don't hesitate to ask. I'll be at your disposal.'

Tom and Lane assured him they would ask if they needed anything.

After they collected their luggage from the driver, they watched in silence as the limousine pulled into the traffic. When it was out of sight, Lane sighed with relief at being alone with his friend.

He seems like a good man, but his personality is overpowering. It's tiring.

'Sure is,' Tom replied, picking up his single item of carry-on luggage and pushing Lane's towards him with the toe of his boot. 'I guess it gets lonely at the top of the pyramid where everyone else tends to be either a yes-man below you or someone sitting atop a neighboring pyramid waiting for you to fail so they can stick the knives in.'

Lonely billionaires. That sounds like a country and western song.

They both laughed and entered the hotel inventing lyrics for their new song.

***

Dibby and Rev

The horse trucks pulled up near the pens, and the two palominos eyed them nervously, pressing close to each other. Over the past few months, they learned that horse trucks meant they were moving. The drivers loaded them, locked them in, and took them to another strange place to mix with more horses and more people who didn't seem to like horses.

'Will they be right there till morning?' one of the drivers called out to the ex-jockey who managed the privately-owned quarantine facility.

'Yeah, mate, no worries,' he gave a thumbs up. 'Get some rest. I'll see you first thing.'

'See you then.' The driver locked his truck and left.

When the tractor drove past the horse pens leaving hay in the bins for the horses, Dibby and Rev watched the other horses start to eat before they chose a space and put their heads between the rails to eat, their muzzles almost touching as they munched on lucerne. If the mean-natured chestnut mare moved, Dibby stopped eating to watch her in case he needed to duck out of her way. Rev occasionally laid his ears back at a horse that invaded their personal space, but he wasn't an aggressor; he merely defended.

When Dibby released a massive sigh, Rev briefly touched muzzle-to-muzzle to comfort him. As long as they had each other, they would be alright.

CHAPTER THREE

I don't know for certain if we have souls that go to heaven, but I'd like to think that's the case. I know that if heaven doesn't have a place for horses, dogs, and all the other animals, I don't want to go there. If a good dog and a fine horse aren't allowed in heaven, then it's no paradise. For me, heaven is an all-or-none deal.

Lane Dimity on The Morning Show when asked if he believed in Heaven.

Back Together

Are you there? Lane texted Karen within seconds of shutting the door of his hotel suite. His phone pinged almost instantly.

Always, came the reply.

Lane smiled at the memories that flooded back with those words. Even when they were adversaries, fighting over the fate of the horses in her family's laboratories, he promised to be there for her, always. It became her promise, too.

Where is there? Lane asked.

There is here.

Lane chuckled as he threw himself down on the bed. She often made obtuse remarks for comic effect, and he found them amusing. Karen was the most intelligent person he knew, and he revered her intelligence as much as he loved her sense of humor.

His fingers flew as he typed the next message. *Are there and here both in New York?*

Yes, they are. At the airport, to be precise. I'll be on the direct flight within the hour and in Australia with you twenty hours after that. I love these new non-stop flights.

I'd love it more if it left twenty hours ago and you were here with me now.

Karen sent him a series of heart emojis and a Tardis to show she wanted to travel in time.

I'll meet you at the airport tomorrow since I don't have The Doctor's number to arrange a trip to yesterday. Is Joe coming?

Sure is. Karina is staying with Mum at Bisente.

Lane smiled at the thought of Joe's teenage daughter in the company of Karen's mother, Isabella. Karina's obsession with horses would be satisfied while at Isabella's farm, Bisente. The two horses he and Tom accompanied from the U.S. were bred at Bisente and had competed internationally before being bought by the Lomond family in Queensland. Once the horses completed their quarantine, they would fly north to Brisbane and travel to Wunya near Gatton, where Lane would work them for their first week until the Lomond riders took them over.

I bet Karina is having the time of her life.

Mum's already given her a horse. I'm not game to tell Joe yet - I think it's a secret between Karina and Mum.

Horse secrets are always the best kind.

Is that a way of telling me you have a new horse?

A bubble of laughter burst from Lane. He wanted to tease her a bit longer, so he texted, *I'll call you.*

Knowing she would assume that he had a new horse, he grinned as he rolled off the bed and grabbed his laptop from the suitcase. Clicking open his text-to-voice app, he called Karen. When she answered, he could see her face on the screen with the airport terminal behind her.

'Hello, gorgeous,' a voice with an Australian accent spoke as Lane's fingers flew over the keyboard. 'And, no, I haven't bought a horse.'

'You can buy ten horses if you want.' Her remarkable dark blue eyes were flecked with grey, and they shone as she looked at the man she loved. 'How was the flight?'

'Apart from the turbulence that had a twenty-million-dollar horse upside down in his stall? It was good.'

'You're kidding!' Karen looked off-screen to ask Joe Kaiphas, the head of security of Pilatos, her family's company. 'Did you hear that?'

Joe's dry voice replied, 'It's a bit hard to miss when you're sitting two inches away.'

'G'day, Joe,' the artificial voice spoke in a surprisingly natural manner as Lane typed the words. 'Looking forward to seeing you tomorrow.'

Karen tilted her phone, so Joe's stony expression came into view. He nodded at the screen. 'Good to see you, Lane. I hope you've been staying out of trouble and didn't do anything stupid like climb into a stall with an upside-down horse at thirty thousand feet.'

'Funny you should mention that,' Lane shot an abashed look at Karen, 'but it all ended well. The horse is fine, and the owner is happy.'

'Who owns the twenty-million-dollar horse?' Karen asked.

'Brian Farley-Wells. The horse is Sucre Noir.'

'Nice.' Karen remembered seeing the horse run in the States. 'That's a *nice* for the horse, not the owner. He'll get the money back in service fees in no time. I've heard of Brian but haven't met him. What's he like?'

'He's your everyday, run-of-the-mill billionaire.' Lane waggled his eyebrows at the screen. 'He likes fast horses, big limousines, and impressing people with his wealth and power.'

'You're not doing much of a job selling him to me,' she grimaced. 'That sounds like my father, and we're not exactly on speaking terms anymore.'

'Brian likes horses,' Lane assured her, remembering how her father sanctioned the suffering of the horses at his Pilatos laboratories. 'You'll get to meet him when his horse Quest runs in a few weeks.'

'His horse, Quest?' Karen opened her eyes wide, waiting for more information.

'He's a fine horse. He was underneath Sucre Noir on the plane. I hope he's slow so I can have him.'

Karen laughed. 'I knew you'd have a new horse tied up somewhere in this. What's he like, this Quest?'

'He's a bay with a question mark on his forehead and intelligent eyes. I liked him.'

'I can tell. Love hearts are forming over your head as you're talking. I never worry about you falling in love with another woman, but I do have to compete with the horses you fall in love with.'

'You'll always win that competition,' he assured her.

'I don't have to win. I'm fine with coming second to a horse now and then.'

Knowing that Joe could hear them prevented Lane from pursuing a more intimate conversation. Instead, he told her about their plans for the coming weeks, including visiting his station in the outback.

'You know I'm happy to do anything with you in my time off, whether that's going to the races or camping in the wilderness. But maybe not watch football with you. Those Australian games are far too confusing.'

'I can live without football.' He paused before clarifying his statement. 'Of course, if we're talking about State of Origin, that's different. We have to watch that.'

Karen gave a dramatic groan.

'Also, if we have time, I might look into why two lots of dead horses were dumped – fifty in each place. It might be nothing, but it seems odd.'

'I heard about that.' Karen narrowed her eyes in thought as she searched her memory. 'In South America somewhere.'

'No, here in Australia. Around the Hunter Valley.'

Tilting her head, Karen squinted at the screen and pursed her lips. 'A mass grave of horses? No - it was definitely South America - Venezuela. Outside Caracas. There were close to one hundred horses with the brands cut off, found in an abandoned quarry. They'd been covered up, but heavy rains washed some of the dirt off. Julian was telling me about it. One of the Bisente riders came from the region and got the goss from her parents.'

'That's an unusual coincidence.' Lane's mind went into overdrive as he tried to think of possible connections between the sites in New South Wales and the one in Venezuela. Were there others out there? It seemed unlikely that this had only happened three times, and they learned of all three – how many other places were yet to be found?

'I can see the cogs in your head turning over. It's just a coincidence until we learn otherwise, so don't lose any sleep over it. People breed too many horses the world over, and if they don't want them going to pet food, they might just put them down and bury them. It's not a crime – it's just a coincidence.'

'Or maybe a quantum connection.' He gave her a look of speculation as he considered how often seemingly random events were connected.

'Maybe. And maybe we'd better stop talking as I have to get on a jet and fly to Australia to meet a crazy horseman.'

'I'll be waiting at the airport tomorrow.'

Karen narrowed one eye to look at him with suspicion. 'Are you sure? I have the feeling you're going to be busy chasing down information about all those buried horses. You might forget to make it to the airport.'

'Cross my heart; I'll be there.' Lane made a crossing motion over his chest. 'Though, I may use some of my spare time trying to find out more about this.'

'I bet you will,' Karen chuckled. 'I have to go. I'll message you when I'm on the plane. I can't wait to see you.'

Instead of typing the reply for the artificial voice, Lane held up his right hand with his thumb, index, and little fingers raised, and the middle and ring fingers folded down. *I love you.*

Karen brushed the backs of her fingers against her cheek and flicked them forward. *Always.*

For several minutes after the phone call ended, Lane stared into space, thinking about Karen Lawford and all she meant to him. He'd fallen in love with her the moment they met over a year ago, though it had taken considerably longer for her to return the feelings. She ran Pilatos after removing her father from power when he risked everything to produce a drug that slowed aging in men. Such was the allure of the fountain of youth that he bred a genetically unique line of horses that remained in stables all their lives so they could provide the blood required for Stablex. When Karen learned the truth of what happened with the horses, she conducted a coup and took control of the company. Her father retired to a foreign country with his personal supply of Stablex, and Karen managed to restructure the company to bring it back from the brink of bankruptcy.

In all those long months she dedicated to reshaping Pilatos into an ethical company that cared about its employees, the environment, and the welfare of animals, Lane remained at her side. He massaged her temples when she suffered from migraines, he cooked for her, and he held her as she cried in frustration and despair at trying to keep the company afloat without causing job losses and distress to the workforce. It was far easier making money by ignoring the rights of workers and the value of the environment than it was trying to provide equity for all and a sustainable approach.

This was their first full-length holiday together since they had three weeks alone on his station in outback Queensland after the Stablex horses were set free. He wanted it to be perfect for Karen. She deserved an incredible holiday without stress or other issues, but he couldn't stop wondering about those horses.

Before going next door to see Tom, he sent a message to Julian asking him if the South American rider would be available to answer a few questions about the horses buried outside Caracas. He was curious about whether the horses had been shot or killed by lethal injection and if they represented one breed or many, like those in Australia.

Do you want to order something for lunch? Lane asked when he joined Tom in his rooms.

'Sounds good.' Tom reclined on his bed and pointed to the hotel information folder. 'Pick something from that. There seem to be dozens of places nearby that deliver meals. Pizza, Thai, salad – whatever. I'm easy.'

Vegemite sandwiches it is.

A pillow hurtled from the bed, and Lane barely managed to raise his hands before it hit his head.

'Don't you dare feed me that vile stuff.' Tom pulled a face at the thought of the black spread enjoyed by so many Australians. 'I know there's something seriously wrong with you lot when you enjoy that goo.'

Lane grinned at him. *And I don't understand why you don't like it.* He handed Tom a menu from a local Vietnamese restaurant. *But since you're that fussy, order something from this. I'll have Bun cha, thanks.*

After Tom placed their order, Lane told him about the horses discovered in South America. Like Karen, Tom doubted there was a connection.

'People overbreed. They buy them because they're cheap, then they can't afford to feed them. You know all the stories. There are probably plenty of places around the world where people have buried the victims of their horse dreams.'

I guess, Lane shrugged, unconvinced. *I still want to find out more. Can you speak to someone on the council where they were found?*

'Find me some phone numbers, and I'm on it.'

It took less than a minute for Lane to find contact numbers for the two New South Wales councils. He listened in amusement as Tom used his Arizona charm on the employees. They transferred him to several different people at each office, but no one could provide any information. He left his phone number in case they learned anything new.

'No one seems to have any knowledge apart from the fact that they were there.' Tom put the phone down and frowned. 'They don't know how they died. They don't know if anyone ran any tests to see if there was any contamination of any sort. They don't know where they came from or how long they were there. One of the men I spoke to has horses, so he was interested in the story, but the police told him it wasn't worth investigating, and the RSPCA weren't interested as there was no indication of animal cruelty.'

How could they know if no one did any examinations or tests?

'I know. It seems it wasn't considered important enough to investigate. Perhaps, when tens of thousands of horses end up as pet food, seeing one hundred put down and buried didn't seem a big deal.'

Lane's mouth tucked to one side in distaste at that thought. *You'd think they would at least want to charge someone with illegal dumping. All those carcasses would be a contamination risk.*

'Well, they didn't. It's been swept away like it never happened. The horseman I spoke to was surprised it didn't rate much of a mention in the news. Word of mouth has been spreading it among horse people.'

A knock at the door heralded the arrival of lunch. While they were eating, the conversation switched to the books they were writing. Lane's collection of stories about horses he had known had a release date a few months away, and he needed to focus on finishing it. Tom's book covered indigenous knowledge about weather and climate in different parts of the world, and he was doing his final edits.

After lunch, Lane remained in his room writing while Tom went to the airport to meet Vicki, who was flying in from Adelaide. She had taken several weeks' leave to join Tom in Australia and had agreed to cover an event in Adelaide for her newspaper before meeting him in Melbourne. She disliked leaving her animals for any length of time, but she wanted a holiday with Tom, so her family helped out. Her dressage horse and her dog were at her parents' farm near Redding in Connecticut, and her sister was staying in her New York apartment to mind her two cats.

When he saw her striding through the arrival door with her light brown hair swishing around her face as she spoke animatedly to the person next to her, he smiled. The harsh expression he usually wore melted at the sight of the feisty and funny journalist who stole his heart. He watched her head turn as she began to scan the waiting crowd looking for him. When her large hazel eyes landed on him, they lit with delight. She waved and grinned, looking more like an excited teenager than a mature and respected journalist.

Fighting the urge to run to her and sweep her up in his arms, he walked with studied casualness, his gaze so focused on her beaming face that everything else blurred into meaningless sound, movement, and color. When he reached her, he wrapped his arms around her and tilted his head so he could continue to meet her eyes.

'It's good to see you,' he managed to say before she stood on tiptoes and pressed her smiling mouth against his.

'It's even better to kiss you.' Her eyes sparkled with bedroom promises as she pulled away from him. 'Have I mentioned that I don't like being away from you?'

Tom took a few seconds to control his emotions. His mother used to tease him about how his life would change when he fell in love. She tried to describe the feelings to him, and he laughed at the thought of feeling weak at the knees or having his heart thump so loudly that it felt as though everyone could hear it. Nothing she said prepared him for the exquisite sensation of seeing and holding Vicki, whether they were together every hour of the day or seeing each other after a week apart.

'Maybe,' he murmured against her hair. 'I'm happy to hear you say it as many times as you like.'

He wanted to say something more meaningful. His inner voice spoke eloquently of achieving happiness if time stopped right now and he spent eternity in this moment, feeling her body against his forever, but the words remained silent.

'I don't like being away from you,' she repeated with a chuckle. Leaning back, she looked up into his smoldering eyes, and an involuntary shiver ran through her. 'Let's get back to your room. Do you have a car?'

Tom shook his head and tapped the phone in his pocket. 'We're Ubering. It's all organized.' Picking up her travel case, he started towards the bag collection area.

'You distracted me so much I forgot I had luggage to pick up.' Vicki trotted at his side, marveling at how his long legs covered the ground so quickly.

Flashing a grin at her, he waggled his eyebrows in the way she found so charming on his usually stern face. 'The sooner we get back to the room, the quicker I can work on distracting you even more.'

'Promises, promises.'

Several hours later, with their hair still wet from showering and their eyes devouring each other, they knocked on Lane's door. When the door swung open, he looked from one to the other, quirking an eyebrow at the afterglow shining from them.

He tapped the wall next to him. *These walls are far too thin.*

Vicki shot him a mortified look as she thought of her very active reunion with Tom.

Lane laughed. *Kidding. Sorry.* He reached out to hug her, laughing even harder when she slapped him on the back and called him an unsavory name.

'I want to say I'm pleased to see you,' Vicki sniffed as she walked through to the main room, 'but I don't think I will now. When does Karen arrive?' She looked over her shoulder so she could see his answer.

Early tomorrow. We're heading up to Sydney in the morning to meet her and Joe.

'Good. I can play that thin walls joke on Karen and see if she finds it funny.'

Lane held out both hands apologetically before signing, *We're flying straight to Brisbane when she arrives. All of us. You won't have time for that joke. Sorry.* He winked at her, clearly not at all apologetic.

'We're spending a few days at Wunya Stud near Gatton,' said Tom. He threw himself into one of the armchairs and grinned at Lane. 'Of course, it will mean you won't have time for a private reunion, my friend. It'll be a quick hello in public and a rush to Gate Nine.'

I can handle that. Lane was unperturbed by Tom's teasing. Once Matthew and his twin Andrea joined them, the clown factor would increase by ten, so this bit of joshing was beginner level. *Coffee? Have you told Vicki about the dead horses?*

'Excuse me?' Vicki turned incredulous eyes on Tom. 'Is there a newsworthy story that I don't know about?'

Tom shook his head. 'I don't think so. When it comes to horses, Lane sees conspiracies where we see coincidences. You know that.'

'I know nothing of the sort,' scoffed Vicki, plonking herself down on Tom's lap and planting a quick kiss on his cheek. 'I do know that even when I'm on holiday, my editor expects me to keep looking for stories, and it looks like you're sitting on one. Spill it.'

While Lane made coffee, Tom told her about the buried horses in Australia and South America.

'So that's it,' he finished. 'So un-newsworthy that our newspapers and tv stations haven't bothered with it.'

Vicki harrumphed and met Lane's eyes as he handed her a cup of coffee. 'You think there's something to it, don't you?'

With a non-committal shrug, Lane put his and Tom's coffees on the low table and sat in the chair opposite his friends. *I don't know enough yet. I want to learn more.*

'So do I,' Vicki nodded at him and elbowed Tom none too gently. 'And you think it isn't worthy of being news - this is going to make the New York news.'

Before Tom could retort, his phone rang. He looked at the screen before answering. 'It's Binky.'

As he took the call, Vicki mouthed *Binky?* to Lane.

His new girlfriend, Lane ignored Tom's fierce glare and ducked when a cushion flew at his head. *She was helping transfer horses from the air stables to trucks this morning. She told him about the horses.*

'Then my journalistic nose has just gone into bloodhound territory,' she playfully sniffed around Tom's ear as he tried to listen to what Binky was telling him. 'I smell a story.'

'Is that right?' Tom said to Binky as he raised a warning finger at Vicki, who was doing a bloodhound impersonation at his collar.

She bit his finger, Lane laughed, and Tom rolled his eyes at them both.

'You stay safe, alright?' Tom told Binky. 'Don't go drawing

attention to yourself. In fact, don't do anything. We'll handle it.'

He finished the call and examined the tooth marks on his finger. 'Vicki bit me, and that really hurt, Vicki.'

Vicki snorted at the perfect British accent coming from the Arizona man. One of the most endearing things about Tom was the playfulness under the stern exterior. 'Here's a note for future reference - don't raise a finger at me, and it won't get bitten.'

'I'll never raise a finger against you,' Tom promised, then shook his hand dramatically. 'Not if I risk getting bitten.'

You live and learn, Lane smirked. *You need a strong-minded woman who won't put up with your alpha male, finger-shaking ways.*

'Exactly,' agreed Vicki, wriggling on Tom's lap and laughing at his discomfort. 'Those sweet little things who think men have the right to rule the world would apologize to the finger and, before you know it, you'd be lording it over them as they apologized their way into insignificance. Me? I bite.'

'I noticed.' Tom grimaced at her, his dark eyes dancing with mirth. 'And I deserved it. I was out of line. I apologize my way into insignificance.'

Vicki dug him in the ribs. 'You are never going to be insignificant.'

Making a gagging noise at their banter, Lane signed, *What did your stalker have to say?*

'Stalker?' Vicki shook her head, trying to take in the new information. 'I thought you said Binky was his girlfriend.'

Tom frowned at their joking. 'She's not a girlfriend, and she's not a stalker. She just appreciates what an incredible person I am and chose to learn a lot about me.'

'She's a stalker,' chortled Vicki.

'She has some interesting news.'

'News?' Vicki sat upright on his lap.

Tom's lips twitched in amusement at her sudden attentiveness – she was ever the journalist. 'Binky's uncle works in one of the coal mines not far from the mine where the horses were found. She asked him about it, and he said that no one should be able to truck in horses and operate machinery to bury them because they have locks, alarms, and security patrols. He also said that a few weeks ago, one of his workmates joked about some easy money burying horses, and he disappeared the next day.'

'No way!' Vicki removed herself from his chair and sat on the settee opposite, leaning forward eagerly as her newshound senses kicked in. 'Is this something the workmate often does, or do we have a murder?'

'Binky's uncle says it's out of character for him, and he hasn't contacted work or family. The story slid past the newspapers and tv like the horses. No one was interested.'

'I'm interested,' Vicki's eyes glowed. 'I could easily make a that's-not-news call on the horses but a man who claims he was paid to bury horses and then vanishes, now, that is something worth chasing up.'

'Binky is on her way to the Hunter now with some horses. I asked her to be careful. Maybe the missing man has just gone fishing, but if he has gone missing because of that easy money, this could be dangerous.'

Vicki tapped her fingers against her knees as ideas ran through her mind. 'Can you text a few questions through to your buddy Binky? I'm after some names and times so I can start researching.' She turned to Lane. 'What's your gut feeling on this?'

There's a story here. Lane stood and stalked to the window to look out over the city. The bright lights of Melbourne made him long for the outback. He turned to his friends and continued signing, *I think there are more buried horses and more missing people because this feels like the start of a pattern.*

'If people are going missing because of the horses,' Tom pointed out, 'it implies that this is not a case of horse people getting rid of excess horses. Something else has to be going on. You don't remove people because you couldn't feed your horse.'

Laundering drug money? Lane suggested. *Perhaps they buy cheap horses then claim to sell them for big money, but the money is from drug sales, and the horses need to disappear.*

'Good theory,' commended Vicki. 'Even if that's not the case with these horses, I'm sure someone will be doing that somewhere. What about laboratory research gone wrong? We've already had the run-in with the Pilatos laboratories. If we're following a trail of coincidences, maybe we're dealing with something like that again. Pilatos didn't want the world knowing about all the horses dying in their stables, and some of their employees were capable of making people disappear. I could imagine them quietly burying animals en masse if they thought they could get away with it.'

What about trying to hide a disease outbreak? Lane thought of the range of equine viruses that an owner or group of owners might be desperate to hide. *If a riding school or knackery or even a stud learned some of their horses had Hendra, they might put down everything that showed symptoms and hope the authorities didn't find out about it and put down all their other horses as well. Or it could be African Horse Sickness because that is creeping closer to Australia.*

'Or Equine Infectious Anaemia,' added Tom, 'or another outbreak of Equine Influenza, or Nipah.'

'Remind me again – why do we have horses?' Vicki wrinkled her nose at all the deadly equine diseases, the worst of which were zoonotic and could pass on to humans. 'Any of those could certainly motivate someone to dispose of horses quietly. Where's the connection between the ones here and the ones in South America, though?'

Tom scratched his head, trying to think of a possible link. 'Maybe someone traveled between the two places and carried the disease. Could the one owner have horses in both places?'

Taking out her phone, Vicki began searching for links between horses and the two countries using various combinations of keywords. While she searched, she made the occasional noise in her throat to express frustration, surprise, disagreement, or interest. The two men continued to throw ideas between each other.

'Well, that's interesting.' Vicki lowered her phone and narrowed her eyes, deep in thought as she sorted through the information in her head.

I think she's going to keep us in suspense, Lane signed to Tom. *Or maybe she didn't find anything, and she's pretending.*

Slanting her eyes up at him, she twisted her mouth to the side. 'I have peripheral vision, you know.'

Lane winked at her. *I know.*

'OK, smarty-butt,' she feigned annoyance but couldn't prevent a smile from surfacing. 'Once I removed references to individual racehorses with Venezuela in their name, there were a few links that kept showing up. Both countries are big on racing. Then there is Venezuelan Equine Encephalitis, a zoonotic disease with horse-to-human transfer and a high death rate. That might support your virus theory. There are also Olympic horses and riders mentioned from both countries, as well as individuals involved in show jumping and polo. Any chance they were all polo ponies?'

'If Binky's descriptions are accurate,' replied Tom, 'they were a mix of horses and ponies, including some heavy horses, so that's unlikely.'

'There are a few owners who have large numbers of horses both here and in Venezuela, including racehorse owners, Arabian breeders, and others – I've copied their names to a list you can go through later. A cutting horse facility outside Caracas has imported at least a dozen horses from Australia over the last few years, and four of them are from one of your friends, Lane – Cameron O'Shea. There's a photo of you standing with one of the horses before it left Australia.'

He's a good man. He wouldn't be involved in having big numbers of horses put down and buried.

'F.L.W., Lane,' Vicki warned.

He gave her a questioning look.

'Famous last words,' she explained. 'I can't tell you how many times I've said *he'd never* or *she wouldn't*, only to be proven wrong. But, moving on, the charity Rescuing Equines Everywhere has riding centers in both places where they give challenged children and those living in poverty the chance to learn to ride. Several international horse transport companies, including Horse Air Transport Company, have offices in both countries. They are the ones you flew with, aren't they?'

Tom nodded. 'HATCO. It's a big company that's flying million-dollar horses around. I can't see a reason for them to kill a bunch of horses and ponies and bury them.'

'I'm not saying that - I'm merely bringing up names that came up in relation to horses in both countries. There's also a Wunya connection that might be worth checking out. Ernie, the eldest son of your friends Henry and Sheree, is based in Caracas and has several Wunya horses doing show jumping. There's a coincidence for you.'

There are too many coincidences. Lane shrugged. The horse world was a small place, and the region occupied by high-profile breeders, trainers, riders, and associated businesses even smaller. If there was something nefarious linking the dead horses in both countries, and it involved well-known horse people or businesses, there was a good chance he would know them.

'Here's a recent newspaper article about Grace Walker from Horse Helpers Australia visiting Caracas,' she turned her phone around so they could see the photo of a woman with light brown hair and glasses frowning at the camera as she patted a horse. 'Apparently, she was looking at some of their horse rescue facilities.'

'I've heard her name a few times today.' Tom reached for the phone and examined the image of the serious young woman who looked more like a librarian than a horse person. 'That's curious in itself. Is there anything linking her to the Hunter Valley?'

When he handed the phone back to Vicki, she ran a quick search. 'Here you go. She has a Horse Helpers depot for rescue horses not far from Singleton.'

The men exchanged *ah-ha* glances.

'And look. Here's a photo of her with Ernie Lomond and one of his show jumpers at a competition in Caracas.'

This is doing my head in, Lane complained as the connections began tangling in his mind.

'I've only scratched the surface,' said Vicki, putting her phone back in her pocket. 'Who'd have thought that there were so many equine connections between Australia and Venezuela? We don't even know if there is a link between the horses dumped here and the ones there – they could be unrelated.'

True, Lane acknowledged. *My instinct is that the same people did it. In both cases, the brands were cut off. They didn't want anyone to trace the horses through their brands.*

Vicki felt sure a story lurked in the information. 'I'll do some more research tonight after dinner. Are you coming with us?'

Looking at their faces still glowing from the pleasure of being back together, Lane shook his head. A romantic dinner always went better with two. *I want to write another chapter, so I'll stay here. Thanks.*

That evening, while Tom and Vicki held hands across a candlelit table, Lane wrote about how horses feel grief. He described a horse that refused to eat when his rider died, and another that suffered from extreme depression when his paddock mate, a goat, passed away. Horses could display classic signs of grief in much the same way as humans understand the emotion. As he typed, he wondered about the buried horses – unknown horses intended to be forgotten. Did they have friendships? Did they grieve for horses and people they had lost before being killed and disposed of like rubbish?

He went to sleep thinking about the unknown horses and wondering how many more lay forgotten in mass graves.

In the morning, they returned to the airport early and flew the hour to Sydney. Once there, Lane attempted to appear cool, calm, and collected but, on the inside, he felt like a six-year-old on Christmas morning waiting for his parents to wake so he could open presents. While Vicki and Tom wandered off to shop, Lane watched the planes land, occasionally glancing at the list of scheduled arrivals.

Once her jet landed, she messaged him. He wrote and deleted four replies before hitting on one that seemed to balance looking forward to seeing her without being too needy.

How many messages did you delete before you came up with that one? Karen's reply made him chuckle. She knew him so well.

Four. I deleted too clingy, too casual, too insecure, and too jokey, and went for the classic factual approach.

The weather details were an added bonus. I appreciate them. That's a fact.

Who's getting jokey now? He grinned as he sent the words, imagining her laughing at their exchange.

But it wasn't too jokey like the messages you deleted. I think mine struck a good balance. The seatbelt sign is off – see you soon.

Flying Business Class meant that Karen and Joe had a fast-track through customs. Lane had to work extra hard to maintain his nonchalance as he caught sight of her leading the way into the area where friends and family waited to greet passengers. Her classic elegance in black pants, a cream silk shirt, and an emerald jacket set her apart from travel-weary passengers in crumpled clothes. He raised a hand to catch her eye and felt the usual punch to his chest when she looked at him and smiled.

It's good to see you, he signed as she approached.

And you, she returned, as she strode towards him on long legs.

He took her in his arms, and she melted into his embrace. A sense of coming home swept through them both as they held each other. Words were unnecessary as they exhaled the stress and tension of life and inhaled the strength and wonder of being together again.

'I missed this so much,' she whispered in his ear.

'I know,' he breathed into her hair.

There were moments when the barriers of the selective mutism dropped, and words found his voice. Although the option to speak aloud was switched off by his mind, on occasions, it appeared for a few seconds. It was beyond his control. Specialists, psychologists, and psychiatrists failed to open the pathways, and he rarely missed the ability to speak since there were other effective ways to communicate.

As he held her, he was grateful that some of the *voice-on* moments occurred when they were together. Before Karen, horses were the only ones to hear his voice, which seemed fitting. It was because his voice couldn't save his beloved horses when he was eight that it went away, returning briefly to help soothe a horse that needed more than his touch.

Joe Kaiphas, one of the trusted heads of Pilatos Industries, coughed politely and shuffled from foot to foot while his boss and her lover embraced. Once in charge of security, he now worked as Karen's second-in-command. He understood how the company ran on all levels and was determined to maintain the ethical and sustainable approaches that Karen introduced after taking control.

Stepping slightly away from Karen while keeping one arm around her, Lane held his right hand out to Joe, smiling with the genuine delight of seeing a good friend.

'Good to be back in Australia.' Joe shook his hand and gave him a fatherly slap on the shoulder. 'Any chance we can have a real holiday without drama, problems, and danger?'

The sheepish look Lane shot him was correctly interpreted by both Americans.

'Really?' Karen laughed, amused by the abashed expression on Lane's face. She kissed him on the cheek. 'I'm assuming this is about those buried horses. What else have you found out?'

By the time they met Vicki and Tom in an airport cafe, Lane had updated them on the buried horses and the missing miner. Over coffee, Tom listed some of the horse-related connections between Venezuela and Australia while Vicki emailed the information they'd gathered so far to everyone, including Matthew and Andrea.

On the flight to Brisbane, Lane and Karen held hands most of the way, remembering their first flights together as they traveled to Austria. Joe thought the hand-holding was sweet while Tom pretended to put fingers down his throat, an action that prompted a slap on the arm from Vicki, followed by making him hold her hand. Lane and Karen didn't care about what anyone else thought; they were in their own world where only the other existed.

When they disembarked at Brisbane, Matthew and Andrea were waiting. Like an over-excited Golden Retriever puppy, Matthew jumped around hugging, handshaking, and patting backs. At twenty-six, he and Andrea were the youngest in the group. His youthful energy made him seem adolescent, while his twin's dignified reserve gave her the appearance of someone far older. Their fashion reinforced the differences. Matthew wore the checked shirt and Wranglers preferred by young rodeo riders, and his black hair hung in unruly curls to his collar. His sister had her sleek black hair pulled back, and the blue jeans, white t-shirt, and black jacket lent her the look of a model on assignment.

The pair had flown in from northern Australia, where they spent two weeks twice a year volunteering at Doomadgee, the Aboriginal reserve where they grew up. They taught the children about handling horses and photography, and tried to act as positive role models. On this visit, Andrea brought a dozen cameras from one of her sponsors so the Doomadgee children could work on their photography and email her the results. She intended to publish a book of their photographs, with all profits going back to their schools.

Matthew had a Toyota Kluger waiting so they could drive to Gatton. Fortunately, Matthew's driving was less erratic than his bouncing behavior, and he safely negotiated the Brisbane roads, from the Airport Tunnel and the Legacy Way, out to the Warrego Highway, which led west from Brisbane. After driving through Gatton, they turned down the Mt Sylvia valley, driving past some of Australia's finest vegetable-growing properties.

As the valley narrowed and the hills began to close in, they reached the gates of Wunya, a five-hundred-acre property sprawled across the valley floor and up into the mountains. The farm had white railed fences, a covered arena, and dozens of horse pens with immaculately presented stables. Large Warmblood horses watched with interest as the car pulled up near the main house.

The owners, Henry and Sheree Lomond, had several guesthouses which they turned over to Lane and his friends whenever they visited the area. Lane and Karen had a one-bedroom cottage, as did Tom and Vicki, while Matthew, Andrea, and Joe shared a three-bedroom bungalow, all scattered through the expansive gardens of the horse stud.

After putting their bags in the house, they joined the Lomonds and their sons in the main house for pre-dinner drinks. Lane was keen to hear if the Lomonds could offer any insights into the mystery of the buried horses.

***

Dibby and Rev

The driver delivered the horses to the Horse Air Transport Company facility and passed along his notes about them. Grooms checked the horses for injuries and swapped the headstalls for the padded HATCO ones.

As a hard-faced woman removed Dibby's headstall, he gently nudged her hoping for a scratch or some kind words. He loved the sound of human voices talking to him.

'Cut that out,' she snapped and punched his neck.

Dibby tensed and held his head slightly turned away from her as she adjusted the headstall. Rev's soft intelligent eyes regarded the woman as she moved to him, and he stood like a rock as she changed his headgear. She didn't pat him before moving to the next horse.

Once she was gone, Rev nudged Dibby, and the two stood, nose to nose, breathing each other's breath.

One of the female grooms appeared and looked around to make sure no one was watching. She took out her phone and started taking photos of each of the horses. When another worker arrived to check that all headstalls were on correctly, she pretended to look at her messages. When they left, she returned to photographing the horses and their brands.

CHAPTER FOUR

We need to remember that when we win, our horse should also be winning. Sometimes, people are so focused on winning that their horse loses: the training is harsh, the punishment extreme, and the horse's joy forgotten. You can both win. You don't have to break him to train him - you can build something joyful when the two of you work together in harmony. When that happens, you both win with every ride.

'Horse Dreaming' by Lane Dimity, p. 88
International bestseller

Horse Charities

'I don't have time for any of the charities,' declared Matthew with a scowl as they discussed fundraising tactics in the large Wunya kitchen. Sharing photos of ancient horses suffering numerous illnesses to increase donations seemed wrong to him on many levels. 'The organizers seem to think running a charity is a license to do what they want while spending other people's money. They pull everyone's heartstrings with stories of sick and infirm horses, many of which would be better off put down, just to raise funds which mostly go to pay for the horse hoarder's lifestyle.'

'They're not all like that,' insisted Sheree as she turned out a loaf of fresh-baked bread to accompany dinner. She wanted to tell him about their neighbor but realized it might not be the right time, so let him continue his rant.

The seven guests stood around the enormous country kitchen, which was filled with delicious odors of French cooking. Sheree was cooking her way around the world, and this week's menu covered European regions.

'Most are.' Matthew held strong opinions about horse rescues and charities, and the more he learned of them, the less he liked. 'Sure, I know there are some that do a good job, but you have to admit, most of them are a total rort. They're about making money for the organizers, not doing the right thing for the horses. I recently looked at one in the States, and they were bringing in hundreds of thousands of dollars, but only five percent of it was going to the horses.'

'I thought that was the accepted margin most charities operate on,' reasoned Henry, putting Sheree's bread on a breadboard and moving it to the dining table in the adjoining room. 'Ninety-five percent goes to running costs, advertising, administration, office space, car hire, wages, and so on, and five cents in the dollar goes to the people or animals the donors want to help. It's not just horse charities that do that, and it's usually a better ratio than that.'

'I understand,' said Matthew, 'but it's the horse ones that irk me at the moment. I'll get on my high horse about the others later. They rake in money hand over fist because people want to help the horses. The people running the charities live the high life on the donations while they use the suffering of horses to make an income for themselves.'

That's a bit harsh, bro, Lane put his wine down so he could sign. *How many do you really know? It's easy to repeat social media complaints when they aren't true. We heard of some good ones yesterday.*

'Brian Farley-Wells donated to a couple in our names,' put in Tom. 'After Lane risked his life like a twenty-first-century hero of the skies,' he grinned when Lane pulled a face at him, 'and saved his gazillion-dollar horses, he wanted to reward us, and since we wouldn't take his money, he decided to donate to some horse charities. I wouldn't imagine he'd donate to them if they weren't legitimate. He seemed the sort of man who would check things out carefully before giving away money.'

'Who did he support?' Matthew asked.

'Rescuing Equines Everywhere and – maybe - Equines In Need Of Funds. I looked them up today. REE does some great work saving horses and giving the sound ones useful lives teaching disadvantaged children to ride. Equines In Need Of Funds seems just as good.'

'Did you check out their financial reports?' Matthew remained suspicious of the entire industry of equine charities.

'Sure,' Tom arched a brow at him and took a sip of his coffee. 'I allowed my paranoia to guide me, and I spent ten hours today poring over their financial statements and researching the destination of every dollar they receive.'

His sarcasm almost caused Vicki to snort her gin and tonic down her shirt.

Matthew was unimpressed. 'Maybe you should have looked at them. They'll be a con; they all are. Show me a horse rescue, and I'll show you a horse hoarder or a con artist tricking people out of their money.'

'All horse rescues are horse hoarders or criminals?' A new voice with a hostile edge joined the conversation.

Everyone turned to see a woman in tight black jeans and a red shirt standing at one of the kitchen entrances. She rested her hands on shapely hips as she glared at Matthew, who was similarly dressed in jeans and a red shirt. With her chin raised combatively and her shoulders squared back, she looked as though she was ready to stride into battle. Her straight brown hair was pulled back in a ponytail, and her hazel eyes flashed with sparks of green through her glasses as she sized up the dark-eyed man who spoke with such contempt about horse rescues.

'Pretty much,' he flashed her one of his smiles that usually charmed everyone.

It had no effect on the feisty woman in the red shirt.

'And you've had experience with every horse rescue in Australia, have you?' Her voice remained as belligerent as her stance. Part of her acknowledged that his face was ridiculously handsome when he smiled like that, but she detested sweeping generalizations, and a charming smile was not about to distract her. 'You've met every single person who runs them and know for a fact that they're either a horse hoarder or a criminal?'

'I don't need to.' Since charm did not affect her, he glided seamlessly into infuriating insolence, ignoring the audience who seemed bemused by the clash of words between the redshirts. 'I see them begging for funds when they can't afford to feed all the horses they bought. Here's one for you – the first rule of horse ownership: if you can't afford to feed them, don't collect them. The horse rescue people go to auctions and get into bidding frenzies over horses they want – that isn't rescuing, that's buying. They're outbidding people who want to buy the horse, not pet food buyers. And I know some of the people who run the charities earn more money from the charity than what the donors earn in their jobs. It's a crooked business of horse hoarders and con artists, and you won't convince me otherwise.'

'I wouldn't bother trying,' she narrowed her eyes and reached for an insult that could dent his arrogant demeanor. None was forthcoming, so she defaulted to one of her grandmother's sayings.

'You can only educate those capable of learning. There's no point trying to teach a turkey how to tat.'

If she expected to rile him with her words, she was sorely disappointed. Instead of taking umbrage, he burst out laughing, his deep brown eyes glowing with merriment as he chortled at being likened to a turkey. Even the menacing presence of Joe Kaiphas seemed to soften at the sight of a woman squaring up to Matthew and smacking him about the head with words.

'Tat?' Matthew spluttered. 'What the heck is that? Maybe turkeys can do it.'

'It's making lace,' replied Grace scathingly, 'and, no, turkeys can't make lace.'

Sheree took the opportunity to introduce the newcomer. It was unfortunate she walked in as Matthew had his mouth in top gear about horse rescues, but it couldn't be helped. 'I'd like everyone to meet our neighbor, Grace Walker. She runs Horse Helpers, which is next door to us.'

'Surprise.' Grace offered Matthew a cold, fake smile, her anger burning hot beneath the cool facade. 'I'm one of those horse-hoarding criminals.'

'At least you admit it.' Matthew waggled his eyebrows at her.

Grace was not amused.

'It's always a pleasure to see you, Grace,' Sheree stepped in front of Matthew to try and break the conflict before it escalated. 'If I'd known you were back from Sydney, I would have invited you for dinner.'

'I'm finding myself rather relieved that you didn't.' Grace's smile warmed marginally as she looked at her neighbor.

Sheree proceeded to introduce everyone. Like most people in the horse world, Grace knew of Lane and his friends. She was a fan of Lane and followed him on social media but refrained from mentioning that while a certain pair of unnerving dark eyes mocked her.

'And our outspoken friend here is Matthew McLeay, Andrea's twin. Once he gets to know you, he'll realize you're neither a horse hoarder nor a criminal, so don't be too offended by his words. They're not personal.'

'They seemed that way.' Grace shot Matthew a sour look. He grinned at her. A pacifist by nature, she was surprised by the strength of her desire to punch him.

'Perhaps you'll have time to tell us about Horse Helpers.' Karen smiled at Grace, finding herself liking the fiery woman whose eyes launched knives at Matthew. 'I haven't had much to do with any horse rescue facilities, so I'd be interested in learning more.'

'You are welcome to visit if you have the time.' Grace's attitude improved considerably when she met the calm gaze of the head of Pilatos. The previous year, she followed the story of the Friesian stallions bred by Pilatos, and she approved of Karen's changes since she took over the company. 'I understand some people are wary of horse rescues, so I am always open to inspections and questions.' Sending a dark look at Matthew, she added, 'And my financials are always available if you want to find evidence of my criminal activity.'

Unabashed, Matthew winked at her. 'Much appreciated, Grace. I wouldn't mind examining them to see what we come up with.'

'I assure you, Grace is one of the good ones.' Henry put a glass of white wine in Grace's hand and patted her shoulder. 'Drink up, neighbor. He mightn't seem so irritating after a few glasses.'

'I'll drink to that,' Andrea raised her glass in Grace's direction. 'A few drinks always make it easier to put up with my brother. Finish the bottle, and you might decide he's a decent bloke.'

'I'd have alcohol poisoning before I reached that point,' Grace said caustically, causing Andrea to laugh.

'Will you stay for dinner now that you're here?' Sheree asked her. 'I'm in France tonight. *Potage Parmentier* and fresh bread, followed by *Boeuf bourguignon*, and finished off with *Tarte Tatin.* I cooked for an army, so there's plenty. Please stay.'

Glancing around at her hosts, their four sons already sitting at the dinner table, and the seven guests in the kitchen, Grace shook her head. 'Thanks, Sheree. I'll take a rain-check on that.'

'Don't leave on my account.' Matthew gave her a lopsided grin, enjoying seeing her eyes spark when she looked at him.

'I'm not likely to do anything on your account,' she told him sharply. 'I came over to let Sheree and Henry know that a couple of their cows were out on the road.' Her voice softened as she looked at Sheree. 'They didn't want to come back here, so I've popped them in one of my paddocks. They'll be fine until you have time to get them.'

'Thanks for that,' said Sheree. 'I'll send the boys over in the morning. Before you go, can you tell our visitors what you think of REE? They are interested in learning a little more about the nature of horse charities.'

'Don't get me started.' Grace took a mouthful of her wine and looked around at everyone, seeing curiosity in their expressions. 'I meant that literally. It's really not a good idea to get me started talking about them. Anyway, I'm sure I don't know anything that you wouldn't discover, given a few days and the right questions.'

'We're not that interested, to tell the truth,' said Tom, throwing an amused glance at Matthew. 'Matt is the one with charity issues. But can we get you started on those two lots of horses found buried in the Hunter region?'

Grace's eyes widened at the abrupt change in subject. 'Three, you mean.'

'Yeah, we know about the ones in Venezuela, too.'

'Venezuela?' Grace's brow creased in confusion. 'I meant three in Australia. Someone uncovered another burial site this morning in an old quarry out past Scone. A friend who lives near where they were found contacted me because she knew I was trying to do something about the first two. I don't know how many, maybe another fifty. According to the person who found them, all sorts of breeds with the brands cut off. When the police arrived, they told her to leave.'

'This is becoming newsworthy,' murmured Vicki, her eyes ablaze with interest.

Grace shook her head. 'It won't make the news. I don't know what's going on, but no one seems interested in it apart from the horse magazines and horse people. The police are treating it as though it's nothing. I mean, it's not like they're finding dead people. Animal welfare groups have taken the line that the horses have been put down humanely and don't appear to have suffered, so there's no evidence of cruelty. REE claim to have looked into it and decided the deaths are a by-product of too many horses and not enough feed, and as long as there was no cruelty, they won't do anything except tell people they'll gladly provide a home for any unwanted horse. I'm surprised they haven't turned it into a fundraising platform, telling people to donate money so they can buy more unwanted horses, then owners won't have to put them down.'

'That seems a decent idea to put forward,' said Karen, glad that the charity gave horses the chance to live.

'I trust them about as far as I could spit them,' Grace's lips curled in disdain. 'It wouldn't surprise me if they were the ones dumping the horses. They get hundreds of millions of dollars in donations – they are a corporate-level charity like we've never seen before. They grandstand about how many horses they save. I don't think they can possibly give all those horses the wonderful homes and happy retirements they boast about. I could see them putting the excess horses in the ground because there's not a lot of accountability about what happens to the horses after they've saved them. They could easily fill the internet with their before-and-after photos then shoot them. They're all about the appearances because that brings in donations, and I'd like to know what happens to all the horses when they've finished the *after* photos.'

'So, let me get this straight,' Matthew decided to push her buttons a little more, though he wasn't sure why, 'you're honest and not a horse hoarder, but they are dishonest, and instead of hoarding, they kill them off? It sounds like you're a little jealous of the successful end of the horse rescue market.'

Grace pointedly ignored him. She looked at Vicki and continued, 'REE have become everyone's darling and can do no wrong. They're the international savior-of-the-horses. People go on about how wonderful they are, saving horses from death and rehoming them around the world in their riding centers for the disadvantaged. There are even documentaries about how the children in developing countries thrive by learning about horses and riding because of REE. Everyone looks at the surface, but who knows what is going on behind the scenes? They are about as transparent as mud.'

'What do you mean?' Vicki leaned forward, keen to catch every word. If the buried horses fizzled out as a story, perhaps there was one worth following with the charities.

'Just that,' Grace shrugged. It was difficult to explain her frustrations and suspicions about the corporate-scale charities. 'The big charities like Rescuing Equines Everywhere, Equines In Need Of Funds and that new one, Caring About Horses And Ponies, seem to have a different set of rules when it comes to reporting. I've been running Horse Helpers for over ten years, and I have to jump through all sorts of hoops to meet the requirements of being a charity. Every cent I receive as a direct deposit, a cash donation, or as the result of selling something to help pay for feed, has to be accounted for in my financials. You should look at their financials – they are a complicated maze of smoke and mirrors with trust funds and off-shore accounts, unspecified categories where funds go, obscure payments, and page after page of incomings and outgoings associated with companies owned by discretionary trusts.'

'That's not breaking any laws, though, is it?' Matthew asked. 'It seems like they are jumping through the same hoops as you.'

'But they're not,' Grace insisted. 'I can't prove anything, but I've looked at the financials that they make public, and I know there's something wrong - I just don't know what it is. There are the cash donations, for instance. At least twenty percent of my donations are cash from people putting money in collection boxes at horse shows, demonstrations, and visits to our rescue centers. None of the big three have discernible cash donations, but I know they all have people collecting for them. Where's the cash? If someone is pocketing that illegally, then it won't be the only thing that's wrong about those charities.'

Before anyone could ask her more, Sheree banged a spoon against the soup tureen. 'I was ready to serve this up five minutes ago. Stay, Grace, and continue this discussion over dinner. It's interesting. Vicki clearly wants to know more. I want to know more.'

Grace waved a hand over her attire. 'I'm not exactly dressed for dinner, Sheree.'

'Nonsense.' Sheree pointed down the corridor towards the bathroom. 'Go and wash your hands and join us. You won't have anything at home to eat if I know you, but I bet you've fed the horses already.'

'Of course.' Grace only had a dozen low-care horses on her farm at present. They were quick and easy to feed with hay and concentrates.

'Then stay,' insisted Henry. He always enjoyed Grace's company, and it was twice as entertaining with the electricity arcing between her and Matthew.

'Yes, do join us.' Karen smiled at her in a way that made Grace want to do anything for her. The New Yorker was tall, beautiful, and charming, making Grace feel short, plain, and awkward in comparison, but Karen looked at her with such kindness that she felt special.

'I don't want to intrude...' Grace made her last feeble attempt to leave. The aromas of Sheree's French cooking made her stomach growl with the desire to stay and eat.

Lane signed something and seeing Grace's perplexed look, Karen explained, 'Lane said he'd like to hear more about the charities. You need to understand that Lane believes in quantum connections. Before yesterday, he hadn't heard of Horse Helpers or you, but the charities you've mentioned, as well as you and your rescue, have been spoken about several times by different people in two days. Until you walked in on Matthew being so boorish about charities, we had no idea you lived next door. Don't you think that's an interesting quirk of fate?'

'I guess.' Grace wasn't sure what to make of being seen as a coincidence.

'Jasper!' Sheree called to one of her sons. 'Can you set another place for Grace? Thanks.'

'How are ya, Grace?' Jasper's youthful voice yelled from the other room, followed by a chorus of hellos from Darcy, Frankie, and Felix.

Rather than shouting hellos back to them, Grace excused herself from the kitchen and stopped by the younger Lomonds on her way to the bathroom.

The extended dinner table sat fourteen comfortably, and Sheree declared that it was a much better number than thirteen. Grace was relieved to be sitting at one end near Sheree, Karen, and Lane while Matthew was at the far end where she couldn't see him. The potato and leek soup and bread helped calm the conversation's combative nature, and the main course soothed the way into affable table-talk. Sheree explained to Grace how Lane had agreed to help the two Bisente stallions settle into their new life at Wunya after they came out of quarantine.

'And the rest of us,' Karen informed her, 'are having a break. Lane and I are going to his property out past Longreach in a few days and will head to Melbourne when the stallions come out of quarantine. Then, we'll accompany them back here.'

'Your mother owns Bisente, doesn't she?' Grace asked.

'She does.' A smile touched Karen's lips as she thought of her vibrant and remarkable mother, Isabella. She explained to Grace how the connections worked. 'Ernie Lomond rode at Bisente for six months before moving to South America, where he's currently based. He told his parents,' she nodded at their hosts, 'about Bajoran and Barabel being the sort of stallions that would complement the Wunya breeding program. It was a happy coincidence – there's that word again – that they and Lane go back many years, and so we all end up here together.'

The mention of Ernie prompted Grace to turn to Tom. 'You mentioned Venezuela earlier, and I know Ernie's based there. I visited him last year. Were horses found there, too?'

'Yes. Just like the ones found here.' Tom tore off a piece of bread and examined it, thinking about the links between the two countries. 'They have an over-production of horses, too, so it could be a case of someone choosing to put their horses down rather than send them off as horse meat.'

A skeptical grimace crossed Grace's face. 'I doubt it. You do realize that REE have one of their international riding centers there, not too far from where Ernie lives? If you're into looking at quantum connections, I suggest you look more closely at them.'

Matthew leaned forward at the other end of the table so he could look at Grace. 'I'm interested in looking more closely at a lot of these horse charities. It seems you're all happy to take donations to fund your lifestyle.'

Not one to back away from confrontation, Grace met his gaze and decided to wave a red rag at him. 'Yes, we are happy about that, and there's not a thing you can do about it.'

Henry smothered a chuckle as he and Jasper cleared the main course plates. He knew that all donations to Grace's charity went to the horses. She inherited an estate from her parents that paid for all her living costs, and she channeled a lot of her personal income into the charity. If Matthew wanted to accuse her of living off donations, he was going to be sorely disappointed. Looking at Grace's determined chin, he decided to let them figure things out for themselves - when two people struck against each other like flint and steel, it was often best to let them handle their own sparks rather than get caught in the ensuing flames.

'Why don't you go over to Grace's tomorrow, Matthew?' Sheree was well aware that Grace was provoking him. She'd rather they fight at the farm next door than at her dinner table. 'You can start your examination of equine rescues with Horse Helpers. I think it's one of the best, so I'll be interested to hear your take on it once you have a look around.'

'I think I will.' Matthew gave Grace a triumphant look as though he'd made the winning move on the chessboard. 'If Grace doesn't have any objections.'

Grace fluttered her eyelashes at him and put a hand to her heart as she added dramatic fear to her words. 'Goodness, I am having conniptions at the thought of what misdeeds you will find if you investigate my affairs, Sherriff.' She narrowed her eyes to slits and changed her voice to a hostile tone. She knew she had the checkmate move in this game. 'Bring it on.'

'Dessert, everyone?' Sheree's voice was loud and bright as she attempted to calm the mood.

The talk returned to neutral topics around the table as they ate the caramelized apple tart. Grace, Vicki, and Tom insisted on clearing the table and tidying the kitchen so their hosts could enjoy some after-dinner time with their guests.

'Matthew isn't usually so antagonistic,' Vicki assured Grace as they stacked plates in the dishwasher. 'He's normally quite a sweet person.'

'Really?' Grace snorted in disbelief. 'He gave me the impression of being a Spanish inquisitor looking at a woman accused of dancing naked with cats during a full moon.'

Tom laughed in appreciation of her humor. 'You sure got under his skin. He's usually one to charm the opposite sex whenever possible.'

Wrinkling her nose at him, Grace said, 'Yeah – not feeling it.'

'You're not too bad at throwing the verbal punches yourself,' Vicki told her.

'It's from growing up with a bunch of rowdy cousins,' explained Grace. 'I had to fight my way physically and verbally against a dozen male cousins who played rough. By the time I was twelve, I could drop any of them like a suitcase with words or a kick.'

'Remind me not to upset you,' Tom grinned at her. He liked her candor. 'Maybe I should warn Matt not to push you too far.'

'Let him go,' said Vicki. 'I'd rather like to see Grace drop him like a suitcase.'

'I wouldn't do it to a stranger, even though he's an annoying youngster.'

'Youngster?' Tom quirked an eyebrow at her. 'You both look the same age. He's twenty-six.'

Throwing her hands up as though discovering the answer to a problem, Grace replied, 'There you go then, he's just a youngster. I'm thirty. I feel as though my four years seniority may as well be a few decades, though. He seems very boyish. Immature, even. Child-like. Young and prone to emotional outbursts. Just the sort of youngster who'd stand at the kitchen door and think I couldn't see him as I talked about him.'

She turned her head and gave Matthew a flat stare. He leaned against one of the entrances to the large kitchen, his mouth stretching into a huge smile. At first, he thought he had stumbled onto Grace talking about him, but her final words and gaze made it clear she intended the words for his ears.

'You're welcome to call it boyish charm,' he invited.

'Thank you, but no.'

'Perhaps thirty is too old to appreciate my youthful ways,' he teased, enjoying seeing how her facial expressions flowed through various emotions, none of which approved of him.

'It's old enough to recognize your nonsense.'

'You just haven't had enough wine yet. Drink up. Andy is right – I appear better the less you're capable of thinking about me.'

His twist of self-deprecating humor undid Grace's resolve to stare daggers at him, and a hoot of laughter forced its way from her throat. Immediately, she covered her mouth with a hand in an attempt to stop her odd laugh, but the damage was done. Tom and Vicki laughed, and it was infectious. Her laughter broke out in a series of hoots and gasps that had Matthew doubling over in amusement.

'Your laugh,' he pointed at her, 'that's the funniest laugh I've ever heard.'

'I hate it,' she hooted and wheezed as tears started to run down her cheeks. 'It's so stupid.'

'It's brilliant,' Vicki chortled uncontrollably.

'I sound like,' Grace tried to catch her breaths between laughs, 'a flock of asthmatic geese.'

Her comment increased the others' hilarity, and as their laughter grew, her own changed gear into something akin to someone machine-gunning a seal.

'I can hear Grace laughing,' Henry called from the dining area where amusement was rippling around the table. 'It's impossible not to join her.'

Ending on some snorts and wheezes, Grace finally gained control of herself. 'I'm sorry,' she apologized to Tom and Vicki, ignoring Matthew. 'I hate it when that happens. Having an abnormal laugh is a pain.'

'It's fabulous,' Vicki assured her. 'Who'd want a boring old chortle like mine when yours spreads mirth like a plague?'

'Yeah, that's not convincing me it's a good thing, but thanks for trying.'

As Tom closed the door on the dishwasher and Vicki took a phone call from her editor in New York, Sheree walked into the kitchen taking orders for coffee and tea.

'Not me,' Grace shook her head. 'I'm going to head home. Thanks for dinner, Sheree; you outdid yourself.'

'I'm glad you enjoyed it. Are you sure you won't stay for coffee?'

'No, I'll get walking. Thanks all the same.'

'Walking?' Henry entered the kitchen behind his wife. 'I'll drive you. You're not walking a kilometer at this time of night. Or Matthew can take you, and you can continue your arguments without an audience.'

For a moment, Matthew considered the idea. He wouldn't mind the opportunity to make her laugh again. The total craziness of the sounds she made appealed to him. As he opened his mouth to offer to drive her home, she cut him off.

'Absolutely not,' she said firmly. 'If Matthew wants to continue his inquisition tomorrow, that's fine, but right now, I'd much rather my own company and a long walk.'

With a cool look directed at him, she strode past to say goodnight to everyone at the table and departed before any more offers of a lift home were made.

'She's something, isn't she?' Henry started placing coffee mugs on a bench. 'Best neighbor anyone could wish for.'

'Having a heap of rescue horses next door doesn't worry you?' Matthew asked, curious to know more about her. He wasn't prepared to change his opinion on horse charities, but it wouldn't hurt to learn more about hers.

'Grace is a horsewoman who knows horses.' Sheree glanced at

Matthew as she made a pot of tea and brewed coffee. 'She's not the corporate level charity that you see with REE, EINOF, and that new one, CAHAP, and she's certainly not a misguided horse hoarder using donations to fund her obsession.'

'You know her better than I do.' Matthew remained guarded in his opinion of the neighbor. 'I'll have to take your word for that.'

Looking out the window to make sure Grace had left, Sheree continued. 'I know she'd hate me telling you this, but it might help you understand her. Ten years ago, Grace was one of our leading young event riders. Her horse, Donegal, was her obsession. She was offered several million for him by a Japanese buyer, and she wouldn't consider it for a moment because she thought of him as family. They fell at a practice jump on her farm next door, and Grace broke her back in two places. Donegal broke both front legs. It was about five hours before her boyfriend found her, and I can't bear to think what she went through in that time.'

Sheree turned to look at Matthew since the story was for his benefit. 'The doctors said she wouldn't walk again, but she defied the odds because that's Grace. She spent two years in a wheelchair and another three with a cane, and I have no doubt she still suffers pain, but you'll never hear her whine about it. Horse Helpers was started because losing Donegal broke her heart, and she coped by saving other horses and giving them a chance. I don't know what those other charities do, and I don't care, but Horse Helpers is good. Grace doesn't take a single cent for herself. In fact, she puts a lot of her own money into the rescue. Everyone is a volunteer, and even most of the vet work is done on a volunteer or cost-only basis. If you want to look for corruption in the charities, start with Horse Helpers to see one that isn't tainted in any way.'

Her words shook Matthew. For some reason, he hadn't expected the person in charge of Horse Helpers to be an accomplished horsewoman. Many of the rescue operations he saw around the world were run by people who professed to love horses, but they only had a basic knowledge of them. Thinking of Grace walking home in the dark with pain as her companion made him feel guilty. If he hadn't been quite so obnoxious to her, she might have allowed him to drive her home. But who was he kidding? Until he heard her personal history, he hadn't been interested in doing anything for her.

'That's one heck of a story.' Matthew scowled at himself for being such an oaf in his approach to Grace. 'If I'd known, I wouldn't have been such a tool.'

'And Grace would hate you to be nice to her just because you felt sorry for her,' Sheree pointed out, beginning to regret telling him about their neighbor's background. 'If you go over there tomorrow, don't be all soft and syrupy because you feel sorry for her now that you know her story. She's more likely to kick you than thank you for treating her with care and concern. Just tone down the aggression a little bit, OK? She's not the enemy.'

'Who's not the enemy?' Vicki put her phone back in her pocket and tuned back into the conversation.

'Grace, apparently,' Tom grinned at her. 'Obviously, she's not Sheree's enemy as she's a great neighbor, but Matthew behaved as though she was his despised adversary.'

'Because she runs Horse Helpers?' Vicki raised her eyebrows at Matthew, who raised his hands defensively.

'It takes two to tango,' he tried to justify his behavior even though he knew he had no excuse for being rude to Grace. 'She gave as good as she got. In fact, if you were awarding points, I think she won most of the rounds.'

'You can have a few more rounds with her tomorrow.' Vicki winked at him before announcing to those in the kitchen. 'My editor wants me to do some investigation into the horse charities. I told him a bit about it this morning my time, which was his evening, and now that he's slept on it and did some checking, he thinks there's a story here.'

An amused sigh escaped from Tom. He knew Vicki wouldn't be able to have a holiday without finding a story. 'What about the buried horses?'

'Two stories.' Vicki grinned and rubbed her hands together in anticipation. 'Even better.' She began to plan aloud. 'I want a list of the major charities, and then I'll get into their financials to see where the money comes from and where it goes. And horse numbers. I need to know how many horses they save and how they choose them. Also, how accountable are they for what happens to the horses for the rest of their lives?'

'Sounds like a job for a journalist,' he threw her a cheeky grin, 'not a climatologist.'

'There'll be work for you,' she promised.

Tom's phone vibrated in his pocket. He took it out and saw that it was Binky ringing. He thought she might have new information, so he excused himself and went outside to take the call.

By the time Tom re-joined his friends, they were back at the dining table enjoying coffee, tea, and some classic *petit gâteau financier aux amandes* – small almond cakes. He stood watching them, his face pale.

Lane caught his attention and asked, *What is it?*

'That was the police.' Tom's voice was heavy. 'They're going through Binky's phone, calling anyone she spoke to or texted in the last week. We've been talking and texting. Binky was found dead around midday, near the mine where those horses were found. Someone strangled her.'

***

Dibby and Rev

The palomino geldings shared an air stall with a tired taffy-colored pony gelding. The pony, Dusty, was built like a tank on legs. When Dibby, who stood in the center of the three sections, greeted the pony, he merely sighed and looked away, his interest in life gone.

He'd served many owners faithfully through his life then, several years earlier, his owner didn't want him wasted in the paddock, so loaned him to a friend who gave him to someone who sold him at a horse sale. The people who bought him knew little about horses and treated him cruelly, starving him and belting him any time they thought he did something wrong. Dusty only did what they told him to do. The problem was that they didn't know they were telling him to trot, canter, turn, or stop, and they punished him for following their commands.

Perhaps if Dusty's silver gene had him looking more like a silver dapple with a rich chocolate coat and cream-colored mane and tail, he might not be part of the cargo bound for distant shores. As it was, his unremarkable coat of mud-brown matched his brownish mane and tail, and when he went through the next horse sale alongside prettier colored horses, they sold well, and he went cheaply to another inexperienced home where they mistreated him.

Somewhere along the line, as he changed hands, received beatings, made friends with horses around him, then lost them again as he moved on, he shut down emotionally. He remembered being loved. He remembered gentle hands that groomed him and hugged him. He remembered carrying young riders with care and keeping them safe. As people mistreated him, he retreated into his memories of life when it was good, and people loved him.

When the scissor lift raised the air-stable into the Boeing 747-400 cargo plane, Dibby nickered nervously. Rev flicked an ear towards him and cast a soft eye his way, making a small reassuring sound in his throat. Taking comfort from Rev, Dibby lowered his head and snorted, resigning himself to whatever was happening.

For a moment, Dusty looked up at the two big golden horses, a passing light gleaming in his eye. He remembered having friends who cared for him. Long ago, there were horses who shared his paddock; they stood nose to tail with him to keep the flies off each other. They were friends who scratched his wither with their teeth in return for a scratch. If he ever saw them again, even after all these years, he would know them instantly, but they were gone.

Dusty lowered his head, his eyes growing dull. He had no idea where he was going, but humans had taught him that it wouldn't be a good place.

CHAPTER FIVE

You improve your training by understanding your horse. You understand your horse by listening to what he tells you and respecting his voice. He speaks silently and eloquently with his expression, his ears, his eyes, his reactions, every movement, and every whisker. Learn his voice so that he enjoys learning with you.

'Connecting with Your Horse' by Lane Dimity, p. 202

Early Plans

Soon after Tom's announcement, the seven guests retired to the largest of the guest houses. They didn't want to worry the Lomonds with their concerns about a girl Tom barely knew. They offered their hosts a brief explanation before walking through the gardens, letting the cool night air clear their minds. Once in the spacious lounge, Joe Kaiphas discarded his usual reticent exterior and paced the floor, asking questions and gathering information, his razor-sharp mind arranging everything in his mind.

'Tell me again exactly what Binky said to you.' Joe's brow furrowed in concentration as he listened to Tom recount his conversation with the groom at the airport. Tom had already gone through it twice, but Joe knew that a story told several times often revealed new information that the speaker overlooked or forgot in earlier versions.

Holding a hand to his forehead, Tom tried to remember every word Binky said as Joe walked back and forth across the polished timber floors.

'I don't know what is going on,' Joe tapped his fingers together as he sorted through the puzzle, 'but it's international. Those horses in Venezuela have to be related to the ones here. What sort of horse operations are international and deal with big numbers of horses?'

'Big studs and racing,' suggested Andrea.

'Any of the bigger disciplines,' said Matthew. 'Polo, jumping, eventing, dressage, cutting, endurance – heaps of them.'

Joe sat down at the table in the large open living area and began writing down their ideas. 'What else? Keep throwing them out there, so we have them all.'

'International horse transport,' said Karen, thinking of Tom and Lane flying with the Bisente horses.

'Travelling shows that have horses, like circuses.' Andrea scrunched up her face at her idea. 'But they wouldn't have hundreds of horses to get rid of, so aren't likely suspects.'

The horse meat market, Lane signed. *They deal in hundreds of thousands of horses each year.*

'That's the best guess so far,' Tom nodded at Lane. 'All the others have hundreds or thousands of horses, but they tend to be a particular type. The horses found were said to be a mix of horses and ponies, light and heavy boned. That doesn't fit racing or dressage or even a horse stud.'

'What about pharmaceutical companies?' Andrea looked at Karen. 'I know Pilatos bred all those Friesians because of a specific gene, but other companies use horses for other things. There's the pregnant mare urine market for women's hormones, and don't they use horses to create antivenom for snake bites? And the companies that develop treatments for equine diseases must have a variety of horses and ponies that they use for testing. What if some new test went wrong and they had to dispose of a lot of animals but didn't want authorities to know about it?'

That's plausible. Lane narrowed his eyes in thought. It was possible that one company, or even different ones, had accidentally caused the deaths of their test animals. Rather than deal with animal welfare and public condemnation, they could have buried the mistakes and replaced them with another range of horses from the saleyards. *Why remove the brands? If they kept a record of their brands, it would be easier to change the records than cut off the brands.*

Andrea tapped her teeth together as she considered the problem. 'Maybe because studbooks, breeders, and previous owners would recognize the brands.'

'It's worth investigating.' Joe met Andrea's eyes and inclined his head slightly to indicate she should follow that line of inquiry. 'I imagine horse pharmaceuticals are a billion-dollar business. If they make mistakes with their test animals, whether it's the spread of a disease that shouldn't be in the country or unexpected deaths, they could try to destroy the evidence. Did anyone test the dead horses for disease?'

Tom shook his head. 'No one seems to be interested. The police, the welfare groups, and the media seem prepared to accept that it's just some owner who had too many horses and chose to put them down instead of sending them off for meat.'

'Which may be the case,' reasoned Vicki. 'We could be making mountains out of molehills. Binky's death might have nothing to do with this – she could have been the victim of a robbery or assault that ended in murder. The missing miner might be on a bender. And the Venezuela horses could be completely unrelated.'

They fell silent, considering the sense in her words. Lane thought of someone killing the horses, and he wanted to know the story behind it. He owed almost everything good in his life to horses: his friends came to him because of their shared love of horses, and his wealth came from his books about horses. His concern about the Pilatos horses led to him meeting and falling in love with Karen.

If an owner could no longer care for their horses and put them down humanely before burying them, he wanted to know so he could reach out to other owners in a similar situation and offer them alternatives. If another pharmaceutical company was doing the wrong thing by their animals, he wanted to stop it.

It was a mystery that needed to be solved. *You might be right,* he signed to Vicki, *but my gut feeling is that there is something connecting everything. I think the miner was killed because he knew something, and Binky was killed because she asked something. I believe powerful people are pulling strings to keep the story quiet.*

'That could be a pharmaceutical company, then.' Matthew knew that profits could be a strong motivating factor behind crime. 'Could the people running some of these horse charities be that powerful? They deal with all types of horses and ponies, and REE is international with their riding centers. Grace said they had one in Venezuela.'

What time is it there? Lane looked to Karen. She always seemed to know the time zones in the Americas.

'It's nearly eleven here, so it's almost nine in the morning there.'

You know Ernie, Lane smiled winningly at her as he signed. *Could you give him a call and ask him what he knows?*

Tom frowned at them. 'So he can end up like Binky? That doesn't seem like a good idea.'

'It sounds like young Binky went snooping,' put in Joe. 'I'll find out more tomorrow when I get on to some of my contacts. You're not going to ask Ernie to investigate anything; you're just going to ask him what he knows and tell him to lie low.'

'That's a good point.' Karen reached into her handbag for her phone. 'If I *don't* phone him about this, he might be curious and ask questions. It's only right I call him and tell him not to ask around about the horses.'

'What if he's involved?' Matthew had a knack for looking at situations from different angles. Karen was assuming Ernie's innocence, but, as they'd often pointed out, the horse world was surprisingly small, and there was a strong chance they already knew some of the people behind this. Maybe Ernie was one of them. 'We have horses dead here in Australia and an Australian in Venezuela where others died in similar circumstances.'

Karen didn't consider the possibility of Ernie's connection for a moment. She remembered him when he was riding at Bisente, and he was a good and decent person, like his parents. 'There is no way Ernie would be involved in anything as nefarious as en masse killing of horses. He is the nicest man you could ever hope to meet, present company excepted, of course.'

'Of course,' Matthew grinned at her.

Holding a finger to her lips to ask everyone to be quiet, she found Ernie's number and tapped it. It rang twice before a cheerful Australian voice with the slightest touch of American on the vowels answered.

The first words from Ernie indicated he knew Karen was at his parents' property. 'Are Mum and Dad OK?'

'Everything's fine,' Karen tapped the speaker option so everyone could hear Ernie. 'I'm putting you on speaker, alright? Your mum and dad are great. We had dinner with them, and now we're in one of the guesthouses talking, and we wanted to ask you something.'

'Really?' He sounded surprised, and they could almost hear the shrug in his voice. 'Whatever floats your boat, I guess. How are you, anyway? And Lane?'

'We're good. And you?'

'Living the dream. I'm sitting here on Wunya Jack after a great training session wondering what's so important at eleven at night over there.'

'It's about the horses in those mass burials. Three lots here and one lot over there.'

'Two,' Ernie grunted as he dismounted, his feet making a satisfying thump when he landed on the grass beside his horse. 'Not far from here, actually. It's a bit bizarre.'

'We only heard about one over there,' Karen met Lane's eyes, intending to communicate her interest in Ernie's news. Instead, she lost herself in their depths for a second before struggling to extricate herself from their hold. She needed to hurry and get through this so she and Lane could get to bed. 'Three here. So far. The authorities seem to think it's just someone who put them down rather than sell them.'

'Interesting.' Ernie paused. 'Do you want me to ask around? No one seems to know much about the ones over here. There's nothing in the news about them.'

'No. Whatever you do, do not ask around. We have a missing man and a murdered girl, both associated with the horses. The last thing you should be doing is drawing attention to yourself.'

'And yet you're asking around.'

Karen stifled a snort. He had a point. 'But I'm only asking you. We wanted to know if you had any information at all and if you could think of anything that connected those horses to the ones here, like a horse stud or company.'

They talked for several minutes, discovering that the police, welfare organizations, and news outlets in both countries seemed disinterested in the horses. Ernie mentioned that an earthmoving company completed burying the horses, and no further investigations were taking place. Karen ended the call by asking him to contact her if he thought of anything relevant and reminded him to avoid asking questions.

'What happened with the horses here?' Andrea asked. 'I mean, we know someone found them, but what then? Did the councils try to remove them or leave them?'

'Here's something.' Matthew looked up from his phone. He'd been searching for any information on the subject, but it was almost non-existent apart from some social media chatter between horse people. 'Some members of a horse group in the Hunter are discussing the petition started by Grace...'

He was interrupted by Joe. 'The Grace we met tonight?'

Matthew nodded. 'She started it last week when she heard about the first lot of horses. It's a letter to local politicians asking for an investigation, and the people in the group are arguing whether it's a good idea or if it's something better left alone. Some want to know if the horses had a disease that they need to be aware of, and quite a few said they were glad the council covered them quickly so they could rest in peace.'

'That answers that, then.' Andrea took the phone from her brother to skim through the comments he'd been reading. 'They were quick to cover up the evidence. That seems suspect. Do you think there are more out there that someone buried properly, and no one knows about them?'

Maybe. Lane stood and held out a hand to Karen.

'We'll talk more tomorrow,' Karen said as she held Lane's gaze, her heart flipping wildly as it did every time he looked at her with that mixture of tender love and simmering heat. 'It's been a long day for me, so we might turn in.'

Looking at how their eyes devoured each other, Andrea realized that they were hungry for some time alone. 'Yeah, you two go and catch some shut-eye. I won't be long out of bed either.'

'Goodnight, all.' Karen raised a hand in a wave.

Lane took her hand in his, and they left.

The sudden cold breeze from the door opening caused Vicki to glance up from her search on Australian and American horse rescues. She blinked to adjust her eyes away from the screen. Once she started researching a story, it was easy for her to become lost in the information. 'We might call it a night, too,' she patted Tom on the knee, 'what do you think?'

'I think whatever you want me to think.' He raised and lowered his eyebrows several times at her.

'Yeah, right,' she drawled, chuckling at him. 'Like anyone could control you.'

'Yup,' Matthew leaned over and scruffed Tom's hair, earning a scowl. 'Might as well try and hold back a storm as try and control our environmental warrior.'

Tom cursed him in friendly tones, and Matthew laughed.

'Tomorrow,' said Vicki, standing and looking at Matthew, 'I want you to do some work for me if that's alright with you.'

'I could do with the money.' He gave her a cheeky look. 'How much are you paying?'

'A bottle of cheap Australian wine.'

'I believe that's my going rate,' he laughed. Vicki knew he made a substantial income from being a social influencer and having popular video clips. He wouldn't accept payment from a friend no matter how hard she tried, which she had done in the past, and he made it clear that he always had time to help friends. 'What can I do you for?'

She rolled her eyes at his tired and worn-out play on words. 'I think there's a good story in these horse rescues, and I want to get some more angles on everything. Can you go over to Grace's and…'

'Do I have to?' Matthew cut in, feeling uncomfortable about meeting Grace again. After she dismissed his offer to drive her home, he knew that she would not welcome his presence. He acknowledged that she had a right to feel that way - he'd been out of line with the things he'd said. It would be a sensible move to avoid meeting her again.

Frowning at his interruption, Vicki continued. 'Yes, you do. For that bottle of cheap wine I'm paying you. I thought you were going over there, anyway, to snoop around.'

'I changed my mind.'

'Change it back, please. I want you to go over there and do a little bit of investigating for me. Not so much into Horse Helpers as I think hers is a good operation, but keep your eyes open just in case she has everyone fooled. I want her opinion on some of these other rescue charities, particularly the big ones. Names, rumors, leads – anything and everything. I don't have a lot of direction with my report yet, but I know there's a story here.'

'He's scared,' Andrea teased her twin. 'Frightened of an itty-bitty girl with a big attitude.'

Matthew scowled at her in an attempt to look fierce. Her sparkling eyes made it clear that he failed dismally. 'And what if I am scared of her? It takes a big man to admit to being frightened.'

'Then be the big man and go over to her place tomorrow and gather some information for Vicki.'

'And what will you be doing?'

Putting her hands up in front of her face as though holding a camera, Andrea made a clicking noise as she pressed a finger on the imaginary shutter button. 'Taking photos of the Wunya horses for their advertising as well as for a Horse Deals article. So, you can run along to Grace's place and talk to her without me. I don't think she'll bite you.'

'I'm not totally convinced about that,' Matthew grumbled.

Outside, Lane and Karen wandered across the lawn to their accommodation. The entire world seemed to teeter on the point where their hands clasped, thought Lane. Stopping under a lemon-scented gum, he raised her hand to his mouth and pressed his lips against her skin. Closing her eyes, Karen shuddered at the sensation of his breath on the back of her hand. It never ceased to amaze her that every thought and every worry could twirl away into nothingness when he touched her. He made her feel safe in an increasingly crazy world, and his unwavering goodness shone like a beacon in the darkness.

To him, she represented courage, morality, and hope for the future. He believed that the thousands of years of wars and greed overseen by men could evolve into something better with powerful women like Karen making changes to the world.

'I missed you so much this past week,' she whispered, finding it difficult to speak as he released her hand, placed his fingers against her cheek, and met her moonlit gaze.

Instead of replying, he widened his eyes fractionally and inclined his head ever so slightly. To the casual observer, the movements would have passed unnoticed. To Karen, she knew he was saying that he missed her, too, and suggested they hurry to the bedroom. At first, it surprised her how much he could communicate with a few small movements of his facial muscles. It was as though he spoke the words into her mind. Now, she was used to it and continued as though his message came to her as words.

'Let's go then. We can remind each other what it is we've been missing.'

Lane grinned at her, sending her heart tumbling again.

In their cottage, they gave in to the passion that burned at the heart of their relationship. Next door, Vicki and Tom lay talking about ideas for the story she wanted to write. In the larger guest house, Andrea drifted off to sleep, planning the photo shoot. Joe lay on his back staring at the ceiling, organizing all the information they had so far on the dead horses. On the one hand, the fate of some unwanted horses seemed too trivial to concern one of the heads of Pilatos Industries. On the other, in the year he'd known Lane and his friends, he learned that their compassion for horses represented something the world needed – more kindness for those who did not have a voice. If Lane wanted to find out what was happening with these pits of dead horses, he would devote his energies to helping.

Matthew lay on his side in his room, his arms wrapped around a spare pillow that he hugged to his chest in a childhood habit. It made him feel secure. He stared at a moonbeam on the wall, images going through his mind of Grace lying in the paddock with a broken back while her horse struggled nearby with broken legs. It tore at his heart, and tears dampened his pillow as he thought of the suffering in those hours.

He managed to maintain the clown's façade with the others around - the fool, the comic who amused them with his words and jokes. Lane and Tom brought out the best in him and allowed him to shine. They didn't dismiss his Aboriginality with notions of *we don't see color.* They acknowledged his Indigenous heritage and respected that he was a First Nations person, like Tom, and they valued it, which made him feel whole. When he spoke or laughed with his friends, he saw himself with their eyes and was confident and optimistic. By himself, alone in bed in the dark, he was full of insecurities and worries. The scars from growing up indigenous in a white world retained the power to cause pain in the lonely hours.

He wiped away the tears that fell for a young horsewoman who couldn't help her horse, and he knew that must scar her soul. Did she lie awake and remember those hours? He felt apprehensive about meeting Grace again. There was a measure of shame for his outspoken opinions at dinner, and he knew she must despise him for being an ill-mannered idiot. He drifted off to sleep, beating himself up for everything he'd done wrong instead of seeing all that was right.

***

Dibby and Rev

With eighty-six horses on board, the cargo plane accelerated down the runway before lifting into the sky. To the horses, it seemed little different from the horse floats and trucks they'd encountered during their lives. They all remained calm except for the big bay clumper.

Baron, as he'd been named at birth by the family who bred heavy performance horses, called out nervously, stomping his massive hooves down and kicking back at the rear of his air-stable. In his life, he'd gone from experienced homes where his ability to carry heavier riders was valued, to people who knew little about horses. He was starved, sold on, and poorly treated until his trust in humans eroded into fear and apprehension.

After being forced into a horse float too small for him so that his head hit the roof, he became a nervous traveler. Twice, he'd fallen in floats after being loaded in bays with solid-to-the-floor sides that prevented him from spreading his legs. He'd scrabbled madly, trying to keep his balance, finally falling and lying awkwardly until the horse float stopped and the people hit him hard enough and long enough to make him stand.

Being trapped in an air-stable that tilted as the jet took off caused him to panic. His kicking and stomping became an explosion of hooves battering his stall and terrifying the smaller horses on either side.

'Get the humane killer,' called one of the air grooms as Baron reared, snapping the clips on the two leads that kept him cross-tied. It was clear they wouldn't be able to sedate him.

Dibby and Rev listened to the commotion behind them, their ears flicking back and forward rapidly and their heads raised in alarm as they tried to understand the threat. The distressed cries from Baron told all the horses that danger was nearby.

An air-fuelled thump from the bolt-gun stopped Baron's noise.

Rev strained against the cross-tie that prevented him from touching

Dibby's nose. He knew his tall friend needed to touch nostrils and share breath so he could find calmness, but they couldn't reach each other. Rev exhaled and gave his friend a long look. They were going to be alright.

CHAPTER SIX

Calmness is a great tool when working with horses. With nervous horses, use your voice softly and be sparing with your movements. The calmer you make your core, the more the horse will trust you. Loudness, a high voice, waving arms, and a quickly turning head and eyes all scream messages at your horse that neither of you understands.

'Ride With Heart,' by Lane Dimity. P. 129

Horse Helpers

On the following morning, everyone helped to feed the Wunya horses and clean stables. Henry and Sheree insisted that their guests didn't need to work but, being horse people, they refused to stand by and watch others do the work. Joe was the only one to avoid the chores because of his limited experience with horses. Instead, he sat at a table in the Wunya gardens and used his phone to collect information about the dead horses and the horse charities. He wasn't convinced that they were connected, but Grace's words about REE indicated that they had enough horses to dispose of some without drawing attention.

After breakfast, Andrea began her photo shoot, assisted by Lane and Karen. Tom and Vicki borrowed a car to explore the local area while Joe continued making phone calls to discreetly gather more details about the horses in the Hunter region. Using a spare phone with a number that wasn't connected to him if anyone searched for it, he invented various characters, from a PETA welfare officer to an equine journalist, to ask questions and follow leads.

Meanwhile, Matthew set out to walk to Grace's property. Wearing jeans, a blue checked shirt, and Ariat boots with an Akubra on his head, he looked like a typical Australian horseman. The sun peeked above the hills to the east of Wunya and evicted the cool night air from the valley. When he left the driveway and began walking along the road, he stopped to remove his boots and socks. He believed it was essential to connect to the earth, and the simplest way to do that was to walk barefoot on the ground and feel the earth under his feet.

Looking up at the hills, he saw the horizontal lines of ancient lava flows and was aware of the prehistoric seabed under his feet. Twenty-five million years earlier, the shield volcano near Cunningham's Gap erupted for a few million years, pouring out low viscosity lava that spread across an enormous region, including the Scenic Rim and the Lockyer Valley. The lava flows over millions of years formed immense basalt plains across south-eastern Queensland, covering the sea beds from earlier times. With tens of thousands of years between some of the eruptions, layers formed between flows.

After the eruptions ceased, millions of years of erosion carved valleys into the lava plains and ate away at their edges, reducing them to mountain ranges like the Main Range and the Little Liverpool Range. As the mineral-rich rock eroded, it left behind rich soils, and the region was famous for its vegetable production and other crops.

Matthew knew the geological history and, as he walked barefoot on the grass at the edge of the road, he felt the land tell its own story to his soul.

When he reached Grace's driveway, he put his socks and boots back on so he looked a little less feral. The property looked to be set out as neatly as Wunya, with railed fences and well-maintained horse shelters in paddocks. Birds gathered in the trees along the driveway, chattering and singing as he passed.

Everything was neat and organized. Looking around at content horses and the well-kept property, he sensed the serenity of Grace's farm. It felt welcoming.

'I was kind of hoping you wouldn't come.' The soft voice behind him wasn't at all welcoming.

Turning, he saw Grace appear from behind a hedge of flowering Callistemon, carrying two buckets filled with horse feed. The red flowers that covered the bottle-brush trees buzzed noisily with bees. Two Border Collies trotted at her heels and, once they saw him, raced over, their tails wagging.

'And yet you invited me,' he countered, bending to pat the dogs. 'Can I carry those buckets for you?'

'You can,' she cocked head to one side, a glint of amusement in her eyes, 'but the question is, *may* you carry them? And you may not. I'm perfectly capable of carrying a couple of buckets.'

'A grammar lesson? Really?' He narrowed his eyes and adopted a school-teacherly voice. 'You should know that the word *can* has become accepted as the replacement for the more formal *may* in relation to questions regarding possibilities. Of course, there are still fuddy-duddy old English teachers who like to correct students, but it isn't necessary.'

The corners of Grace's mouth twitched, and she repeated, 'Fuddy-duddy,' before snorting in amusement. 'Touché on the *can* and *may* thing, though. If you want to help, there are another two buckets of feed in that shed behind me. They're for the horses down this side of the driveway.'

Giving her a mock salute, he strode off through the trees to collect the buckets. Grace scowled at the traitorous Collies who decided they'd rather be with him and bounced around his legs. When he returned, two of the horses were eating from feed bins attached to the fence.

'Those are for the Clydesdales down here,' Grace swung an empty bucket to point out two baldy-bay faces looking at them expectantly. 'Bill and Ben believe they'll starve to death if they aren't fed immediately.'

They walked to the nickering Clydesdales, whose anxiousness about breakfast grew exponentially as the buckets approached. Taking a bucket, Grace poured the contents into a feed bin on the fence while Matthew emptied his into the next bin. The horses drove open mouths into the feed like steam shovels.

'Steady on there, boy,' Matthew chuckled at the large horse's desperate dive into his breakfast. 'You'll give yourself choke if you eat like that.'

'It comes from being starved,' Grace informed him. She stood next to the rails, her blue shirt, jeans, boots, and Akubra a feminine reflection of Matthew's outfit. 'When they arrived here, they were skin and bone. I wasn't sure I could save them. They were abandoned in a paddock out past Dalby. Three other Clydesdales in the paddock had already starved to death.'

Matthew winced at her words. The horses had the well-rounded condition of show horses, and it was hard to imagine the gentle giants at the point of starvation.

'You've done a good job to get them back to this.' He rubbed the gentle face in front of him. 'What happens with them now?'

'They live,' she responded, resting a hand on the broad forehead of her Clydesdale. 'REE are the ones obsessed with making horses do something. I'm happy for them to live comfortably and just be horses.

Horses don't sit around wishing they were useful to humans – they want to eat, drink, have companionship, feel comfortable and safe, and have the occasional play. I think the horses that come to Horse Helpers have suffered enough at the hands of humans, and they've earned the right to live their own life and stop serving us.'

It was quite the speech, and Matthew could find no fault with it. He often thought that horses were happiest with humans serving them rather than the other way around. 'I'm interested in learning more about REE and their objectives.'

'Aren't we all?' Grace scoffed as she reached for the buckets, stacked them together, and headed back to the feed shed. 'Let me know what you find out. I think it's messier than a redback's web, and I get the feeling that there's a whole pack of redbacks hiding there, ready to bite anyone who puts their hand in. But that's just me, and what was it you said? That I'm jealous about their success? Maybe I am. Anyway, I'll introduce you to the other horses and ponies here so you can decide if you think I'm doing this for them or simply using the charity to give myself the horse hoarder's lifestyle.'

Catching up to her, Matthew knit his brows, trying to think of the right words to convey his regret about the things he'd said. He sensed if he merely apologized, she'd rebuff it. 'This looks successful. I don't think you should be jealous of anyone.'

'Is that your way of saying sorry?' She tilted her head to look up at him, arching one brow.

'It might be,' he hesitated, unsure of her reaction, 'if you want it to be.'

She laughed. Not the full-blown machine-gun seal-massacre laugh, just a couple of hoots and gasps, which she quickly smothered with a hand to her mouth. 'That's a true Clayton's apology, that one, isn't it? You *could* be sorry for calling me a jealous, horse-hoarding con artist, but only if I *want* you to be sorry.'

'I didn't mean it like that,' Matthew started, silently cursing himself for being awkward with words at the wrong time.

Holding up her hand to stop him, she grinned. The flashes of green in her eyes communicated humor at his discomfort. 'No need for more clumsy attempts at fixing what's already been said. Although I am surprised – the articles about you always imply you are a genius with words.'

'You've read articles about me?'

'Don't get excited, youngster. I didn't read them because they were about you. I just like to read every article in a horse magazine when I've bought it.'

With his ego suitably deflated, Matthew grunted, not sure what to say next.

'You're here now,' Grace dropped the buckets outside the feed room, intending to clean them later, 'so let's make the best of this. Come and meet the horses and see my horse hoarding habit in action.'

Once the conversation moved to horses, Matthew was able to speak intelligently and knowledgeably. He asked about each horse's history and what treatment she'd used to get them to their current healthy and happy states.

'They are all settled into their new lives here,' Grace scratched the wither of a palomino pony as he ate from a full hay feeder in his paddock, 'and they'll stay here unless someone has the right facilities to foster them.'

'You don't sell them?'

'Never. Horse Helpers owns them for life, so they can always come back here or to one of the other farms if their foster homes aren't working out for whatever reason. No horse ever leaves here to live alone – foster homes either take two or more or already have a horse. Companionship is one of the essentials that we provide all horses.'

'What do the foster homes have to pay?' Matthew remained curious about the financials of any horse charity.

'Nothing to us, but donations are always appreciated, of course. They do have to demonstrate knowledge of what a horse needs and have the ability to pay for basic care. Most of our foster homes are people who'd rather give their time and effort to helping a horse than donating money, and they know they can return the horse if they're no longer able to feed and care for it.'

They began walking towards the house, a large Queenslander raised off the ground with verandas all around. The Collies raced ahead and used their noses to open the front door.

'Good security, as you can see.' Grace shook her head at the dogs.

'Smart dogs. You mentioned other Horse Helpers places.'

'I did? Well, yes, there are. This is my property, left to me by my parents and nothing from Horse Helper's income goes towards it. There are a few people with farms who reached the stage in life where they wanted to help horses, and they've signed ten-year leases on portions of their farms for us to use.'

'How much do you pay for that?' Matthew wondered if it was a viable income source for the landowners.

'A dollar per hectare per year. A nominal fee. They could make a thousand times that amount from other uses, but Horse Helpers is all about people doing something for nothing. Almost all our workers are volunteers, unlike REE and EINOF, which pay tens of millions in wages and salaries to employees and the redbacks hiding in the web. Keep in mind, we are tiny compared to them. They are international corporate-level charities. We are people who care enough about horses to give up something to help them.'

'So, you have no money at all going out as wages?' Following her example, he removed his boots and followed her into the house, his socked feet padding softly on the polished wooden floors.

'We pay vets, though they work for reduced rates and do a lot for free. We pay transport companies when they charge us, but they don't always charge. And there's one wage. We have quite a few facilities in four states and only one wage – the rest is volunteer work.'

'That's impressive.' And he was impressed – he had imagined dozens of people drawing wages. 'Do you pay their costs and expenses?'

'Some of them, like feed and vet expenses. We don't expect people to be out of pocket, but I think that notion of organizations being a top-down affair works here.' She stopped at the open-plan kitchen and held up a kettle to ask if he wanted tea or coffee. He nodded, and she continued talking while she made morning tea. 'For what it's worth, I'm at the top. I don't draw wages; I don't have my car, phone, or anything else paid for by the charity. I get paid fifty dollars a year for the fifty hectares I've leased to the charity, and I put a lot of my own money into it rather than take money out.'

She held up a jar of coffee and a pack of teabags. Matthew pointed at the coffee and replied, 'White and one. Thanks.'

'If people see someone at the top making lots of money from a charity – having their car provided, having expenses paid, living the high life on donations – they are more likely to try and get their pound of flesh. They see me giving, and they are more likely to give.'

'And you think all charities should operate like this?' Matthew accepted the mug of coffee and sat at the chair indicated by Grace as she placed a plate of homemade cookies between them.

'No, of course not. I understand charities need to cover costs and pay people, so I don't have an issue with people being paid from donations, but it's not what I do. The lines become blurred once you start providing lots of things for people from the funds. An old vehicle that does the work, a new reliable vehicle with a warranty, or a luxury car that is a status symbol? A meeting in Sydney to discuss changes in funding or a three-week study tour around the world looking at how other charities are run? Providing basic accommodation for a worker on one of the farms, or renting mansions for managers and their families?'

'Do some of them pay for mansions and study tours?'

Grace gave him a flat look before biting into her cookie. She didn't trust him and wasn't about to tell him of her suspicions, though she could hint at them. 'You need to look at what some of the charities do with their funds. Some start with justifiable expenses and seem to grow more generous with how they spend donations. A few seem to be providing the best of the best for everyone who works there, including those expensive business class study tours.'

'Like REE?'

'You need to do your research,' she waved a finger at him. Reaching behind, she grabbed a stack of papers from the kitchen bench and put them in front of Matthew. 'Starting with this. These are my financials. There are the financial reports from the charity, and there are also my personal taxation details.'

Looking embarrassed, Matthew pushed them away. 'I don't need to look at this.'

'You do.' She pushed them back. 'I'm going outside to work, and I expect you to spend the next hour looking through those. I'm not going to have you looking at me, wondering if I'm telling the truth or lying about funds. Believe me, plenty in the charity business lie about funds and where the money is going, and that's not just our little corner of equine charities. So, you're going to sit there and go through them. It might be fun to play games and pretend to be something I'm not just to see how you react, but I can't be bothered. If you're half as smart as all your fans think you are, you'll understand those figures and will work out how Horse Helpers operates financially.'

'There's no need.' Matthew's discomfort caused him to wriggle in his seat like a child eager to spring up and run away.

'There is,' she disagreed as she stood and headed to the door. 'Stay there and go through them. I don't particularly care about what you think about me, but since you'll be talking to your journalist friend and she may write something in the future, I do care what people read about Horse Helpers.'

Before he could object further, she pulled on her boots and left the house with the Border Collies at her heels. He smiled because she had to call her dogs to make them follow as they wanted to stay with him. No doubt that irked her.

With a resigned sigh, he started looking through the pile of documents. In no time, he became absorbed in reading page after page that told the story of a woman who turned over a large portion of her income to horses. There were lists of volunteer hours for workers at the various Horse Helpers sites, which would have converted to millions of dollars if they were on a payroll. It seemed Grace led by example, and others followed without expecting compensation for their time. Payments to vets and farriers were surprisingly small considering the work they did, and even feed bills were minimized with donations of hay and grain from farmers. One modest wage was paid to a bookkeeper to keep everything in order across the charity branches.

A reputable firm of accountants prepared the financial reports and Grace's taxation, and he was positive they would not be a party to any misleading figures. For a fleeting moment, it occurred to him that these could be doctored copies and not the ones the accountants prepared. It would be easy to scan the originals to a computer and then alter figures, so he only saw the fakes. He dismissed that idea. The Lomonds knew Grace well, and their confidence in her reassured him that the reports were accurate.

Checking his watch, he saw that the hour had passed and Grace had not returned. He stacked the papers and went looking for her. As he left the house, two older women, one grey-haired and the other with rainbow curls, led a couple of plump ponies to a small, bare yard. He watched them release the ponies.

'They eat too much,' explained one of the women when she saw his interest. 'Grace likes them to have six to eight hours a day off grass with just some dry hay and water.'

'I've had ponies like that.' He offered the women the charming smile that failed to impress Grace. He was glad to see it had the desired effect on them, and they smiled back, their eyes lighting up. 'I'm Matthew McLeay.'

He strode towards them, his hand outstretched. They shook hands and introduced themselves.

'I thought I recognized you,' said one. 'You're Lane Dimity's friend, aren't you?'

It never worried Matthew that so many people equated him with being Lane's friend rather than a successful horse trainer in his own right. It was a privilege to be one of his inner circle, not because he was famous and had over seventy-million social media followers, but because he was simply the best person Matthew had ever known. There was something so pure and good about Lane that Matthew often thought of him as a light shining in a dark world. Sometimes he remarked to his sister, half-joking and wholly in earnest, that if his epitaph read, *Matthew, friend of Lane Dimity*, he would feel that his life had meaning.

'That's me. Do you know where I can find Grace?'

'Is Lane here? And Tom?' The rainbow-haired woman looked around as though hoping to catch sight of them.

Her face fell when he replied, 'Nup. Just me.'

'I didn't mean that it isn't great to meet you, too,' she rushed, realizing how her words may have sounded. 'I've watched all of your training videos and love your work. I just thought it would be amazing to see all three of you. And your sister, too, of course.'

'I'll let them know.' He decided against telling them that they were next door. 'Now, Grace?' He gave them a questioning look.

'She's over the other side of the main stables.' The grey-haired woman pointed to a large building obscured by trees. 'The new horse, Shelley, is proving a bit of a problem.'

'Thanks.' Matthew touched a finger to his forehead in a loose salute and left them before they started explaining about the horse. He could see they were eager to talk.

Making his way through the park-like gardens, he rounded the end of the block of ten stables to see Grace standing in the center of a round-yard while a palomino mare trotted around the rails, her head high and her ears alarmed. Matthew froze, knowing she wouldn't see him in the shadows of the trees. He wanted to see Grace in action.

She stood behind the eye of the mare in the spot that kept her moving forward. After a few circles, Grace lowered her eyes from the mare's face and took a step back, disengaging the forward movement and inviting the horse to step towards her. The mare slowed and faced her, snorted, and shook with fear. Grace raised her head to look at the mare and moved half a step, opening a hand. It was enough to send the horse trotting in the other direction.

Matthew recognized what she was doing. Join-up was a useful tool with horses that didn't want to be caught. It involved moving them away from you until they indicated that they were ready to make contact, and then you let the horse come to you. He knew from experience that a horse as scared and worried as this mare might not respond as expected because her adrenalin overrode all other reactions. She wouldn't tire, and she wouldn't relax. A wild horse that had never been touched responded surprisingly quickly to the method, but this mare's body language spoke of being abused by humans to the point that her terror blocked her from accepting the quiet woman in the yard with her.

'Do you have any magic that will work?' Grace spoke to him without looking away from the mare.

He wondered if she'd been aware of him all along.

Stepping out of the shadows, he approached the fence. The mare hadn't noticed him earlier and panicked when she caught sight of him, almost throwing herself at the rails on the far side of the yard.

'She has some bad memories,' he guessed. Leaning against the rails, he watched the mare as she trembled, her head high and her ears flicking forward and back. Grace kept her back to him as she watched the mare.

'Her owners tied her to a post and beat her with steel pipe because she was hard to catch. Repeatedly. The neighbors reported them, but welfare didn't do anything as they hadn't seen the beatings, and they could see she had feed and water. They told me, and I bought her for a stupid amount of money, but I had to offer something that the owners wouldn't turn down. Look at her.' Grace wiped her cheeks, and Matthew realized she was crying. 'It's hard to imagine what they did to cause that level of fear. She's been here three weeks, and I can't do anything with her. We brought her here on a cattle truck, and I have to put her in the race before putting a headstall on her for the vet to tend to her, but she is terrified the whole time. I'm failing her.'

Her shoulders slumped, and she took a step back from the mare to give her more space.

'You're not failing her.' Matthew slid between the rails and moved to stand next to Grace. He didn't look down at her as he understood she might be embarrassed by her tears. Instead, he kept his eyes on the mare, who stared back with dread. 'She's safe. She just has a long journey to recover from what they did to her. You haven't failed her.'

'I don't want to ride her or do anything with her,' Grace tried to justify her efforts to work with a horse that wanted nothing to do with people, 'but I want her to be comfortable with being caught. It's not fair to make her terrified every time we need to have her hooves done or a vet check. I can't put her in the race and tranquilize her every time she needs attention, but nothing I try has worked. If you can do anything, please do.'

Grace turned away from him and left the yard, wiping at her face with a sleeve. It hurt her to see the suffering of the traumatized horse, and she felt helpless after weeks of failing to win even a small measure of trust.

'I gather there's not much point moving her around and expecting her to lower her head and grow calm.' He spoke to Grace as he watched the mare. 'She's so frightened of what might happen that she'll run all day. Adrenalin is one heck of a fuel. There are a few things that might help or might not. Lane could help.' He looked over at Grace, who leaned on the rails from outside the yard. 'He really is magic. It's like he talks to horses on a level that no one else understands. But I have some tricks if you want me to try.'

'Please do.'

'Can you get me something long, hard, and light to lift?' When he saw Grace's lips clench together to hold back a giggle, he rolled his eyes and shook his head at her wayward thoughts, though his eyes gleamed with shared humor. 'Like a curtain rod or even a long piece of poly pipe.'

'Got you.' She winked at him and ran off to the stables, returning in a few minutes with a piece of wooden dowel nearly four meters long, which she passed through to Matthew.

'Perfect.' He stepped away from the mare as her fear level increased when she saw what she perceived as a weapon. 'Now, I'll just stand here for a moment with the end on the ground near you so she can see it isn't attacking her. What I want to do is make it an extension of my arm and, hopefully, touch her gently while I'm still far away from her. She's so terrified of what will happen if one of us touches her that she's making sure we can't get near her. So, her nightmare is going to come true. She will get touched by me, and she'll discover that it's not as bad as she thought. Once she's accepting the touch of the stick, then I slowly move towards her until it's no longer the extension of my hand touching her – it is my hand. I do a whole lot of approach-and-retreat stuff, so it may get boring to watch, but I want her to have it in her head that I'm not trapping her. I always move away from her and leave her free.'

As he talked, he slowly moved the stick up in the air until it was two horse lengths from the mare, then moved it away again. He repeated the move ten times, each time moving the stick slightly closer.

'I know you're worried, girl,' he spoke to the horse as though she understood English, 'and we're going to try and get past that. I want you to be so bored with what I'm doing that your fear level is going down. I'm not taking her to a panic point,' he pointed out to Grace, who was watching with interest. 'I'm trying to keep her below that with the constant retreating. I'm not looking at her because that makes her think I'm a predator. I'm looking to the horizon beyond her, and my body language is saying that I'm watching for predators and I'm keeping her safe.'

'I think I understand,' Grace nodded. She had read most of Lane's books, and he often wrote of how human body language speaks to horses.

'You're welcome to go and do something else if you want.' Matthew took a step towards the mare, then two steps away from her. 'This is going to take an hour or more. But I promise I'm not going to scare her, and I won't be angry if it fails.' He flashed her a grin. 'I'm OK with failure because that means I call Lane, and you'll get to see him work his magic.'

'I'd like to stay if that's alright with you.' Grace was curious to see what he did with the mare. She wanted to trust him, but she knew mild-mannered people could lose their temper when frustrated by an uncooperative horse, especially when there weren't witnesses, so she trusted him more while she stayed watching.

It took twenty minutes of Matthew stepping closer to the mare, then disengaging and walking away before he held the stick close enough to touch her wither gently. The mare shuddered but remained standing because he almost immediately stepped away and removed the stick. Each time he approached her, he could feel her rising fear in his chest as though she were pushing him away, and he always retreated before she reached the point of running from him. As he stepped back, he sensed her dread decrease instantly. After five approaches with the stick touching her wither for a second, he walked back to Grace to allow the horse to understand that she was still free and unhurt.

'The continual moving away from her is the main part of this,' he said as he rubbed the stick along Shelley's back and retreated. 'I'm watching her panic level and getting away before she reaches it. She's not going to think once she starts to panic, but she's thinking and learning while we're staying under that level.'

'I'm impressed that she's standing and not in full flight.'

'I'm boring her senseless,' he chuckled. 'It's my approach to women in general. I rabbit on harmlessly until they're nearly asleep, and then I ask them out. I think they say yes to shut me up, but I'll take that.'

Grace snorted at his self-effacing humor. The man was handsome with a smile that should be licensed, so she was reasonably sure any woman would say yes if he asked her out. Not her, of course, she told herself. She had no interest in dating anyone.

At the fifty-minute mark, Shelley was standing with a hind leg resting as Matthew placed the stick on her wither and stepped forward along the line of the stick until his hand replaced its touch. He rubbed her lightly and retreated.

When an hour passed, he could walk up to the relaxed horse, rub her along the neck and shoulder with his hands and a rope before stepping away. Grace held her breath when he explained he was going to catch her once and end the session. With the stick on the ground, he walked up to Shelley, rubbed her shoulder, put the rope around her neck, and held her for five seconds before removing it and exiting the arena.

'Impressive,' Grace took the rope from him.

'It's not a cure for what ails her. You'll have to do shortened versions of that each time you catch her for weeks, maybe months. Try to keep her below her panic-and-flee point. For the next week, do the approach and retreat, then catch and hold her for a few seconds as the very last part of the routine. That should help her associate being caught with the end of a lesson rather than the start of her nightmare.'

'That makes sense.' Grace led the way back to the stables to put the halter and rope away. 'Thank you for helping Shelley.'

'Any time. Thank *you* for sharing those financials with me. It gives me an idea of what to look for if we check out some of the other rescues. You didn't have to show me your personal financials, though.'

'Maybe I wanted to impress you with my wealth.' She stopped and looked up at him, her eyes doe-like as she licked her lips and dropped her gaze to his lips. Her voice became soft, almost breathless. 'I thought that, maybe, if you realized how much I was worth, you might find me more attractive. Did that work? Do you find me attractive?'

Matthew froze. Words fled his mind as he felt an overwhelming urge to flee.

Placing a small hand against his chest, Grace gave him a light shove and burst out laughing, pleased to have a little revenge for his horse hoarder and criminal comments. 'You look petrified.' Her amusement increased until she slapped a hand over her mouth to control the quick-fire bang, wheeze, and squeal of her unique laughter.

Replacing the alarm with disapproval, Matthew glared down at her. He wanted to be unamused by her prank, but her laughter was irresistible, and the corners of his mouth began to twitch.

Waving her other hand at his face, she managed to gasp out, 'You looked like a rabbit caught in the headlights.' She paused her hilarity long enough to open her eyes and mouth wide in an imitation of Matthew's horror before another outburst of crazy laughter overcame her.

This time Matthew joined in. She didn't seem at all offended that his reaction to her fake flirtation was fear. He wanted to explain that it was fine if she flirted with him, that it was just the implication that he would find her money attractive that distressed him, but after they stopped laughing, the opportunity never arose. He was due back at Wunya for lunch, and Grace needed to train several new volunteers who were waiting.

***

Dibby and Rev

Grooms brought feed and water to the horses in flight. One of the younger women spoke to Dibby and Rev with reassuring sounds, and they looked forward to seeing her again. The others worked without any compassion.

There were no other incidents after they silenced Baron, and the horses traveled calmly as they soared over the ocean. Air turbulence caused some nickering, but they settled quickly.

Dusty dozed, dreaming of days gone by when the laughter of children on his back was the sweetest sound in his life. Dibby and Rev took turns exhaling as they tried to share each other's breath. They closed their eyes and recalled a lifetime of sharing breath in a ritual of friendship.

CHAPTER SEVEN

When your horse doesn't learn, don't accuse him of being stupid or stubborn; instead, look to how you need to modify the lesson. The horse can't always adapt to your teaching – you need to adapt your teaching to the horse.
Lane Dimity, social media post. Shared two million times.

Moving Forward

As he walked back to Lomond's property, Matthew took out his phone and looked up the financials of a few high-profile horse charities, keen to compare their figures with the Horse Helpers' numbers that were fresh in his mind. He stopped halfway between the properties, standing in the shade of a Moreton Bay ash as he scanned the documents.

There were many differences. The donations to REE were in the hundreds of millions, while Horse Helpers brought in a few million. REE was international with facilities in eight countries, and, judging by the Australian expenses, he realized there had to be other financials for the overseas sections. The overseas rescue facilities, called Equine Wellness Centers, received a fraction of the money allocated to the Australian centers, indicating they had their own source of income not covered in these reports.

Over thirty million dollars was spent on transporting Australian rescue horses to the riding centers around the world. Matthew estimated it would cost fifty thousand dollars for the transport and quarantine costs for one horse, even with the HATCO discounts, so that equated to about six hundred horses. He wondered how they could continue to send that number of horses to their riding schools year after year – were the facilities continuing to grow, or were they selling the horses, or worse?

The transport costs seemed a justifiable expense given that so many people donated *because* of the help given to disadvantaged children in those countries. The media articles he skimmed showcased the almost miraculous changes in the lives of the children who worked with the REE horses in countries where most were denied access to horse riding. The largest number of horses going through REE seemed to be ex-racehorses – gallopers and harness horses. Most of those were donated by owners who didn't want their horses going to pet food. Matthew could understand that giving their horses to a charity like REE sat easier on their conscience than selling them for a few hundred dollars to a knackery.

Where close to ninety-five percent of donations to Horse Helpers went to the horses, on the surface, it appeared only about five percent of donations to REE went to the care of the horses while the rest went to the expenses like wages, transport, agistment, advertising, vehicles, office space, accommodation for workers, seminars, travel, promotions, consultancy fees, and a myriad of other costs. It helped him appreciate how Horse Helpers spent their money. He understood that five cents in the dollar was the accepted percentage that went to the cause donors thought they were helping, but it seemed a lot of people were making a good living from REE.

He couldn't find published financials for EINOF or the latest charity, CAHAP. Two other rescue organizations seemed to function along the lines of Horse Helpers, only with wages paid to workers and substantial amounts paid to vets, farriers, agistment centers, vehicle costs, advertising, and trainers. A rough perusal of their figures indicated that more than half the donated money was going directly to the care and upkeep of the horses. The multi-national REE stood out for the hundreds of millions spent on expenses not directly related to the maintenance of rescue horses. He was curious to learn more.

When Matthew arrived back at Wunya, Lane and Karen were finishing a dressage session alongside the Lomond boys, Jasper, Felix, Frankie, and Darcy. Sheree instructed, Henry heckled from the side, and Andrea took photos. Seeing the horses undertake half-passes, shoulder-ins, and single flying changes, Matthew deduced they were training at Medium level. He didn't see canter pirouettes or several flying changes in a row to indicate higher levels, and there were no attempts at passage or piaffe, so he doubted they were FEI-level horses.

'What do you think of our Grace?' Henry asked as the six riders trotted single file across the diagonal, showing lengthening of stride.

'I'm prepared to admit that she doesn't seem like a horse hoarder or a criminal.'

Henry chuckled at his careful words. 'She's a good 'un. I find it odd that there are so many rumors about Horse Helpers being crooked. I know from experience that most problems in any business or institution are a top-down thing, and with Grace at the top, I know it has to be good all the way down.'

Narrowing his eyes in thought, Matthew considered that theory. 'It makes you wonder who's at the top of those big charities. REE has hundreds of millions of dollars to work with each year. That's an awful lot of money.'

'And believe me,' Henry tapped the side of his nose, 'follow the scent of that much money, and you'll find corruption. Crime likes to make nests in places where there's a lot of money.'

'I think we need to find out more about them. Hey, Lane!' Matthew called to his friend as he rode past at a trot.

Lane guided his horse into a six-meter volte to return to Matthew and halted next to the rail. He raised one eyebrow in query.

'Any chance you and Karen can give up your trip to Ellamanga to look into these charities?'

Rather than remove his hands from the reins to sign a reply, Lane glanced at Karen, who was cantering along the far side of the arena. He smiled in admiration of her riding skills and shook his head. He had been planning this trip home to Ellamanga for months, and the rest of the world could wait.

'What if these charities are linked to the dead horses and that murdered girl? You know they seem to be one of the few horse owners who could have that number and variety of horses and ponies.'

Lane looked to the skies as he thought about that, then moved an index finger away from a rein to point at Matthew.

'Aw, come on, Lane.' Matthew kicked at the sand like a schoolboy upset about being told he couldn't play at lunchtime. 'You know I want to go to Ellamanga with you. I don't want to be stuck chasing up facts and figures about horse rescues.'

Raising one shoulder slightly, Lane tilted his head to show that it didn't worry him what Matthew decided to do. He could come to Ellamanga or do some research; do both or do neither. He wasn't one to tell his friends how they should spend their free time. They all had several weeks' holiday and, apart from helping the Lomonds with the two Bisente stallions when they were out of quarantine and watching Quest race, there was nothing else scheduled on his calendar.

'I suppose I should find out more.' Matthew sighed and waved at Lane to continue. 'You finish riding. I'm going to talk to Joe to see if he's learned anything.'

Raising his right thumb off the nearside rein, Lane signaled his approval before gathering his horse back up and moving forward into a collected trot.

On his way through the garden to look for Joe, he found Tom and Vicki on a bench under a jacaranda tree. Tom sat upright while Vicki lay on her back, resting her head on his legs. They focused on their phones: reading, tapping, and swiping.

Matthew paused near them, shaking his head at the fact that they hadn't noticed him. 'Now, there's a twenty-first-century love scene if ever there was one. Lovers sitting in a beautiful garden, lost in their smart devices.'

'I'm not lost in it,' Tom muttered without glancing up. 'I knew you were approaching.'

'I was,' Vicki grinned and sat up, shaking her phone at Matthew. 'There's a story here. A big one. Do you know how much REE received in donations last year?'

'As a matter of fact, I do. I've been looking them up, too.'

Vicki's eyes shone with a fanatical light. When she was chasing a story, she tended to become a little obsessive. 'I want to visit one of their riding centers and speak to their people. And EINOF as well. I have a lot of questions.'

'So do I.' Matthew could see his holiday on Luke's property transforming into a fact-finding mission for Vicki.

'How'd you go over at Grace's? Did you learn anything?'

'I did.' Matthew gave her a summary of how Horse Helpers operated, their financials, and what he'd learned of REE.

'After this morning,' he finished, 'I'd have to say that I think there's a story there, too.'

'I agree.' Joe's voice surprised them.

He managed to arrive without anyone noticing him. Matthew often thought he moved with deadly silence like an assassin. He once light-heartedly asked him if he had killed many people, and the chilling look he'd received in reply ensured he never enquired again. They'd known Joe for over a year now, though Karen had known him most of her life, and he remained a shadowy figure even when they traveled together. After seeing how Joe's teenage daughter, Karina, wound her father's heart around her every smile, Matthew accepted that the man was intrinsically good. Scary but good.

'Did you find out something about Binky?' Tom looked hopeful. The death of the girl weighed heavily on his mind. If he hadn't shown interest in the mystery of the buried horses, she wouldn't have been asking around. He feared her death was a consequence of her interest and not a random attack.

Joe shook his head, his face solemn. 'What I didn't learn tells me more than what information is available. Her case is described as drug-related, which tends to decrease the urgency of trying to find her killer.'

'There's no way she was a drug user.' Tom shook his head, upset that someone tarnished the reputation of the bright and eager groom. 'She was the sort to be high on life. I wouldn't be surprised if she avoided taking ordinary headache tablets because she was so clean living that she didn't want any sort of drugs in her system.'

'She made an impression on you.' Vicki laid a sympathetic hand on Tom's arm. She knew that behind the hard warrior's face that he turned to the world lay the gentlest of hearts. Even though he met the young woman briefly, she trusted his perception. If he said Binky wasn't the type to use drugs, she believed him.

'Not only that,' Joe frowned, 'there was an accident with the crime scene evidence, and it was mislaid. Convenient. No one wanted to talk about it.'

'Do they know we're the ones asking about her?' Matthew looked concerned as he considered that whoever killed Binky may be prepared to kill again.

'Yes,' Joe offered him a flat stare. 'I used your name and phone number in all my inquiries.'

For a second, Matthew felt a sense of panic, then the faint twinkle in Joe's eyes gave the game away. 'Very funny. Not. I was about to pack up and leave the country.'

'There is no way for them to trace any inquiries back to me,' Joe explained softly, 'or to any of us. I have phones that aren't connected to Pilatos or me in any way, and I use VPNs. Whatever is going on involves people spending a lot of money because you don't buy silence cheaply. Someone is paying for silence, and whoever is getting paid is making sure that either no one talks or they don't have the information that enables them to talk.'

'Is that just in relation to Binky?' Vicki asked, making some notes on her phone. 'What about the horses?'

'Same results.' Joe told her. 'I spoke to councils, welfare organizations, and police, and they all put it down as a result of the drought and don't want to take it any further since farmers are facing enough problems without victimizing them for humanely putting down livestock. Their words, not mine. The same words from different sources, so I think they are parroting what they've been told.'

'Do you think the two are connected?' Tom looked up at Joe, his expression bleak.

Seeing the younger man blame himself for Binky's death was a shame, but Joe wouldn't sugar coat it. He was positive that if the girl hadn't been asking about the horses, she would be alive. 'I believe they are. And the missing miner as well. His family says it's not like him to go missing, but the police claimed he left the area, and there's nothing to indicate a crime.'

'So, what do you do next?' Tom looked at Vicki.

'I'm going to learn more about the charities. That's the story I'm chasing at the moment. Maybe it will connect with the dead horses and Binky's death somewhere along the line – stranger things have happened. Do you have any leads, Joe?'

'I made a few calls,' he replied, his face the usual mask of neutrality. 'According to my contacts, the two organizations to trust are BJ Rescues over near the Gold Coast and Horse Helpers next door. They hinted at a collaboration of some sort between REE and EINOF. Given that they are both multi-million-dollar enterprises, it could be expected their management know each other.'

'BJ Rescues?' Vicki noted the details on her phone.

'Two sisters, Kat and Kaz. They won a big lottery and used it to start their rescue. Apparently, they are quite outspoken about corruption among the equine rescues, as well as crime in other horse areas including racing and the horse meat industry.'

'Outspoken horsewomen?' Matthew scoffed, throwing a wry grin at Tom. 'That would be unusual.'

Vicki kicked him. 'Hey. I'm a horsewoman.'

'Ouch. A most unusual and wonderful one.' Matthew slathered the charm on her.

'You're forgiven. Now, how committed are you to going out west with Lane and Karen?'

'I think I'm about to become uncommitted, judging from the look on your face.'

'You're right,' Vicki gave him an unapologetic grin. 'I'd love you to go on helping with this story since you already have a foot in the door at Horse Helpers.'

'Grace may have jammed the door on that foot,' Matthew glanced morosely at his feet as though they caused him pain. 'And stomped on them for good measure. I'm not sure if I'll be much good to you on that front.'

'Of course, you will.' Vicki nudged him with her foot, gently this time. 'No one can resist your charm. You and I will go back over there tomorrow and play good cop, bad cop.'

'Can I be the good one?'

'I wouldn't have it any other way. I want to apply a bit of pressure to Grace to see how she reacts. We'll use that as our litmus test for people from other charities.'

Tom tilted his head to look at her as though peering at something he didn't quite recognize. 'You scare me sometimes.'

'Good.' She blew him a kiss. 'If all men were a little scared of women, the world would be a more balanced place.'

'If you'll excuse me from charity-chasing,' Tom continued, 'I'd like to find out more about what Binky was doing. There might be a story in that, too.'

'If you turn up something about those horses that's worth writing about, I'll try to get my editor on board with it. At this stage, if people are saying that they are farmers putting down stock because of the drought, then that isn't sensational enough for my editor. It's too much of a no-go area because maybe they had no choice except to euthanize their livestock.'

'That isn't the case with these,' Tom argued. 'The horses weren't starving, according to what Binky said. The area where they were found still has grass.'

Matthew looked to Joe. As the oldest and most experienced with investigations, he might have suggestions. 'Where do we go with that one, Joe? It seems you just found dead-ends, so is there any way forward?'

'Running into walls has been a way forward, of sorts,' Joe gave a half-shrug. 'It means someone is paying to build walls. We need to look at who has that sort of money and why they are going to such an effort to hide everything. Where did the horses come from? And why didn't they do a better job of disposing of the horses in the first place? There wouldn't be any questions if they did that properly.'

With a snort, Matthew provided an answer for that. 'It's our Australian work ethic, Joe. They paid some Aussie blokes to bury the horses. Those fellas were going fine until they looked at their watches and thought it was nearing beer o'clock, so they decided close enough was good enough and knocked off. The horses were covered but not well enough to withstand the rainfall and people with a good sense of smell.'

'If the missing miner is one of those men, there should be another one, if not more.' Joe tapped his fingers against his thigh as the thought. 'We should be trying to see if any other machinery or truck drivers are missing.'

'Maybe they punished him for talking,' pointed out Tom, 'rather than because he did a sub-standard job. There might not be any other victims, just people too scared to talk or too well paid.'

'It's still a way of moving forward.' Joe considered his options. Karen wouldn't need him once she was safe on Ellamanga with Lane, and he'd rather be working than sitting on a veranda waiting for them to come back from riding horses. 'I might head down into the Hunter Valley region and have a look around.'

'Like Binky?' There was worry in Matthew's voice.

'Like someone who has dealt with billion-dollar corporate crime for decades, and all the dangers that go with it.' Joe gave him a dry look. He appreciated Matthew's concern, but the Australian had no concept of what Joe handled for Pilatos and earlier employers.

'Well, be careful,' Matthew urged, knowing his words were lame, but the sentiment behind them was powerful.

Joe patted the younger man on the shoulder in an uncharacteristic show of affection. 'Thanks. I will.'

'I might come with you.' Tom offered.

Knowing he spoke from a place of guilt about the groom, Joe shook his head. 'You stay here and ask the sisters at BJ Rescues about horse-related crime. I've been assured they know the Australian horse industry well, including the underbelly. Whoever disposed of those animals had a reason to do what they did. They owned that mixed bag of horses that no one missed, they have money, and they are dangerous. That narrows the list of suspects considerably. The sisters might be able to give you a list of possible suspects while I'll nose around down there. If I can get one of you to run me into Gatton later, I'll find my way down to the Hunter.'

'I can take you to the airport,' offered Matthew.

'I think you need to find out as much as you can from your new friend next door.'

'We're not friends.'

'You will be,' Joe winked at him. 'Trust me.'

Taken aback by Joe's unusual show of friendliness, almost playfulness, Matthew fell silent, unable to think of a comeback. By the time he thought of something amusing, Joe was halfway back to the house.

That afternoon, Matthew and his sister took Joe into Gatton, where he caught a bus to the airport. Vicki spent several hours hunting down more information on charities while Tom looked into laboratory facilities in New South Wales that used horses of different breeds and sizes. He hadn't dismissed the possibility of a company trying to cover up a mistake or a disease by burying the evidence.

Most of the Lomonds continued working horses, while Henry took Lane, Karen, and Andrea for a drive to Glen Rock National Park located at the end of their valley. They explored the walking trails and took photos of kangaroos, wallabies, and a dozen varieties of birds. Andrea was always on the lookout for photos to add to her portfolio as, though she was renowned for her horse photography, her clients often requested non-horse subjects.

In the evening, they enjoyed another big family meal with their hosts. When they moved to the veranda to talk over coffee, Tom received two phone calls.

'That was Joe,' Tom informed them after the first call. 'He hired a car and is on his way to the Hunter region.'

When the second call came in, he looked at the number, raised his eyebrows, and stepped inside to speak in private.

'Tom Claw here.'

'Hi there, Tom,' the jovial voice of Brian Farley-Wells greeted him. 'Brian here - the eternally grateful owner of the horses you and Lane saved on the flight the other day. How're things going with you?'

'It's always good this side of the grass.' Tom wondered why Brian called but didn't want to ask. It had become a habit to create silences that others filled with their words.

'Great to hear. I thought I'd call your phone rather than Lane's. Mind you, I know you said he has text-to-voice capability with it, but this is easier.'

'I suppose it is,' Tom paused, waiting for the words to flow into the empty space.

'I just wanted to let you know that Quest has recommenced training in quarantine and is looking good for a start in a fortnight. I'm hoping you'll both take me up on my offer and fly down to watch him run. With your friends and significant others, of course. All on me. I owe you that and more.'

'Lane is keen to see Quest race, as am I.'

'We'll lock it in, then.' Brian paused before continuing in a more somber voice. 'Did you hear what happened to the young woman you were talking to at the transfer point?'

Tom's interest heightened, but he kept his voice casual. 'Binky? Yes, I heard. Tragic.'

'Absolutely. She's helped with a few of my horses over the last year. Always pleasant. A lovely girl. She didn't deserve that.'

'I don't know the details.' Tom pretended ignorance in the hope that Brian would share information.

'You don't want to. It seems she was involved with shady people, and it went bad. It's hard to believe. She seemed such a sweet thing, but you never can tell.'

'I only spoke to her for a minute, so I wouldn't know.'

'I was thinking of paying someone to look into it, just in case the police reports are wrong. I don't suppose you or Lane do that sort of work?'

'Like private investigators?' Tom snorted softly, trying to picture himself and Lane as a P.I. duo.

'Something like that. I don't think her family has the money to pay someone to check what happened, and I want to make sure it doesn't have anything to do with her work with racehorses. Just quietly, we're getting some unsavory types in racing these days. I guess they follow the money. I'd like to know that none of them were involved in this.'

'I don't think we'd be any use.' As he spoke, Tom wondered if Joe would discover anything but declined to mention that their colleague was doing some investigating. 'If you find out something, though, I'd be interested.'

'That goes both ways. If you happen to hear rumors about her, I'd appreciate it if you'd pass them on to me. The Australian horse world is a small place, and you never know what you might hear while you're in our little corner of the globe. I know I'm not the sheriff of the racehorse world, but I still want to keep it as clean as possible.'

'And run the bad guys out of town?'

Brian guffawed at the question. 'If I can, I will.' He adopted an American cowboy drawl. 'This town ain't big enough for the likes of them and me.'

Laughing politely, Tom glanced up to see Lane standing in the doorway. He held the phone against his ear with his shoulder and used his hands to sign Brian's name. Lane cocked his head to one side in interest.

Tom continued speaking into the phone, 'It's good to know that people are trying to keep crime out of the horse world.'

'We do what we can. Now, if you and Lane and your friends want to stay at one of my places before Quest runs, let me know. Happy to have you stay on one of the farms or in the city. And there's a nice beachside place over at Eden if you're after quiet.'

'I'll let the others know, but I think we have our time already planned.'

Lane raised his eyebrows at Tom, who merely shrugged in reply. He would explain when the call finished.

'Whereabouts are you staying? I think you mentioned something about going to Queensland.'

The question hit a jarring note with Tom. He couldn't see why Brian needed to know where they were, and general nosiness seemed incongruent in a billionaire whose time was precious.

'Here and there,' he replied. 'We're in the southeast corner at the moment but may head out west to Lane's station soon.'

'Good. Mind you, I don't have any places out there that I can offer to you, but when you come back, make yourself at home at any of my properties. I mean it.'

'We'll certainly consider it.'

'I'll stay in contact so we can organize getting you all here to see Quest run. It's always good talking to a horseman outside the racing industry. You tend to have a different view of things.'

'I suppose we do.' Tom didn't think they'd explored any of his views.

After a few more pleasantries from Brian and non-committal rejoinders from Tom, the phone call ended.

What did he want? Lane asked as soon as Tom put the phone in his pocket.

'I'm not sure. Partly to remind us about your horse running.'

He's not my horse.

'He will be.' Tom grinned. 'When you have your heart set on a four-legged friend, it almost always comes to pass that you end up with that horse.'

I can hope.

'He sees himself as the self-appointed sheriff of Racehorse Town and wants to find out what happened to Binky. He offered to pay us to do some snooping.'

Interesting. Lane scratched his head and looked at the floor as though it could provide answers to his questions. *Does he want to know, or does he want to find out what we know?*

'That, my bro, is what I've been wondering. If you approach any crime with the notion of not trusting anyone, it makes you paranoid about everyone's motivations. He says he's worried in case it's related to the racing industry – no mention of the dead horses.'

Perhaps we need to assume guilt and innocence at the same time.

'Deep.' Tom's eyes danced. He tapped his nose and pointed at his friend in a gesture that said *Lane knows things.* 'What are the chances he's involved?'

He owns horses. He knew Binky. He knows some of the horse charities. He has money. If he isn't involved, I bet he knows who is, though he may not realize it.

'And maybe he's just a wealthy racehorse owner who wants to keep crime out of his industry.'

More crime. Lane pulled a face to emphasize the first word. *I'm fairly sure there's already plenty there.*

'Fair enough. If all those dead horses were Thoroughbreds, it would make this so much easier to work out. We all know that the racing industry produces more horses than it can look after.'

They are cleaning up their act and rehoming more these days. I bet some of the dead horses were racehorses. They cut the brands off, didn't they? And the easiest horses to trace through brands are racehorses.

'It's the ponies that throw me. Who needed to kill ponies?'

Lane nodded and frowned. *Someone. We'll find out who.*

'And then what? If the police and welfare authorities don't think there was a crime involved in euthanizing those horses, it achieves nothing.'

There is a crime. Binky. It leads us to who murdered Binky.

'I'll be interested to see what those BJ Rescue sisters have to say.'

Me, too. We're looking at a scattered jigsaw puzzle with missing pieces. We need to gather all the pieces and start organizing what we have.

***

Dibby and Rev

As soon as the cargo doors opened, the air that swept in told the horses they were in an unknown place. There were no smells of eucalypt forest or Australian paddocks. As tired as Dibby and Rev felt, they widened their nostrils to sniff the air for messages about their location.

Dusty raised his head to look at the two golden horses whose presence had provided comfort during the flight. His heart was heavy. He knew that life only gave him friends to rip them away. They would be gone from him soon. He whickered softly, and Dibby looked at him with kindness. Something about the two palominos made Dusty feel safe. He closed his eyes and sighed. It wouldn't last. He knew that. Nothing good ever lasted.

CHAPTER EIGHT

Don't ever forget that it's alright to have fun with your horse – it's not all about hard work and training.

Lane Dimity on Twitter.

BJ Rescues

In the morning, Matthew returned to Horse Helpers with Vicki. As they walked along the quiet road on the valley floor, he explained all he knew of the charity. She noticed he went to lengths to make it clear that his low opinion of many horse rescues did not apply to Grace and Horse Helpers.

Her lips twitched when he described how Grace spent a large percentage of her income on the rescue horses. 'She certainly seems a cut above the usual horse hoarders you loathe.'

'She's not one of those,' he replied, unaware of Vicki's teasing edge.

Half an hour later, after Grace had given her a tour of the facility and introduced the horses in residence, Vicki began asking probing questions, partly to see Grace's reactions but also to gauge Matthew's feelings. She hadn't seen Matthew behave so oddly around anyone before. He stumbled over words and displayed uncharacteristic awkwardness in Grace's presence. It occurred to her that he had no idea why his usual charm had transformed into gawkiness, and pushing Grace's buttons might help him understand himself.

'Where do you bury the horses that can't be saved?' Vicki's sharp gaze pinned Grace as they stood next to the round yard where Matthew had worked with Shelley the day before. 'Clearly, when dealing with this number of rescue horses, you must have those who don't make it. What happens to them?'

Vicki knew the answer. In her research into the various rescues, she knew this was a point that REE and others used to attack Horse Helpers. It didn't surprise her when Grace's expression hardened.

'If we decide that the horse or pony isn't able to have a reasonable quality of life, for whatever reason, then it is put down. It isn't something we do lightly. We have at least one vet and one independent trainer work with us before we make that decision.'

'Seems reasonable.' Matthew accepted her account without question.

'Put down or sold for meat?' Vicki shoved her empathy aside and adopted an interrogative tone. 'You don't bury them here, do you? They end up in the pet food industry, don't they? I wonder how you reconcile that with your rescue status.'

Judging by the furious light in Grace's eyes, Vicki knew she was about to see raw emotion and hear straightforward facts from the woman. Not the polished version that most people wanted to hear, but the simple truth that was far more interesting.

'I do what is right for the horses. It's not always easy or even palatable to those who want fairy-tale endings, but sometimes death is not the worst option.'

'Really?' Vicki narrowed her eyes and goaded the Australian woman further. 'REE claims your rescue horses become dog food far too frequently. They pride themselves on saving every horse while you give up on the difficult cases.'

The tough questioning made Matthew uncomfortable. He looked at his feet and shuffled them as though contemplating running from the confrontation.

'Look around.' Grace pointed at her paddocks. She glared at her visitors, hostility rolling off her in waves. 'I rarely keep more than twenty horses here as that is all I can care for when volunteers don't turn up. And sometimes they don't turn up because they're tired, or it makes them too sad to see a horse that has come from hell and is still recovering. The other Horse Helpers branches operate much the same, with one person giving over part of their farm to the horses and only taking on the number they can care for alone when volunteers don't show. Unlike the corporate rescues, we don't pay people, and I certainly don't pay myself a million-dollar salary. We just try and do the right thing by the horses, and sometimes that means euthanizing them, and when we do that, no, I don't bury them. If death is a kindness – and sometimes when a horse is in extreme suffering it is - I arrange for them to be put down here, and their bodies are used to feed rescue dogs rather than feed the worms.'

Using her journalist's tactic of provoking more words from a person with an expression of disbelief, Vicki murmured, 'Interesting.'

Seeing Vicki's skeptical look, Grace continued, her voice burning with anger while tears threatened to burst through her fury. 'It might not seem pleasant to people who expect happy endings all the time, but it's sensible. I can't save all the horses I rescue because sometimes they are too injured or too dangerous to themselves and everyone around them, including other horses. If I can't save them, they help feed dogs that people have abandoned. I don't sell them to the knackery - I donate them to dog rescues that operate like mine. It's not my fault that people breed foals and puppies without any thought of their future. Don't blame me for the people who don't want a dog once the cute puppy has grown up. Don't blame me for trying to take care of one small piece of what humanity ruins. The bodies of the horses that we can't save can either rot in the ground or help the dogs. They are put down humanely here without fear or mistreatment, and their bodies are used rather than wasted.'

'What do you mean by corporate rescues?' Vicki picked up on the term that interested her, hoping Grace's emotional state would cause her to speak without filtering her words.

Grace did not disappoint.

'Those thieving, crooked, mongrels who pretend they're the angels of the horse world.' Her words were laced with venom. 'They're using the suffering of horses to make themselves rich. If they were even partly honest, they wouldn't have to go around trying to trash the reputations of all the smaller rescues. And you can't tell me that the men running them aren't in cahoots with each other. There are just too many similarities in how they do things.'

'Do you mean Rescuing Equines Everywhere and Equines In Need Of Funds?'

Realizing she had said too much, Grace tightened her lips together and looked at Matthew, who immediately dropped his eyes to his feet. He didn't want to be a part of this.

'Is that who you mean?' Vicki probed.

'Is that who you are working for?' Grace countered, her suspicions rising. 'I've had them send spies here before, but this is a whole new level if you are working for them. I shouldn't be surprised, though - they are more powerful than I thought possible.'

'We're not working for them.' Matthew could no longer stay silent. He understood that Vicki wanted her story, but he didn't want Grace thinking he was lying to her. 'Vicki's editor wants a story on horse charities, and we're curious about those big ones. I've told Vicki that your financials check out, but there seems to be a lot of grey areas with those others.'

'Grey areas,' Grace snorted, her lips twisting to one side. 'Those people are dancing in the shadows. There's more than just grey areas.'

'The REE centers for helping disadvantaged children seem to be an interesting concept.' Vicki threw a quick warning glance at Matthew. She didn't want him overplaying the part of the good guy. 'What objection do you have to the horses being used to help children in developing countries?'

'I don't object to it; I just don't believe everything they tell us. All those expensive ads on television showing the magic of children learning about horses seem…' Grace searched for the words to describe the uncomfortable feeling she had when those advertisements played.

'Fake?' Matthew offered. He felt uneasy about the exchange between the women and didn't know how to add to the conversation without making it worse, so he tried to stay silent. He hoped a single word might not upset his friend or new acquaintance.

'Not exactly fake, but overdone. Too saccharine and perfect. And expensive. I know they have big sponsorships from a lot of companies, but sending rescue horses all around the world like that? If they kept the horses here, they could use that money to save twice as many if saving horses is their aim.'

'Do the children help open the wallets of those big corporate sponsors?' Vicki believed they did, but she wanted to hear Grace's views. 'When they think they're giving disadvantaged children in developing countries this amazing opportunity, isn't that the incentive to give more money?'

'Yes, but it's more than that.' Grace wrinkled her nose, trying to explain her suspicions. 'I don't know. Maybe I'm wrong, but my gut instinct says that the whole helping-the-children thing is a front. Most people think it's incredible that they donate money that saves a horse, and then that horse goes overseas and saves a child, but it's all too movie-script perfect to be real life. There's something else going on. I'm sure of it.'

'Want to help us find out what that is?' Vicki leaned forward in a conspiratorial manner. 'I think there's a story here, and I want to uncover it.'

'So, you've finished upsetting me, and now you want me to team up with you?' Grace looked unimpressed. 'I'm sure you'll understand if I decline. I don't want to play games with you,' her gaze switched to Matthew, 'or you.'

'I understand,' Matthew muttered, wanting to shuffle his feet like a little boy in trouble.

Holding up both hands in a sign of surrender, Vicki tried to soothe her. 'I apologize for coming in hard before. Matthew assured me you were one of the good guys in this charity business, but I like to pressure people to see how they react.'

'Playing games, in other words.'

'Not quite, but I can understand where you're coming from with that. What I'd like is to have some of your honest opinions of the other charities.'

'I'm sure you can work out your own opinions.' Grace didn't feel inclined to help Vicki after the interrogation over the horses she couldn't save. She wanted to save them all, but she knew that some horses had so much damage, physically and mentally, that putting them down was kinder than making them suffer through a year or more of rehabilitation and vet care with no guarantee of a good life. The horses couldn't understand that the pain and stress might cease in a year or more; they only understood the present, not some possible future. Still, thinking about the horses she put down made her feel like she'd failed them.

'Would you at least give me a quick overview of how you see the whole horse rescue and charity industry in Australia?'

'I can try. You can't think of it as a binary system of good and bad – it's a sliding scale, like just about everything else in this world. Down one end, you have the ordinary horse owner who takes on a rescue horse and puts all their own money and effort into giving that horse a good life. I'd say more than half of Australian horse owners have rescued a horse at some stage and given it a haven without any thought of recouping the money spent on it. Then you have those who rescue a few horses and maybe get a bit of help from friends. You also find some horse hoarders.'

She paused and glanced at Matthew, her eyes narrowing momentarily. He gave her an apologetic look.

'Horse hoarders,' she continued, 'who use fundraising platforms to try and have other people pay for the horses they own. I'm not sure you can call them rescues, but they think they are. You work up to rescues like mine. We're a registered charity, so donations are tax-deductible. The people running the Horse Helpers centers are doing it voluntarily and running it on their land. There are a few more about our size that pay basic wages and all expenses to managers and employees from donations because they don't have the resources that we're lucky enough to have, and most are doing a good job. Some rescue managers receive a large salary from donations, and I'm not saying they don't deserve it. They are putting in the hours, and they deserve their salary. You only have to spend a few hours on some of the horse groups online to learn about them.'

'I'll look into that.' Vicki gave Grace an appreciative smile, hoping she'd continue talking.

'Finally, you have this new wave of corporate-level charities that have taken rescuing horses to a whole new level. There are government grants as well as donations in the millions from international companies and the racing industry. They exploit every possible way to obtain money from everyone, right down to having children pledge their school lunch money. They pride themselves on saving most of the racehorses that used to go to pet food, and they take in any horses that people are no longer able to care for and give them an incredible life, or so they claim. REE send hundreds overseas to their riding centers. EINOF have bought up great parcels of land, and their horses and ponies are retired to paddock lives. Now there's the new one, Caring About Horses And Ponies. It's also producing glossy brochures and fancy promises. REE, EINOF, and CAHAP have turned horse rescues into a business worth hundreds of millions of dollars, and not much of that money goes to the horses.'

'And I want to find out a lot more about them,' promised Vicki. 'I have some leads, but I'd like to hear who you suggest we contact.'

Grace's mouth twisted to the side in a crooked smile as she thought of the most outspoken people in the rescue business. 'You need to speak to Kat and Kaz. I'll hold back details that could result in a defamation claim. Those sisters will give you the names, information, and rumors while raising the middle finger at threats of slander. Nothing silences them when it comes to issues in the horse world.'

Thinking of the good times she'd had with the sisters over the years, she knew that wasn't entirely true. A couple of bottles of good wine, and they stopped talking horses and turned their minds to hilarious revelations about ex-husbands and future flings.

'We've heard of them,' said Matthew, wishing his contribution didn't sound quite so lame.

'I'm glad you suggested them.' Vicki clapped her hands together, pointing an index finger at Grace as though announcing she had won a prize. 'We're going to their place after lunch. It would be great if you came with us. The only thing better than two outspoken horsewomen is having a third one who is sensitive to defamation laws, so I know when facts become unsubstantiated suspicions.'

'You're on your own.' Grace began heading towards the stables, where a wheelbarrow and stable rake waited for her. She had turned the horses out earlier and needed to clean the stables. 'It's been interesting meeting you, but I have work to do, and all my volunteers called in sick today, so I have a full day ahead of me. If you'll excuse me – I'm sure you know your way home.'

To her surprise, Vicki strode along beside her. 'Come on, Matthew. We'll give Grace a hand so she can get her jobs done and come with us.'

'I'm not sure that's what Grace wants,' said Matthew as he picked up a shovel and fork and placed them in one of the wheelbarrows lined up in an empty stable. 'I'm fairly sure she's dismissing us.'

'You're right,' Grace entered a stable and began sifting the wood shavings onto the long prongs of the fork to remove the clumps of manure. 'I was trying to be subtle about it, but I think I need to be blunt and tell you both to go away.'

Vicki laughed and began expertly removing manure and wet shavings in the next stable. 'I like blunt. I'll ignore it, though – I'm a journalist, it's what I do. Matthew is more sensitive; he'll be cringing at forcing ourselves on you.'

'I am,' agreed Matthew. 'My mother taught me that if a woman tells me to go away, I go away. This hanging around and annoying you feels wrong.'

'We're helping Grace,' Vicki pointed out, 'not annoying her.'

Grace made a derisive sound.

'I don't think she agrees with you.' Matthew set to work on cleaning the third stable.

'I'm missing my dressage horse,' Vicki changed the subject in the hope she could engage Grace in a less confrontational discussion. 'I ride a Bisente horse related to the ones that the Lomonds have in quarantine.'

'I'm looking forward to seeing them.' Grace decided that even though they were irritating, she would rather have them helping than send them away when she had a lot of work to do and no volunteers. It would serve them right to do some farm work after grilling her over the horses she couldn't save. They might be famous and important people, but, as her father used to say, picking up poo was a great leveler.

A stifled laugh came from Grace's stable.

'What's so amusing?' Vicki looked over the divider to see Grace chuckling to herself.

'The fact that I have an award-winning U.S. journalist and the famous Matthew McLeay cleaning my stables.'

'She called me famous,' Matthew boasted to Vicki.

'Calm the farm,' Vicki replied dryly, 'Jack the Ripper was famous. It might not have been a compliment.'

They finished cleaning the half dozen stables before unloading a truckload of hay into a shed. After completing a few more tasks, Grace relented and agreed to go with them to see Kat and Kaz.

'It's not because I want to help you.' Grace pushed her glasses up her nose slightly so she could give Matthew a stern look. 'It's because I haven't seen them in a while, and I want to hear what they have to say about the charities as well as those buried horses. They always seem to have interesting inside information on everything in the horse world.'

An hour later, Grace was driving Matthew, Vicki, and Tom to BJ Rescues outside Canungra. She offered to drive since she knew the route well and was happier negotiating the twisting roads herself than worrying if the driver understood the conditions. Located in the mountains near the Gold Coast, the region was renowned for its beauty and, like a tourist guide, she pointed out interesting landmarks to the passengers.

The hundred acres of BJ Rescues consisted of lush creek flats and several hillside levels that resembled a tropical jungle with small clearings set amongst it for horse pens. Grace drove up the steep winding driveway and parked next to an expansive sandstone house that suggested the tens of millions won by the sisters didn't all go on the horses.

As they exited the vehicle, two tall, blonde women in skinny jeans and tight white t-shirts stepped off the veranda and waved excitedly. Kat and Kaz looked more like catwalk models than horse women with their tanned skin, long legs, and perfect hair.

'Grace!' One of the women squealed her name and ran forward to envelop Grace in a hug. Her words came out in a flat Australian drawl despite her obvious enthusiasm about seeing her friend. 'You've gotta come and visit more often, Luv.'

'Brilliant to see you, hun,' the taller sister flashed her exceptionally white and even teeth in a beauty-contest smile.

'Kat,' Grace indicated the taller one first, 'and Kaz, this is Vicki, the journalist doing the article on Australian horse rescues, and Tom and Matthew.'

They spent several minutes on the usual introduction niceties as they walked around the house to the back yard, where a palomino mare grazed on the lawn next to a marble statue of a Pegasus.

'What a gorgeous horse.' Vicki eyed the big mare with a critical eye and couldn't find fault with her.

'This is Barbie.' Kat clicked her tongue, and the horse walked to her. 'She is perfection in gold. We have a friend who judges palominos, and she said Barbie would win at any level in Australia – her color, conformation, movement, and behavior are all exceptional.'

'And this is Barbie when she arrived.' Kaz held up an A3-sized photo of an emaciated horse with sores on her hips and shoulders from rubbing on the ground when she was too weak to stand.

'You want information on some of these so-called charities?' Kat looked into Vicki's shocked eyes. It was difficult to believe that the beautiful animal had ever looked like the photo. 'Then here's one. This mare was donated to EINOF by her elderly owner who only had a few months to live. She didn't want to sell Barbie and think of her changing hands several times and ending up in a bad home. Barbie looked pretty much as she does now when she arrived at EINOF. They promised that she would live in luxury for the rest of her life, and they received a sizeable bequest from the lady when she passed. It was enough to keep fifty horses in luxury for twenty years. A year later, someone took this photo of one of the starved horses dumped in a paddock out whoop-whoop somewhere, and we recognized her.'

Kaz took up the story. 'Her brand proved her identity. EINOF claimed someone stole her from one of their equine paradises, but there were scores of horses where she was found, and we know some of them were EINOF rescues because they used before-and-after photos of them to pull in more donations and show people how their money is used. Only the photos were in the wrong order. The horses arrived looking good, and EINOF used the photos of the neglect that took place while they had them as the before photos.'

Holding up three large photos of a uniquely marked black and white pinto, Kat thrust one forward, showing the horse in good condition with the words *After three months of EINOF care* across the bottom. 'This was the horse the day he arrived at that rescue. This was not after three months with them. Note that there is no injury on his near fore.'

She swapped it for an image of the same horse standing on three legs, a V-shaped cut on a knee, and its ribs poking through its bite-marked coat. Across the top of the photo, it stated, *Arrival at EINOF*. 'Now, look at that leg injury and those bite marks and compare them to this third photo.' She held them side by side. 'Everything matches. Our friends took this photo when they found these horses starving in a paddock. EINOF took in a healthy horse, starved it, allowed it to be injured, then took photos and pretended it arrived like that and they fixed it; meanwhile, they left it to die in a remote paddock in outback

New South Wales.'

The sisters paused as they let the enormity of their information sink in.

'You have to ask yourself,' Kat held up the other photos of starving horses, 'if they did that with the pinto, did they also do the same with all these horses? Did they acquire healthy horses under false pretenses and deliberately neglect them to create the *before* photos that they use to increase donations? If they did that with these horses, how many others have suffered so that EINOF can make money? And if EINOF do this, what is REE doing? It's an even bigger corporate charity focused on making money.'

As soon as Kat stopped, Kaz started speaking again, her blue eyes glowing with zeal for their equine cause. 'And we want to know if those three lots of dead horses found buried in the Hunter region are from REE disposing of their excess horses. We started making inquiries but were warned off, and that had us asking more questions. Who doesn't want us finding out the truth about those horses? Why are they important enough to cause police and welfare to tell us they'll take action against us if we interfere in this matter?'

'Police *and* welfare?' Vicki cocked her head to one side as she considered the implications of this information. Was someone controlling them? Who was pulling the strings behind all of this?

Kaz nodded. 'Yep. We had an animal welfare official turn up here and imply that we were close to being shut down. Between the lines, it was fairly clear that we were being warned off. Someone is controlling them.'

'The council workers didn't want to talk, either,' Matthew reminded them.

'And you think EINOF or REE have something to do with it?' Vicki took the photos from Kat and examined them.

'I think they rescue more horses than they can handle.' Kat led the group through the cool interior of the home that looked to be a contender for House of the Year with its clean lines and vast windows offering views of the valley. 'They take in thousands of racehorses a year. Thousands of them. Plus, all the horses and ponies that people can't look after anymore. That probably adds up to thousands as well. Trying to find out actual numbers from them is like looking for a particular grain of sand in a storm – you know it's there somewhere, but there is so much other stuff thrown about that you have Buckley's of finding it.'

'They are experts at pulling the wool over everyone's eyes,' added Kaz as she indicated for everyone to sit at an enormous hewn wood table laden with an afternoon tea of cakes and savories.

'Like I said,' Grace sent her three new companions a flat look, 'I have to jump through hoops to keep my charity status, with every detail available for public scrutiny. Somehow, those big charities manage to provide so much information that it ends up obscuring the details we want to know. Where is all the money going? Where are the cash donations? And give us the actual figures of horses coming in and where they all are.'

'What she said,' Kat jabbed a finger at Grace and winked at her. 'There was always a bit of rot in some of the horse rescues. Little stuff, like some lady with mental health problems hoarding horses and saying they were rescues and expecting others to pay for their expenses, or youngsters with dreams but no means of saving all the horses.'

Grace slid a loaded glance at Matthew, whose mouth quirked apologetically back at her.

'Some we had doubts about, but they were helping horses, so most of us ignored the minor complaints. These corporate-level charities are a whole different board game, though.'

'Do you know who is behind the big charities?' Vicki looked up as she tapped some notes into her phone.

'No one does.' Kaz handed her glossy pamphlets advertising REE and EINOF. 'REE appeared out of the blue maybe ten years ago and grew exponentially compared to anything else around at the time. EINOF followed their business plan a few years later. They are money-making machines. They have high-profile fronts and spend millions on advertising with tv ads and pretty things like these pamphlets, but it's impossible to find out who is benefitting from all that money. It's not all going to the horses, that's for sure.'

'Wine?' Kat reappeared with two bottles of wine and a handful of glasses. 'Or juice? Mineral water?'

Vicki nodded at the wine while Tom, Matthew, and Grace opted for lighter choices.

'But not breakfast juice,' Grace told the sisters in warning tones.

Kat reproached her, 'You know it makes the day so much better when you add breakfast juice.'

Pulling a face at her, Grace shook her head. 'Not when it's half vodka, it doesn't.'

'Half vodka makes everything better.' Kaz chortled. Seeing the perplexed expressions on the faces of the other guests, she explained, 'It's how we got the name BJ Rescues. Occasionally, we'd start the day with breakfast juice laced with vodka, and one day, after a few glasses, we picked our lotto numbers and won. So, BJ for breakfast juice. But Grace has never been one for imbibing.'

'I'm not a teetotaller,' Grace defended herself, 'but swilling vodka for breakfast is not my style.'

'We don't *swill* it,' Kaz placed a carafe of orange juice on the table, along with some mineral water, 'we mix it with juice and enjoy a healthy start to the day. It's the breakfast of champions when we have to cope with idiots.'

Matthew raised his eyebrows at the sisters. 'I hope that doesn't mean you needed a few glasses this morning before we arrived.'

Slapping him on the back, Kaz grinned and assured him that was not the case. 'We're huge fans of you and Tom. And Lane and Andrea, of course. This,' she held up the glass of wine Kat handed to her, 'is my first alcoholic beverage of the day. Scout's honor. We wanted to meet you with clear heads, not sitting sloshed in the corner from our breaky juice.'

Kat dropped an arm across her sister's shoulders. 'Although, we are highly entertaining when we reach normal operating levels of alcohol, so I recommend hanging around until we polish off a few of these.' She raised her wine glass.

Finding the Australians amusing, Vicki smiled across the top of her wine before bringing the conversation back to the reason for their visit. 'Do you have anything concrete on these charities,' she tapped the pamphlets on the table, 'or is it all just a feeling that something isn't right with them?'

In reply, Kat took several sheets of paper from the bench behind her and handed them to Vicki. 'This is taken from REE. It names the Directors and some of the managers. They seem to be a mix of decent people genuinely concerned about horses and complete unknowns. I wouldn't be surprised if they were homeless people who were given a few bucks to sign up. Under their names is a list of associated parties, but they're mainly trust fund entities and two-dollar companies that lead to other empty entities, and you can't find the people behind them.'

Vicki quickly scanned the papers. 'What about their financials?'

'They're available online,' Kat's mouth twisted dismissively, 'but they are a tangled web of information with hundreds of sections for expenses. Money comes from overseas as donations and goes back overseas as expenses related to their horse centers, but there are separate financials in each country for those horse centers that we can't access. We can't work it out.'

Pouring herself another glass of wine, Kaz chuckled. 'It's enough to drive us to drink.'

'Face it, sis,' Kat held out her glass for a refill, her eyes glinting with amusement, 'we've been driving that particular bus for years.'

They both laughed and continued outlining some of the main points of the REE financial reports, including tens of millions paid to agistment centers, vets, and farriers when they estimated those expenses to be a tenth of what was claimed.

'Then there's tens of millions paid to transport companies,' Kaz tapped the relevant figures on the page Vicki was perusing, 'even though they supposedly gave discounted rates as their sponsorship.'

'They don't name any particular company,' noted Vicki.

'No,' Kat glanced at her sister and received a nod, 'but we know some of the grooms who work at airports for a few companies, and the word is that HATCO flies hundreds of nondescript horses and ponies out of Australia...and in. They're not stud animals, and there are no other horses on those flights. We think they are the REE horses. Phillipson's may be transporting them, too.'

At the mention of the horse transport companies, Tom sat to attention. Lane always pushed the notion of quantum connections, and this seemed to fit right in with his theories. Narrowing his eyes, he tried to remember everything that passed between them when they met Derek Anderson.

'Lane and I met the HATCO owner the other day.' His solemn gaze rested on the sisters. 'He mentioned offering discounted services to REE.'

'That confirms it, then.' Kaz took a pen and sheet of A4 paper, drew a circle in the center, and wrote REE in it. Drawing a line to another circle, she wrote Derek's name, then added several empty boxes around that. 'Find out who his friends are, and you might find a few more of the missing links.'

'He has connections in the racing industry,' said Tom, remembering him mention being part of a racing syndicate.

Kaz wrote *racing* in the top left-hand corner of the sheet. 'We know a lot of donations come from the racing industry, and REE take in thousands of ex-racehorses, so it's worth chasing up. We've had racehorses in the past – you'll meet them when we show you around the paddocks – and we knew a lot of the movers and shakers in the racing industry. Derek Anderson made a sudden appearance around the time that REE started up. He had a few horse trucks for road transport, and suddenly he had a fleet of planes, and I don't think he won the lotto.'

'What about Brian Farley-Wells? Lane saved a couple of his

racehorses on the flight.'

'He's a good bloke.' Kaz paused before writing his name in the top right-hand corner. She added a smiley face above his name and a sad face over Derek's. 'He's been big in the racing industry for at least ten years. We met him a few times, and he was always friendly. I could be wrong, but he seems to genuinely care about his horses.'

'Don't go into a stable with him, though,' added Kat, 'if you know what I mean. You men should be fine, but he's a player. Or a predator. I wouldn't want to be a pretty young thing working for him. He slapped me on the butt at the races once, and I told him I'd stab my stiletto into his groin if he touched me again. We both laughed, but I think he could be quite intimidating to a woman with less backbone. But, hey, men in his world are often like that, so focus on how he's nice to his horses rather than how he'd like to treat women.'

Putting a finger on Derek's name, Tom thought back to the cheerful man he met. 'Do you think he'd be capable of murder?'

'Do you think I'd be capable of murder?' Kaz countered, her blue eyes twinkling with mischief.

'Premeditated or a crime of passion?' Tom raised one eyebrow at her.

Kaz chuckled. 'I think I'm capable of both. I know Kat is. You should see us when we're in a full-out brawl with each other. It's quite on the cards that we could commit murder. Mum was always terrified that one of us would pick up a knife.'

'I love you, too.' Kat blew her sister a kiss. 'She's right, though. Given the right circumstances, we could be murderous. Murderers.' She wrinkled her nose at how similar the words sounded. 'Murderous murderers. If you're talking about the groom who was murdered in the Hunter, then it's unlikely to be any of the heads of whatever company is responsible for those horses. If Derek's involved with either REE or those dumped horses, he's one of the heads – he's not the guy pulling the trigger.'

'She was strangled,' Kaz pointed out.

'He's not the guy grabbing the throats,' amended Kat.

Matthew decided to pursue a different tack. Since the sisters seemed to know so many in the horse industry, they might be able to help. 'Do you know of any laboratories that have both horses and ponies? I wondered if some treatment failed or if there was a disease outbreak, and they covered it up.'

'Interesting,' Kat pursed her lips as she considered this. 'We've been assuming it was one of the big horse rescues because of the mix of breeds, but you might be on to something.' She looked at her sister.

'Who's down that way with large numbers of horses and ponies?'

'Not the plasma or snake bite people,' Kaz eliminated some possibilities. 'They only use big horses. What about that new one that is specializing in vaccines for zoonotic diseases?'

Unable to remember the name, Kat spent twenty seconds searching on her phone. 'Menningala Vaccines Limited. Interesting. They're developing new vaccines for humans and animals against zoonotic diseases, principally those spread by bats. They work with horses. They claim their animals have the highest levels of care, and they work closely with welfare groups to ensure their standard of excellence.'

'Let me guess,' Matthew sent Tom a dry look. He remembered how the international group Animals Deserving Our Respect gave their approval to the treatment of the stallions in the Pilatos laboratories as long as enough money changed hands. 'It's ADOR who says their welfare is fine.'

'You're right.' Kat sounded surprised. 'They are mentioned several times and claim all horses at Menningala are happy, content, and well cared for.'

Tom grimaced. 'They say that if you pay them enough.'

'They have horses and ponies of different breeds,' Kat continued, 'to see how treatments and vaccines work on them. They also have cattle, sheep, pigs, cats, and dogs, as well as some exotics.'

'That's just great.' Matthew's words dripped with sarcasm. 'They're testing on the entire farmyard as well as our companion animals and paying ADOR to approve everything. If those dumped horses came from them, I'd hate to think what bat virus they've unleashed.'

'What's so important about bat viruses?' asked Kaz.

'Tom's our scientist,' Matthew waved a hand at his friend. 'The abridged dumbed-down version, please, Tom, because that's the only one I understand.'

Tom knew Matthew did not require an easy explanation, but he kept it simple all the same. 'Bats have an incredible immune system as well as an ability to limit inflammation. They developed those because the energy required to fly is huge, and they needed to overcome toxins that build up from that muscle use, plus cope with the raised temperatures. Their ramped-up systems are so good that they protect them against most viruses. Keep in mind, a virus only wants to live and replicate; it doesn't really want to kill its host because then any viruses in that host are likely to die.'

Everyone nodded like well-behaved students at a lecture.

'In the bats, viruses must mutate and develop increasingly strong defense features just to survive. By the time they've adapted to living in that hostile bat environment, they are a super-bug that can live in almost any animal system – they are zoonotic. Humans and most other mammals don't have the super-powered immune systems and anti-inflammatory abilities of bats, so when a bat virus jumps to us, we get very sick or die. Ebola, Marburg, the coronaviruses, Hendra, Nipah, rabies, lyssavirus, and others either originated in bats or find a safe reservoir there and can emerge at any time into other animal populations. What is even more concerning is the unknown viruses they harbor which may be worse. Imagine an airborne version of Ebola that spreads before showing symptoms and doesn't weaken over time.'

The thought of such a virus made Grace shudder. 'That explains why we have a facility like Menningala. Perhaps someone should check to see if they have a sister operation in Venezuela.'

'Good thinking.' Matthew knew her mind had jumped to the dead horses found there. If there was a link, it stood to reason that the people responsible were in both places. 'It brings us back to REE, though, doesn't it? They have facilities in both places.'

Tom held his phone screen up for everyone to see. 'Here you go. Menningala have an address outside of Caracas. So, they are present at both places.'

'Derek Anderson's HATCO has offices there as well,' Vicki reminded them, 'and since they might tie in with REE, it makes them look suspect. And we have Venezuelan Equine Encephalitis, which may fit in with the vaccine company – maybe they had some mistakes that they tried to bury. Literally. There's also Lane's friend Cameron O'Shea who is based there and has a farm in the Hunter, and Ernie Lomond, of course.'

Kaz whistled and raised both her perfect eyebrows. 'That's a lot of connections.'

'It almost makes me want to go back and visit Ernie again,' Grace mused, her eyes wistful as she remembered how much she enjoyed her time in Venezuela.

A strange emotion plucked at Matthew, and he wondered if Grace and Ernie were in a relationship. Perhaps that was why she visited South America before, and now she wanted to return. The pensive look that crossed her face hinted at longing to go back there. He tightened his lips. It was none of his business, and he didn't care if she and Ernie were an item. It didn't worry him one bit.

'What's wrong with you?' Vicki reached over to tap Matthew on the shoulder. 'You look like you've eaten a lemon.'

'I was just wondering about what is going on in Venezuela. That's all.'

Both Vicki and Tom flicked their eyes to Grace, who remained dreaming about her visit. They looked at each other, smiles tugging at the corners of their mouths. Matthew was too easy to read, and it was clear that the feisty horse-loving Grace was getting under his skin.

'You should go there, Matt,' suggested Tom, a wicked glint in his eye that had Vicki turning away before she laughed. 'You know if you run it past Lane, he'll tell you to get on the next flight and check it out. We have a few weeks clear, and we all want to know what's going on with the horses. Just go.'

'Do it,' Vicki urged, controlling her humor. On the one hand, it was fun to tease Matthew; on the other, she could see the positives in Tom's idea. 'You can inspect REE's riding facility while you're there. I want to know if it's everything they claim. Is it a good use of donations, or are they just shipping horses there and killing them, so there's room for more horses?'

'Don't tempt me,' stated Matthew without conviction.

Vicki smiled at him. 'I'm not tempting you – I'm telling you to go. I'd love to have you on the ground over there reporting back to me.'

'Just go,' said Kaz. 'I want to know what REE are doing over there, too. Kat and I can pay for your airfare right now if you like.'

Matthew waved away her offer. 'No need for that.'

'He's loaded.' Tom grinned at his friend who was considering heading to South America. 'Even though he's a young pup, he can afford to travel.'

'I'm sensible with my money,' Matthew defended himself. 'I don't smoke, hardly ever drink, never do drugs, and I'm not big on restaurants, energy drinks, or takeaway coffee, so that's like fifteen thousand saved each year, maybe twenty.'

'I like your style.' Kat raised her half-empty glass of wine to him. 'I probably spend thirty thousand a year on that stuff. Just as well I won lotto, otherwise, I'd be up poo creek in a barb wire canoe.'

Kaz snorted. 'Or on a corner down in Surfers trying to drum up trade.'

'Shh,' Kat thumped her sister's arm. 'No one needs to know about my weekend job.'

The sisters laughed.

'Are you really thinking about going?' Grace eyed Matthew doubtfully. It seemed such a spur-of-the-moment scheme, and she suspected he was joking.

'Maybe.' The idea was fast growing into a plan, and he found himself liking it. 'Lane introduced me to Ernie years ago, and we're staying with his parents at the moment. I imagine he'd be OK with me turning up. Joe is checking out the cases in the Hunter Valley, and I'd like to know if the ones over there are the same. I think I might go.'

'Make sure you let me know what you find.' Grace twisted her lips to one side, then the other as she envied him heading off to South America on a whim. It took weeks of planning before she could leave the farm. Not that she minded. She loved her life, but there was something remarkable about being so free that a trip across the world could evolve from an idea to a plan in a matter of minutes. 'I haven't been able to achieve anything worthwhile concerning those dead horses. I started a petition that I hoped would influence the police or newspapers to do something, but once it reached five thousand signatures, it disappeared. Someone shut it down.'

'You should go, too, Grace.' Tom ignored Vicki's kick under the table. 'We can look after everything at your place while you're away. I gather you've known Ernie most of your life, so it would make it easier for Matthew if you went.'

'It's impossible.' Grace shook her head firmly. 'I can't up and leave at a moment's notice. Let's not even think about it. We came here to learn more about the horse charities for Vicki's article, so let's get back to that.'

They spent another half hour going over details of horse rescues in Australia and overseas as Vicki took notes. Before leaving, they met the horses at BJ Rescues. The palomino Barbie seemed to have run of the farm, and she followed along as they walked around the lush paddocks in the rainforest setting. It was evident that the sisters took great care of the horses and were knowledgeable horse people.

Vicki accepted that if there were a sliding scale of corruption in the business of horse charities, Kat and Kaz were located at the honest end since all the money used to buy and care for horses was their money. What she wanted to know was the level of corruption at the other end of the scale. It seemed that the big players like REE and EINOF had secrets that she wanted to uncover.

***

Dibby and Rev

The last of the air stalls were unloaded and the horses placed in secure pens at the livestock transfer facility awaiting the next leg of their journey. Dibby, Rev, and Dusty stood together in a yard of fifteen horses watching the grooms disinfect the air stalls before new horses were loaded and placed in the cargo plane.

The horses leaving looked exhausted. One reminded Dibby of a horse that once lived next to their paddock, but none of the horses responded. Their ears drooped, and they seemed unaware of their surroundings.

Dibby eased closer to Rev, pressing against the smaller horse and drawing courage from his steadfastness.

CHAPTER NINE

There are seven thousand human languages and one equine language. Put horses together from any country in the world, and they will understand each other. Their communication is universal, and we need to learn it.

Lane Dimity in an article on equine communication.

Two to Venezuela

'Matt's going to Venezuela,' Tom announced when he, Vicki, Matthew, and Grace walked into the Wunya kitchen that evening.

'I might not be,' Matthew protested.

'That would be wonderful!' Sheree clapped her hands together. 'I have a few things I want to get to Ernie, and you can take them for me. When are you leaving?'

'I don't know that I'm going.'

I think it's a good idea, Lane signed to him, grinning at his friend's discomfort. *You like South America.*

'As do you,' Matthew glared at him, 'so why don't you come too? Leave your trip to Ellamanga until we get back.'

Karen met Lane's eyes, laid a hand on her stomach for a fraction of a second, and shook her head slightly. Tom, Vicki, and Matthew noticed the protective gesture of her hand. Everyone else in the crowded kitchen was busy cooking, talking, or organizing drinks. The message conveyed in the secret communication was a surprise to the three friends, and they struggled to keep the joy off their faces and pretend they knew nothing.

I need to go home, Lane's hands spoke. His gaze, filled with love, remained on Karen. *But you should go, Matt.* He glanced at Tom. *Are you going?*

'I'm helping Vicki with her exposé on the horse rescues.' Tom dropped an arm across Vicki's shoulders, and she snuggled against him. 'Her editor wants the teaser in tonight, so I'll be chief coffee-maker and shoulder-massager as Vicki drums the keyboard.'

'Do you have enough information already?' Karen eyed her dubiously. She didn't think that visiting Horse Helpers and BJ Rescues provided enough substance for an article on the entire rescue industry.

'It's just a lead-in to tease the readers and get them buying newspapers, downloading copies, and talking about it. It'll be sensational and questioning rather than fact-filled. Depending on the response, my editor will decide where the finished pieces will run. There's not just the main newspaper, there are regionals as well as a couple of horse magazines.'

Sheree paused her stirring of a pot on the stove and turned to Vicki. 'Is there really that much interest over there in what happens with some horses here?'

'You'd be surprised. If there's anything untoward about these big charities – and that certainly seems to be the case – then readers will go crazy for it. Australia plus crime and intrigue equals a winner in the ratings.'

'Only if you write it,' Karen pointed out. 'The readers want you as much as they want the topic you're reporting. You are the award-winning journalist, chased by the paparazzi – which seems a little cannibalistic if you ask me. Plus, you're dating the famous, enigmatic, and much-desired environmental warrior, Tom Claw.'

Tom grinned at her. 'Where were you in high school when I was the nerdy kid studying too hard? Maybe if someone had described me as enigmatic and desirable back then, I wouldn't have had to take my cousin to the prom.'

'It's hard to imagine you as the ugly duckling.' Sheree looked him up and down, seeing perfection in his tall frame and chiseled features.

'He's fishing for compliments.' Vicki dug her elbow into his ribs. 'I've seen his high school yearbook. He was already doing modeling jobs and half the girls in his year listed marrying him as one of their life ambitions. Plus, his cousin is his second cousin who was Miss Arizona at the time and favorite to take out Miss America.'

'My version sounded better.' Glancing down at Vicki, he chuckled, his dark eyes shining with amusement and love.

Grace felt a tug at her heart as she witnessed the love and friendship between this group of people. As much as she wanted to be a part of something like this, she had work to do. 'Thanks for taking me to see Kat and Kaz, everyone. I need to get home and feed up.'

'It's all done.' Henry raised his hand in a stop sign. 'The boys went over earlier and did everything so you can join us for dinner.'

'We're experiencing Morocco tonight,' Sheree informed them over her shoulder as she went back to stirring. 'Henry, it's time for the mint tea. Wash your hands, travelers, and we shall enjoy some traditional mint tea to cleanse the palate.'

'That sounds pretentious,' muttered Henry as he poured hot water over mint leaves in cups.

Changing her voice to a broad Australian drawl, Sheree repeated her message. 'We have some beaut Moroccan food, so scrub up, fellas, and get some of that mint tea into ya.'

'Better,' Henry winked at his wife and offered her the first cup.

'I should go.' Grace took a few steps towards the door.

'Go with Matthew to visit Ernie?' Henry handed her a cup without waiting for her to wash her hands. 'Excellent idea. The boys will look after everything at your place. Don't think about it, just go.'

'What a wonderful plan!' Sheree's voice bubbled with excitement. 'You know Ernie will love seeing you. And it's about time you did something impulsive instead of planning everything to death until you decide not to do it.'

'I'm not…' Grace began, only to be cut off by Sheree.

'The Harira is about to be served. For those who care to know, it's lamb, tomato, and lentil soup, and it's delicious.'

Deciding it was easier to capitulate on the dinner invitation than continue the struggle to leave, Grace fell in with the Wunya crowd. As Sheree promised, the soup was excellent, and Grace was glad they railroaded her into staying. Most of the time, she enjoyed being alone, but there were nights when aloneness dipped into loneliness, and she was glad of the entertaining company around the table.

Sometime, between the chicken tagine with olives and herbed couscous and the date cake with orange syrup, the collective mind at the table decided that Grace would visit Venezuela with Matthew. The flood of reasons as to why this was a good idea threatened to drown Grace, and she kept her head above water by giving up the fight against the current and going with the flow. She knew she could back out of it once alone, so it didn't hurt to go along with them now. A small voice behind all the sensible voices of reason in her head whispered that it could be exciting to do something as insanely impulsive as heading across the planet with a man she barely knew.

Matthew wasn't quite sure why he was agreeable to the notion of Grace joining him. He told himself that it was a logical decision. She knew Ernie and that region of South America. Her interest in finding out about the horses in the Hunter extended to learning about those near Ernie's base. If REE were involved, Grace's knowledge of the charity could be significant. Plus, he enjoyed her company.

That last reason kept creeping in to color his thoughts. If she were a man, he told himself, he'd be just as keen to have her company. The fact that her open and honest face was easy on the eyes had nothing to do with it. His desire to hear her crazy laugh again was irrelevant. The way his heart rate increased when she looked at him – or glared at him – was immaterial. It was simply logical to have a knowledgeable person join him on a fact-finding mission.

'You should organize flights now,' Karen advised as they sipped the final cup of mint tea after dessert. She remembered her first flight across the world with Lane when she wanted to dislike him, and he was already well into his plan of winning her heart. It was a good plan. She had a hunch it was an equally good plan for Matthew and Grace. 'That old saying about strike while the iron is hot is worth following. Book the flights - he who hesitates is lost.'

Putting her cup down, Grace gave Karen a cautious look. 'I'm more of a *look before you leap* kind of person. I also believe that fools rush in where angels fear to tread.' Her gaze hardened and flicked to Matthew at the word *fools*, but something about his earnest expression softened her resolve to irk him. Her lips moved into a smile, and he grinned back.

This is not good, she told herself when Matthew's grin sparked off internal fireworks. Not good at all.

Suspecting that Grace's doubts about going would cement into a resolve to stay home, Karen gave Lane an intense look. As though reading her mind, he inclined his head slightly in approval of her thoughts. Karen placed a hand over his and squeezed lightly. She loved that they shared ideas without needing words and that he always supported her.

'I don't know if you're aware of it, Grace,' Karen began, 'but over the last year, my family's company Pilatos set up a foundation that seeks to improve the welfare of all animals that are involved in laboratory testing. Understandably, the focus is on horses because of the Friesian stallions at our laboratories. Given the possible link between the Menningala Vaccine company and the horses here and in Venezuela, I'm keen to investigate further. Joe will chase up that angle here, and I'm hoping you'll accept the task of looking into it over there. The Foundation will cover all travel and accommodation expenses, as well as any other costs, and we pay consultancy fees.'

'What about me?' Matthew's voice held an indignant edge as he sensed an unfair deal favoring Grace.

'You're one of the directors of the Foundation,' Karen reminded him, her eyes twinkling in amusement.

Matthew smacked a hand against his forehead. 'Duh. I forgot. Sorry about that.'

'Which is why I'm hoping Grace will accompany you.' Karen smiled kindly at the younger man. Over the last year, she had grown fond of Matthew and his twin. 'Something tells me she is organized and unlikely to forget things like being a director of the Foundation. You only need to submit the correct reimbursement forms for your out-of-pocket expenses, and everything will be covered as it is a legitimate use of Foundation funds.'

'I'll just pay for my trip.' Matthew pulled a face at the thought of all the paperwork involved with the reimbursement forms. 'You know I hate trying to account for everything I spend.'

'Which is why I'm going to have my right-hand woman Sandy book the flights for you right now.' Karen took out her phone and gave Grace a pleading look. 'Please say you are willing to do this for me. I'm serious about ensuring laboratory animals, particularly horses, are treated well, and if there's a link between those horses and the vaccine company, we'll see them brought to justice.'

The doubts of the Australian farmer had no chance against the persuasive skills of the New York lawyer. It suddenly seemed imperative to visit South America and check on what happened there. Grace nodded. Before she could think any further, Karen dialed Sandy and requested two business class seats from Australia to Venezuela on the earliest available flights.

Karen smiled warmly at Grace as she ended the phone call. 'All sorted. You simply need to send Sandy your details, and she'll get back to you with the arrangements. Sandy is amazing. She can organize anything with a minimum of fuss, and she thinks of everything. I am so relieved you are going.'

'We'll make sure everything is fine at home,' Felix assured her. 'We'll probably do what we did last time you went away. A couple of us can stay at your place each night, so you don't have to worry about the dogs being alone or anything.'

Unable to think of any excuse that wouldn't be cast aside by her neighbors and their friends, Grace sighed and accepted that she was going to South America.

'I'm glad that's sorted.' Vicki stood and started collecting some of the dishes from the table. 'I'll give a hand with these and then head back to our cottage so I can write the teaser. I wouldn't mind heading to Sydney tomorrow to speak to some of the companies associated with the big charities. I need some facts rather than opinions and guesses.'

Lane caught Tom's eye. *Be careful. It might not be one snake; it might be a whole nest of vipers.*

'Careful is my middle name.' Tom ruffled his friend's hair as he stood to help Vicki clear the table. 'I'm curious about how they operate, and I want to catch up with Joe to see if he's learned anything about the dead horses.'

'You could just ring him, you know.' Karen gave him a wry look.

Tom tapped two fingers under his eyes and pointed them at Karen. 'Yeah, but I like this face-to-face stuff. Plus, I had a call from Binky's father today.' A pained expression crossed his features as he recalled the sobbing father begging for any information that might lead to finding his daughter's killer. 'He's going through every number in her phone trying to find someone who knows something about what happened. He said the police aren't investigating properly. They're saying it was a random killer, but he's sure it has something to do with the buried horses.'

Shaking his head as he imagined the grief of Binky's father, Lane signed, *He's lucky the police gave him her phone.*

'They didn't,' said Tom. 'It was on the detective's desk, so he turned his phone off and swapped them. They're not even the same brand of phone, so it's clear the police aren't doing much of an investigation after their initial phone calls. It seems as though someone has called them off.'

'Poor man,' murmured Vicki as she headed to the kitchen with a stack of plates. She knew Tom worried that he was partly responsible for Binky's murder and understood his concern. 'Maybe it was just a random killing.'

'I wish that was the case,' said Tom as he followed her, 'but my instinct says it's because she was asking questions about those horses, and she was doing that because she wanted to report back to me.'

After placing her dishes on the sink, Vicki patted his arm. 'She was already interested in this before you spoke to her. It's not your fault.'

Grunting a sound of disbelief, Tom began rinsing the plates and placing them in the dishwasher.

The dinner party disbanded. Vicki spent two hours writing the piece designed to whet the curiosity of readers. It implied that nefarious, even criminal, actions were taking place in Australia's horse charities and hinted at the revelations to come in the following articles. While she was writing, Tom gathered information about the Menningala laboratories, including the fact that they used a large variety of horses and ponies. Interestingly, on the list of diseases they studied, he found Venezuelan Equine Encephalitis.

Sheree drove Grace home, chatting excitedly about the things she would send over for Ernie. When she was alone in her house, Grace stood for ten minutes staring at a wall as she replayed the dinner conversations. As she ran through everything that was said, she realized she had been manipulated into agreeing to the trip.

Objections about going rose in her chest, and she decided to tell Karen that she had changed her mind. Sitting down at her laptop, she went to her emails, intending to send one to Karen immediately. An email was preferable to a phone call as she knew how persuasive Karen was in conversation.

Noticing an email from one of the volunteers at the Hunter Valley branch of Horse Helpers, Grace decided to read it before writing to Karen.

Hi Grace, it's Sharyn here. I have a bit of an unusual case for you. I don't know if you can help. You know how I've been searching for Image after my parents sold him in the drought? And the last we knew, REE bought him at a sale? And how they claimed they didn't have him? Well, I think he's turned up - in Venezuela of all places.

My cousin was over there on holiday, and she saw a horse at a show and thought it looked like Image, so she took some photos. Look at the photos (I've attached them). I've enlarged the one of his shoulder to show his brand - that's Image's brand. And there's that W-shaped scar on his neck from when he was caught in the fence. The white on his legs and face are identical. There are the three unusual white spots on his hip that made us joke about him turning into an Appaloosa. That's Image. He was outside Caracas doing a jumping competition with a junior rider and has a different name, but it's definitely him. I'd stake my life on it.

I did some digging around, and I learned REE have one of their riding centers over there. They insist they didn't buy him at the sale, but I spoke to the auctioneer, and he said they did. The person I talked to at REE also said that any horses they send to their riding centers are there for life. They were adamant that they don't sell any of their horses. So, how did Image turn up over there?

I know you're friends with Ernie Lomond who's in Caracas, so I was hoping you could ask him to keep an eye out for Image.

There were another few paragraphs that Grace skimmed. Leaning back in her chair, she closed her eyes and pinched her lips together as she considered the coincidence of receiving this email tonight. Maybe Lane was right about the power of quantum connections. Looking at the photos, there was no doubt that Sharyn's horse was in Venezuela, and she wanted to find out how he ended up there. If REE had bought him and shipped him to Caracas for their riding center, why deny buying him? And why was he no longer with them? She sighed – it seemed she was going to South America to find out.

***

Dibby and Rev

Workers with different speech patterns from the familiar drawled accents of Australians brought hay twice a day. It tasted different, but it was fresh and there was plenty of it, so there was always something to eat. The water was clear, the pens were clean, and there was shelter from the sun. The Australian horses were cared for like cattle in a feedlot as they waited for the paperwork to clear so they could leave the quarantine yard.

Dusty stayed near his golden guardians finding solace in their quiet presence. Some horses became leaders by attacking other horses and fighting for dominance. Dibby and Rev remained calm and pleasant, spreading their leadership like a balm over the horses around them. If Dibby laid his ears back at any horse, Rev looked at him with reproval in his kind eyes. It was enough to remind Dibby that his shorter friend was the leader and he the sidekick.

One by one, the horses around them followed their lead: eating without fighting, sharing the confined space without aggression, and looking to Rev whenever something alarmed them. They felt safe with Rev and his best friend watching over them. Whenever they looked up, one of the palominos was watching the horizons at all times so they could relax.

The horses in that yard became a herd.

CHAPTER TEN

My grandmother met Dr. Mountjoy near Leopold in Victoria in the 1960s. In World War I, he served as a veterinary officer with the Australian Light Horse. He told her about the courage and loyalty of horses that stood over their fallen riders during battle, choosing to stay with their riders rather than flee to safety. At the end of the campaign, the horses could not come home to Australia. Since life in the Middle East could be cruel for a horse, the men chose to put their horses down rather than think of them suffering – sometimes, death is not the worst thing that can happen to a horse. Dr. Mountjoy moved along the lines of horses with his gun, and each horse looked him in the eyes as he raised the barrel. He told my grandmother that they knew what the weapon meant - they had witnessed so much death from the barrels of guns that they knew. He said every horse looked at him with trust and forgiveness before he pulled the trigger. It was the hardest thing he had to do in the war.

One of Lane Dimity's contributions to the anthology, 'Remembering Australian Horse People'

The Putty Road

Monday, Tuesday – Tom and Vicki.

On Monday morning, the band of friends headed to different destinations when they left Wunya. Andrea accepted a last-minute booking for a photographic shoot at a Thoroughbred stud in New Zealand. She traveled with Matthew, Grace, Vicki, and Tom to the airport, where she departed for New Zealand, and they flew to Sydney. In Sydney, Matthew and Grace boarded a direct flight to Chile while Tom and Vicki gathered more information about the charities.

Hiring a car at the airport, Tom and Vicki drove to The Rocks and booked into one of their favorite hotels with views of both the Opera

House and the Sydney Harbour Bridge. Opening her laptop, Vicki began searching for facts and rumors regarding the horse rescues, and Tom phoned Derek Anderson. He knew Vicki was keen to explore the HATCO relationship with REE, so that was his starting point.

'Great to hear from you, Tom.' Derek's jovial voice seemed genuinely delighted. 'How are you enjoying your time in Australia so far?'

'It's always a wonderful place to visit. We've had several days in Queensland, and I'm in Sydney now.'

'Are you? I'm at our Sydney offices this week – how about lunch tomorrow? I still owe you for saving my neck with those horses belonging to Farley-Wells. I hate to think of the insurance claim if either of those horses had been seriously injured or put down on that flight. I don't think I'd want to upset that man. He was good about it, though. Now, lunch – is Lane there with you?'

'No.' Tom glanced at Vicki, who was listening to the conversation with interest. Before the phone call, they had discussed whether or not to explain to Derek about the investigative piece Vicki was writing. He decided against it. 'My girlfriend Vicki is with me. I'm showing her around.'

'Then bring her to lunch, too,' Derek offered. 'My wife's been pestering me to take her to the new Thai restaurant near our main office, so bring Vicki along, and the two women can chat about their girlie stuff while we talk. How about that?'

When Tom looked at Vicki's face, he clenched his mouth with the effort not to laugh. Perhaps Derek didn't intend to sound sexist, but his *girlie stuff* remark seemed like he was assigning them to kitchen and bedroom duties while the men did the important things. Vicki's face looked as though she could shoot daggers from her eyes.

'I'm sure Vicki will enjoy chatting about women-folk stuff.' He grinned at Vicki. She kicked him. 'Tomorrow suits. What time?'

'Excellent. I'll text you the address and time after my girl makes the booking.'

After arranging to meet at the restaurant, Tom ended the call and rested an amused gaze on Vicki.

'Women-folk stuff.' Vicki snorted in disgust. 'Maybe you *should* have told him that I'm an investigative journalist who's going to grill his butt about the money he gets from REE.'

'I considered using those exact words but didn't think they were likely to score us a lunch date. Now you can catch him off guard.'

'I hope so. Now, let's see if we can get some appointments with the people from REE and EINOF and any of the companies that receive more than six figures from them or donate similar amounts. And can you check in with Joe?'

'Can do.'

Stretching out on the bed, Tom called Joe while Vicki moved to the lounge room to start her inquiries. After the usual greetings, Tom asked if he had found anything of interest relating to the charities.

'What's of interest is that there's more going on here than meets the eye. You two be careful.'

'Who do we need to be careful of?'

Joe's voice was hesitant. 'I'm not sure yet. Everyone. A farmer near the Menningala Vaccine facility in the Hunter said truckloads of horses come and go at night, but they're supposed to be a secure facility with one hundred and ten horses maximum, and no livestock should go in or out. He doesn't want them to know he's said anything, though. His words were: *people go missing*.'

'I wonder who else is missing.'

'He clammed up after that. He didn't even want to say any more about the horses that go in and out.'

'There shouldn't be horses going in and definitely should not be any leaving, considering the viruses they're working with. Any chance they were covering mistakes by getting rid of those horses and bringing in replacements?'

'Maybe. Some of their horses came from REE.'

That made Tom sit up. REE claimed they rescued horses from companies that intended to use them as test animals. 'Are you sure?'

'A disgruntled ex-employee who worked at the Menningala stables traced some brands of horses that she liked. They were racehorses whose owners placed them with REE. Her employment contract had confidentiality conditions that she wasn't inclined to break, so she quietly left and never mentioned it to anyone.'

'Except to you.'

There was a brief chuckle, and Joe's voice changed from his New York tones to a Montana drawl. 'Never underestimate the charms of an old cowboy who's buying a pretty lady some drinks.'

'Don't worry, I never underestimate you,' Tom said in all seriousness. He had learned over the past year that Joe was a remarkable man. He could make a fortune as a businessman or an assassin, but he chose to work for Karen because he liked her. 'Any word on who was moving the horses out at night?'

'No transport company I contacted claims to have any knowledge of it, but someone could pay them to keep it secret. Interestingly, both REE and EINOF own large horse trucks that fit the description the farmer gave me.'

The information began to knot around itself in Tom's head. 'So, you think REE or EINOF could be involved with providing horses to Menningala and then dumping others? Is that enough of a motive to kill someone like Binky?'

'Those charities have an annual turnover of hundreds of millions of dollars, and where there's big money, there are usually greedy people and crime. Is it enough of a motive to murder a girl who asked some questions? People have been killed over a few dollars, so yes.'

A frown creased Tom's forehead as he tried to work out where the crime lay. 'There are so many ways to justify needing to put down a hundred or even a few hundred horses, though. It doesn't have to be a crime.'

'Unless killing the horses was a small part of a much bigger crime. I've been looking at their records. There seem to be discrepancies between the horses they claim to save and the horses they have. They allow two hundred dollars a week for each horse's care – that's food, vet, farrier, and other costs. So, if you can claim that for one hundred horses that are no longer around, there's twenty thousand a week for someone. Forty thousand a week if they can get rid of two hundred horses.'

'How many horses do you think are missing?'

'Thousands.'

Tom whistled. That much money was a motive for murder and a reason to be dumping dead horses in pits.

When they finished their call, Tom passed on the details to Vicki, who shook her head at the figures involved.

'I can't get my head around that much money for horse rescues.' She looked at her notebook screen. 'I've found five companies that donate more than ten million a year to REE. That's ten million a year each. And guess what – Menningala is one of them. That's a coincidence, isn't it?'

'I feel like I'm wandering through a maze.' Tom rubbed fingers through his hair. 'Joe said to be careful of everyone, and I'm beginning to think that might be the case. There could be a lot of people with secrets who are willing to kill to keep them.'

'Maybe,' Vicki threw him a cocky grin, 'but I never let that stop me from doing a story before, and I won't this time. Are you ready for a drive? I've found a horse rescue that falls somewhere between the mostly self-funded ones like Horse Helpers and BJ and the corporate giants of REE and EINOF. They're happy to have us visit, so get your gorgeous Arizona butt into gear, and let's get going.'

It took a little over forty minutes along the M4 and then the M7 to reach Horsley Park. Among the small hobby farms, they found the neatly set up Horsley Horse Rescues on five acres. It depended solely on donations to fund it, with the manager, Jody Finnegan, receiving a modest wage and on-site accommodation.

Jody, a short, muscular woman with the intense gaze of a Jack Russell Terrier waiting for someone to throw a ball, showed them around the horses. As they walked, she summarised the history of each one. Afterward, she produced detailed copies of their financials and insisted Vicki keep the documents.

'You'll need them to compare to those other ones.' Jody's piercing blue eyes watched Vicky closely. 'You know, the big charities. There's something wrong there. I don't know what, but something. You heard about Binky, didn't you?'

'You knew her?' Tom gave her a quizzical look. Lane often said that the Australian horse world was so small that either everyone knew everyone else or knew three of their friends.

Jody nodded, her penetrating gaze fixed on him. In the privacy of his mind, a rogue voice chanted, *throw the ball, throw the ball,* as her tense body posture gave the impression that she was ready to race away after something.

'Binky didn't earn a lot, but she tried to donate to us when she could, plus, when she was in Sydney with racehorses, she'd often stay here and give us a hand. She was a beautiful soul. Beautiful. Just quietly, there's a few of us saying that she went to the Hunter to find out about those dead horses there. That's why they killed her.'

'Who killed her?' asked Tom.

Grimacing, Jody held her hands palm up. 'I don't know exactly, but someone who dumped those horses, and we're all pretty sure that has to be REE, or is probably them. Maybe it's them. Well, it could be. That place is all about the money. They only care for horses in their glossy pamphlets and videos. And you know what else is really odd about them?'

Tom and Vicki waited for her to continue.

'I don't know anyone who works for them. No one. I know thousands of people in the horse world up and down the east coast. I know Kat and Kaz. I know Grace has headed off on holiday with your buddy Matthew. I know most of their volunteers who have anything to do with horses. I know competitors, trainers, and breeders. I know a lot of Binky's crew who work with the transport companies. But not one person from REE. None of my friends know them, either. How can that be? How can they be so big, but other horse people don't know their employees?'

'That is strange,' Vicki agreed. 'I've learned from my Aussie friends that there's usually no more than two degrees of separation between everyone in the horse industry here.'

'That's exactly it.' Jody pounced on her words excitedly. 'I was told that they employ the young people who learn in their overseas riding centers, but surely they can't do all the work. You'd think they'd have to employ some local horse people. It doesn't make any sense. When you find one thing that stinks about something, you can bet there's other rotten stuff there. I don't trust them, and I don't want to ask around about them because I don't want to end up like Binky.'

They spent several hours learning about Horsley Horse Rescues. The rescue had a mix of horses that were surrendered to them as well as ones they bought at sales that they saved from the pet meat trade. Jody made it clear that she wasn't against using horses as meat, but she hated seeing healthy young horses ending up there.

'People breed too many horses,' she said as they walked back to their car, 'and a humane death at the knackery is better than slowly starving to death in a paddock. Mind you, many of us, including Grace, have been campaigning to improve the treatment of horses in the meat processing chain. They deserve to be treated with dignity.'

Her words made Vicki wonder about the supply of horses destined for meat. 'If REE and EINOF are obtaining so many thousands of horses each year that were destined for slaughter, is there a shortage of meat horses?'

'The prices have gone up considerably,' Jody acknowledged. 'Thousands of slow racehorses that used to end up as meat now go to the big charities. They claim that they rehabilitate them to their riding centers but, really,' her face creased in disbelief, 'are off-the-track-Thoroughbreds what you want for inexperienced children? Non-horse people get all warm and fuzzy about the pretty horses having rainbow-unicorn lives helping the challenged children in other countries, and it keeps them throwing money at REE to keep the fairy-tale going. Meanwhile, those of us who know a canter from a cantle are making WTF faces and wondering what is really going on.'

It had occurred to Tom that REE's claims of using the Thoroughbreds for children verged on the absurd. On the other hand, he reasoned to himself, he had known some quiet and sensible retired racehorses, and perhaps they were being used to teach handling skills rather than riding skills.

'They claim to save thousands of racehorses each year,' said Vicki, 'and they aren't sending them all overseas. It makes me curious about where they are all located.'

'It makes me wonder,' mused Tom, 'if REE is all about money, and the horse meat buyers are paying so much for horses at present, then wouldn't they find a way to channel their excess horses into the meat trade? If they're behind the horses killed in the Hunter, it seems inconsistent with an organization that will do anything for money. From what we've learned, it's hard to imagine them wasting an opportunity to make money, even if it goes against everything their public profile stands for. Why would they kill and bury them when they could do a deal with the horse meat buyers and make money?'

'Maybe they couldn't be used for meat,' Jody pointed out. 'Testing on meat is done at random, and maybe the horses had something in their systems that meant they couldn't go to slaughter. You can't use gentamicin on animals intended for human consumption. I know you're not meant to give bute to a horse that's intended for human or animal consumption. I use bute like it's going out of fashion on anything with pain or inflammation just to make sure they don't end up as meat. There are probably some vaccines that prevent them from being used as meat, too.'

The mention of vaccines had Tom and Vicki glancing at each other. The ties between Menningala Vaccines and REE were looking interesting.

After leaving Jody, they drove back to the city and spent the rest of the day combing the internet, looking for more connections between the charities and companies like Menningala. Before having a romantic dinner in their room, they emailed their information to Joe, Lane, Karen, Matthew, and Andrea. Their files were growing, but they still had no definitive evidence about criminal activity or who was killing the horses.

On Tuesday, they met Derek and his wife, Sissy, at the Thai restaurant. Sissy towered over her jovial, rosy-cheeked husband, and, at first, Vicki suspected she was the epitome of the trophy wife for the short, wealthy Derek. When they sat at their table, Derek instructed Sissy to have some girl-talk with Vicki while he and Tom talked horses.

'Girl-talk.' Sissy rolled her eyes and grinned at Vicki. 'There are times when I find it difficult to remember why I married the man.'

As she met the intelligent gaze, Vicki's assumption that the stunningly beautiful woman married Derek because of his bank account underwent a revision. 'Not for girl-talk, obviously.'

Sissy laughed. 'Surprisingly, he can talk dresses, shoes, and shopping with the best of them. I think he likes the role of the macho man who tells his wife what to do. I'm sure some of his friends are impressed by it.'

At her words, Derek stopped talking to Tom and chortled merrily. 'It's not a role. I do tell you what to do. You just choose to ignore it.'

'As every good wife should.' Sissy patted his arm affectionately. 'Now, you go back to your man-talk so I can chat to Vicki about dressage and journalism.'

'Be careful she doesn't do an exposé on you,' Derek teased, winking at Vicki.

For the briefest of moments, the cheerful light in his eyes hardened to something more sinister. It was so fleeting that Vicki doubted she'd seen it, but the shiver down her spine told her it was there. Glancing at Tom, she quirked an eyebrow at him. Tom had not mentioned Vicki's background to the Andersons, so it seemed they had been doing some investigating of their own.

'I'm sure you're safe.' Vicki smiled at Sissy. 'I only do exposés on problems that need exposing.'

'Now, that makes me curious about your current project.' Derek chuckled, maintaining the façade of a jolly man, but Vicki remained wary after seeing the flash of menace behind the mask. 'I hope you'll share it with us. Perhaps we'll be able to assist you.'

Again, Vicki saw the hint of something intimidating behind his happy surface.

'Perhaps you can.' She looked down at the menu the waiter placed in front of her, feigning disinterest in the topic. 'Or not. But enough of me and my work. You two men get back to your discussions so Sissy and I can start talking dressage. Do you ride, Sissy?'

Derek watched her, his expression a mask of neutrality. When Tom asked him about his racehorses, his animation returned, and he launched into some amusing anecdotes about racing.

For the first half of the meal, the women spoke of horse people, training methods, and their shared interest in dressage. Although Vicki competed at FEI level and Sissy joked at her attempts to move beyond Preliminary and Novice tests, they both appreciated harmonious relationships between horses and their riders. They admired some of the old school riders and trainers like Reiner Klimke and Nuno Oliveira, and neither were fans of the flashier and more forced movements that were currently popular.

'What do you do with your racehorses when they retire?' Tom moved the conversation towards the purpose of the lunch. He glanced at Vicki to see her listening closely. 'We've noticed a lot of racehorses going to REE.'

'Mine live out their days on one of our farms.' Derek waved his fork in the air to indicate the direction of the farms. 'Up there in the Hunter. We don't have any need to sell them or give them away.'

'Do you ever wonder what happens to all the horses that go to REE?' Tom took a sip of water and watched Derek, who appeared unconcerned by the topic. 'I've heard they get thousands of ex-racehorses every year. I gather you're not flying all of them overseas to their riding centers.'

Derek's bushy eyebrows moved towards each other as he frowned. 'It's nothing to do with me. I like what they're doing and give them a good deal on transport. As far as I know, they have thousands of acres around the country where the horses that are unsuitable for rehoming can enjoy retirement.'

'They do an amazing job,' Sissy broke into their conversation. Her husband's judgemental eyebrows warned her to be quiet, but she continued in an excited voice. 'We donate to them because they don't just help horses; they help children in so many countries.'

Vicki used her words as the starting block for the questions that lined up in her mind. 'Yes, I see that your company has donated ten million to them each year for the past few years. Any reason for such a large amount?'

'It's a tax deduction.' Derek's expression grew brittle as he regarded Vicki. 'Surely, you understand how that works. We donate to them and get the deduction, and they use our services and recommend us to their millions of fans. It's a good investment for us, and it pays off.'

'When you donate that much,' Vicki widened her eyebrows at the amount, 'you must get to meet the people running the charity. What sort of people are they?'

'That's not really for me to say.' Derek snapped his fingers at the waiter and shook his glass to order another whiskey. He didn't ask anyone else if they wanted a drink. 'Why the interest in them? They do a lot of good and don't do any harm.'

'There are a few people who claim they've caused harm.' Vicki decided to throw some suspicions at him to see his reactions. 'I've heard they are responsible for killing those horses found buried in the Hunter. Also, at least one machinery operator who worked for them is missing, and a lovely young woman who worked in the equine transport industry was murdered. I think REE are involved.'

Guffawing at her statements, Derek shook his head. 'You've got to be kidding. I don't know about the machinery operator, but if you're referring to Binky, that had nothing to do with REE. She often worked for us when we had horses coming into Melbourne, and she was a sweet kid who trusted people too easily. She was always on the cards to be the victim of some predator.'

'She was asking questions about the horses found in the Hunter,' Vicki kept her gaze on Derek and noticed that his jolly demeanor seemed forced, 'and there's a lot of talk about them coming from REE, which is why their brands were removed. Brands could prove they were racehorses rehomed with REE.'

'If that's the story you're working on,' Derek's voice remained pleasant though his eyes had a flintiness to them, 'then I suggest you find something more credible to write about. I don't know who is telling you this nonsense, but the people I've met at REE put the welfare of their horses above all else.'

'So, who are those people?' Vicki challenged him. 'I've been looking through their documentation, and most of them are a mystery. It's as though someone pulled homeless people from the streets to fill the positions so that those who actually run it can remain anonymous.'

'I've met them, and I assure you they are above board. If they choose to avoid public scrutiny, then that's their business. I'm not about to jeopardize my business relationship with them so you can sensationalize a story that has nothing to do with them.'

'That's understandable.' Vicki smiled sweetly at him. His strong reactions interested her, and she decided to change tack before he shut down. 'Ignore me - I'm only fishing for a story. I don't really know anything about REE, but I've often found if I throw some hand grenades into a room, something blows up. Not in this case, obviously.'

'There's nothing there to cause an explosion,' Derek said, matching her smile with an equally false radiant beam. 'But I understand how journalists work – your editor wants a story, so you bait your hooks and see who bites.'

Vicki laughed and chose to compliment him. He struck her as a man who enjoyed flattery. 'You seem far too intelligent to take bait dangled in front of you by a journalist. Perhaps I need better bait and a stronger line if I want to fish in your part of the pond.'

Glowing in the light of her admiration, Derek leaned over to pat her hand. She struggled to leave her hand on the tablecloth and not snatch it away.

'There's nothing here for you to catch,' he assured her in warm tones. 'We transport horses. REE save horses. We often transport their horses. And we're not the only ones. Phillipson's Transport move as many or more. We might be in competition with each other, but I know for a fact that they are good people who care about horses, so there's no story there, either.'

With a slightly ditzy sigh that had Tom almost choking on his drink, Vicki gazed at Derek with shining eyes. 'It was worth a try. I don't know much about the horse transport industry, but when I hear someone praise their rival, I know I'm dealing with good people. I'm used to men who throw their opposition under the bus. Perhaps it's an Australian thing – you Aussies are so much more likable than most.'

'You should do a story on international equine transport,' suggested Sissy. She felt a little threatened by how her husband and the American appeared to flirt in front of her and wanted to steer the conversation away from their one-on-one chat. 'There's no scandal that I know of, but it's interesting. Moving horses around the planet is a massively expanding industry. I think it would interest readers.'

'Lane and I found the experience fascinating,' put it Tom.

'You might have something there,' Vicki said to Sissy. 'I don't know anything about it. Do you sedate horses to fly them?'

The tensions eased as Sissy answered Vicki's questions while the men watched in silence for a few minutes. When Derek was convinced that their discussion avoided controversy, he and Tom began talking about the merits of American and Australian football.

After lunch, just before they parted ways, Derek reminded Vicki that there was no scandal or crime associated with REE, and he hoped she would stop looking for any. As the Australian couple walked away, Vicki shuddered. She sensed a threat in his final comment.

'He's up to his neck in it,' murmured Tom when he was sure they were out of earshot.

'I agree,' nodded Vicki. 'His reactions told me more than his words. There's more to his relationship with REE than a straight-forward business association.'

'He gets a ten-million-dollar tax deduction for donating to a charity that pays him to fly horses around the world. What are the chances he's one of the mystery men behind the charity?'

That seemed a possibility, thought Vicki. There were a lot of puzzle pieces to fall into place, and she wouldn't be surprised if the jovial little man was more involved than he claimed. 'Next stop, Phillipson's. I want to learn something about their arrangement with REE.'

'Have you made an appointment?'

Vicki gave him a wolfish grin. 'I'm going for the surprise attack. Let's catch them off guard and see if anything drops from the tree when we give it a shake.'

They put the address into the car's guidance and drove to Phillipson's Bankstown Airport offices. Tom tried calling Karen and Lane a few times, but their phones were out of range as they traversed the outback. He would tell them about Derek later.

The unimposing single-story building housing Phillipson's Equine Transport was crammed between an auto repair shop and plumbing supplies. It had the look of a small industrial business rather than the offices of an international transport group.

They parked outside, and Vicki frowned at the exterior, noticing that the previous company's name was visible under the Phillipson's sign. 'How can this company afford to donate ten million to REE? This looks like the headquarters for a two-dollar company that will disappear at the drop of a hat.'

'Maybe they'd prefer their tax deductions in the form of donations than office leases.'

'I guess.' Vicki exited the car and hooked her handbag onto her shoulder. 'Maybe their Melbourne offices are grander than this.'

They approached the glass front of the narrow building and pulled the sliding door open. Inside, some posters of racehorses decorated the walls of the large reception room. The bright orange carpet clashed with the three red chairs. At the reception desk, a young woman stared intently at her computer screen, checking social media sites. It took a full minute before she turned her attention to the visitors.

'Hi. I'm Zoe.' She spoke in a flat Australian drawl. 'How can I help you today?'

'Hello, Zoe.' Vicki spoke briskly. 'I'm Vicki Marshall, and this is Tom Claw. We're researching an article on international horse transport and wanted to speak to one of your managers here. We're particularly interested in the quarantine side of things and how you cope with potential virus outbreaks.'

Tom admired her fabrication skills. He almost believed her himself until he remembered that she was investigating horse charities, not transport.

'They said you'd be coming.' Zoe's mouth pursed tightly in disapproval. She took a folder from the desk and passed it over to Vicki.

'Who said?' Vicki glanced at the plain manila folder.

Zoe avoided the question. 'No one is available to see you, Miss Marshall. That folder contains information about Phillipson's, as well as press releases. If you need any other information, send us an email, and we'll forward it to our lawyers.'

'How very defensive of you.' Vicki raised her eyebrows at Tom. He arched one back at her. 'Perhaps if I just have a quick word with one of your senior staff.'

As she spoke, Vicki started walking towards the door that led to the offices at the back of the building. Zoe jumped up and sprinted around to stand in front of the door, holding her hands out like someone running defense in basketball.

'You are to leave this premises.' Zoe's brow furrowed as though she was trying to remember the words she'd been instructed to use. 'I will call the police and have you charged with trespass if you don't leave immediately. Management at Phillipson's will not communicate with you.'

'Easy now,' Vicki smiled at the younger woman. 'I only wanted to find out a bit about companies like Phillipson's, and it seems I have.'

As they left, Zoe picked up the phone to call someone.

Outside, Tom whistled. 'That was unexpected.'

'It was bizarre. Who told them we were coming? I'm assuming it has to be our red-cheeked little friend, Derek, since we had lunch with him. Who else could it be? No one else knows we're looking at REE and the companies that made large donations.'

'Jody, or Kat and Kaz,' suggested Tom, not believing it for a moment. 'Maybe Grace spoke to a friend about what we were doing, and they passed the information on. Derek does seem the likely choice, though.'

'I don't know why Derek would say anything. Why help the competition?'

'Because they're not competition.' A soft voice from the car parked next to theirs made Vicki jump.

'Sorry to startle you,' Joe drawled through his open window. 'Apparently, we're chasing up the same leads.'

'Should we be open about speaking to you?' Tom asked as he stood next to the driver's door of his vehicle, looking at the passing traffic rather than at Joe. 'Or should we be all secret-squirrel about this?'

'I always fancied Secret Squirrel, myself,' replied Joe, looking at a racing magazine.

In response, Vicki and Tom climbed into their vehicle and lowered the window next to Joe's car. It was unlikely a casual observer would realize they were talking to each other.

'I learned that they donated ten million to REE,' said Vicki, explaining why they were there. 'I thought I'd come out and find out about them, but they don't want to talk to me.'

'Any idea who would have told them we were coming?' Tom glanced at Joe, who studied an article on popular sires.

'If you've spoken to Derek, then I'm sure he's the one who warned them.' Joe turned some pages. 'He and the two Phillipson brothers own a racehorse together. Coincidentally, at least five of the other owners in that syndicate own or are directors of companies that made large donations to REE and Equines In Need Of Funds.'

'That's some coincidence.' Tom's eyes widened at the implications. 'They're working together? Are they the ones who control the charities?'

'I don't know yet.' Tossing the magazine onto the passenger seat, Joe adjusted his rear-view mirror. 'I can tell you that at least three of the companies make enough money to warrant donating millions to these equine charities, but they don't appear to have any assets or office space any more than what Phillipson's has here. Two of them handle the advertising for both the big charities, and those accounts are worth more than what they donate each year.'

'Are they using the charities for money laundering?' Vicki chewed at her bottom lip, trying to work out the money trail. 'Or just money-making? All those hundreds of millions of dollars in donations coming in, and most of that is going back out to transport companies, advertising agencies, feed suppliers, and others. I bet one of the big donors is a horse feed manufacturer and earns back far more than he donated.'

Joe tapped his nose. 'Spot on. They allow two hundred a week for the upkeep of each horse in their care, and about half of that is for feed. I can't pin down how many horses they own, but let's say they have five thousand spread around the country. That's possible since they claim to save several thousand racehorses a year. That's half a million a week on horse feed, or twenty-six million a year.'

'And how profitable for everyone,' Vicki nodded slightly, her eyes narrowed, 'if a few hundred horses go missing now and then but stay on the books. The money still gets donated for them. The money still goes to the feed merchants and everyone else. Only, there's no money going to the horses because they're dead.'

'You might have something.' Joe saluted without looking at her. An observer would think he was simply adjusting his hair. 'I'm heading back to the Hunter now if you want to meet up at Singleton tonight. We can go on to Scone tomorrow.'

'We might follow you.' Vicki looked to Tom for agreement. 'We'll head back to the hotel for our stuff, so if you're leaving now, we'll be a few hours behind you.'

'Phone me when you get into town.' Joe started his car, looked around, and reversed out of the car park.

'I think that theory could explain everything.' Tom watched Joe's car as it disappeared around the corner. 'It's all about the money, not the horses.'

'Isn't that the case with lots of things relating to horses?' Vicki rested her head back and closed her eyes. 'It's about making money from them or winning something because of them. When I'm competing, is it really about the horse or about me winning?' She opened her eyes and looked at Tom with genuine concern. 'How do I know I'm not doing the wrong thing with my horses?'

Tom thought back to his years on the show jump circuit. He asked himself the same question many times. 'I think it's partly a question of priorities and mainly a question of knowing your horse. I made a promise early on that if my horse was not happy doing what I wanted, and if I put winning ahead of his welfare, then it was time to step away.'

'How do we know when the horse is happy, though?'

'We know. Our horses talk to us all the time. If they are fighting us with every step, laying their ears back – not just the ears-back-because-I'm-listening-to-you action, but the angry flat-back position – and kicking at the spurs on their sides, then we know they are not in a good place mentally. I'm not talking about the occasional episode of *I'm-cranky-today,* like a child not wanting to go to school on Monday, to which you respond with *too bad, you're doing it*. I mean a genuinely unhappy horse that dislikes his rider, dislikes the work, and has to be forced to perform every movement. You would know.'

He started their car and headed back onto the roads that led into the city.

'None of mine ever reached that.' Vicki thought of the happy expressions her horses displayed during training and competition. 'Is this something you've always known, or did joining Lane's circle make a difference?'

'Lane always makes a difference,' Tom chuckled, 'but it's something I always knew. Lane helped me understand it more. My parents threw us on horses from the time we could walk, and we raced around bareback like wild things. We had harmony with those horses before we had any idea of what that was. We *thought* canter, and they sprang into action. It was teamwork. Synchronization. An agreement of minds. It didn't matter if we used bits or rode with a string around their necks - we worked together without force.'

'Like Ahlerich and Klimke at the Olympics when they won gold.'

'Exactly.' Tom thought of the video that Lane often played to demonstrate the harmony between horse and rider. 'Winning the gold was the rider's hope, and I could be wrong, but it never looked as though he placed his ambition above Ahlerich's wellbeing.'

'It seems that REE have people putting money above the wellbeing of the horses. It almost looks as though it's a scheme cooked up to make money. The horses are merely the means to their increasing wealth.'

Taking his hand off the steering wheel momentarily, Tom touched the back of his fingers to her cheek. Keeping his eyes on the road, he replied, 'We've already learned how far some will go to create more money than they need. It's quite possible that these particular charities are for wealth creation rather than horse welfare.'

Leaning into his touch, Vicki smiled. 'And if that's the case, we're going to expose it.'

Two hours later, Tom concentrated on negotiating the narrow winding Putty Road that started near Windsor and crossed the mountains to Singleton. One of the staff at the hotel reception recommended taking the scenic Putty Road rather than the main highway. The road zig-zagged in blind bends up and down the mountains, and Tom wished they hadn't taken the advice.

Wincing at the drop at the edge of the road, Vicki eyed the bend ahead with trepidation. 'You know we're going die if there's a truck coming the other way, don't you?'

Tom grinned without taking his eyes from the road. 'I'm aware of that possibility. I'm amazed that people bring their horse trucks this way. We must have passed four already.'

'Australians are crazy.' Vicki's hand crept up to hold the safety bar above the passenger door. 'And here I was thinking these handles were for just for coat hangers. I want to grip this like there's no tomorrow. And that's not an indictment of your driving; it's the terror of seeing someone come round that bend in our lane.'

Glancing in his rear-view mirror, Tom frowned at the cars behind them. He'd first noticed the three four-wheel-drive vehicles when they drove through Windsor. They made him uneasy. On a small straight section, he slowed and pulled to the left. The first of the vehicles overtook him and pulled away quickly.

A sense of relief washed over him as it disappeared around the next bend. He increased his speed again. He felt more reassured when the vehicle at the back pulled over and parked at the side of the road.

'I'm glad they're gone.' Vicki shared his slight sense of paranoia. 'It was beginning to feel a little threatening.'

'I know what you mean.'

After a few more minutes, Tom's eyes flicked to his side mirror, where he could see the remaining car pulling out wide as though to overtake on the double white lines. His mouth turned down in disapproval. What was wrong with them? It was madness to try and overtake along this section.

He slowed and pulled as far to the left as safely possible. Vicki ogled the plummeting slope an arm's length away as the beige four-wheel-drive roared up alongside them.

'Go around,' Tom mumbled as he slowed further to allow the vehicle to overtake. 'Don't just sit there in the wrong lane.'

The vehicle swerved sharply to the left, slamming its bullbar into his door. Tom fought with the steering wheel to keep the car from heading down the side of the mountain. Braking hard, he tried to duck behind the attackers.

Matching his deceleration, the other vehicle jerked sideways again. This time the bullbar pierced through the gap between Tom's door and the front panel, locking into place. It started pushing their car off the road. Desperately trying to avoid going over the edge, Tom braked, then accelerated, and turned the wheels into the attacking vehicle. Nothing he did shook the bullbar loose. The heavier vehicle gave one final shove, and their car ripped free of the bullbar as it was airborne over the side of the mountain.

Instinctively, Tom threw out his left arm to protect Vicki. They looked at each other with a million unsaid words. There was nothing they could do or say in those seconds to change what was about to happen. Everything seemed strangely quiet and frozen as they plummeted through the air. The vehicle clipped a tree in mid-flight, pulling it into a roll down the hill. The nose of the car hit the ground first, digging in and setting off the airbags. The momentum flipped them end-for-end several times before tree trunks snapped it back into a sideways roll. It hurtled down the slope, snapping off small trees and taking a landslide of dirt and rocks with it.

Eighty meters from the road, the tumbling car slammed into two aged eucalypts that held fast against the force of the collision. The front and rear of the vehicle wrapped around the trunks while the roof fitted between them. The underside of the car pointed up the slope.

From the road above, it appeared as though the fall had crushed the car. The driver who caused the accident stood staring down the mountain, debating about whether or not to climb down to ensure the targets were deceased. As he watched, the two-way radio in his vehicle crackled.

'Taken care of?'

He hesitated to answer. What if they survived? It seemed unlikely, but perhaps he should go down and make sure they were both dead. His lip curled in distaste at the thought of the descent and, worse, climbing back up.

A fuel leak in the crashed vehicle ignited, and a fiery explosion pushed hot air up the mountain. The man nodded in satisfaction: there was no need to climb down now.

He returned to the car and picked up the two-way. 'Taken care of. There's a fire, so you might hold the traffic for another ten.'

'Understood. The traffic controllers will let drivers know there's some burning off in the area.'

He sat in his car, watching the fire spread outwards from the wreck. If there was any chance they survived the crash, the fire finished the job. Once the traffic started to move, he would join it and take a scenic drive back to Sydney via Maitland.

A kilometer in either direction, forgettable men in the reflective gear of roadside workers explained to the drivers about the burn-off, turned their STOP signs to SLOW, and allowed the handful of cars they'd held back to start moving. Once the road was clear, they placed the signs back in their cars and drove away.

There were no witnesses to the incident on Putty Road.

***

Dibby and Rev

'No sick horses?'

Rev pricked his ears at the drawling tones of an Australian voice. Following his lead, the horses in his yard and the ones on either side came to attention, listening to the voice that reminded them of home.

A voice with a Venezuelan accent answered that the horses remained in good health.

Three men with folders moved along the pens, writing notes as they looked through the rails at the animals.

'Another few days here, then we'll move them to the farm,' continued the Australian. 'They have to clean everything up before they're ready for them at the plant.'

Moving to the rails, Rev watched the men pass. Nothing about their body language showed care for horses. He neither called to them nor wished they'd return. They were like the passing of a predator in the night, and his ancient instinct told him that prey animals like horses did not try to attract the attention of predators.

When Dibby moved to stand next to him and Dusty tucked himself against his other side, Rev stepped back from the fence. He kept watching the horizons, like a good protector keeping his herd safe.

CHAPTER ELEVEN

Like us, horses have a sense of home. At the end of a long day mustering, drop the reins, and your horse will take you home. Most of us have ridden a horse that is overly keen to get home. Some are so attached to a place that they stress when asked to leave it. We had a twenty-year-old horse come back to the station after being sold as a two-year-old – eighteen years away, and when released, he went straight to the stables, pushed the end door open, and broke into the feed room like he did when he was two. He knew he was home.

'Horses Think, Learn, and Remember' by Lane Dimity, p. 54

Going Home

Monday and Tuesday – Lane and Karen

At Wunya Stud, after the travelers heading to South America, New Zealand, and Sydney departed, Lane and Karen made preparations to go home. Ben, one of the workers from Lane's property, Ellamanga, brought a station vehicle down to Gatton to start his holiday, and Henry drove them into town to meet him.

'We'll see you next week,' Sheree told Lane as they hugged before he left Wunya. 'We really appreciate you helping us out with the stallions. I'm sure they'd be fine, but having you travel with them and settle them in here means the world to us.'

Always happy to help, he signed. *Thanks for letting us stay.*

'It was exciting seeing you all together. Some people love their movie stars, but you guys are horse stars, and that's better than actors any day.'

The Lomond offspring said their boisterous farewells, waving and calling goodbye as they drove away. The narrow floor of the valley opened up into wide, rich farming land on the approach to Gatton.

The Lockyer Valley earned its reputation for being the nation's salad bowl: thousands of acres of food crops flourished in the black soil.

As arranged, Ben waited for them outside the Transport Museum near Lake Apex. They swapped news and discussed the road conditions between Gatton and Longreach, and then Henry drove Ben to the bus stop in the center of town while Karen and Lane started their road trip west.

In the passenger seat, Lane's fingers flew over one of his text-to-voice devices so he could converse with Karen without her needing to take her eyes off the road.

'If you drive as far as Dalby,' the pleasant Australian voice spoke to her from the device, 'I'll take over from there.'

'Nonsense. I enjoy driving. Plus, if I'm driving, we can talk. If you're driving, I'd much rather you keep your hands on the steering wheel than chatting to me.'

'Miles, then. Drive to Miles, and we can swap there. I don't want you getting tired.'

Karen laughed. 'I'm a corporate lawyer, remember? I thrive on long hours. I'll drive so we can talk. When I get sick of talking to you, then you can drive. That should be in about seventy years.'

It was Lane's turn to laugh. He loved that she saw their future as together forever. It was how he saw it, but he knew that not all couples shared the same views on their future. 'Junior will be close to turning seventy by then. How strange. Junior isn't even born yet, and I'm thinking of him or her at seventy.'

Karen's left hand moved momentarily to rest over her abdomen. 'I think we should have told everyone. You know they'll be excited.'

'I think they've already guessed. Andrea was fussing over you yesterday, and I saw Tom looking emotional a few times when he looked at us.'

'Tom emotional? Then he must have guessed. He likes to keep that macho mask in place most of the time. Tell me about this road. Is this the way the bus brought you home from boarding school every holiday?'

Remembering those teenage years brought a whimsical smile to Lane's face. Jill and Trevor Moreton, the neighbors who found him in the horse yards on the day his parents died, raised him with infinite love. They didn't have children of their own and doted on him. Not once did they question his inability to speak after that day when his voice couldn't save his horses or his father. When the school pushed for more counseling and more specialists to help him speak so that he could have a normal life, they challenged the definition of *normal* and insisted Lane could live outside those parameters.

Sometimes, Jill would lightly touch the birthmark on the back of his neck and point out it was the exact shape of wings because he would fly. He thought they were the wings of a bird, but Jill said they were the wings of an angel placed there by heaven as a sign he would achieve wonderful things in his life. She explained that by *wonderful things,* she didn't mean becoming rich or famous or even being a doctor or scientist unless that was his ambition; she meant he would achieve great acts of kindness because that was the gift of the angels.

'This was the road,' he replied, typing the words faster than the device could speak them. 'It was later in the afternoon when we passed through here. We'd stop at Withcott up ahead to pick up passengers. Then it was up the range. Not the by-pass road we'll take today, but the original range crossing that takes you into Toowoomba. We used to joke about having to get out and push the bus up the range.'

'Did you have friends on the bus?'

'Lots. Almost every high school-age person from home went to school in Brisbane. The kids I grew up with were on the bus. We didn't all go to the same school, but we tried to catch the same bus home at the end of term. Sometimes we flew or someone's family drove a few of us, but mostly it was the bus. It was a party bus. The bus driver must have hated the end of term.'

Karen stretched a hand over to grip his arm and squeeze gently. 'If the kids were like you, I imagine the drivers loved those trips. Country kids excited about going home sound like a recipe for good times, not trouble.'

'Maybe,' he gave her a lopsided smile and decided not to tell her about the kids who smuggled alcohol onto the bus.

They climbed the range on the Toowoomba by-pass and continued sharing stories about childhood as they passed Oakey. Ninety minutes after leaving Gatton, they stopped in Dalby for a coffee and to stretch their legs. They drove through Chinchilla then stopped for a meal in Miles.

Are you sure you don't want me to drive? Lane signed when they returned to the vehicle.

'Positive. I'm loving talking to you like this - no interruptions from flight staff, friends, or your fans. Doing this drive is a great idea. I'm seeing the country. I'm driving on the right side of the road, which is the left, so it seems wrong, not right.' They both chuckled. 'And I'm thinking that Ellamanga would be a good place to raise our children, so I want to see the road that they will be traveling.'

They? He looked sideways at her.

'Of course. This one may have been a little unexpected, but I think we should aim for a basketball team, at least.'

We play polocrosse out west, he grinned at her, *so we might need six players.*

'Done. Did I really agree to that?' Karen snorted once at the thought of having six children and again because she realized it would be fun to have a large family.

We're both only children. It makes sense we'd want our children to know a big family. A happy family.

'We'll know happiness.' Karen promised as she motioned for him to get into the car. 'Let's keep going. I want to see all these other towns that trigger memories for you.'

As they passed through the country towns, he shared the past with her. The Drillham polocrosse team, his school friends from Dulacca and Yuleba, and the horse the Moretons bought him from Wallumbilla. They refueled at Roma, and then it was Muckadilla, Amby, and Mitchell. Karen took a selfie at the sign for Mungallala because she loved how the name rolled off her tongue.

At Morven, they had a drink at the pub and checked their phones. They had missed calls from Tom, but when Lane phoned him, it went unanswered. For several seconds he stared at the phone, a bad feeling creeping through him. Shaking it off, he rang again and left a message explaining that they'd be in and out of phone reception until they were at Ellamanga.

As they sipped their drinks at the bar, Lane showed her a map of the area on his phone and signed, *The bus used to go straight ahead to Charleville, but if we're not going to stay the night there, we may as well take the Morven-Augathella Road and cut the corner.*

'I say we keep driving. I'm feeling as fresh as a daisy. Is there a motel in these towns?' Karen pointed at the map.

Lane shrugged. *Motels or pubs. All the pubs have rooms. Ben put our swag in the back so we can sleep anywhere. Just not on the Morven-Augathella Road.*

'Why is that?'

It's childhood nonsense. We used to say the road was haunted or that yowies lived there.

Karen frowned at the unfamiliar word and sounded it out in her mind before saying it aloud. 'Yowies? I'm a New Yorker, remember – you need to explain these things.'

Australia's version of Big Foot.

'Ah. Gotcha.' She rolled her eyes. 'I'm reasonably sure we are safe from yowies.'

Ten minutes later, as she guided the car along the road in question, she understood Lane's words. Somehow, although it didn't look much different from the land for the past few hundred kilometers, it felt a little more isolated, a little less populated, and faintly eerie. She was happy to keep driving so that the stretch of road was behind them.

They spent the night in a motel at Tambo. Lane told of playing polocrosse there and waking in the morning with a thick crust of frost on the swags. She always imagined Australia's outback was permanently hot, so it came as a surprise to learn of frosts in winter.

In the morning, she noticed the extra spark in Lane's eyes as he stood outside and gazed around. Although still many hours from his Ellamanga, all of this was his home - this was the outback. In the year she'd known him, she learned that the ancient heart of this land beat inside Lane. Here, in his land, she could almost hear the thump like tribal drums when she looked at him.

Wedge-tailed eagles. Lane pointed to the east, where a pair of huge birds spiraled on the early morning thermals.

His eyes glowed as he watched them, and she realized that he didn't just admire the birds; he *loved* them. In all her life, she had never met anyone so filled with love as this silent horseman. It flowed from him like light from the sun.

Touching the birthmark wings on the back of his neck, she murmured, 'They left their mark on you when you were born.'

My angel wings?

'I see the wings of an eagle.'

He reached up to take her hand gently in his own. Bringing her fingers to his lips, he kissed each one, meeting her eyes. She felt the love flow from him and marveled at how he made her feel both weak and strong in the same moment. Weak because she thought she could not survive without him, and strong because he made her feel capable of anything.

'I love you,' he said, his voice soft.

It never failed to move her that the rare occasions he found his voice were when he wanted to express his love for her. She knew that sometimes his voice worked for horses when they needed reassurance, but she was the only human who had heard his voice since he was eight years old.

'And I love you more than I thought possible.' She pushed his unruly hair back from his glorious eyes. 'You brought me to life.'

The towns stretched over an hour apart after Tambo. They drove straight through Blackall. At Barcaldine, instead of taking the main road west to Longreach, they continued north to Aramac and on to

Muttaburra across the flat downs country sprinkled with gidyea trees and acacia. Approaching the small outback town, Lane leaned forward and gazed around the land as though devouring it with his eyes. Karen was glad she insisted on driving. Not only did it allow Lane to use his text-to-speech device, but it gave him the chance to look across his land rather than focus on the road.

'The long crossings are ahead,' the voice she associated with Lane spoke to her as he typed. 'Most of the channels of the Thomson will be dry, but in the wet season, they can be kilometers wide.'

It was difficult to imagine the dry creek beds joining together to form one wide brown flood, but he assured her it happened.

She drove through Muttaburra and admired the small one-pub-town that offered so much to the locals. On the other side of the town, she followed Lane's directions and turned off the main dirt road to property tracks which wound through different stations. The individual paddocks were several thousand acres or larger, and each property averaged around forty thousand acres. Lane knew them all, telling her about the people who lived there now and when he was a child, their horses, their dogs, the schools they went to, and other details that she found strangely interesting. It seemed to be an area as large as one of the smaller U.S. states, and he not only knew everyone in that area, he knew the details of their lives.

When she saw the property sign for Ellamanga, she stopped the car before crossing the cattle grid into the property. She suspected he might enjoy a moment to savor his return to Ellamanga, and she was right.

With the smile that always disarmed her, he got out of the car and stepped onto Ellamanga. He raised his chin and looked at the horizon because the property ran beyond what he could see. Karen saw a vast rolling plain of dry grasses dotted with acacia bushes and hardy native trees. Imagining the same scene through Lane's eyes, she saw paradise.

Lane leaned over, picked up a handful of dust, and threw it into the breeze. It reminded her of a child's response on the first day of a summer beach holiday. The innocence and joy that set Lane apart from most of the people she knew formed part of the reason why she loved him so much and why she felt the need to protect him from the ravages of the world. She would be happy living here in the outback, undertaking her work remotely and knowing he walked on the land that called to his spirit.

Thank you, he signed as he returned to the car. *I've always loved the feeling of the first footsteps on home.*

Karen drove with caution along the dirt track. On her previous visits, she learned that kangaroos, emus, or cattle could run out in front of the vehicle, and she found that far more disturbing than driving in city traffic. The Ellamanga Hills appeared on their right, jutting up out of the plains, their red sides eroded from ten million years of weather.

'I remember the day I arrived here by plane after months of believing my father killed you. You sat on a horse at the top of those hills,' she flicked a finger towards the flat-topped cliffs, 'and we flew over. You didn't have a shirt on. I watched you ride your horse bareback down the side of hills, like a wild thing, and I worried that I'd traveled across the planet to see you, and you were going to break your neck riding off a cliff.'

'Our horses are like mountain goats,' he replied via the device in his hands. 'They race up and down those hills for fun. As a rider, the trick is to sit without unbalancing them. I was doing it from the time I could crawl onto the back of a horse.'

'Which makes me rethink raising a child here.' She pulled a face at the thought of watching their son or daughter riding up and down those steep slopes. 'Maybe city life isn't so bad.'

Lane grinned at her teasing. He didn't care where they raised their child as long as they were together. When he wasn't on Ellamanga, he carried the outback with him, and so would his children.

'Your driveway is so long. It's certainly easier arriving by air.'

'It's only eight kilometers from the grid to the house. Not that long.'

'It is long, and you know it.' She slanted him a wry look. 'You Aussies like making remarkable things sound commonplace when you know they're not.'

Lane pointed ahead at a bare patch of ground next to the road where a dozen kangaroos lounged in the shade of a tree.

'I see them.' Karen slowed, worried they might hop in front of the car. 'I think I've seen at least ten thousand kangaroos on this trip. Who knew there were that many kangaroos in all of Australia?'

Lane waggled his eyebrows at her and pointed at his chest.

'Well, of course, *you* knew,' she gave his arm a light thump. 'You traveled that road scores of times, but the great Australian road trip is a new thing for me.'

'Did you enjoy it?'

'I loved it. And I'm proud I drove all the way. I know you wanted to drive, but I wanted to know that I could do it myself.'

They arrived at the Ellamanga homestead to a bounding and bouncing welcome from six kelpies. Lane immediately went to his knees to hug them, and they wriggled excitedly as they crowded against him for attention. Jill and Trevor Moreton, his foster parents, came down the homestead steps, their faces bright with smiles to see their son home. They lived next door on their property but helped run Ellamanga when Lane was away.

To Karen, it felt like she was coming home, too, and most of the worries of the outside world dropped from her shoulders as Jill's motherly arms wrapped around her.

'It's so wonderful to see you again,' enthused Jill as she held Karen's shoulders and admired her.

Without thinking, Karen's hand went to cover her stomach as Jill scrutinized her. Jill noticed the gesture along with the boy-with-a-secret glint in Lane's eyes. Delighted at the thought of having the role of grandmother, Jill hugged Karen again to hide the sudden moisture in her eyes.

'We have Scott and David over at our place for a few days,' Jill told them as they went indoors. 'We thought you two would like some time alone here without those two getting up to their shenanigans.'

Thanks for that. Lane grinned at her. The two station-hands were excellent workers, but they were as excitable as the kelpies and every bit as keen to follow Lane around. *I hope they didn't mind.*

Trevor laughed. 'Mind? They're dying to have some of Jill's cooking for a change. And they had plenty of *nudge-nudge, wink-wink* nonsense to say about you two, so they're happy to give you some space.'

They walked up onto the veranda that wrapped around the homestead, and Lane paused to look back at the road leading to the stockyards. For a painful moment, he imagined an eight-year-old running barefoot down that track, leaving footprints in the dust. The gunshots rang out from the yards as he ran, his birthday presents forgotten as the meaning of the shots fractured his soul.

'It's with us all,' Jill murmured, placing a gentle hand on his arm. She recognized the pain on his face as he looked down the track. That day haunted her as well. The relief of finding him alive when they thought he had died alongside his father and their horses was an unimaginable joy on the darkest day of their lives.

Lane thanked her with a smile and continued to the heart of the house, the kitchen. He checked his phone to find a text from Tom about their activities in Sydney. Outside, a murder of crows flew from the cypress trees, making their mournful *ark-ark* cries as they took to the sky. He shivered. They called like that the day his parents died. He pushed the ancient superstitions aside and managed to laugh as Jill described the latest adventures of her pet kangaroo that believed it belonged inside.

***

Dibby and Rev

As he snoozed in the Venezuelan sun, Rev dreamed of Mel's hands running over his coat, checking him for marks and scratching him on the wither in the place he loved. The sound of the tractor bringing hay woke him, and the pleasant feeling of being looked after by Mel evaporated. He looked down at Dibby who lay in his shadow and dropped his nose to his ears, gently lipping the tips like mares sometimes do with their foals.

Dibby yawned and rose to his feet, shaking himself to release the last of his sleep.

Men threw hay into the feed bins along the fence, and the horses waited until Rev started eating before they followed suit. His calm strength seeped into the pens around him until even the short-tempered horses that once fought to eat first looked to him for leadership.

CHAPTER TWELVE

You cannot change the past, but you can learn from it. You live now, in this moment. You have the power to change the future. Now is when you can start the change.

Lane Dimity, social media post.

Venezuela

Monday and Tuesday – Grace and Matthew

'I've never flown business class before.' Grace looked around at the spacious seats and accepted a flute of champagne from the flight attendant, who explained there was a ten-minute delay. 'I'm not disapproving, mind you, but I always tried to find ways to put more money into the horses. Traveling back there,' she waved a hand behind her, 'meant a few extra thousand for the horses.'

'I don't always travel in this section,' Matthew assured her, 'but I was hoping to impress you.'

Grace narrowed her eyes at him, and he chuckled.

'Alright, that bit's made up.' He raised his glass to hers. 'When Karen organizes things, she always pays the extra for us to travel business. She says it's worth it as we arrive fresher and more capable than the walking zombies who traveled economy.'

'I am not a walking zombie when I travel economy,' she informed him tartly.

'No, of course, you aren't. You cross the world crammed in a tiny space with people sardined all around, and you arrive as fresh and sharp as an Antarctic blizzard. I arrive like the walking dead, but you are immune to such earthly things as tiredness and jetlag.'

'Finish my sentence,' she scowled at him, though her dancing eyes did not match the angry slant of her lips. 'Don't be a …'

'Funny person?' He grinned and took a sip of champagne. 'Amusing raconteur? Don't be a delightful travel companion?'

Grace tapped her finger against the air as though pressing three buttons. 'No, no, and no. I can't even commend you for trying.'

'Do you want to plan our moves once we reach Caracas, or will we just wing it? I used to like planning things, but working with Lane for a few years has shown me the fun of throwing everything into the air and seeing where it all lands.'

Grace snorted at him. 'That's probably not the best metaphor when we're getting ready for take-off.'

'Are you a nervous flyer?'

'I wouldn't say nervous.' Grace took a mouthful of champagne and tucked one corner of her mouth in as she considered her flying experiences. 'Let's say that I enjoy the level flying when I can convince myself that it's no different from being on a train. I'm not so keen on the take-off and landing when it's obvious I'm inside an object that is clearly too heavy to be in the air.'

'It's all just a balance of weight, lift, thrust, and drag. The heavier the plane, the more thrust we need, and the wings provide the lift by causing different air pressures above and below the wings.'

She chuckled at his explanation. 'So, you're a pilot now?'

'For a few years.'

Grace was growing used to his nonsense and shook her head to show she didn't believe it for a moment.

'Seriously. We all have our pilot's license. Even Lane, though he's restricted to aircraft and flights where the radio isn't needed. I'm an MEA IFR pilot.'

'Throwing random letters at me doesn't prove you're a pilot.'

He smiled at her skepticism. 'Multi-Engine Aircraft and Instrument Flight Rating, so I can fly, say, a twin-engine Beechcraft at night. I can show you my license if you don't believe me.'

Her lips twitched back and forth as she regarded his open expression. 'No, I believe you. Could you fly this plane if something happened to the pilot?'

'I could fly it,' his eyes twinkled, 'but landing it would be a whole other matter. Luckily, there's a co-pilot up there.'

'I had you picked for someone who can drive cars, maybe a truck, and ride horses. The pilot thing is unexpected. Surprise me some more.'

Matthew looked into the greens, browns, and flashes of gold in Grace's eyes as she pressed a finger against the bridge of her glasses to adjust them. 'Are you interested in learning about me, Miss Walker?'

She met his dark brown gaze and mentally kicked her heart to stop it from backflipping around in her chest. This was not going anywhere, she told herself firmly, no flirting and no fanning the flames of desire. 'Don't get too excited, cowboy. The plane is moving, and I want something to stop me from thinking about the take-off. They're not playing movies yet, so you're the next best thing. Talk.'

Her feisty attitude amused him. The whites of her knuckles as she clasped one fist on her lap and squeezed the stem of the champagne flute with the other told him she genuinely needed a distraction.

'Have I told you I'm a scuba diving instructor?'

As the plane backed away from the terminal, Grace gave him another of her doubtful looks.

'We should take an extra day and head out to the Islas Los Frailes.' Matthew almost laid a hand over her clenched fist but refrained from touching her. Even if he intended it to be reassuring, it was too invasive of her personal space. 'It's an archipelago out from Isla de Margarita and a great place for diving. Have you dived before?'

Grace shook her head, her lips tight as they taxied to their runway.

'We'll go there if we have time and get you started.' Matthew proceeded to entertain her with anecdotes about diving, flying, horses, and his various jobs with circuses around the world.

The take-off was uneventful, apart from a few patches of turbulence that had Grace clenching her jaw. Empathetic to her fear, Matthew chatted away without expecting replies. When the plane leveled off, she breathed a sigh of relief and murmured a heartfelt thanks to her travel companion for his help. She appreciated that he did what she needed - he didn't tell her not to be scared or give her advice on how to control her fears; he simply trotted out a series of surprisingly engaging stories.

As he told her about a one-legged Russian trapeze artist, she looked at his quick-to-smile face and realized that it wasn't just his stories. *He* was surprisingly engaging. What had she been thinking when she agreed to this crazy plan? They had to land in Sydney, change planes, take off again, land in Santiago, change planes, and head to Caracas. Almost all of the next twenty-four-plus hours would be spent whisper-close to the handsome, annoying, perceptive, and amusing man. Part of her mind looked forward to it; the sensible part waved warning flags and rang sirens.

The flight to Sydney took an hour. During landing, Matthew's ability to entertain and distract proved effective for controlling her fears. They had coffee at the airport before boarding the international flight and taking their seats near the front of the plane. Despite her intention to remain serious and businesslike, she jiggled her legs and grinned excitedly at Matthew when the steward brought them slippers and pajamas.

'And you fly like this all the time?' Grace rubbed her cheek against the silky sleepwear and knew they'd be comfortable.

'Not all the time. When Pilatos is paying, I do. If it's a long-haul flight like this, I pay the extra. These seats are like beds, and you can actually sleep.'

'I thought I was OK as far as finances go, but I'm not in the fly-business-class league. Well, I suppose I could afford it, but I couldn't justify it when that money could feed a horse for a year.'

'Now you're making me feel guilty. Do you realize that one of my Instagram posts makes enough to pay for these tickets? You can think of it feeding a horse for a year which makes me feel bad, or see it as the money from a photo and a few seconds of writing a comment which makes it look like it's nothing much at all.'

'Can you make that much from a photo?' She was aghast at that sort of money for posting a selfie and some words.

'I'm a social influencer,' he winked at her, amused at her reaction, 'but that's nothing compared to what Lane makes every time he gets on a social media platform.'

Grace had no idea that people like Lane and his friends were paid for their presence on Instagram and elsewhere. 'If it isn't too rude to ask, how much are we talking about? Like, last year, do you know what you made from that?'

Usually, Matthew avoided questions about his income, but he saw innocence in Grace's curiosity. Part of him wanted her to know his worth. Perhaps it was his ego or vanity, but he wanted to impress her.

'I don't know the exact figures, but a few million. Maybe five. That's just from social media, not from my books or investments or anything else. And mine is a fraction of what Lane makes.'

Fitting this new information into her knowledge about Matthew and his friends, she looked him up and down. He wore riding boots, jeans, and a shirt – the sort of outfit that a Gatton local might wear to a rodeo.

'You don't look like millionaires.'

'Good.' Matthew chuckled. 'We're the same people we were before businesses started paying us for everything we do. I'm the same Aboriginal kid who studied hard at school and dreamed of working with horses. Lane's the kid who grew up in thc outback dreaming of saving horses because he couldn't save his when he was eight. The money hasn't changed us.'

Narrowing her eyes, Grace looked meaningfully around the business class section. 'Really?'

'OK,' he flashed her a smile, 'so it might change how we travel, but not who we are. If it all disappeared tomorrow, we'd still be the same people with the same friends doing what we can to make the world a better place one piece at a time.'

The conversation moved forward, twisting and evolving, and Grace barely noticed the jet's acceleration down the runway and the ascent. They talked about childhoods and horsey dreams. She told him about the months when she thought she'd never walk again, and he told her about his volunteer work with the indigenous children at Doomadgee. They stretched their legs, enjoyed the five-star food, and talked some more, their heads close together so that their voices didn't disturb their fellow passengers.

As the jet cut its way across the skies over the South Pacific, the cabin lights dimmed, and they adjusted their seats into beds. After changing into the pajamas provided by the airline, Grace returned to her seat, glad that Matthew wasn't back from the bathroom yet. It seemed strangely intimate to wear sleepwear next to a man she met a few days earlier. What if she snored? She snorted as she thought of worse noises she could make while sleeping. Maybe it would be safer to stay awake.

When Matthew took his seat, they watched a documentary and drank hot chocolate before adjusting the seats into beds.

'Have you come up with a plan of action for when we arrive in Caracas?' Grace whispered, her eyes on Matthew, who lay with a blanket pulled up to his chin.

His dark eyes glinted with humor as he turned to look at her. 'I have no idea what I'm going to do. But that's fairly typical of how I approach most things these days – I'll just make it up as I go along. Hire a car and head to Ernie's place. Try and see the places where those horses were buried. Find out about the REE riding center. Maybe follow up on some of the other connections we found between Australia and Venezuela. It'll all fall into place one way or another. What are your ideas?'

'You know how I feel about REE, so I want to check their facility. And I want to find out about Image, the horse bought by REE at a sale, though they deny it. He's turned up in Caracas.'

'Yeah,' Matthew inclined his head, 'that's weird.'

'I want to find what the dead horses there have in common with the ones in the Hunter. It can't be a coincidence. It just can't.'

'I agree.'

'You look worried about something.'

He flashed her a smile and blurted the truth without thinking. 'I'm worried I'm going to snore. Promise you'll dig me in the ribs or punch me or something if I do.'

Grace widened her eyes. 'Oh, I know!' Keeping her voice pitched low, she leaned in closer to him and confessed, 'I'm so worried about snoring. Don't make fun of me if I sound like a deflating balloon; just wake me up. Please.'

'If you snore, it will be cute. If I do it, it'll just be annoying.'

'I've heard my cousin snore, and she's way prettier than I am, and there's nothing cute about it.'

As if on cue, the older man seated in front of them made a series of strained engine sounds as he breathed in and exhaled like a leaf blower.

Exchanging amused glances, they settled back into their beds and waited for sleep to sneak up on them. In Matthew's mind, voices argued about what he should have said to Grace and offered suggestions for things to say next time they were talking. Similarly, Grace's mind was preoccupied with replaying her conversations with Matthew, only she was now far wittier and more interesting than when they occurred.

Neither was aware of the point when consciousness tipped softly over into sleep.

When Grace woke a few hours later, the background noise of the jet that penetrated her waking haze reminded her that she was not at home in her bed. Looking at her travel companion, she saw he remained lost in sleep. With his head half-turned towards her, it provided the opportunity to examine him.

For several minutes, she studied his face. The angles spoke of strength while the soft lines of his mouth hinted at empathy and passion. Her eyes traced the outline of his lips, and a shiver ran down her spine. Perhaps it was best not to dwell on a mouth as kissable as his. He looked innocent and younger than his twenty-six years. She smiled. He was only four years younger than her, but at times he seemed almost childlike with his enthusiasm and cheek.

His eyes opened, and he immediately focussed on her. There was an eternity in the silent two seconds that followed, then he smiled. 'Are we there yet?'

'Halfway. Go back to sleep.'

'I had a bad dream,' he confessed, his expression disarmingly open. 'I don't think I want to go back to sleep in case it continues.'

'Poor baby.' She pouted in mock sympathy. 'They're not real, you know.'

'How do we know? How do we know that this isn't the dream and the dreams are real?'

'Because we wake up to a reality that has constancy and continuity, and we remember the dreams which break the laws of physics, time, and the universe.'

He regarded her with his dark brown eyes and sighed away the bad memories of the dreams. 'That is good. I want to remember that because it makes sense. Do you know why we dream?'

'Lots of reasons.' She stopped herself and looked at him doubtfully. 'Are you just funning with me? I imagine you know why we dream.'

'I probably do, but I want to hear your explanations. I think you make the world easier to understand.'

Grace's lips twisted one way then the other as she considered his words. Not entirely convinced he was genuinely interested in her thoughts, she proceeded with caution. 'The reasons include the brain sorting through memories of the past few days and filing them away. It also likes to play out scenes that make us feel strong emotions as though it's preparing us for things that can happen. What some people think is a premonition of bad things, even death, is more likely the brain playing out a hypothetical to see how we react. There are lots of other reasons. Sometimes your subconscious seems to enjoy playing out pleasant scenes that make you feel good, and other times it wants to scare you.'

'So, you don't think they're premonitions?'

'I guess there could be a case where the subconscious sees all the factors and variables of a situation and gives you insight into what might happen. Not so much a premonition of events as a case of, *given all the variables, this is a likely outcome*. Then if it happens, people assume it was a precognitive dream when it was simply a logical one.'

Matthew gazed at her as though hypnotized by her words. She made so much sense in the middle of the night. He wanted her to keep talking forever. With her glasses, she looked beautiful, but here, in the night without her glasses, the intimacy lent an air of ethereal loveliness to her looks. 'I was dreaming about truckloads of horses, one after the other, driving past all of us as we stood helplessly at the side of the road. The horses were screaming for help, and we didn't do anything to help them. We just watched them go. Truck after truck, after truck. I wanted to help them, but I couldn't move.'

Seeing the distress in his eyes as he recounted the dream, Grace moved her hand from under the blanket and lay it over his. 'That's a perfectly logical dream. We're all scared we won't be able to help the horses, and we worry that more horses are going to die for whatever reason the others died. Your mind is playing out a perfectly reasonable summary of the events we're currently in.'

'That makes total sense.'

'I'm a sensible person.'

'What do you dream about?' he asked, his voice soft as he began drifting down from consciousness.

'I dream about riding my horse Donegal.' Tears pricked her eyes as she remembered the horse she loved. It wasn't only her back that broke the day he died.

Matthew's eyelids grew heavy as a wave of sleep washed over him and began pulling him back into the ocean of slumber. He rolled his hand over so they were palm to palm and squeezed lightly. Her hand felt so small in his.

'I wish you were here every night when I wake up from a bad dream,' he murmured as his eyes closed. 'Your logic chases away the fear.'

Grace watched the lines on his face relax as he went back to sleep. If he remembered his words in the morning, she was sure he'd regret them. Telling a woman that he wanted her next to him every night was a quantum leap from accusing her of being a con artist and a thief. She closed her eyes, acutely aware of his hand still holding hers.

***

Dibby and Rev

'The paperwork's been cleared.' The Australian leaned on the rails and scanned the horses. He didn't like horses. They came in handy for this, but he wouldn't go out of his way to pat one. 'We'll be taking them out to the farm tomorrow or the next day.'

'Any of them going straight to the plant?' The man responsible for distributing the hay did like horses. He saw how much they changed when it was time for them to leave Venezuela, and he felt sick as he wondered about what was done to them. The money was good, though, and he kept his mouth shut.

'Nah. They'll spend some time at the farm before heading there. None of them are losing weight?'

'They're all good, boss. Quietest mob of horses we've had through here. Easy to handle.'

'Good to hear.'

'Those two palominos in the third yard – any chance I could take them out for my family? My daughters would like a pair of horses like that.'

'Not a chance, mate.' The Australian slapped him on the back. 'We need all of them at the plant this time around. Tell your girls to take up soccer. Not as expensive as horses.'

When they were gone, Rev lowered his head from a defensive position and relaxed. When he first heard the Australian voice, it conjured up memories of people who cared. The more he saw and heard the man, the more his instinct warned him of danger. This was a man who walked with death on his shoulders.

CHAPTER THIRTEEN

At the end of your life, you won't remember the money - you'll remember the moments. Don't spend all your moments counting the money - make the moments count.

'Top 20 Lane Dimity Quotes', Australian Equestrian Magazine; April 2021.

Carolina

When they landed in Santiago after almost fifteen hours of flying, the time in Chile was only one hour after their departure time.

'Crossing the International Date Line always plays havoc with my brain,' Matthew complained as they disembarked and made their way through the terminal. 'We left Sydney at three in the afternoon, fly all night, and here it's four in the afternoon of the same day we left, but it's six in the morning of the next day at home.'

'Just adjust your watch to local time and don't think about it,' Grace advised without sympathy. 'We have five hours to fill in before the flight to Caracas, so I'm going to find a quiet spot somewhere and do a bit of research. I'd better give Ernie a call, too, to make sure he's still OK with us staying there.'

'I have some contacts in Venezuela. I'll make some calls and see if they know anything about the dead horses.'

'Do you have friends in every country?'

'I doubt it. There are nearly two hundred countries. On every continent, I would.'

'Antarctica?'

He met her smug look and grimaced. 'You are such a smarty-pants, aren't you?'

'I try to be,' she replied happily, leading the way to a quiet corner in an eatery that she remembered from her last visit.

They caught up with their emails and phone calls while drinking locally made coffee and eating Thousand Layers Cake, which they both agreed was their favorite Chilean sweet food. After a shopping session, they tried a couple of the airport bars and ended up giggling like teenagers at each other's jokes. Grace told herself it was the alcohol making Matthew seem like the most entertaining person she'd ever known, but when she saw the envious glances from women at other tables, she knew it was more than just the wine.

Not that it matters, one of her internal voices chided, *you are here on business. Horse business. You are not getting involved with this man no matter how good-looking he is. He can have the pick of any of these gorgeous women at other tables who are drooling over him. Why would he be interested in a little plain-Jane from Gatton who spends more time sparring with him than fawning over him?*

'Ground Control to Major Grace.' Matthew sang the corrupted song lyrics to break into her thoughts.

'Sorry. Thinking about horses. Did you manage to get Lane or Tom on the phone?'

'No one wants to speak to me. Tom sent a text but isn't answering his phone now, and I'm guessing Lane is out of range between towns on his road trip.'

Grace glanced at her watch that displayed both local and Queensland times. 'It's nearly seven here, and close to nine Tuesday morning there. What are Tom and Vicki doing today?'

'Chasing down leads around Sydney. They visited a charity called Horsley something yesterday.'

'Horsley Horse Rescues? They do a good job. Jody, who runs it, is down to earth. Are they going to see REE?'

'I think so. And EINOF. They'll be like a pair of bloodhounds. Nothing will get past them.'

When their flight was due to leave, Grace found that her nervousness had almost vanished. Whether it was the jet lag and tiredness or Matthew's company, or a bit of both, she managed to talk with him during take-off rather than sit frozen in fear. Even the turbulence didn't worry her as much with Matthew beside her.

The seats did not change into beds, but they adjusted to a comfortable sleeping position. When Grace fell asleep, her head rested on Matthew's shoulder, and she felt neither awkwardness nor embarrassment about the contact.

The flight to Caracas took eight hours, and they arrived at five in the morning. Picking up their hire car, a sleek BMW, Matthew drove along the Caracas–La Guaira highway with confident ease. The road wound through the mountains that separated Caracas from the ocean, with tunnels punching shortcuts through the rock. The scenery was spectacular, and they both pointed and exclaimed at features as the car snaked along the road.

They sliced through the city of Caracas. With a population of over two million, it was the largest city in Venezuela. The crowded buildings they could see from the highway were a mix of old and new, with closely packed housing estates and industrial areas smothering the hills. The modern office buildings and vibrant city center provided a stark contrast to the poverty-stricken areas with their graffiti-covered walls and air of desperation.

Ernie's training facility lay south of the city, not far from the famous racecourse, the Rinconada Hippodrome. The horse-riding establishments in the area did not have the lush green paddocks of Bisente in Kentucky or Wunya in Queensland. They were smaller, with horses kept in pens and stable complexes, not large paddocks.

An hour after leaving the airport, they drove through the large white gates of Ernie's training center. A security fence topped with barbed wire surrounded the three-acre property, and cameras high up in the trees glinted in the sunlight. Ernie loved Venezuela, but he was not blind to the dangers of living in a land where kidnapping and crime were common - when the front gates were locked, his place became a fortress.

The sun was well into the sky, and the arenas were active with horses and riders as they moved slowly along the driveway. Brightly colored show jumps decorated two of the sand arenas, and three riders worked between jumps in one arena while another four schooled horses over jumps in the other.

As one of the riders cantered his horse towards a four-foot oxer, Grace pointed at him. 'There's Ernie. I know that seat anywhere.'

Matthew admired how Ernie sat in the saddle and understood why Grace recognized him. 'You're an expert in his seat?'

'Ew,' Grace screwed up her nose, knowing what he implied. 'That's Ernie we're talking about. He's like a younger brother.'

'He does sit well.' Matthew watched as Ernie approached a double, his hands light on the reins and his body moving in perfect harmony with the horse.

With his ears pricked, the big bay cleared the first jump with ease, landed, took two strides, and leaped skywards over the second obstacle. Ernie's hands moved just enough to ensure no interference with the horse's mouth as he stretched out over the jumps. It was beautiful to watch.

On landing, Ernie allowed the horse to canter another few strides before he eased back into a trot then walk. He called a few instructions to the other riders then, seeing the visitors getting out of their car, waved and trotted towards them.

'Grace!' His voice was as excited as a child spotting kittens. 'So great to see you again.'

Taking both feet out of his stirrups, he sprang to the ground, as agile as a cat. He placed the horse's reins over the arena rails and strode over to them. Wrapping Grace in an enthusiastic embrace, he held out a hand to Matthew behind her back.

'Good to see you, Matt.' He pumped his hand in a friendly shake. 'And so glad you're back, neighbor.' He gave Grace another squeeze before releasing her.

'It was a bit unexpected,' Grace explained, 'but it's wonderful to be back in Venezuela. If I wasn't such a little home-body, I could move here in an instant.'

'You should think about it.' Ernie waved an arm around in an expansive gesture. 'The horse scene is buzzing. Ignore the crime – everywhere is a jungle of some sort, and you simply take precautions. There are so many brilliant riders and horses around. Look at this place – it's alive with talent. What about you, Matt? Could you live here?'

'As much as I could live anywhere outside of Australia.'

Ernie chuckled. His smile and shining brown eyes echoing the looks of his parents. Even if Matt hadn't met him before, he would recognize him anywhere as the son of Sheree and Henry.

'I take that to be a no, then.' Ernie patted him on the shoulder. 'Well, if you ever decide to move out from Down Under, I can recommend this country. Actually, most of the South American countries are exciting as far as horses go. Look at those Brazilian riders. Whether it's rodeo or jumping, they're a force all of their own.'

Their conversation detoured along the path of great South American riders before Ernie told them to head up to his house, and he'd join them shortly. They drove up the palm-lined driveway while Ernie handed his horse to one of the student riders and followed them on foot. A whiteboard in the stables held the schedule of training for the day, and he knew the riders would work through it, ensuring every horse received the set training whether he was watching over them or not.

'It looks like you've doubled the number of horses here since I visited,' said Grace as Ernie joined them on the veranda of his Spanish hacienda-style home.

'Tripled. I had four big wins in a row after you left. After that, horses and paying pupils poured in. Everyone likes a winner. My main sponsor, Caraven Constructions, who paid me to set up here, have sent another six horses as well as several more paying riders.'

He led them to the open plan living area where the Spanish theme continued with terracotta tiles on the floors, dark wooden beams against white walls and ceilings, and splashes of red and orange, adding vibrant color.

'Congratulations.' Matthew eyed the display of trophies and rosettes in a display cabinet. 'Millions want to make a living out of horses, but not many get there.'

'Horses make us money,' Ernie's finger waved back and forth between his chest and Matthew, 'while poor little Gracey here spends her fortune on them.'

'I get by,' Grace objected. 'Anyway, is it really horses that make Matthew's money? From what I've been seeing, it's his pretty smile and social media posts that make the moolah flow.'

'Ouch.' Matthew took his phone out, leaned towards Grace, and pretended to take a selfie with her behind him. 'I need to post about that right now.'

'I'm guilty of following you.' Ernie poured chilled orange juice into three glasses. 'And Lane, Tom, and Andrea, too. I don't suppose your sister has a boyfriend yet.'

'Do you want me to put in a good word for you?' Matthew joked.

'In all seriousness? Absolutely. You and I met years ago, and I keep hoping I'll bump into her somewhere, but it hasn't happened yet, so if you could inform her of my existence, it would be appreciated.'

'Really?' Matthew was genuinely surprised. People often told him that his twin was gorgeous, but no one since high school had asked him to tell her that they liked her. He thought for a second and revised that to no one since primary school.

'I'm sure she knows you exist,' Grace assured him. 'After all, she's been staying at your parents' place for a few days, and they talk about you a lot.'

'It doesn't help me meet her, though.' Ernie pulled a sad face as he handed her the juice, then grinned. 'But maybe she wouldn't like me if we met, anyway, and my ego would implode if that happened.'

Looking at the attractive man who stood as tall as Matthew with a similar mischievous charm about him, Grace doubted that his ego would collapse if one woman rejected him. She was reasonably sure there would be a hundred others ready to take her place.

'If you want to meet Andrea,' Matthew put out his hand to take a glass from Ernie, 'all you have to do is book a photoshoot with her. It's not that difficult. Here, I'll show you.'

He still had his phone in his free hand, so he put the glass down and called his sister while Ernie tried to dissuade him.

'Matthew,' a sleepy voice answered his call. 'It's one-thirty in the morning here. This better be important or I'll thump you.'

'Hello to you, too.' Matthew chuckled at Ernie smacking his forehead. 'You're on speakerphone, sis. I've just arrived at Ernie's place. Say hello, Ernie.'

He meant for Ernie to say hello, and held the phone towards him; instead, Andrea followed his instructions. 'Hello, Ernie.'

'Hi, Andrea,' Ernie mumbled, clearly embarrassed.

Matthew rolled his eyes at his lameness. 'Ernie needs someone to photograph his horses and his clients' horses. Any chance you're coming to Venezuela sometime soon? I told him you were the best in the world at this, and his clients would love your work.'

'One, I'm not the best,' her voice grew more alert as she woke up, 'and two, I'm in Jamaica next month if that would suit. It's only a few hours flying time to Caracas from there.'

'Is next month OK for you, Ernie?' Matthew looked at his host in amusement.

'I'll check my calendar.' Ernie cleared his throat and straightened his thoughts. 'I have a few competitions, but I'm based here most of the month.'

'I'll send you his number,' Matthew told his sister, 'and give yours to him. You two can work it out. He has a nice place. You should stay a while and drum up some other work while you're here.'

'Yeah, whatever.' Andrea yawned. 'Hey, Ernie?'

'Yes?'

'When you do ring, can you not do it in the middle of the night?'

'Sure thing,' he replied.

'See, that's just silly,' Matthew chided his twin. 'How will he know when the middle of the night is for you when he won't know if you're still in New Zealand or England or somewhere else? He'll just have to ring and...'

Andrea cut him off. 'Goodnight, Matt. I'll send you my Jamaica dates, Ernie. Hi and bye, Grace, if you are there.'

'There you go.' Matthew put his phone down and smiled at Ernie. 'Now you get to meet her. The rest is up to you.'

'Am I mistaken,' Grace quirked her mouth as she looked at Matthew, 'or did you just pimp your sister out to a stranger?'

Ernie made a choking sound and tried not to spit orange juice over the table.

Matthew pretended to be offended and spoke in haughty tones. 'I recommended her photography services, so I may have pimped those out if you want to speak so crudely. Anyway, Ernie's not a stranger. Personally, I think she and Ernie would make a wonderful couple, and I'd like to see her happy, but that won't happen if Ernie can't learn to string a few more words together when speaking to her. She does like conversation, you know.'

'You embarrassed him,' Grace defended her neighbor. 'One second, he makes a passing comment about your sister, the next second, you have her on the phone dangling her in front of him like she's a worm on a hook.'

'Pimping metaphors and fishing similes.' Matthew shook his head as though dealing with a child, making Grace long to hit him. He was infuriating. 'If that's how you see a little bit of help from cupid, then you're not a very romantic person.'

'You're no cupid.' She pulled a face at him. 'And I don't think that was helping.'

'Was it helping?' Matthew asked Ernie, who held up both hands to try and stay out of it.

'See.' Matthew and Grace spoke simultaneously, each thinking Ernie had proven their point.

Ernie laughed at them. 'How about you two put your gear in the spare bedrooms down that corridor and then come and meet the horses. I think being cooped up too long in planes is making you a little crazy. Carolina, the woman who can tell you something about those dead horses, will be here in an hour.'

They brought their luggage inside, and Ernie returned to the stables to check how the training sessions were going. His two main competition horses, one of them from Bisente and the other from Wunya, were doing flatwork with students. The riders worked the horses with the lightest of aids, allowing them to position their heads where they felt comfortable for the first ten minutes before asking for collection.

In the second arena, a rider was having difficulty teaching a green horse to canter on the correct diagonals. Ernie spent a few minutes instructing her, reminding her to keep her head up and look where she wanted to go. She was making the mistake of trying to throw the horse onto the correct lead with her body, causing the horse to compensate for her change in balance by striking out on the wrong leg.

'Stay upright with your weight down into your heels and your height up.' Ernie leaned on the rails as she trotted in a circle to the left. 'Forget the circle and ride the full arena. Ride your corners and watch that inside rein as you may need to raise it to stop him from dropping the inside shoulder. Don't lean in or out – you have to remain still and balanced to help him. If you lean where your instinct tells you to, you're making it more difficult for him to choose the correct lead. Bend him into the corner and ask him to canter as he comes out. Go back to the old pony club aids if you like – inside leg on the girth, outside leg behind, feel with that inside rein to keep his flexion there, and one, two, three, canter.'

The horse struck off on the correct lead, and the rider grinned.

'Tell him he's a wonderful horse,' Ernie continued as she cantered down the long side of the arena. 'Give him his head and let him relax into that canter because that is a reward. Now, ease him back to a loose rein walk as another reward, and then you'll try to do it again, but only once. I'm fairly sure he'll go on the correct lead, and you'll reward him with an easy, loose rein canter, then back to a walk, and his lesson's over.'

'But I have another fifteen minutes with him,' the rider spoke in heavily accented English.

'He'll remember that going on the left lead when given those signals results in rest. If you make him do it another twenty times, he'll start wondering if he's doing it wrong because you keep asking him for something. Always be prepared to finish the lesson fifteen minutes or half an hour early if your horse achieved what you wanted for that lesson. We tell him he's a good horse for doing what we wanted and reward him with what he wants, which is to stand around doing nothing. That helps him learn faster than forcing him to endlessly repeat what he just got right.'

'You sound like my father,' she laughed.

'Which is good, given that he is on the World Cup circuit and doing better than I am.'

The horse cantered on his correct diagonal a second time, and the rider followed Ernie's instructions and finished the lesson.

'She rides well.' Grace moved to stand beside Ernie. Wiping the sweat from her brow, she added, 'I forgot how hot it gets here.'

'It's not hot,' Ernie disagreed. 'It's a pleasant twenty-nine Celsius all year round. It gets a lot hotter at Gatton.'

'Well, it feels hot today.'

Matthew looked at the flush on Grace's skin. 'Are you coming down with something?'

She shook her head. 'A bit of a headache from the travel, that's all.'

'Meeting the horses will take your mind off it.' Ernie held out his arm, and she linked hers through it. 'To the stables.'

Matthew followed, trying not to scowl at the camaraderie between the two who had lived next door to each other all of their lives.

After learning about the horses in training and Ernie's competition plans for the coming months, they returned to the house to meet Carolina Rojas.

'One of our stablehands, Luis, is Carolina's younger brother,' Ernie explained. 'I asked around about the dead horses - just casually, of course, I didn't want to sound like I was doing an investigation. Luis mentioned that Carolina found the second lot of horses and reported it, and he said she was scared. She wouldn't tell him about it, but he said she stopped going out apart from work.'

Grace dabbed a cool cloth on her face and frowned. 'Do you think she's scared because of finding those horses? Or something else?'

Ernie shrugged. 'It's Venezuela. Who's to say? Maybe she witnessed a kidnapping or murder. They happen more frequently here than around Gatton.'

'Does the crime worry you?' Matthew thought of the statistics he'd looked up before arriving. It seemed a dangerous country compared to Australia.

'I'm aware of it. At the moment, we have Carmen Vargas, the daughter of the owner of Caraven Constructions, staying here as a student rider. Her father, Ricardo, has a full security team inside the compound. It makes me feel safer. There are eight armed guards with us when we go to a competition because of Carmen, though Ricardo keeps a couple with me even when she's home. He says that both the horses and I could be targets.'

'Training in Australia is safer,' Grace remarked, 'but I know you love the competitions in the Americas. Have you thought of moving to somewhere in North America?'

'Only briefly. Ricardo makes it worthwhile to stay here. He's hoping Carmen will make it onto the Olympic team.'

'Is she that good?' Grace trusted that Ernie wasn't giving the Vargas family false hope. She knew trainers often overestimated the abilities of their horses and riders to keep the money flowing, but she doubted Ernie would be that way inclined.

Ernie nodded. 'She has the right stuff. Several of my riders do, but she has the money behind her to make it happen.'

They continued to talk about horses and horse people while Ernie prepared lunch. Some paracetamol helped Grace's headache, and she enjoyed the salad and cheese put in front of her. By the time Carolina arrived, Matthew had completed the washing up, and the three Australians were in the main reception room having coffee.

After introductions-, Matthew surprised Grace by speaking fluent Spanish to the petite woman with long dark hair and haunted eyes. Carolina's hands wrung together repeatedly as she nodded and conversed, her eyes darting to the door as though expecting trouble. She wore jeans and a white shirt with a colorful scarf around her neck that she pulled over her hair in public.

'I can speak English,' Carolina nodded at Grace, 'if you would prefer.'

'You're clearly better educated than I.' Grace smiled warmly at her. 'I wish I spoke Spanish, but I only know some basic expressions.'

'My mother teaches English and French at a *colegio* – high school. She made sure my brothers and I learn well.'

They spent several minutes talking about high school and languages before Ernie steered the conversation back to the point of this meeting.

'Luis tells us you found one of those mass burials of horses. Matthew and Grace said similar ones have turned up in Australia, and they want to learn more about the ones here.'

Carolina's dark eyes overflowed with fear. 'I trust you because Luis says I can. These horses – there is too much bad about them. When I report what I found, the *policia* were not interested because they are just horses, not people. Animals die. It is not a crime. Then, two days after, a man visits to ask me about what I saw. He pretended to be from a newspaper, but I recognized him.'

She stopped and looked around to make sure that only the three Australians could hear her. Leaning forward, she spoke in a whisper. 'When my youngest brother worked in the cafeteria at Menningala Vaccines, this man was one of their guards.'

At the mention of the vaccine company, Matthew and Grace exchanged glances. It was an interesting coincidence.

'I remember him because one day I was in the car waiting for my brother to finish work when this man starts yelling at one of the workers and pushes him to the ground. He looked like *el matón* – a bully. He threatened to make the worker disappear. Then he comes to my apartment and says he is from a newspaper and wants to know what I found. I lied. I said just horses that a farmer killed. I said I wanted someone to cover them up because they smell and will bring the Chupacabra to the area.'

For a second, her fear faded, and she smiled at her ruse. 'I do not believe in the Chupacabra, of course, but if he thinks I believe in nonsense, it makes me appear more *estúpida* – stupid, simple, not so bright. I tell him stories of the Chupacabra to show I am more interested in that than the horses. Before he leaves, he tells me that he believes the horses belong to one of our big crime organizations, and if I didn't want to attract their attention, it would be best if I forget ever seeing them. There was menace in his voice. A threat. He said it would be very unwise to speak to anyone about the horses because people go missing all the time.'

Carolina shuddered as she remembered the evil in the man's eyes.

'A few days after that,' she continued in a soft voice, 'another man approaches me at work to ask about the horses. He says he is an investigator who will pay me for information, but I believe he comes to test me. I say there is nothing to tell. People who can't afford to bury horses or cows dump them, and that brings the Chupacabra. I say he should be investigating them, and tell him about pigs killed mysteriously in the night in our road. I took a photo of him from a security camera at work. I showed my brother. He said he also worked at Menningala.'

Again, Matthew and Grace looked at each other. What was Menningala doing? Were they disposing of mistakes and stocking up on horses from REE to cover up the deaths?

'Was there anything unusual about the dead horses?' Matthew asked.

'Yes.' Carolina looked around again like a bird suspecting a cat stalked her. 'Their brands were cut off, and they all had surgery.'

Matthew sat up in surprise. His immediate thought was of the stallions in the Pilatos laboratories with the throat surgery to mute them. 'Surgery? What sort of surgery?'

Pointing to her abdomen, Carolina drew a line vertically through her navel. 'Like when horses have *un cólico* – the stomach ache or blockage. That is colic? And the veterinary doctor does surgery.'

'*La cirugía abdominal?*' Matthew hoped he had the correct words for abdominal surgery. 'Did all of them have surgery?'

'All I could see,' Carolina nodded. 'I looked at perhaps twenty. All showed signs of surgery with basic stitching. Not the sort of work that a veterinary doctor does if he wants a horse to live. I know this because I did some research. With colic surgery, the skin is shaved. It was not with these horses. And the stitching should be careful so that the edges can heal together. What I saw was like a child sewing a potato sack together.'

'That's bizarre.' Ernie scrunched his face into an expression of distaste at the fate of the horses. 'If they are coming from the Menningala laboratories, what sort of vaccines are they testing?'

'Maybe they're trying to shorten trial times,' suggested Grace. 'Rather than waiting for a year or two for ill-effects to show in the overall health and performance of the horses, they're cutting them open to look for any damage to the organs. Then they dispose of them because that's cheaper and easier than nursing them through recovery.'

'That's possible,' Matthew tapped his fingers against his mouth as he considered Grace's words. 'REE have an oversupply of horses, so it might suit them to siphon some off to Menningala while keeping them alive in their books. That way, they can continue to collect donations for them,'

To be fair,' pointed out Grace, 'we don't know what REE are doing. We're just hypothesizing what might be possible. Maybe they think they are retiring the horses to one of their properties, and the truck company was doing those night-time deliveries to Menningala without their knowledge. We don't even know if they were REE horses. We have to consider all possibilities.'

'Agreed.' Matthew admired Grace's fairness even though she did not attempt to hide her dislike of the massive charity. 'They could be separate issues.'

Ernie turned to Carolina and asked if there was anything else they should know.

'I do not think so,' she shook her head. 'I don't understand why those dead horses are so important, though. We lose more people around the city without anyone worrying. Why would two Menningala men want to make sure those horses are forgotten?'

'Some of the vaccines they work on could be worth hundreds of millions of dollars, maybe billions,' Matthew explained. 'If it became known that the vaccines were killing horses, damaging hearts, causing tumors in the liver, or something like that, then it could cause enough of a backlash to shut the company down. If that was happening to those horses, and they are just killing them here and in Australia rather than giving them the correct level of care, then the repercussions would be immense. It could be worth tens of millions or more to keep the information about those horses hidden.'

'People would kill for that much money.' Carolina sat back in her chair and ran her fingers through her black hair. 'I trust you will tell no one that I spoke to you about this.'

'You have our word,' Matthew assured her.

'Did you want to see Luis ride?' Ernie stood and extended a hand towards Carolina. 'I can have someone run you back to your home whenever it suits you.'

'No, no,' she smiled at him. 'I have my car here. I will watch Luis, and then he can come with me when I leave to save him a walk.'

The four of them went to the arenas and watched the next riding session. Ernie convinced Matthew to join in, but he didn't ask Grace as he knew she stopped riding after her fall. As Matthew followed Ernie's instructions, Grace had the opportunity to watch him. As soon as he sat in the saddle, his body seemed to meld with the horse so they moved as one. Even though he'd never met the towering young Warmblood before, he seemed to form an immediate rapport with him.

'Your boyfriend rides well,' commented Carolina as she stood next to Grace.

For an instant, Grace wanted to set her straight, then realized there was no harm in him being her boyfriend in Carolina's mind. 'Yes, he does.'

The session ran for thirty-five minutes and included a few jumps over four-foot obstacles. Matthew's riding skills were on a par with Ernie's, and both men laughed and joked as they casually schooled the horses over the jumps. It was obvious that Ernie enjoyed having a fellow Australian riding with him. When they finished, some junior riders took the horses to cool them down, and Matthew and Ernie brought Luis over.

'Your sister is going to save your legs and give you a lift,' Ernie patted him on the shoulder. 'Good riding today, Luis. You've formed a good partnership with Jazz. I think we need to start looking for your first competition.'

The boy's eyes glowed. It was his dream to compete for his country, and Ernie's generosity might make that happen.

Luis and Carolina climbed into her little yellow car and waved as they left. The three Australians leaned against the fence and watched the car stop in the gateway before pulling onto the road. A few seconds later, a semi-trailer carrying shipping containers roared past the gate. Almost immediately, the sound of a collision and the scream of metal against metal shook the neighborhood.

Matthew, Grace, and Ernie exploded into action, running full speed down the driveway. As he ran, Ernie yelled at the riders to call for an ambulance. Several other workers dropped tools or dismounted from horses and ran behind the Australians.

Before the scene became visible from behind the trees, they could hear the truck engine revving as it continued forward. The screeching of metal grinding against the road surface hurt their ears. When they reached the gate, they paused as they took in the horror of the scene.

The remains of the little yellow car appeared from under the back of the truck. As the last of the semi-trailer's wheels bumped over the mangled wreck, the unseen truck driver changed up a gear and accelerated away.

Ernie ran to the wreck while Matthew held out an arm in front of Grace to stop her.

'They can't be alive.' He pressed a palm against his forehead and squeezed his eyes shut as though that could change the scene. 'We can't do anything.'

'Ernie!' Grace called to her friend of many years. She knew Matthew was right. Already, she could see blood forming rivulets with the fuel and water leaking from the squashed and distorted mess of metal. 'Come back. Don't look. They won't be…'

Her voice trailed off when she saw Ernie reach the wreck and immediately turn aside to vomit. He took another few steps away from the car and fell to his knees.

'Go get him, please.' She squeezed Matthew's arm and looked up into his eyes with trust. 'He's still so young.'

'I think we're the same age.'

'I know, but you're…' she gripped his arm a little tighter as she tried to find the words to explain her feelings. For most of the time since she'd met him, she thought of him as young. Not just younger than her in years, but so much younger in his attitudes. It occurred to her that beneath the deceptively shallow surface ran great depths. 'You're like an old soul. You seem so much older.'

Unsure whether that was a compliment or not, Matthew walked forward from the gathering circle of spectators and stood next to Ernie without looking at the car. He didn't need to look to know that human bodies inside the vehicle would be as broken as the twisted, flattened metal.

'Come on, mate; there's nothing we can do.' He spoke softly in the voice he often used to soothe upset horses. 'It was an accident. You need to speak to the riders who were friends with Luis.'

'An accident?' Ernie looked up at him. His skin was pale, and his eyes were shocked. 'Do you really think that? She came here to talk to us, and now she's dead. They both are. That wasn't an accident.'

'We don't know that.'

'The truck driver didn't even stay around.'

'But he could have been scared. Maybe he was on drugs and didn't even know he ran over their car. We can talk about it later. For now, you have to be a role model for all the people who work at your place. They're looking to you.'

Ernie nodded and rose to his feet.

They walked to the others who remained well back in case the fuel ignited. While Ernie talked to his riders and other workers, Grace and Matthew silently regarded the car. In the distance, sirens grew louder.

'Binky, and now these two.' After replaying the accident in his head, Matthew thought it was likely the truck had been waiting for Carolina's car to leave.

'They couldn't have known she was here to talk to us about the horses, though, could they?' Grace's brow creased as she thought about what happened. 'As far as anyone knows, we're just Ernie's friends from Australia, and Carolina was here to pick up her brother. If they killed her because she talked to us, then they'll try to kill us, too, won't they?'

'I don't think so,' Matthew reassured her. 'If this relates to the horses, I imagine they killed her because they suspected she had seen more than she let on. It was going to happen regardless of our presence. No one from Menningala or REE or any crime syndicate would know who we are or that we wanted to find out about those horses.'

His phone buzzed in his pocket. He considered ignoring it but decided to check the caller first. It was Joe. He answered and did a quick calculation of time differences – after lunch Tuesday in Caracas made it close to 4 am Wednesday on the east coast of Australia.

'Hey, Joe.'

'Are you and Grace safe?'

'We are at the moment, but we're standing close to what might be a double murder.'

'To do with those horses or the charities?'

'The horses, maybe. Why? What's happened?'

'I haven't told Lane yet as I want him and Karen to have a few days of peace on the station before I wreck things. They'll be safe there.'

He paused, and Matthew felt the adrenaline kick his heart into overdrive. What had happened?

'It's Tom and Vicki.'

***

Dibby and Rev

The sense of danger grew as the hours passed. Rev watched some new men in city clothes walk along the fence, looking at the horses and making notes. Their language and speech patterns were strange to him, and their eyes held a threat. They looked at the horses like killer dogs eyeing a pen of chickens.

Rev took a few steps back from the men and lowered his head, looking away. Dibby and Dusty copied him, averting their eyes from the men who stared hungrily and talked with cold voices. No horse stretched out a friendly nose as they passed. Once Rev had shown his aversion, all the horses stayed back, avoiding them as though death walked past the yards.

One of the men, a veterinary surgeon, noticed the horses withdrawing from them as they walked by. Long ago, he liked horses. After losing his wife in a fall from a horse, he blamed all horses for her death. The world was better off without them, and these horses would be dead soon enough.

For the briefest moment, he caught one of the palominos watching him, and he shivered. It was as though the horse looked into his soul and saw the blackness there. The horse saw him – saw into him - and looked away.

It didn't matter, he told himself. They would all die, and he would make more money. Of course, money did not buy happiness, but what it did buy helped drown the misery.

CHAPTER FOURTEEN

Life is a rollercoaster ride. Highs follow lows follow highs. Enjoy the views when you're at the top. Hang on while you're falling, and know you'll climb again. Stay in your seat until the ride stops and the operator tells you to leave – don't try and leave while the ride is still going. Enjoy the ride because that is life.

A message to the Rosewood High School graduating class from Lane Dimity.

The Putty Road

The vehicle slammed to a halt against the trees, and the airbags deflated. Vicki took a shuddering gasp of air. She looked around to get her bearings. The car was on its side. She was in the seat above Tom, held in place by the seat belt. Blood dripped from her nose, but she could feel and move all her limbs, so she assumed she had avoided serious injury.

Tom, on the other hand, looked to be in a bad way. His eyes were shut, and blood gushed from a cut on the other side of his head. The rhythmic spurting of the blood proved his heart was beating, and she was grateful for that. His body slumped loosely in unconsciousness, and she knew she had to get him out of the vehicle. The smell of petrol was strong, and while the battery remained connected, any loose wire might spark an explosion.

Vicki forced the confusion out of her head and focused on one thing – getting Tom away from the vehicle. The repeated rolling left the windscreen shattered and scattered, providing her with an exit. She made sure she could stop herself from falling on Tom before she released her seat belt. Bracing her legs against the steering column in front of him, she pushed up to release the pressure on the seatbelt, then unclipped it.

There was very little grace in her scramble through the smashed windscreen, and she landed on her hands and knees in the forest mulch that was damp from the previous night's rain. Looking up, she was relieved to see that the car shielded her from the road above. Unless they came down to inspect the vehicle, they would assume the occupants died in the crash. *Good,* she nodded to herself, *let them believe we're dead.*

A box of tissues rested on the side window next to Tom's head. Grabbing it, she pulled out a handful and pressed them to Tom's temple. Although the bleeding had slowed, his pulse still pushed out a spurt of blood with every beat. The smell of fuel spurred her to remove him from the car and worry about his injuries later. Pushing against his body to ease some of the strain on the seatbelt, she reached over and unclipped it. Tom's weight sagged against the door and window that lay against the dirt.

Grunting and heaving, she pulled him out through the front of the car, glancing up frequently to make sure the killers didn't appear around the ends of the vehicle.

'You are a lot heavier than you look.' She kept her voice to a whisper as she struggled to maneuver him through the opening. It was almost impossible to move his limp body, but fear gave her extra strength.

Once he was out of the car, she started pulling him down the hill. With gravity helping, it was easier to slide him along over the leaf matter. She scuttled back, inches at a time, pulling him towards her and repeating. Occasionally, she threw handfuls of leaves and sticks over the drag marks to disguise their tracks. Desperate to put distance between themselves and the leaking fuel as well as the men who tried to kill them, she pushed through her pain barriers and kept moving.

Judging their distance from the car as safe, she crawled from behind Tom to return for their phones, wallets, and luggage. Before she had time to move more than an arm's length from Tom, a wire sparked in the engine, and a great WOOSH of flame exploded into the air. Turning away, she shielded her eyes with one hand and put her other in front of Tom's face to protect him from the initial blast of heat. The flames soared into the branches of the trees, setting them alight. They also began dancing and crackling across the forest floor, drying the damp leaves in front before igniting them.

'Phones. Passports. Cash. Credit cards. Clothes.' Vicki hung her head in a moment of despair for losing all those things. A glance at

Tom reminded her of what mattered – their lives. The sound of the approaching fire prompted her to keep moving. The oil in the eucalypt leaves fuelled the flames, but, thankfully, the dampness slowed them so that they had time to flee.

'Can you wake up?' Vicki grunted as she doubled her efforts to drag Tom down the hill in an inch-back-and-pull action. 'I would *really* like it if we could avoid being burned alive. You won't be so handsome if that happens.'

Her breath came in ragged gasps as she pushed herself back down the slope, hauling Tom with her. The burning body of the car hid them from the view of anyone on the road, and she hoped the fire would discourage them from checking the wreckage. Behind her, the slope disappeared into bushes. Before the noise of the fire, she heard the sound of water beyond the undergrowth and knew she must reach it.

When thorns pricked her back, she turned to see a bank of blackberry bushes blocking the way. A path formed by kangaroos, wallabies, and rabbits wound between the stems and canes. Muttering curses about Brer Rabbit and the blackberry bush, she followed the narrow tunnel through the thorns, trying to ignore the pain when they snagged her.

'It's probably not a good time to wake,' she told Tom as a thorn dug into the arm of his shirt. 'Once we're on the other side, you won't know if the blood is from the crash or my Brer Rabbit impersonation. Just so you know, it's from the crash. I'm the one getting blooded by the blackberry. Not far now.'

The wall of leaves protected her from the growing furnace on the other side. She wondered if blackberry was flammable, and the thought of being caught in a combustible tangle of thorny bushes encouraged her to work harder. She continued talking to Tom because her monologue helped calm the panic that bubbled beneath the surface.

On the other side of the blackberry thicket, the hill dropped sharply. She held Tom against her chest, her legs on either side of him, as they slid down the mud to land on flatter ground. Leaving him for a minute, she scooted back to throw loose leaves and sticks over the track they'd created. It might not pass a close inspection, but it was harder to see than the muddy gouge from their backsides.

Tom remained unconscious, and she took a moment to inspect his head. The swelling on his temple, where the blood continued to seep, was an alarming size, but his breathing appeared normal. Dropping a light kiss on his lips and uttering a soft prayer, she returned to pulling him towards the creek.

The long grass and reeds were the next barrier. It was not that they were difficult to negotiate, Vicki thought as she inspected the lush growth, it was the fact that she knew what lived there. Eastern brown snakes. Tiger snakes. Red-bellied black snakes. Lane had taught her about the Australian snakes, and she held a healthy respect for the venomous reptiles. Not fear, she tried to tell herself, just respect.

As she pushed through the damp overgrowth moving closer to the sound of running water, she shuddered at the thought of the snakes that were probably around her. Not probably, she grimaced as she saw their ideal habitat in the long grass where frogs and small mammals lived – they were definitely here.

'They're more scared of me than I am of them,' she told herself, banging her hand against the ground a few times to let any nearby snakes know that something big moved here. Too big for them to think of attacking. Big enough for them to avoid. 'And they only want to live. They were here long before humans walked the earth, so they have the right to live here.'

Repeating Lane's information did little to quell the worry as she pushed backward through the grass. Relief flooded her when she reached the rocks at the edge of a running creek. The rain the night before had the water flowing rapidly over the rounded stones, its sound drowning out the crackling of the fire.

Trusting that the mountain water was clean, she scooped some up in her hands to drink. She removed her bloodied shirt and rinsed it before using it to wipe Tom's face. His eyes remained closed, and she carefully placed her shirt under his head. It seemed more important to cushion his head than to cover her skin and bra from the gaze of the bushland animals.

The fact that he remained unconscious for so long disturbed her. Without a phone to call for help or any sign of houses nearby, she would have to deal with it herself. His pulse and breathing remained steady. Unbuttoning his shirt, she put an ear to his chest and was comforted by the sound of clear lungs. The diagonal bruise across his chest from the seatbelt was a mirror image of hers. There didn't seem to be any broken bones, and most of the blood on his clothes was from the head injury and blackberry thorns.

He needed to wake up as she couldn't leave him like this to go for help. Anyway, where would she go? The men who tried to kill them might still be at the road above. The fire appeared to be dying out as the dampness of the forest slowed it, and no sirens heralded the arrival of a fire brigade. The area around the creek looked as though no one had walked there in years, so she couldn't expect hikers to wander along.

If she left Tom to go for help, she might be gone for hours. She couldn't leave him. But she had nothing here that could help him.

Bowing her head, she silently asked her God and Tom's Holy People for help. Once, when she visited his family in Arizona, she spent an afternoon with his grandmother, learning about their traditional beliefs. She learned of the Three Worlds the Diné passed through before arriving at this, the Fourth World. There were curious similarities between the Diné beliefs and her own. A Great Flood forced the First Man and First Woman to leave the Third World to arrive here, in the Fourth World.

His grandmother spoke of the importance of restoring balance and harmony as a way of securing good health. Songs and dances were a vital part of healing ceremonies, but Vicki knew none of them. Neither her beliefs nor his could help.

A flash of blue pulled at her peripheral vision, and she turned to see four kingfishers on a branch overhanging the stream. The brilliance of their turquoise feathers shone a light into her heart. Tom's grandmother spoke of the importance of the number four: the Four Worlds, the Four Sacred Mountains, four times of the day, four songs for a ritual, and the four original clans of the Diné. It was a sacred number.

Four sacred kingfishers in the color of the stones valued by the Navajo for good fortune and protection from evil perched above the water.

Her scientific mind laughed at her fanciful thoughts – a family of kingfishers, no matter how beautiful, could not help with a head injury.

One of the birds tilted its head to look at her, then dove into the water. Vicki sighed, wishing she could find significance in its actions, perhaps a message, but it was a kingfisher – diving into the water is what they did. The bird returned to its perch and cocked its head as though waiting for her to respond.

Twice more, it repeated its dive into the cold mountain water before all four birds flew away. *The cold mountain water,* Vicki repeated the phrase in her mind. Cold slows bleeding and reduces swelling. If the blow to Tom's head had caused bleeding or swelling, cold water might help. She recalled one of her favorite childhood horse books. The injured horse fell in the brook, and Ken sat in the water all night holding her head so she didn't drown. He became ill, but it saved Flicka. Cold water.

Moving with care, Vicki slid into the creek, pulling Tom with her. The rocky bank sloped steeply enough that she was able to sit in the water cradling his head while his legs remained dry at the edge. She positioned him so that his eyes, nose, and mouth remained above the surface while the flowing water chilled the rest of his head. Holding him tenderly, she bowed her head and prayed for him. She hoped that his ancestors had sent a message with the kingfishers, and she wished for the water to have healing power. Human hopes and wishes seemed inconsequential notions against the ancient background of the Australian bush, and she longed for a phone or friendly voice.

The light faded, and the bush noises changed from daylight chatter to the still of the night. She shivered in the cooling air. The sounds from the occasional car or truck on the Putty Road filtered down to her. The dampness of the bush extinguished the fire, and only the smell of smoke remained. A few times, she called out, hoping someone would hear but fearful that the men who wanted them dead were still around. No one answered. No one came. It seemed like they were alone in the world.

She leaned over to kiss Tom lightly on the forehead. She couldn't leave him, but this wasn't achieving anything. Perhaps it was time to place him somewhere dry and walk for help. But where could she go? Should she climb back up to the road and stop a passing car? What if the killers were still up there? Maybe she should follow the creek and hope she found a house.

'I wish you were here, Lane,' she whispered, thinking of the man who inspired such loyalty in his friends. They followed him because they believed in him, and they loved him. 'If you were here, you'd know what to do. Tom needs you.'

When you choose not to act, it is still an action, Lane once told her. It seemed relevant now. She chose to stay with Tom rather than seek help, and perhaps he would die because of her inaction.

Lane often made profound statements, she mused, her mind wandering as the cold crept into her core. A journalist at another newspaper once mockingly called him *the Jesus of the Horses.* At first, she thought it was an irreverent remark, disrespectful to both Jesus and Lane. After some thought, she saw the parallels between their lives. She pointed them out to Tom, and he showed no surprise. He told her that Lane was a man worth following as he had more kindness and strength than any person he'd ever known.

Vicki believed that Tom was a man of those qualities, too. She had given up on love when he came into her life and shone like a sun, brightening everything. The thought of losing him was unbearable.

'We need you, Lane.'

Her tears fell on Tom's cheeks. He opened his eyes to the night. The crushing headache that filled his brain blurred his thoughts, but he was aware of being in the water and of Vicki's hands cradling him. His last memory was of the car ramming them off the road.

'Why do I need Lane?'

The sound of his voice caused her to gasp in relief. He was awake and talking. The overwhelming fear of him dying in her arms began to ease.

'We all need him,' she smiled down at him. 'Right now, I just wanted someone to tell me what to do with you. I thought Lane would know.'

'He'd tell you to get me out of the water to start with.' Tom snorted and tried to sit up. Dizziness swirled around him, and he fell back into Vicki's arms. 'And he'd tell me to trust you.'

'Good.' Vicki helped raise his head. 'Your legs are mostly dry, so I'm going to try and keep them that way.' She shuffled him out of the creek. 'I'm sorry about the water, but you wouldn't wake up, and I thought the cold might help your head injury.'

Hearing the desperate note behind her voice, Tom understood her fears and turned to humor to ease them. 'I would have assumed I had a much thicker skull than this. Matthew is always calling me a thickhead. One little blow and I'm out for,' he paused and squinted at the darkness. 'Just how long was I out?'

'A few hours, I think.' Vicki sniffed and tried to quell her emotions. She failed. 'The car burned. We've lost our phones and cards. I couldn't wake you. I thought you were going to die. Then the kingfishers said to try the cold water.'

'The kingfishers?' Fighting the throbbing in his head, Tom sat up and lay a comforting arm across Vicki's shoulders. She leaned against him, shivering, and told him about the birds.

'I woke up, so maybe they did have a message, or maybe your subconscious knew that the cold water would help, and it looked for a way to communicate with your conscious mind.'

'You are too sensible,' Vicki complained without rancor. 'I have a wonderful spiritual story, and you make it mundane.'

'Don't worry, part of me believes in animal messengers, so I'm not completely logical.' The tremors in Vicki's body increased, and Tom became concerned about hypothermia. 'You're freezing. Let's get moving. My head is clearing by the minute. I think I'm ready to walk.'

'Can you climb up to the road, though?' Vicki peered into the darkness where the shadowed shapes of treetops moved against the starry sky. 'It's a long way.'

'I'm tough. I'll make it. We have to get a message to the others. Whoever tried to kill us might try to kill them, too.'

'It's possible,' Vicki agreed as she rose stiffly to her feet. 'I'm glad Karen and Lane are out on the station. It should be safe out there. Andrea should be fine because she's not doing any investigating. Do you think Caracas is safe?'

'It depends if whoever is behind this is also over there.' Tom winced at the effort of thinking, talking, and moving, all at one time. He wanted to find a warm spot and go to sleep, not focus on the intricacies of this dangerous puzzle. 'It might be easier to get away with murder in Caracas than here.'

'Now we know beyond doubt that they're capable of murder - Binky, probably the missing machinery operator, and this attempt on us. There must be a lot at stake for them to use murder to remove problems.'

'It'll all come back to greed. There's a lot of money at stake.'

They moved slowly, resting often. Vicki detoured around the blackberry thicket rather than risk the thorns a second time. Step by step, frequently crawling on their hands and knees, they made their way up the mountain to the road.

Sometime after midnight, they stood at the side of the road, watching carefully to assure themselves that the killers had left. When they finally stepped into view to wave down a car, it seemed drivers did not want to stop for two ragged people in the middle of the night on the Putty.

In the space of fifteen minutes, four cars and a truck passed without slowing. A cyclist changed their luck.

As the tiny headlight approached and the whirring of spokes met their ears, they stepped back off the bitumen to let him pass. It wasn't as though he could give them a lift to town.

The bike rider hit his brakes as he came closer, veering to the other side of the road to keep a safe distance between them. It was sensible to be wary of people on a country road at night, even when six foot six and built like WWE champion.

'Youse two okay?' the extreme-Australian voice drawled.

'We had an accident,' Vicki explained. 'Our car went over the edge.'

'Jeez! Youse okay, though? Do you have a phone?'

His accent ran the words together so that it sounded like, *D'yavva phone?*

'No, they were in the car. Do you?'

'Sure thing, Luv.' Her American accent seemed to assure him that they weren't planning on robbing him. 'Do you want the police or an ambulance? Or both?'

Tom thought of the way the police suppressed the investigation into Binky's death and shook his head. If there were any chance police were involved with this, they needed to avoid their attention.

'We have a friend in Singleton,' said Vicki. 'It would be great if we could give him a ring. He'll come and get us.'

The cyclist removed his helmet and screwed up his face as he looked at Tom in the dark. 'You sure you don't want me to call triple-zero? Your buddy there looks pretty banged up.'

Tom forced himself to smile. 'It looks worse than it feels,' he lied. 'Anyway, our friend will get us to hospital quicker than an ambulance.'

'Sure thing.' The stranger wheeled his bike over and held out his phone. 'Just swipe right to unlock it. Out here for a holiday, are ya?'

'Visiting friends,' replied Vicki as Tom turned away to call Joe. 'We really appreciate you stopping to help.'

'Too easy.' the rider held out his hand. 'Call me Moz.'

Vicki accepted the shake, her hand tiny in his grip. 'As in mosquito?'

He laughed, 'Nah - Moses. But everyone calls me Moz.'

'I'm Vicki, and my banged-up friend is Tom.'

Moz looked her up and down. 'You been in the creek or something?'

'Actually, yes.' Although mostly dried, there were still wet patches.

'You must be freezing.' Moz quickly unzipped his jacket and handed it to her. 'Here, warm yourself up. You'll catch your death out here in wet clothes. I'll turn around, and you change into that. It's some space-age stuff that'll warm you right up.'

Vicki quickly stripped out of her shirt and shrugged the jacket on. The warmth was bliss after the chill of her clothes, and it hung halfway to her knees.

Moz poked around in a saddlebag attached to his bike and produced some energy bars and a microfibre towel. 'I thought I had a spare shirt packed, but if your buddy puts this against his skin under his shirt, it'll give him some warmth. And eat these. You look like you've had a shock, and me mum always said to get some sugar into people who've had a shock.'

After coping with all that had happened that afternoon and evening, the kindness of a stranger was Vicki's undoing. She took the offered items and sniffed before bursting into tears. She felt a fool, crying in front of a stranger.

'I do the same,' he chatted as though she wasn't sniffing and sobbing in front of him. 'Y'think everything's good, and you've handled it all, then one small thing opens the flood gates. My dad never used to cry, and he ended up having a stroke. Mum always said it was because he never let the stress out in tears. Me? No problem with that. I cry. Someone tells me their dog has died, and I cry. I watch a sad movie, and I cry.' He chuckled. 'Just as well I'm built like a mountain, or the kids at school would've belted me senseless.'

Once Tom finished speaking to Joe, he handed the phone back to their Good Samaritan, and Vicki introduced him to Moz-short-for-Moses. Tom remembered Lane telling them that quantum connections can join seemingly random pieces of life in remarkable ways. Having a man named Moses turning up in the wilderness to keep them safe seemed unusual enough, but Tom decided to press further.

'Any chance you heard of those dead horses in the Hunter? The ones buried in pits about the place?'

'The Menningala horses?'

His response stunned the Americans.

'Is that where they came from?' Vicki immediately became the investigative journalist, her tears forgotten. 'How do you know that?'

'My cousin Isaac drives a truck for Menningala. Just general freight in a small truck, like supplies going in and shipments of vaccines going out. One of his mates, Leroy, used to drive the B-dubs – B-doubles, the big trucks. He quit after taking live horses into the facility in the dead of night and carting them out on other nights in tippers like they were rubbish. Awful business. No one wants to talk about it, though, especially after a few people disappeared.'

'A few?' Tom raised his eyebrows. 'I thought there was one machinery driver who went missing.'

'You know about that?' Moz looked from one to the other in the faint moonlight. 'People 'round here are generally a bit tight-lipped about it.'

'We heard,' said Vicki. 'We're horse people. A few friends have horse rescues, and they think the whole business is odd. No one seemed to know for certain that Menningala were involved, though.'

'Small world,' Moz marveled, then shrugged, 'or not. I live in Singleton now, but I was born up the road in Scone and have like thirty cousins around the place; most of them are into horses, so chances are someone in the family would work for a big employer like Menningala. And, yeah, there was the machinery driver, but Leroy reckoned a couple of workers who looked after the horses went missing, too. Leroy didn't give notice or anything, Isaac said, just didn't turn up one day. Isaac spoke to him afterwards - he was up in croc country in the Gulf driving cattle trucks.'

'Sounds like he was smart,' said Tom. His voice was flat with tiredness, but he wanted to know more. 'It's interesting to get that perspective on the vaccine company, though. Do you know what else they do?'

'As far as I know, they only work on developing vaccines for horses and maybe people. Do you think they do something else?'

'No idea – we're just gathering information. Vicki's a journalist. She's keen on doing an article on the Australian horse scene. Learning what happens to the horses that go in and out of Menningala when they're not supposed to have any movement of horses would be interesting.'

'You've got me thinking about that now, too.' Moz flashed a grin at them in the dark, his white teeth bright against his skin. 'But I'm not going to ask around. Too many people go missing. I'd rather mind my own business and not know.'

Vicki wondered if Moz's appearance was more than a coincidence. What if he was sent there by the people who tried to kill them to feed them false information? She thumped a palm against her forehead to punish herself for overthinking everything. If they sent someone, it would be to complete the job, not talk to them. She looked at the tall man with apprehension - maybe he was going to finish the job. The air seemed several degrees colder as she considered the possibility. Once he found out what they knew, he might kill them.

Moz stayed with them at the side of the road, out of the way of passing cars, until Joe arrived. After the introductions, they offered him a lift into Singleton, but he assured them it was his personal challenge to ride home from Sydney, and it would feel like cheating if he accepted a ride.

'Besides, it's mostly all downhill from here.' He adjusted his helmet and mounted the bike before handing a card to Vicki. 'Stay safe, OK? My number's on there if you guys need a place to stay or anything. When you're far from home, it's good to know a local. Don't be a stranger – give a call, even if you just want to catch up for a beer or something.'

'Will do.' Tom shook his hand and thanked him again.

'Your jacket,' said Vicki as she began to take it off, forgetting she only had a bra underneath.

Moz held up a hand to stop her. 'Keep it, Luv. Stay warm.'

When the bike shot away down the road, Vicki breathed a sigh of relief. A small part of her had worried that he intended to kill them all when Joe arrived.

'Tom needs to go to hospital.' Vicki helped him into the back seat of the car, where she instructed him to lie down. 'He was unconscious for more than an hour.'

'Normally, I'd say yes to that,' Joe narrowed his eyes as he thought of what he'd learned that day, 'but I think we should avoid it if possible. How bad is the headache, Tom?'

'Not as bad as it was.'

'Good sign.' Joe opened the door near Tom's head and leaned over him, shining a torch in one eye then the other. 'Your pupils are responding well. Another good sign.'

Joe and Vicki took their place in the front seats, and Joe steered the car back onto the road. The headlights sliced through the darkness as they snaked down the road towards Singleton. They soon caught up to Moz. Vicki wound down her window and waved as they passed the speeding bike.

'If the pain in your head gets worse,' Joe told Tom, 'let us know. I'll check your pupils a few more times tonight, and I have a blood pressure monitor in my bags at the hotel. If you went to the hospital, they'd observe you overnight, and we can do that in the hotel. At this stage, I feel it's best if we avoid the hospitals. I know there are police on the payroll, and maybe they pay someone in the hospitals to report unusual admissions, like an American tourist with a head injury. I'd do that if I was them.'

'And who are they?' Vicki asked.

Joe exhaled with a slight whistle through his teeth. 'That's still the question. At this stage - the shadowy people behind REE and a few other organizations. I'm far from knowing them all, but I can guess at some of the names.'

'Is Menningala involved?'

'It looks that way.'

'Our new friend Moz knew of them. He said Menningala have a lot of horses moving in and out for a facility that shouldn't have any horse movements.'

'The dead horses here were most likely trucked out of Menningala. I don't know about the ones in Venezuela, but it's a heck of a coincidence that REE and Menningala have a presence in both places.'

Tom stirred in the back seat. 'We need to warn Matt. They tried to kill us, so it's likely they know about our group, and everyone is in danger.'

'And Lane and Karen,' added Vicki. 'They need to be kept in the loop.'

'Not necessarily,' Joe glanced sideways at her. 'One of Lane's problems seems to be that when he knows there's an injustice, he has to get in the thick of it. Karen isn't far behind him these days. I think it would be a good idea to keep them in the dark for now. They're out of the way on the station, and I don't fancy seeing either of them in danger at present.'

'You've guessed she's pregnant?' Vicki felt protective of Karen and could imagine Joe, who'd known her since she was a child, felt a strong drive to keep her safe.

'They haven't said anything, but it doesn't take a genius to read their body language. I think we'd all agree with keeping them at a safe distance from whatever is going on here. And you, too,' Joe waved a hand at Vicki. 'I don't expect you to put yourself in danger. What happened this afternoon is not to be repeated. You and Tom can sit this out from here. I'll get a few of the Pilatos security team to help.'

'Good luck with that,' said Tom, amused at the thought of Vicki on the sidelines. In their year together, he learned she did not shy away from danger. 'I've noticed that Vicki doesn't respond well to threats of violence.'

'I respond perfectly well,' Vicki retorted. 'I don't hide from it if that's what you mean. I prefer to turn and face it.'

'And charge to meet it.' Tom snorted.

'It's the best way to get stories,' she looked over her shoulder at him and winked. 'It's hard to write a great exposé if I'm huddled in a corner, unable to see the action. What they did today has made me more determined than ever to drag them all into the light so everyone can see what's going on.'

'Nobody puts Vicki in the corner,' Tom chuckled and groaned as the pain in his head tore through him.

'How's that headache?' Joe asked.

'At prime hangover levels.' Tom closed his eyes. 'Not brain-bleeding-out levels, so don't panic.'

'I don't panic,' Joe replied coolly. 'We'll get you settled in the hotel, and once I'm sure you're OK, I'll give Matthew a call. He needs to know that we've been poking at the nest enough to bring them out fighting. It might be best if he lies low over there and doesn't attract any attention.'

'Yeah,' Tom shook his head slightly, 'that's not going to happen. Matt's as bad as the rest of us. First sign of danger, and he's fired up and racing in to meet it.'

Joe smiled. Matt and Andrea were the youngest of the group, and he had a soft spot for them. At least Andrea was out of the line of fire taking photographs in New Zealand, but Matt was likely to draw attention to himself. He made a mental note to have a Pilatos security team sent to Caracas to support him. Knowing Matthew, he was going to need them.

***

Dibby and Rev

The horses were relieved once the men left, and they were able to eat and drink without being watched. Rev and Dibby stood nose-to-tail, scratching each other on the back with their teeth. Dusty stood next to them, occasionally glancing up at the two palominos to make sure they hadn't spotted any danger. Now and then, Rev would drop his muzzle to Dusty's wither and give him a quick scratch.

Rev's eyes rested on the rails around them. The fences were beginning to feel like a trap rather than just a pen. He'd rattled the gate with his mouth a few times, but the locks in place weren't the simple ones he could open. At home, in his stables, he could grab the barrel bolt and slide it back to open the door of his stall. Mel used to laugh when she found him in the feed room or out on the grass when he was supposed to be safely locked away.

The rails were too high to jump and too solid to rub down. Several times he'd pressed his hind quarter against the fence and pushed, but they didn't budge. There was no way out.

Each day, he sensed danger approaching, and there was no way to avoid it.

CHAPTER FIFTEEN

The more we learn about horses, the more we realize there is to learn. When starting out, we often have the arrogance to believe we know a lot because we know so much more than when we knew nothing. As the years pass and we continue to learn, we grow humbler as we realize how much we don't know. Ask a person who has been riding for six months about horses, and they'll often boast of their experience. Ask a person who's been riding for six decades how much they know, and they'll often say, 'I've learned a bit along the way, but not as much as I need to know.'

Lane Dimity, 'Hints For Horses,' p. 5

Venezuela

Fear gripped Matthew at Joe's words. He turned away from the crash that claimed Carolina and Luis to focus on the conversation. 'What's happened to Tom?'

'I'm hoping he's going to be fine.' Joe's voice remained calm and reassuring. 'He and Vicki spent yesterday asking about REE and some of the businesses that work with them. Keep in mind, it's about four in the morning Wednesday here. I know it's early afternoon Tuesday there. They were heading to the Hunter region from Sydney yesterday afternoon when they were run off the road.'

'Deliberately?'

'Yes. No doubt about that. Their car rolled down the side of a mountain, but Vicki managed to get them both out before the fuel went up.'

Matthew uttered a swear word, and Grace looked at him sharply. She hadn't heard him use profanity before, so she knew Joe's news was alarming. She strained to listen to what he was saying.

'Tom was unconscious for some time. He's asleep now, and I'm monitoring him. We didn't want to go to the hospital because we don't know where the informants for this organization are. I believe there are police on the payroll, and the doctors would be obliged to report a badly injured man. For now, it's best if they believe both Vicki and Tom are dead.'

'He needs a doctor. Head injuries aren't like cut fingers.'

'I understand that, Matthew.' Joe spoke with patience. 'I have one coming up from Sydney now. He'll be here within the hour. He's a retired naval doctor I once worked with. He can be trusted.'

'Do you think they know about Grace and me?' Matthew looked at Grace, who raised her eyebrows at his words.

'I think you have to assume they are aware of all of us and are prepared to do anything to stop us from exposing their affairs. They have a lot of money at stake. It might be best if you and Grace lie low and return home as soon as possible. I can send some Pilatos men to protect you, but they won't reach you for a day or two.'

The thought of going into hiding did not sit well with Matthew. 'It seems there's a big spider in this web who doesn't like us pinging his threads. I'm not inclined to back away because of a threat. I want to keep on pulling and breaking threads until the spider comes out, and we can all see him.'

Joe wasn't surprised at Matthew's attitude. None of Lane's friends were the sort to go to ground when the fists started swinging. He wished they would this time. 'This is not so much a spider in one web as a cluster of spiders in a tangled mess of webs. They want to stay unnoticed in a dark corner where they can continue making their wealth from everything that comes into their webs. We're talking hundreds of millions of dollars. These men will do anything to protect what they've built – including murder.'

'I understand, but I'm here now, so I may as well try and find out what I can.'

'Think of Grace,' Joe urged. 'You and your Dimity gang have consciously decided to take risks to help horses, but she hasn't signed up for this.'

'Yes, I have.' Grace leaned forward to speak into the phone. 'This has been my life long before I met Matthew and the others. Being around horses is dangerous – I should know. I want to find out what is going on, not sit back and wait for others to tell me about it.'

'Seems like your group has grown by another member.' Joe expressed his exasperation with a snort. 'At least lie low until some of my men can get to you. You are in an area where it's easy to organize a hit on a couple of tourists.'

'We'll keep our heads down,' Matthew assured him with empty words.

'What happened with the double murder you mentioned? And how is it related to this?'

Matthew briefly recounted what Carolina told them about the surgery on the horses and the fact that employees from Menningala Vaccines had questioned her twice about what she'd seen.

'Her brother Luis worked here for Ernie.' He grimaced as he thought of the smiling young horseman. 'He was a rider with a big future. They drove out of here in Carolina's car, and a truck ran them down. It could have been an accident but, if it wasn't, then it was beyond callous to take out a boy who had nothing to do with this.'

'These men are desperate to hold onto their empire. It seems both REE and Menningala are tied up with it, and maybe the transport companies that move these horses around the world. If Carolina was killed because of what she saw, and they suspect that she spoke to you, then I can't stress enough how important it is for you both to hunker down at Ernie's and stay off their radar.'

'We'll be careful.'

After saying goodbye to Joe, Matthew put a hand on Grace's elbow. 'We might go back to the house. If there's any chance they don't know about us being here, then I'd like that to continue.'

'So, you're going to lie low as Joe suggested?' Grace looked at him enquiringly. Somehow, hiding to avoid danger did not seem typical of Matthew.

He motioned to Ernie that they were returning to his house before he answered her. 'I don't want to continue standing around here on the street in case we attract unwanted attention, but I don't intend to stay locked away. I want to check out the REE facility tomorrow. I'd say today, but I think Ernie will need our support after this. You don't need to come, though. I'll see if Ricardo Vargas has any connection to REE, Menningala, HATCO, or any of the other companies that could be tied up in this. If he's clean, then you should be safe with his security team.'

Screwing up her face in an expression of distaste, Grace glanced up at Matthew as they walked back up the driveway. 'Do we have to be suspicious of everyone we come in contact with?'

'I've always found a bit of paranoia improves your chances of living when you walk through dangerous places.'

'Deep.' The slight mocking tone to her voice informed him that she was not impressed by his observation.

'I thought it was until two seconds ago.'

Grace apologized, 'I default to sarcasm too easily. Ignore me.'

As he took in the colors of her eyes, he knew *that* wasn't going to happen. 'Will you stay here tomorrow?'

'No way. Whether those security people are safe or not, I'm looking for Image tomorrow. He's doing show jumping, so I'm sure Ernie will know of him. Plus, I'll visit REE with you because I want to bring those mongrels to their knees now that we're sure they're behind it. Well, fairly sure. Keep in mind, there's a good chance what happened with Carolina was an accident. The truck driver might have kept going because he didn't want to face the police. That's a reasonable explanation.

'Reasonable, yes,' Matthew rocked a hand back and forth as though weighing the suggestion, 'but I've learned that when there's a bushfire raging, it's best to assume any smoke you see is related to that fire.'

'I'm not quite that paranoid, but I get what you're saying.'

He looked back at the street, glad that the trees hid the scene of the accident. 'Believe me, when I'm driving, I'll be watching the traffic carefully.'

Grace frowned at the thought of being mowed down by a truck. The thought of hiding and doing nothing seemed worse than facing danger, though, so she was determined to go with Matthew.

Ernie finished telling the police that Luis worked for him and Carolina was his sister, before passing on the contact details of other family members. When he returned to his house, his face was pale. Grace made him a cup of strong sweet tea and assured him it would help. She wasn't sure if the brew helped the person in shock or if the routine of making the tea helped the support person.

'Some of the witnesses said the truck was parked up the street.' Ernie took a sip of tea and sat back in one of his green velveteen armchairs, his face pinched in concern. 'They said the driver pulled out and accelerated quickly, running over Carolina's little car as though it was a target. They thought it looked deliberate. The police sounded like they wanted to find and charge the truck driver but, after a few minutes, the officer in charge came over and called it an unfortunate accident. He blamed Carolina for not looking where she was going. I don't think they'll even look for the truck or driver.'

'That seems to be the pattern in Australia, too.' Grace sat in the chair next to him and patted his arm consolingly. 'The men behind this seem to have contacts in the media and the police. When something deserves media or police attention, they put a lid on it. That takes a lot of money and influence.'

'So, nothing will be done?' Ernie's voice reflected the helplessness he felt at the situation.

Matthew shook his head. 'Not by the people whose job it is to do something, but we'll take care of it. Whoever is behind it - and we are ninety-nine percent sure it's the people who run REE - will regret catching our attention.'

'What can you do?' Ernie's expression indicated his doubts about their ability to achieve anything.

'On the surface, we look like a few horse-mad people who never grew up, but the power Lane carries with his social media presence, and the force that Karen brings to the table with Pilatos is huge. Then there's Joe, who's like a dark angel watching over everyone – the man is scary, and anyone who raises a hand against Karen and her friends needs to be scared.'

Closing his eyes for a moment, Ernie took a few slow breaths. He felt swept along in currents he didn't understand. 'Is there anything I can do?'

'Just carry on as usual,' said Matthew, 'or as usual as you can manage. You might let Carolina's family know that Pilatos were going to offer Luis a riding scholarship, and they'll transfer that money to them. Karen would want the family taken care of since it's likely they died bringing information to us. In fact,' he leaned over to remove his wallet from a back pocket and counted out a wad of notes, 'here's thirty-five hundred *bolívars*. It's only about five hundred Australian dollars – maybe tell them that was the first payment Luis was to receive this week, and I'll have Karen organize something.'

Tears pricked Ernie's eyes at Matthew's kindness. He knew Luis's family struggled to make ends meet, and they would appreciate the money.

Seeing his emotions threatening to overcome him, Grace stepped in with a request to side-track him. 'I need you to help me find a horse, Ernie.'

After describing Image and explaining how he was part of the puzzle regarding what happened to the horses that went to REE, Grace was pleased to see Ernie search for the contact details of the new owners. He recalled seeing Image at show jumping events and knew the family who bought him. He also rang the REE facility and asked if two of his visitors could look at the work they were doing with local children and the Australian horses.

'We were thinking of doing some fundraising for REE,' Ernie fabricated a story seconds before the words left his mouth, 'so we hope to get some photos of my friends with the children and horses. They are quite well known, and there is always some media interest in what they do, so my apologies if any paparazzi are there taking photos. Still, publicity for a good cause is always helpful.'

'Paparazzi?' Grace questioned him after he finished the call.

Ernie shrugged. 'I figured that if they thought you were high profile people who might have photographers following you around, they might be less likely to do something to harm you.'

'Good thinking,' said Matthew. 'And, as strange as it may seem, I have been photographed by paparazzi before, so it's not stretching the truth that much.'

'Really?' Grace looked at him in surprise.

'It's mainly because of Lane,' he explained, downplaying the demand for his photos. 'He has millions of fans around the world, and some of his popularity spills over onto the rest of us.'

'If Grace used the internet more,' Ernie looked at her fondly, knowing she used it sparingly as a business tool but not much else, 'she'd know how famous you are. She's not big into social media or checking up on people.'

'I'm not famous,' protested Matthew.

'Have you ever Googled him?' Ernie asked Grace.

'Why would I? I'd heard of him before I met him at your parents' place. It's not like I live under a rock - I'm a fan of Lane and the work his group does.'

'So, you'd heard of him, and you like his work, but you're surprised that photographers might pop up from behind the bushes to snap his picture?' Ernie handed over his phone after typing in Matthew's name and selecting an image search. 'You didn't do this, though, did you? Have a look through those.'

'Don't.' Feeling embarrassed, Matthew reached to stop Ernie, but Grace was already scrolling through the images.

'The President's daughter?' She looked up at him, her eyebrows reaching for her hairline.

'We're just friends.'

She flicked through more photos, seeing him with politicians, movie stars, and royalty. Her first impression of him the night they met was not flattering, and perhaps that shaky start stopped her from going to the effort of finding out more about him. Most of the time she spent with him, he seemed like an unassuming horseman, but clearly there was more to this man. She wasn't sure that she liked seeing him as someone far removed from an ordinary outback man who enjoyed spending time with horses. The celebrity in the photos seemed different from the man she was beginning to know.

'You know all these people?' She turned the phone to show a photo of him with a group of A-list actors. They were standing around him as though they were his fans.

It was difficult to explain his friendships with the actors while Grace was blinded by their fame. 'I've worked with the horses on some of their movies, and we became friends. You're seeing them as their fame, but that's not really who they are. They're people like us who enjoy riding horses and who are trying to cope with what life throws at them.'

'They're not like us.' Grace's lips twisted to one side. 'At least, they're not like me. It looks like you run in their circles, though. Did you really date her?'

She indicated a photo of him kissing a megastar of the singing world.

'It's friendship. That's all.' He squirmed in discomfort. Life would be simpler without the internet exposing private moments and friendships. 'She had a problem with one of her horses. I helped her, and then we went to a few things together. As friends.'

Observing the devotion in the singer's eyes, Grace had her doubts, but she had no intention of arguing the point. She wasn't jealous. She absolutely was not, she told herself. It simply meant that she had to adjust her understanding of the man who seemed like the typical boy next door when he was someone who mixed in circles far beyond her reach.

'See?' Ernie took his phone back. 'Matthew is the sort of person who might have photographers hiding around corners, so reminding REE of possible witnesses might make them behave, assuming, that is, that they are involved in any of this. That,' he tilted his chin towards the road, 'could have been a genuine accident.'

'Maybe,' said Matthew, thinking of how many accidents had occurred involving people with connections to REE and Menningala Vaccines. 'I don't suppose there's any way of finding someone from Menningala who'd talk to us? A worker who handles the horses, or maybe a truck driver who knows about the comings and goings of horses?'

'I'll see what I can do.' Putting down his empty cup, Ernie sighed and rubbed a hand across his eyes. 'I'm trying not to think of Luis and Carolina, but I need to see their family. They'll appreciate this money. Thanks, Matthew. I'll add some to it and let them know about the Pilatos offer if you're sure it will eventuate.'

'It will,' he promised without reservation. Over the past year, Karen had made it clear to the group that she had funds set aside to help anyone they deemed in need. A struggling family losing two members because of crime in the horse industry fitted her parameters.

Matthew and Grace stayed in the house for the remainder of the day, going over documents that Joe emailed them. There were details about REE, Menningala, and some of the companies associated with them, along with estimates of the number of horses that went into the charity and the much smaller number in the riding centers and rescue paddocks. Joe included a diagram of relationships between various companies showing money moving back and forth between them and the charity.

His information didn't provide any hard evidence of corruption in the organizations since most of it showed acceptable, if expensive, costs. It was common for only five percent of the money flowing into a charity to go to those for whom it was intended, and REE seemed to stick to that figure.

They needed to find something so sensational it would ensure media exposure, police action, and justice for the people and horses that had died. Without evidence, supporters of the charity would claim they didn't care how much money was wasted as long as they saw some horses saved.

In the morning, after helping Ernie feed the horses, Grace leaned on the railed fence watching the two Australian men and the local riders exercise the showjumpers. Matthew rode a bay Warmblood mare, and though he joked around, she could see he rode as well as if not better than Ernie. Judging them from the side as they put their horses over a series of jumps, she decided that Matthew could have chosen a career in show jumping.

'Are you sure you don't want to compete on the weekend?' Ernie asked him as they rode back to Grace on a loose rein, their horses relaxed and happy. 'That mare can be a right cow to ride, but she was going sweet for you. Her owners would love to see her win, and I think you could make that happen.'

'I'm hoping we're heading back to Oz by this weekend,' said Matthew as he dismounted and began sliding his stirrups up. He stroked the mare's neck as he moved to her other side. 'She's good to ride and fairly flies over those jumps.'

'They looked great together, eh, Grace?' Ernie handed his reins to one of the grooms, who also took Matthew's mare. 'Do you think you could convince him to ride here for a season?'

'I don't think I could convince Matthew to do anything.' She watched him remove his helmet and shake out his hair. When he grinned at her, little butterflies of emotion moved in her stomach.

'That's where we differ,' Matthew teased, his eyes shining. 'I'm pretty sure you could convince me to do just about anything. I'm still making it up to you for having my foot jammed so far in my mouth the night we met that I put a dent in the back of my head.'

They looked at each other with humor about that night and the things said the next day. Ernie cocked an eyebrow at the glance that gave him an insight into his friends. He checked his watch and cleared his throat. 'You two need to get cleaned up and head over to talk to Image's owners. You'll like the area around La Castellana and Altamira. My main sponsor, Ricardo Vargas, has found a good property not far from the Scuderie del Caracas Country Club, and I'm hoping to move there next year.'

'This is a good setup, though.' Grace looked around at the stables, riding arenas, and horse pens crammed onto the small property.

'It is, but it's more up-market over that way – swimming pools in back yards sort of thing. Have a look at the country club while you're there, and you'll see what I mean.'

'Country club and swimming pools?' Grace asked. 'Somehow, that doesn't seem to fit in with the reputation of violence, crime, and poverty that we're told about when it comes to Caracas.'

'Sure, there are problems,' conceded Ernie as they headed back to his house, 'but there are two million people each day who *aren't* kidnapped or murdered in Caracas, so the odds are in our favor. Just take precautions – lock your car as soon as you get in, don't behave like wealthy tourists, don't be naïve, and don't get involved with gangs or the drug scene.'

Grace shook her head in mock sadness. 'And here I was thinking that joining a gang and buying cocaine was my entertainment for this afternoon.'

***

Dibby and Rev

Cattle trucks rumbled into the facility, and the first one backed up to a loading ramp. Rev and Dibby watched as men with stock whips opened the first pen of horses and drove them along a laneway. They shut them in a loading yard before forcing them up the ramp and onto the truck.

Their hooves rattled on the floor of the truck, and several horses called out in fear. Rev called back, his loud neigh offering comfort to the horses who heard him. He had no idea what this next leg of their journey would bring, except that he felt an impending sense of doom as hard-eyed men shouted and cracked whips. These were not people who cared about horses.

CHAPTER SIXTEEN

Horses change lives. It doesn't matter if you are young or old – they can lift your spirits, your soul, and your health. They can give children more confidence and increase their self-esteem. They can give you a reason to get up in the morning. If your soul is troubled, horses can provide peace and serenity. Horses can give us hope.

The Horses I Have Known by Lane Dimity p.46

The drive across the city took longer than expected because of frequent stops with traffic issues. There were several accidents, and the Bolivarian National Guard stopped them to check the vehicle registration, proof of insurance, and their passports.

It seemed a city of extremes with poverty and overcrowding set against the wealth of high-rise buildings and shops. Homeless people created a vertical village from an unfinished office tower while luxury cars passed, keeping their occupants away from the hardship around them.

As they passed a truck and car locked together after a collision at an intersection, Grace frowned. 'Maybe what happened yesterday was just one of those things. There are heaps of accidents on these roads.'

'A lot of drivers don't seem to be observing the road rules,' Matthew growled as he scanned the road for erratic driving.

Patting his arm placatingly, she adopted a soothing tone. 'You are doing a wonderful job behind the wheel. I wasn't game to drive when I visited.'

'Does that make me a bit of a hero?'

Grace snorted at the hope in his voice. 'A bit. A little bit. A very little bit. I mean, you're driving a car along a road; we're not talking saving babies from burning buildings.'

'I'd do that, though, if the opportunity arose.' His mouth twisted to the side as he replayed his words. 'Perhaps *opportunity* isn't the right word for that, though.'

'Maybe not, but I know what you mean. Watch out!'

Two children ran onto the road chasing a dog, and cars braked and swerved to avoid them. Matthew managed to dodge around pedestrians and other vehicles and, as he checked his side mirrors to make sure they were safe, he noticed a white delivery van with a crooked bumper two cars behind. He'd seen it fifteen minutes earlier, or one like it, before they pulled onto the Valle-Coche, the highway that took them north from Ernie's home.

'What are the chances two white delivery vans with crooked bumpers are in the city?'

'I'd say there's a good chance there are hundreds of them.'

'And what are the chances one was behind us near Ernie's place and a different one here as we weave through the suburbs?'

'Still pretty good, but I like your paranoia. Perhaps pull over and see what they do.'

With his eyes flicking back and forth between the road ahead and the side mirror, Matthew pulled over to the right and pretended to be looking at something on the other side of the road as he observed the van. The driver and a passenger, both dark-haired men in their thirties, appeared to be arguing about something. He felt a wave of relief wash over him. They hadn't been following them. They showed no sign of watching them.

As the van passed, the passenger turned and looked directly at Matthew. It was only for an instant, but the cold intensity of his eyes held a threat.

'That was creepy.' Grace felt like a field mouse in the sights of a hawk that swooped past and noted where she huddled. She checked that their doors were locked. 'They haven't stopped, though. Maybe he just hates tourists.'

'We'll tell ourselves that,' Matthew pulled back into the traffic, 'and hope the universe conforms to the way we want it.'

They continued to the country club and spent a few minutes admiring the expansive grounds used by golfers, horse riders, and others before driving a short distance to where Image and his owners lived. They planned to spend an hour with them before going to the REE riding center and keeping an appointment with a farmer who lived near the Menningala facility. According to Ernie's contacts, he had some information about horses coming and going past his farm.

After entering through the security gates of the private home, they saw a show jumping arena with stables to one side and a large Spanish villa on the other. Mature trees provided shade that spread across the courtyard where they parked.

'They fit everything into such a small area,' noted Grace. 'This can't be much more than half an acre.'

'It looks like an expensive suburb. Maybe a half-acre here is worth more than a hundred out in the wilds.'

'I see Image!' Grace bounced in her seat like an excited child as she pointed to a big bay horse working over jumps.

'He looks like he ended up in good hands,' said Matthew as he climbed out of the car. The young woman on the horse rode with kind hands and a beautiful seat.

A man with a broad smile on his handsome face strode towards them, his hand outstretched. He carried himself like Spanish royalty, and his brown eyes flashed with intelligence and humor. The Australians warmed to him immediately.

'Matthew. Grace. It is a pleasure to meet you.' He shook their hands. 'I am Alejandro Mendez Garcia, and that is my daughter Shay on Futuro Fuerte - the horse you call Image.'

'She rides well.' Matthew watched her send Image over one last jump before trotting towards them. 'Venezuela has some excellent riders ready to take on the world.'

Alejandro inclined his head at the compliment. 'She will be delighted to hear your opinion. She is a huge fan of yours, Matthew. And Lane, of course.'

'Lane deserves the devotion. I'm not so sure about myself.'

After being introduced to Shay, Grace checked the bay's brands against her photos of Image to confirm beyond doubt that this was the same horse. The brands, the W-shaped scar on his neck, three white spots on his hip, and his markings all assured her that he was the Australian horse.

'The lady who used to own him will be delighted to know he has such a wonderful home,' said Grace, patting Image's sleek neck.

'I love him so much.' Shay hugged him, her dark brown eyes gleaming with emotion. 'He may not get me all the way to the Olympics, but we are doing well in the junior competitions.'

'If you're interested,' Grace began writing in a small notepad she'd removed from her pocket, 'this is Sharyn's email address. She'll have lots of photos of him before he left Australia. I'm sure she'd enjoy hearing from you and learning what a great life he has here.'

Shay promised she would email Sharyn that afternoon.

'You have a lovely place here, Alejandro,' Grace smiled at him as Shay led the horse back to the stables.

He shrugged as he looked around. 'It is home. We have good neighbors. Crime is not high in our streets, but we do take precautions. Security fences, gates, cameras, dogs. My cousin who lives in Los Angeles has similar security, so this is not just a Caracas problem.'

'I don't even lock my house,' said Grace, 'in fact, I'm not even sure it can be locked. If I lived in the city, it would be different, though.'

'Is there much crime in Australian cities?'

'Let's just say I would lock my house in the city.'

Alejandro led them indoors, where he offered them coffee and *bien me sabe*, a layered coconut cream cake that Grace remembered fondly from her previous visit. The house's interior showcased a sense of Spain with terracotta tiles on the floor, white walls with splashes of bright color in the paintings, ornaments, and throw rugs, as well as arched doorways and windows.

Their small talk moved from crime rates and government reforms to the subject of REE horses once Shay arrived from the stables.

'Image ended up at a sale in Australia after Sharyn's parents sold him during the drought,' explained Grace, 'and the charity REE – Rescuing Equines Everywhere – bought him at a sale. They claim they didn't, but the auctioneer states they did. They fly suitable horses to their riding center here in Caracas, which could explain why he ended up here, but REE claim they never sell the horses that come into their care. Clearly, that isn't true since you purchased this one. If they do that with one horse, it makes us wonder how many others changed hands.'

'What is the point of that?' Alejandro's dark eyes puzzled over the scenario. 'It must cost them tens of thousands of dollars to fly a horse across the world. Why then sell him for less than a thousand? It is business madness.'

Matthew conceded it was a good point, and added, 'Unless you receive hundreds of millions of dollars in donations to save the horses, and you want to channel that money into, say, the transport company that flies the horses around and the feed company that is receiving money to feed a thousand horses when they only have to feed one hundred.'

'Ah, I see.' Alejandro nodded with dawning understanding. 'The horses are the means for people to make money. They will make more money if they don't keep the horses but continue to claim their expenses.'

'Exactly,' said Grace. 'We want evidence that proves they are misusing funds and misleading people. Your horse is one piece of evidence. If they sold one horse then denied ever having him, there may be more.'

'There are most definitely more.' Alejandro met his daughter's eyes, and she rose from the table. 'When we bought your Image, the vendors had forty other horses at the sale.'

Shay took a small printed catalog from a drawer in a small desk behind them and tossed it onto the table.

'Have a look at that,' she pointed at the booklet. 'The sellers were not called REE, but if they don't want people knowing they are selling their horses, that would be a smart move. There were close to two hundred horses there, and Toynac Farms, who sold my horse, had forty.'

'Toynac?' Matthew gazed at Grace as he wondered where he'd heard the name before. He pictured the web of connections he'd drawn using Joe's information about the companies associated with the charity. 'Isn't the advertising company that REE uses for their ads, promotions, signs, and printing called TOYNAC? The One You Need Advertising Company?'

Grace widened her eyes. 'What are the chances?'

Matthew flicked through the book, noting that names were written next to some of the horses. On the page where Lot 62, Unnamed Gelding, was listed, dozens of love hearts were drawn along with Spanish words for *love* and *adore*.

'I'll take a guess and say this is your horse,' he held up the page and smiled when Shay grinned at him.

'I fell in love with him the moment I saw him.'

'Yes, she did,' lamented her father. 'I was buying her the Warmblood of her dreams, and she preferred a cheap, unknown horse at the sales to the blue-blooded performance horse I found for her. Who will ever understand horse people?'

'You are glad this happened,' Shay laughed at his pretend sadness. 'My Futuro and I are winning. That expensive Warmblood developed navicular two months after his new owners had him and can't be ridden.'

'That is true.' Alejandro winked at Grace as though sharing secrets. 'Who would have thought a horse-mad daughter would *save* her father money when it came to buying the horse of her dreams?'

'Sometimes horses have a way of finding the place they're meant to be.' Grace thought of the hundreds of dead horses that had possibly gone through REE and Menningala and added, 'And sometimes not.'

Closing the catalog, Matthew asked, 'Do you know anyone who

bought other Toynac Farm horses?'

'Several,' replied Alejandro. 'Shay's riding instructor learned of the horses and took a few of her pupils and their families to the sale. We did not know they came from Australia, though. The word was that they came from Brazil, and their owner did not want to sell them within his country. Good horses being sold cheaply – we did not ask too many questions.'

'I have photos of many of them.' Shay scrolled through the photos on her phone until she came to an album of horses at the sale. She handed the phone to Matthew. 'I took photos of most of them to send to friends to see if they wanted to buy any.'

'I've done the same thing at horse sales.' Matthew smiled as he took the phone.

The horses were a mix of breeds but all good working types. Where there were clear views of shoulders, he enlarged the photo to look for brands. Any brands he found, he showed to Grace to ask if she recognized them.

'That one looks like a Queensland brand.' Grace tapped the screen. 'Three letters over eighteen over six on the near shoulder. The eighteenth horse born on that property in either 2006 or 2016. It could be Thoroughbred or could be any other breed that brands that way. Stations will brand unregistered horses like this for identification.'

Matthew moved through another few photos before Grace laid a hand on his arm to stop him.

'I know that brand. That's a Thoroughbred stud out Toowoomba way. I worked there one holiday.' A touch of excitement entered her voice as she realized what that meant. 'I can look that horse up with the ASB brand search.'

Taking out her phone, she logged into The Australian Stud Book. 'I pay my membership fee because I have to look up Thoroughbred brands all the time. Well, not so much these past few years with REE taking most of the retired racehorses, but it still comes in handy. Here he is. Bay gelding, born 2015.'

The horse's pedigree and race record were there, along with his markings. There was no doubt this Queensland racehorse ended up in a sale yard in Venezuela.

Returning to the photo of the first brand that caught her attention, she entered the details into the brand search and discovered he was a racehorse bred near Brisbane in 2016.

'Can you send us these photos?' Matthew looked at Shay, who nodded eagerly. 'We should be able find the people in Australia who sold or gave these horses to REE with the understanding they'd be taken care of for the rest of their lives, not shipped to another country and sold off. It will be interesting to find if REE still has these horses on their books as being fed and cared for at two hundred dollars a week each.'

'They have riding facilities in other countries,' Grace switched to Googling the REE program for helping children around the world. She thought that it sounded like a worthy cause, and it certainly hauled in donations. 'Myanmar, Cameroon, Senegal, and others. I wonder how many horses are sent to these places and are then sold.'

'Or killed and dumped.'

'That, too.'

'Killed?' Alejandro asked, curious about what they meant.

Matthew explained about the dead horses in Australia, the ones discovered outside Caracas, and the possible link to the charity and the pharmaceutical company.

'And the ones found here had been autopsied?' Alejandro asked, his expression thoughtful.

'It might make the vaccine development easier if Menningala have an endless supply of horses for testing. Instead of being accountable for the welfare of a limited number of horses, they can accelerate testing and kill the horses to look for unwanted side-effects – or desired ones. It does mean they have to hide the bodies so the public doesn't find out what they're doing.'

'It is difficult to imagine all the people involved keeping quiet about it.'

'Which is why,' said Matthew, 'we think several people have been murdered and others are missing.'

'Are you both in danger?'

'Probably.' Grace put her phone down and smiled at the concern on Alejandro's face. His worry seemed genuine. 'We want to stop this before more people and horses lose their lives, and if they know what we're doing, they have a strong reason to stop us.'

Looking up from her phone, Shay asked, 'What happens to all the unwanted horses in Australia if this charity is not taking them?'

'Small rescues like mine save some. A lot go to pet food.'

'So, my horse could have ended up as pet food if this charity had not brought him here?'

The question caused both Australians to stop and think. Image was undoubtedly better off with Shay than fed to cats and dogs, even if REE were misleading their supporters. If their actions stopped the massive rescue business, would they be condemning more horses to death?

'Perhaps,' Matthew tapped his fingers on the table as he imagined the fate of tens of thousands of horses that REE saved from the meat trade. 'Or perhaps he might have ended up in Menningala being filled with drugs and vaccines, then killed and dumped. We still don't know how many have met that fate, or even if that's what happened. We don't know how many are abandoned on farms, but there's at least one case of starving horses linked to REE.'

'If there is anything I can do, please let me know.' Alejandro handed them each a business card. 'If you run into trouble, I may in a position to help, so do not hesitate to call. Now, if you'll excuse me, I have an appointment to meet.'

Both Matthew and Grace stood to leave.

Alejandro waved his hands at them. 'Please stay. If you have time, Shay can show you around the stables. I'm sure she'd like to spend as much time with you as possible while - perhaps take some photos with you.'

'If that would be OK?' Shay looked at the Australians, hoping they would agree.

'We have an hour before we're due at REE,' Matthew told her, allaying her fears, 'and they're only fifteen minutes from here, so photos and stables sound good to me.'

Grace agreed. She could see the hero worship in Shay's eyes every time she looked at Matthew. Selfies with him would be the highlight of her week.

'I wish you luck with your endeavors.' Alejandro shook hands with both of them. 'I will be keen to learn the outcome of all of this. Though I have to say, for the horses, it seems it may be a case of they are damned if you stop REE, and damned if you don't.'

Grace nodded her head sadly, knowing what he meant. Without REE, the horses that the smaller rescues couldn't save would end up as meat. With REE, some had good lives, while too many stood at risk of something worse than a humane death in a killing pen.

'Would you like to see our stables?' Shay asked, plaiting her hands together nervously. She was excited to have Matthew visit and worried she would do something to make a fool of herself. 'We built them when we moved here. There's even a small apartment if you would like to stay.'

'How kind of you,' Grace smiled at her, hoping to ease her nerves. 'I'd love to see your stables. How about you, Matthew?'

'Sounds good to me.'

They followed Shay outside, and she chattered non-stop about her plans with the horse-formerly-known-as-Image, her instructor, and her friends.

'My best friend has a Trakehner, and she's moving from jumping to dressage. She stays here sometimes. She'll be so jealous that you visited. She has posters of Lane all over her bedroom wall.'

'Does that make you feel inadequate?' Grace teased Matthew.

He shook his head, his eyes gleaming. 'I have posters of Lane on my bedroom wall, too.'

Grace was reasonably sure he was making that up, but his smile left her wondering.

'We have pictures of you, too,' Shay rushed her words, worried that she'd offended him with the detail about Lane's posters. 'It's just that there seem to be more of Lane.'

'As there should be,' said Matthew affably. 'My sister takes most of the photos, and she'd much rather spend her photographic talents on Lane than me.'

The stables and accommodation were spacious and well-appointed - a stark contrast to the poverty they'd seen elsewhere in Caracas. Security cameras watched over every angle, and razor wire topped the perimeter fence, reminding the Australians of the crime that plagued the city.

Taking out her phone, Shay clicked open a screen that showed images from the cameras. She held it up to show her visitors. 'Dad works in security, so we have brilliant systems here. He says the criminals will choose easier targets than us, and he's been right so far.'

Grace marveled at how different Shay's life was to hers in a valley where few people bothered to lock their homes. 'Is it hard living with the constant threat of crime?'

'It's not as bad as the media says. They focus on the murders and drugs, but most of my friends and their families do not see that. I think you are more likely to be a victim if you mix in the circles where crime takes place, if that makes sense.'

The visitors nodded, and Shay continued. 'I know I am lucky. We have money, so we don't need to steal or deal in drugs, but many in this city find it hard to put the next meal on the table. When there are not enough jobs and people are desperate to stay alive, sometimes crime seems the only way. I think you'll find that the REE riding center helps many young people escape a life of crime.'

After plenty of photos and promises to stay in contact, they left Shay and took the most direct route to the REE facility. Matthew remained on the lookout for the white van with the crooked bumper, but there was no sign of any vehicle following them.

***

Dibby and Rev

Rev closed his eyes to shut out the sight of the trucks. He didn't want to see the scared horses around him or smell their fear.

A scene played in his memory of a time when he felt safe and happy. He stood with Dibby under a tree on a warm day. The breeze stirred the eucalypt leaves above, and he could smell summer in the air. Mel's voice called to them, and they looked up to see her approaching across the dry grass. She smiled and shook a bucket. Even without the sound of the rattling, they would have trotted over to see her. They always enjoyed her company.

Rev reached her first, and she offered him the bucket. When he had a mouthful, Mel dipped the bucket away from his mouth and held it out to Dibby. For several minutes the bucket went back and forth as they shared the treat.

Mel waved the flies from their eyes as they ate. Her fingers traced lines around their face when she wasn't hunting the flies. Happiness lived in that moment.

Opening his eyes, Rev returned to the stress and fear of starting another journey on a truck without Mel to protect him.

CHAPTER SEVENTEEN

Horses have great power to help a child grow into their dreams. If you have the opportunity to watch a child on the back of a horse, over time you can see them change from a tiny, scared human to a mighty warrior who can conquer the world because of that horse. Growing up is better with a horse that helps you feel significant, worthwhile, and needed.

'Ride with Heart' by Lane Dimity, p. 14

The REE Riding Center

Grace widened her eyes when they stopped outside an equestrian center with enormous white gates and two gold-on-black signs proclaiming *Rescuing Equines Everywhere* and *An Equine Learning and Wellness Center for Children.* 'That is impressive. I could feed all my horses for a year for the cost of these gates.'

A security guard took their details and allowed them in. They could see several large barns built to the highest standards, outdoor arenas, cottages, and a large indoor riding arena. No expense was spared in making the facility first-class for horses and people.

'They have a restaurant at the end of the indoor arena!' Grace gaped at the glass windows and people dining at tables. 'And look at the horse trucks!'

Four large horse trucks with living quarters were parked side by side next to one of the barns. There were six other vehicles in sight – all brand-new four-wheel-drives with REE logos on their doors.

'There must be more than a million dollars in the trucks alone.' Matthew noticed a group of children entering one of the outdoor arenas leading horses. 'And right on cue, it looks like we are going to see what they do with the youngsters.'

A thirty-something man in khaki trousers and a white shirt approached them as they stepped out of their car. He was as tall as Matthew and walked with the effortless grace of a cat. As he passed several stable doors, horses stretched their noses out expectantly, and he caressed each one as he walked, smiling and talking to them. The horses liked him, and he couldn't walk past without acknowledging them with care – which revealed a lot about his character, thought Matthew. When he passed the last stable, he flashed a perfect smile at his visitors.

'Grace and Matthew?' His accent marked him as Australian.

'That's us,' replied Grace.

'I'm Darby,' he shook their hands and then waved in an expansive movement at the buildings and activities around them, 'and this is our Caracas Wellness Center. I've been instructed to show you around and answer any questions you may have.'

'Let's start with the children in the arena,' suggested Matthew. 'I'm curious to know a bit about them and what they're doing.'

'Of course.' Darby inclined his head and motioned for them to walk with him. There was a lush green lawn between the car park and the arena, something they hadn't seen much of so far in the dry region around Caracas. 'We have thirty groups of young horse people who come here, plus many more individuals who haven't been assigned a group yet. Most groups have ten children in them plus two or more instructors. We try to have children of equal ability together to make the lessons easier.'

They reached the white rails around the arena and leaned on them, observing the lesson. Each child wore riding clothes, a helmet, and boots, and their horses ranged in size from ponies through to Thoroughbreds.

'How do they go with the ex-racehorses?' Matthew watched a child of about eight nearly get pulled off his feet as his horse tossed its head in the air. He didn't think pairing such a young child with a Thoroughbred was a good idea.

'Better than you'd imagine. Naturally, the horses have been assessed before they enter the riding program. If they are unsuitable, there are retirement farms in Australia and other countries, which is important when it's time to retire any of these horses. Watch young Carlos once he's on that horse. His size is a disadvantage on the ground, but jockeys rode the racehorses, and many of them are quite small.'

'And quite strong,' added Grace. 'These kids wouldn't have a fraction of the strength of a trained jockey.'

'Good point,' Darby shone his Hollywood smile on her and pushed a stray lock of brown hair off his forehead, 'which is why we assess the horses so carefully. These all have an aptitude for learning and are very tolerant of beginners. One of our beliefs is that students learn more skills with horses that require them to think. If the horses were all old plodders that didn't do anything wrong, then the students don't extend themselves; they just go along for the ride. Carlos has been handling that horse for three months now, and he's improved beyond sight because the horse tests him and pushes his limits.'

There was good sense in what he said, though they were reluctant to admit it. They arrived with a negative mindset about REE and wanted to find evidence that they were right, not indications that they could be wrong.

Grace watched the children tighten the girths, lead the horses around, and then mount. They seemed competent. 'What do their families pay for all this?'

'Nothing. Since most come from low-income families, we provide all their clothing and equipment, so there is no competition between the children about who has the best or the most. The charity provides everything.'

'What happens once the children finish the program?' asked Matthew.

'They have better lives than they would without the program. Part of our work here involves writing exercises, reading, and presentations by the children. It is an excellent addition to their schooling and helps them reach higher than they might otherwise aim. We find their school results improve, the crime level drops or disappears, and they have a much better future than they could have dreamed of before working with the horses. Some have gone on to employment in horse establishments like racing or jumping stables. Some have gone into trades; others are going to university – which is paid for by the charity. We take care of our riders after they've finished here.'

If all of that was true, then it was worth supporting, thought Matthew. As they walked their mounts around the instructors, the expressions on the children's faces told him that they loved being with the horses. Some had the pinched faces of children who missed out on nutrition at a young age, but they smiled, laughed, listened, and, as they moved the horses into a trot, they handled the horses well.

'I don't want to be cynical,' said Grace, 'but do you have proof of all that? With no offense intended, but it's easy to say these things whether or not they are true. I have an inbuilt distrust of charities, so I like to make sure they are doing everything they say before I support them.'

The smile Darby gave her hinted that he knew she wasn't going to support them. She wondered how much he knew about them. Had he bought any of Ernie's cover story, or had the heads of REE told him to be wary of two visiting Australians?

'I understand it does seem too good to be true, and, yes, we do have plenty of proof to show that it happens. We provide it to the media when they visit, and they are welcome to investigate further. The easiest way to show it's all true, though, is to ask the children. I could doctor the paperwork to make it look like we support university students, but if you ask the children, you'll see that their answers are honest and unscripted.'

It seemed a reasonable suggestion. Darby called over a couple of the young riders, introduced them as Angela and JJ, and invited the visitors to ask them questions.

'What a lovely horse,' Grace patted the bay with the brand of a horse bred at a well-known Australian Thoroughbred stud. 'What do you call this one, Angela?

'He is called Storm. He's my favorite horse.' Angela grinned, her dark eyes shining with love for Storm.

'So, you like coming here and riding the horses?' asked Matthew.

Angela's expression darkened with indignation. 'We do not just *ride* them. We learn about them, groom them, clean their stalls, and do classes as well. Anyone can ride a horse. We become horse people.'

'That is wonderful to hear,' Grace smiled at Angela's words. 'And are you the only one in the family who learns here?'

'My older brother Raoul also learned here. He only has one arm, and he rode and worked. He is at university now.' Her face glowed with pride at her brother's achievement. 'REE pay for that. I am studying hard as I want to become a vet, and they will pay for my studies if I keep trying hard.'

Her words came without hesitation. She was telling the truth.

'What about you and your horse, JJ?' Matthew stroked the face of the solidly built brown horse.

'He's called Kangaroo,' JJ grinned widely and flopped down on his neck to hug the horse. 'When I was lucky enough to win a place here, Kangaroo changed my life. He didn't like many people, but he loves me. I am going to become a horse trainer. And a trick rider. Kangaroo and I are learning tricks. Darby knows people in the circus, and they said I could get a job with them.'

'Really?' Matthew smiled at Darby. This was something easy to check. 'I've worked in plenty of circuses myself. Which ones do you know?'

Darby's level of enthusiasm rose by several notches as he began discussing the circuses where he'd worked. His information was correct, and Matthew realized he was telling the truth when he claimed he could help the riders find work there when they were old enough. It was one more legitimate point about this facility and its people.

Grace had one more question before the children returned to their lesson. 'If someone didn't like what REE was doing with these horses, what would you say to them, Angela?'

The rider's eyes flared with emotions. 'I would tell them that these horses save our lives in many ways, and then they make our lives. These are horses that people in your country wanted to throw away. They bred them, some of them they raced, and then they threw them away like rubbish. But these horses are jewels, not rubbish. They come here, and they show us their value. We learn that if throw-away horses are so valuable, then we must be more so. You don't discard horses like that, and you don't throw away children like us – we are important. REE makes that happen when others treat these horses and us like we are garbage.'

The passion in her speech left Matthew and Grace without words. They had been so intent on finding the evil in the horse charity that they forgot that few people or organizations are all bad. The aspects that Angela highlighted were a revelation to them.

When a few more riders came over to talk, it became clear that riding and working with the horses significantly improved their quality of life. They spoke of others who had gone onto university and jobs because of their time at the center. Some of the children had physical or mental challenges to work with, and the charity made a massive difference to their lives.

After the group finished their lesson, the next group came in with their horses. They were more advanced and performed some impressive drills at the trot and canter. Again, when the riders had the opportunity to speak to Matthew and Grace, they told stories that showed the charity turned their lives around and, in many cases, the lives of their families.

'Horse riding can be seen as a hobby of the wealthy,' explained Darby as he showed them through a gallery at the end of the indoor arena. 'When someone struggles to put food on the table and shoes on their children's feet, they can't afford a horse or riding lessons. Those that can afford them are already so far ahead in the race we call life that working with the horses only moves them further ahead. By giving these children the chance to experience horses – to ride them, learn, read, and write about them, and know the feeling of satisfaction that comes from working in harmony with such a beautiful animal – we give them the chance to improve their lives. It gives them skills and confidence previously denied, and that propels them into more successful lives.'

'I can't argue with that.' Matthew looked at the framed newspaper clippings about the success of riders who had gone through the riding center. It did a remarkable job of helping children in many ways. Darby's words echoed opinions that Lane often shared, particularly about how those who already had an advantage in life with money and education widened the gap between them and the less fortunate once they started riding horses.

The riding center embodied many of their beliefs, and he assumed the ones in other countries were similar. Perhaps they were the diamond rings on the hands of the monster called REE. What would happen to these children and horses if they destroyed the monster? These children could lose something wonderful if he stopped REE, but what of the lives of those horses that were killed and dumped? Perhaps some would have ended up as pet food if they didn't belong to the charity, but others would still be alive.

Matthew rubbed a hand across his eyes as he struggled with the consequences of their actions. If they walked away from REE, these children would go on learning. If they stopped REE from their fraudulent dealings with horses, they could harm these children and, perhaps, only condemn the horses to a different death.

Looking through the glass, Matthew watched the lessons taking place in the indoor arena. At one end, ten children were learning how to lead horses. At the other, the group was working horses over small obstacles at a trot and canter.

'Could we be wrong about REE?' Grace murmured at his shoulder. 'This place is genuinely amazing. These kids – look at them. It's giving them the chance to grab a dream that they never knew existed. And those newspaper clippings – there are stories about students from here who've gone on to study medicine, education, mining, and vet science. It does so much good.'

'I know.' Matthew's brows dipped in a frown. 'Can an organization capable of doing so much good also be responsible for murder and destroying hundreds or even thousands of horses?'

'Perhaps this is the reminder that nothing and no one is all good or all evil. Serial killers often have families they love and protect. We're only seeing one face of REE here.'

'And it's a beauty, isn't it?' Matthew watched in admiration as a pint-sized child cantered a Thoroughbred over jumps, handling the horse with the expertise of someone who'd been born to the saddle. He had seen some of the poverty around Caracas and knew what this opportunity meant for the children.

'This is the paddock where we retire our horses once they finish here,' said Darby, indicating a series of framed photos on the wall showing expansive pastures with scores of horses grazing. 'If for any reason a horse isn't suitable or has lameness or something else that prevents it from being used here, we ensure they all have a quality retirement.'

'Do you have any figures on how many horses have come through here?' Matthew looked at the photos and wondered if they were REE horses. It was easy to take pictures of horses in fields and claim they belonged to the rescue.

'That's not my department,' Darby smiled disarmingly at them. 'I know we currently have around one hundred here, and we have another few hundred that we use on rotation so that all horses have several months holiday a year. Everyone I know within the organization is dedicated to the welfare of the horses and the chance it offers these children.'

'Do you know much about what happens in Australia?' Matthew looked him in the eyes, trying to find a hint of deceit, but everything in the young man's expression told of honesty and compassion.

'They told me why you are here,' Darby's voice became grave. 'I know you are trying to discredit the charity or find something criminal. I don't know what happens before the horses come here or before the money arrives to pay the bills, but I know that this is one of the best charity programs I've ever seen. I know that in Caracas alone, we've turned around the lives of hundreds of children and given them hope, dreams, and a future. The same results occur in Myanmar and the other centers because I speak to the managers – they are good people who genuinely care about horses and the children. I can't speak for how the charity gets the money and horses, but here, where I stand, they are doing something incredible.'

The words came from his heart, and they had no reason to doubt him. He claimed he didn't know about the rest of the organization, only what he saw in Caracas. The horses liked Darby, and they seemed to be a good judge of character. There was something likable about the quick-to-smile man who was passionate about helping the young riders.

They spent another half-hour viewing the barns and meeting more of the children. As they drove away, they remained silent for several minutes, digesting what they'd learned. They could understand why REE drew in the big donations – the positive results at the riding center changed lives, and, after seeing it, they wanted to donate as well.

'Could the problem lie with Menningala?' asked Grace, searching for a way to align what they saw at the riding center with what they thought was happening to the REE horses that didn't make it to the centers. 'Perhaps they take horses under false pretenses. Could they have a different company that takes the horses from REE, claiming that they are agisting them on properties and taking care of them? Perhaps REE believe the horses are being cared for and pay this shadow company while it is passing them on to Menningala and killing the excess. Is that possible?'

'Anything's possible.' Matthew felt he had to qualify his words. 'Well, not anything – it's not run by aliens, and the horses aren't flying themselves around the world, but maybe REE isn't the evil entity we were imagining. If it is making a lot of people wealthy from the donations, it can do that without breaking any laws – a lot of charities do that.'

'It's not right.'

'No, but it's not illegal if they are paying for things like transport, horse feed, and advertising, even if it's all at inflated prices.'

'They're selling horses they pledged to care for.'

'Someone is. Maybe there's more to it. I just know that whatever is going on back there,' he waved a finger over his shoulder, 'it is so good that I'm hoping it's not REE who are the bad guys in this. Maybe they just threw around their money too easily and thought they were paying someone to look after the horses.'

With an eye on the vehicles around them, Matthew drove east on the Troncal 9 towards the Menningala laboratories. He was sure no one followed, but he continued to check. The crowded urbanization and industrial estates gave way to treed hillsides, and they turned off the highway to drive between small farms.

Grace examined her phone. 'According to my map, Menningala is at the end of this road up in the hills.'

'We might get there tomorrow. Or not. The place we're looking for should be right about,' he hesitated as he looked at the driveways, 'here.'

The guidance announced they'd arrived at their destination.

A modest stone house crowded by six small sheds hid behind a flush of fruit trees. Most of the other homes they'd passed were set well back from the road, but this stood close to the passing traffic. Two lean, tan dogs ran the fence as they slowed, barking loudly. If the occupants were at home, no one would pass along the road without them knowing.

Eriko Marco Rangel grew small crops on his land. Small of stature and with his face darkened by decades in the sun, he looked every bit the struggling farmer who worked long hours to make ends meet. His son, a truck driver, was dating one of the grooms at Ernie's stables, and he told Ernie that his father often complained about the horse trucks going in and out of Menningala.

'There are supposed to be strict bio-security measures in place,' Eriko complained in Spanish as the three of them stood on the front patio of his home. 'We all have animals here. They are handling dangerous viruses and diseases - animals should not be going in or out of that place.'

'But they are?' prompted Matthew.

'Always at night. Late or after midnight. I have counted four trucks in one night, taking horses away from there. They drove without lights. They did not want people to know what they were doing. I know they are meant to dispose of any animals on site. They have incinerators for that job. There should never be live animals leaving, but every few weeks, they come and go. It is madness.'

'Have you reported it to the authorities?' Matthew asked after translating Eriko's words to Grace

The older man made a sound that was halfway between a spit and a scoff. 'We don't do that here. If a big company is doing something illegal, they also pay authorities to turn a blind eye. And who would be more important? An unknown farmer who grows vegetables or a big company that can splash money around? I am not a stupid man. I know what happens to little people who try to cause problems for those with power.'

Grace listened to Matthew's translation and nodded with understanding. She knew that the authorities were trying to deal with corruption, but there were always individuals who could be bought.

'Ask him if he saw the animals on the trucks – is he sure they were horses?'

'Yes. All horses.' Eriko stated adamantly. 'Sometimes I stand under the orange trees where they can't see me and watch them go past. Trucks with their lights off, loaded with horses. Not always alive, either.'

That caught Matthew's attention, and he asked for more details.

Eriko produced a grubby notebook from his pocket and showed Matthew numbers scribbled down on some pages. 'This shows the times and dates of trucks I saw. I'm not always awake for them, but the dogs bark, you know? They bark and wake me. From under the orange tree, the city lights are on the other side of the trucks, so I can see the shapes of the animals. Always live horses go in. Mostly live horses come out, but here, here, and here,' he stabbed a finger at three underlined figures, 'the horses in every truck were lying down on top of each other. They were dead. They sent dead horses out of a factory that deals with deadly viruses. How is that right? But who can I tell? My son assures me I can trust you, but I must not mention this to anyone else. Anyone at all.'

'Has anyone else asked?' Matthew scanned the figures with interest.

'Someone from that factory comes along this road every few months talking to all of us who live here. They ask if we have any concerns and if we've seen anything we want to ask about. I know what that means. If anyone has a concern or asks about the horses coming and going, that person will disappear. To them, their money is more important than our lives. So, I say that I wouldn't even know the place was there and that I haven't thought of it since they last visited. I tell them my hearing isn't good and my eyesight is worse. Over my life, I have learned that the chicken should not attract the attention of the fox.'

Eriko allowed Matthew to take a photo of his notes after eliciting a promise that no one identified him as the writer. After admiring his fruit trees, chickens, and vegetable gardens, they headed back onto one of the major roads that cut across the city. As they drove, they went over all they'd learned that day, though most of it prompted more questions rather than supplied answers.

When they turned off the major east-west highway to head south to Ernie's, Matthew paused and flicked his eyes back and forth between the road ahead and the rear-view mirror.

Grace noticed his hands clenching the steering wheel. 'What is it?'

'That van is a few cars behind. I can't see the license plate, but I'm sure it's the same one.'

'That is beyond coincidence, then.' Grace tried to sound cheerful, but the thought of the murders associated with this web of crime flattened her voice. 'Are we going straight back to Ernie's place?'

'Maybe. Can you give him a call and see if the Pilatos security team has arrived yet? I don't want to take whoever that is to Ernie's place if there isn't someone to deal with them.'

For several minutes, Grace talked to Ernie, explaining that they believed someone was following them.

'He said to go straight there.' She put her phone down and looked at Matthew's profile, taking in the grim set to his mouth. 'The Pilatos crew aren't there yet, but he's getting the Vargas security people to prepare for trouble. Two of them are taking Carmen home to her father's place so she's not there, and they're organizing more security for us.'

'I don't want to bring trouble to Ernie,' Matthew shook his head. Glancing in the side mirror, he saw the van poking out from behind some cars so the driver could keep an eye on them.

'We don't have much choice. We need to get someplace safe.'

'Maybe it's not the same van.' Even as he said the words, he knew they weren't true. The driver was no longer following at a distance; he was getting closer.

The afternoon traffic was slow with the busy roads and the haphazard approach to road rules. Matthew tried to put distance between them by swerving between other vehicles, but the van followed, ducking and diving between the traffic. They were no longer making any attempt to remain discreet, and Matthew guessed they intended to attack.

'Hang on,' Matthew warned Grace as he veered left at red lights, forcing his way into the flow of traffic. A loud bang behind marked the entry of the van into the traffic. It barrelled into a small car, but instead of stopping, it accelerated and closed the gap.

While he threw the car left and right to weave a path through the traffic, Grace made another phone call to Ernie to give him the details of the van. She fumbled in her handbag for the apple-peeling knife she had picked up from Ernie's kitchen and held it in her hand as she made a call to Alejandro. She wasn't sure why she wanted to speak to him, perhaps because he seemed genuine when he offered to help, plus Shay mentioned he worked in security, and she hoped that meant more than being a salesman for security cameras.

When he answered the phone, he sounded impatient. The voices in the background indicated that he was in a meeting. When Grace explained their predicament, he became businesslike and reassuring, taking the description of the van and telling her to leave her phone on no matter what. He snapped some orders to the people with him then returned his attention to Grace, telling her to lock her phone so that it looked like it was off.

'If they catch you, they will most likely take you alive,' he told her in clipped tones. 'Until they break or discard your phone, I'll need you to keep up a running commentary about what you see or hear, about turns left or right so that we can pinpoint your location. Do you understand?'

'Yes. You sound like you've experienced this before.'

'The company I work for specializes in finding kidnap victims, negotiating, and neutralizing situations. I am not a field operative – I handle the legalities of what we do, but I am familiar with procedures. Do not panic, do not become confrontational, and assume they are not working alone. If you can see that van, there will be a backup vehicle somewhere behind them. If you manage to escape from the first line of attack, there will be a second line in the background to get you.'

Grace grunted as the van slammed into the rear of their car.

'Sorry, sorry,' Matthew muttered as the car went into a spin. He reached out a hand to protect Grace, who struggled to keep the phone to her ear. Picking his moment, Matthew accelerated out of the rotation and sped between the lines of cars.

'Conceal your phone, Grace,' Alejandro ordered. 'Can you hear me?'

'Yes.' She gasped as the van struck them again. This time, Matthew managed to avoid losing control. 'I can hear you. They are ramming us with their van.'

'That is a good thing. If they wanted you dead, they would have shot you already. They want you alive, probably for ransom. When they catch you, I want you to put your phone in the pocket of your jeans or inside your bra. They will find it eventually, but they will be focused on getting you into the van and won't worry about it straight away. Do you understand?'

Screeching sounds drowned out her words as the gap between the lines of traffic became too narrow, and their car scraped against the vehicles either side

'I understand,' she repeated when the screams of metal-on-metal ended. 'I'll keep my phone on, and you will hear what they're saying.'

'Correct. If they get you, I want you to keep talking. Where are you now? We have a car with four men leaving in a few minutes. I'll relay your location.'

Grace named a street they passed and read some advertising signs.

'Good. I know where you are. If our men reach you, their names are…' He stopped and spoke to someone in the background. 'The names they will be using are Fred, Barney, Bam, and Slate.'

'The Flintstones?' Despite the danger of their situation, Grace snorted a laugh and covered her mouth to prevent any further odd sounds from emerging.

'You are correct.' There was no humor in Alejandro's voice, only a calm intensity as he explained the reason behind the names. 'You will easily remember these names. No one else in Caracas will be using them.'

'That makes sense.' Grace braced as the car lurched sideways, changing lanes and avoiding some cyclists. If four men introduced themselves with those names, she would know they were Alejandro's men.

'I will contact the police,' Alejandro continued. 'I know who can be trusted.'

'Tell him about the Pilatos team,' muttered Matthew as he fought the steering wheel to dive through gaps between cars.

'There are some people from the company Pilatos. They are coming to help us.'

'Pilatos Industries? I know of them. I will get someone to contact them.'

'Hang on!' Matthew yelled as the traffic in front came to a halt.

Without enough room to fit between the vehicles, he shoved the brake pedal to the floor. Blocked by trucks, he turned the car and bounced off the edge of the road onto the dirt. This time, when the van hit them from behind, their tires slewed on the gravel, sending the car skidding sideways. A cloud of dust spewed out from the tires as they slid across the dirt and careered into a billboard advertising beer. The sign shuddered, and the car came to a stop against its metal legs. Before Matthew could drive forward, the van drove into the rear door, pinning the car against the sign. There was no escape.

As two men with handguns approached, Grace slipped the phone inside her bra and raised her hands to show they were empty. Matthew marveled at her calmness and apologized for getting them into this situation.

'I'm having an adventure,' she spoke quietly as the gunmen waved their weapons about and shouted in Spanish. They didn't seem inclined to shoot, so she decided that was something positive. 'Nothing like this happens at Gatton.'

Matthew flashed her a smile as he raised his hands. 'We're going to be alright.' His words were more positive than his feelings about the situation.

'If we're not,' she gave him a dry look, 'I'm going to leave a particularly nasty review of Caracas on TripAdvisor.'

***

Dibby and Rev

As each truck filled with horses, another took its place at the loading ramp. The full trucks pulled away and parked, waiting until all were loaded so they could travel together.

The cracking of whips and yelling continued as men chased horses from their pens, along the laneways, and onto the loading ramp. Fear filled the air as the animals worried about what was happening.

When Rev's gate opened, he looked around for an escape, but there was none. He knew going on those trucks was dangerous, and he wanted a way out. A whip cracked across his face forcing him to go out the gate and along the narrow lane between pens.

Dibby and Dusty followed closely, keeping their noses near his flank as the dust rose from their hooves. They needed the security of being close to Rev.

They climbed the loading ramp single file, and once Rev's tail was in, the sliding gate slammed shut, locking Dibby and Dusty out. Rev's truck drove away, and Dibby screamed for his friend. Dusty nudged his tail to tell him he was still there, but Dibby needed his best friend, his protector, his brother. He called out in terror of losing Rev; his *Where are you?* whinny ringing across the quarantine yards.

From the other side of the parking bay, Rev returned his call. He tried to sound reassuring with his, *I hear you, and I'm over here* neigh.

The next truck reversed onto the loading ramp, the sliding gates opened, and the whips forced the horses forward. Dibby pushed forward in the hope he could reach his friend.

CHAPTER EIGHTEEN

Maintaining calmness at your core is soothing to horses. They are drawn to calmness while they fear or are confused by too much noise, movement, and expression. With a nervous or frightened horse, keep your arms and hands still, keep your movements slow, quiet your voice, and keep calmness at your core because the horse will see that as strength and leadership. No matter what life throws at you, when you are with your horse you should feel like the calm eye at the center of the storm.

'Horses, Hope, and Hearts' by Lane Dimity, p. 156.

The Calm Eye

'Is it strange that our friends are barely communicating with us?' Karen sat on a rock next to Lane on the hills overlooking the Ellamanga homestead.

She leaned back to rest her weight on her arms and drank in the outback sunshine that made everything seem brighter than anywhere else in the world. Below them, the vast plains of Ellamanga stretched in a sea of green to the horizon. On her previous visits, the station had been dry and dusty. The lush pastures dotted with wildflowers lent it an air of magic.

They are giving us some quiet time together. Much needed quiet time, he signed, his eyes creasing as a smile lit his face. *They want us to think that no news is good news.*

'But it's not, is it? No news means they are finding things out, but they don't want to bother us.'

And that's a problem because? Lane raised his brows to punctuate the question.

'Because I'm a control freak, and I want to know what's going on.'

Karen chuckled at his mock amazement about her admission. 'I've never hidden the fact that I like being in control of things and I want to know what is going on out there. What are they learning? Are they safe? Are we right to question what is happening?'

So many questions. His smile softened any criticism. *They can function without us – they're big kids now.*

'I'd thump you if I wasn't enjoying this sun so much. Aren't you worried at all?'

I'm worried, but I put it to the side. Worrying won't change anything for them, but it will make our time less enjoyable.

'You are irritatingly wise.'

Is wisdom an irritation?

'It is when you're right, and I'm not.' She grinned at him. 'Very irritating.'

I'm right about our friends, too. I hope. He grimaced slightly at the thought of being wrong. *They will handle things.*

'They're used to you being in control and making decisions. I'm worried they'll be lost without you there.'

I trust they'll do the right thing.

'Maybe you could get on to Joe and have him send you all the updates about what's going on.'

Maybe. The expression on his face indicated that he had no intention of asking for updates. He enjoyed his time with Karen and was happy to keep the rest of the world at bay. *What about you? As the head of Pilatos, it's a big thing to step back and relax on a rock in the outback. Should we cut our stay short so you can get back to Pilatos?*

'Mum and my grandfather can run everything perfectly well. Plus, I have a wonderful team around me now.' She paused, thinking of the men she fired after she took over from her father. 'I don't have any of the sycophants that Dad liked having around – they couldn't function without him telling them what to do and how to do it. I could retire completely, and Pilatos would be fine.'

Realizing he'd maneuvered her into admitting that her company could function without her, just like he'd insisted his friends would operate successfully in his absence, she snorted. 'You don't look conniving, but you are, aren't you? I get it - we can both step back and know everything will continue to run efficiently.'

That's my point.

'I'll want to get back eventually, though. So will you. But it's good being alone in the world for now. You, me,' she rubbed her stomach, 'and baby makes three.'

Lane pointed beyond Karen, and she turned to see two eagles

spiraling upwards on the thermals created by the warm air hitting the hills. The sky seemed so much bluer and more vibrant than her New York sky. The edges near the horizon faded to pale blue, but high where the eagles soared, it was a rich hue that seemed unique to the outback.

'Beautiful,' she murmured, watching them ascend without flapping their wings. 'A land where eagles soar. Should we move here to raise our children? I could leave the States and make this home. You must want to come back here and stay full-time.'

Lane reached his hand out to touch her cheek with the backs of his fingers. There was an eternity in the two seconds that they gazed at each other, then he signed, *My home is where you are. I like living here or America, Britain, or anywhere else, but my home is always wherever you are.*

Sitting up so that both hands were free, Karen placed one over her heart. 'Your words melt me. How is that? Others have rattled off beautiful words that seem so slick they slide right off me. You create words with your hands, and they are like flames on my candle heart.'

Pulling a face, Lane questioned, *Candle heart?*

Karen laughed. 'OK, so it was an awful metaphor. I wanted to create the picture of something melting in a good way.'

I don't think a melting candle for a heart is good. It can't be healthy.

They exchanged looks loaded with humor. It never ceased to thrill Karen when she gazed into his eyes. He was intelligent, compassionate, kind, funny, and everything else she'd ever dreamed of in a partner, and he understood her. Not just the surface layer that most people knew, but the layers all the way down to her core. When he looked at her with such intensity, she sensed he saw all of her, even the parts she'd hidden from the world. He saw her, and he loved her.

'I'm enjoying this time with you here,' she murmured, her eyes soft with emotion. 'This is a magical place.'

Lane smiled. The fact that she felt the enchantment of his ancient land meant a lot to him. *It is magical. Perhaps we should come back up here tonight and look for the Min Min.*

'Can we?' Karen's face shone with the eagerness of a child on Christmas Eve. 'I didn't believe you until I saw them for myself. They don't make sense in a scientific world, and yet they are here. I often read that poem you gave me.'

Anne Morrow's poem?

Karen nodded. Their neighbor wrote an ode to the Min Min that she read aloud at outback gatherings. It discussed the mysteries of the lights and how they called to the souls of all who saw them. 'It reminds me that we don't understand everything in this world.'

Life and events connect in patterns that we don't always see. Lane stopped for a moment and thought of all the quantum connections that danced through his life. *One day, we'll sit up here with our children and show them the Min Min.*

Imagining her husband sitting in the same spot with little mini-me versions of them as they looked for the mysterious outback lights, Karen's heart swelled. How had she been so blessed as to find a man like Lane? And not only find him but have him love her. 'You'll be a great dad.'

I'll try. I trust you'll be honest enough to tell me when I need to improve.

'If we learn parenting skills from childhood, believe me, I'll be the one needing improving. Dad tried to make me the son he wanted, and Isabella absented herself from my childhood.'

She's making up for it now.

Thinking of her flamboyant powerhouse of a mother, Karen smiled. Yes, she was. She helped outsmart Karen's father and turn control of Pilatos over to her, and she packed a lifetime of motherly wisdom into the past year. It was partly her idea to take time away from everything, shrug off responsibility, and be a couple in love putting themselves first.

'She's making sure all Pilatos workplaces are family-friendly.' Karen closed her eyes against the sunlight and thought of her mother's latest change. 'There will be childcare facilities in every workplace so that parents can return to work and have their babies and children nearby if that's what they want. We have flexible hours to allow people to work around their family's needs, and more can work from home if they wish.'

When Karen looked to Lane for a response, he signed, *I'm impressed. Ensuring any parent can work and remain close to their children makes it a workplace designed for all. Good one, Isabella.*

'My grandfather opposed it.'

Of course, he did. He's an older generation. He still thinks if women want to work, they need to change to fit the man's job. Isabella realizes the workplace needs to change to adapt to the workers, whether they are single, parents, or facing challenges.

'I knew you'd like the changes.' She briefly touched his arm before rising to her feet. 'It made me realize that the world changed while most jobs remained designed for an early twentieth-century man who has a wife at home. Two people; one job. One is doing paid work while the other worked the unpaid position at home to support the paid worker. No wonder couples are exhausted when they both work – they don't have someone at home to do the cooking, housework, shopping, washing, and everything else for them.'

Do you want me to stop working and be your home support person? Unwinding his tall frame, Lane stood beside Karen and smiled down at her. *I can be the child carer while you work.*

'I think this child will be raised by a village, not us, so we'll both be able to do as much work as we want. Matthew is still a kid himself – he'll be the play-buddy. Tom and Vicki will be in practice mode for their children.'

Do you think they'll have children?

'I'm sure of it. They both get clucky over babies. Auntie Andie will be amazing – I've seen Andrea with little ones, and they love her. Then there's Joe and his daughter Karina – they will be like family. This will be one lucky baby.'

Noticing Karen touch her temple and wince slightly, he asked, *Another migraine?*

She nodded, aware of the slightly-off aura that started to surround her mind. 'It's been a while since the last one. If we head back to the house, I should be able to stop this with the tablets, but they seem less effective these days.'

In their first six months together, the migraines had retreated, and she thought the calmness that Lane brought to her life had helped remove them. She still felt that calmness, but the migraines were returning. It felt as though pressure was building inside her skull. Without medication, the light would start to hurt her eyes, and every sound was magnified. Then, nausea would peak, she'd vomit violently for a few minutes, and it would all recede, leaving her washed out.

You need to have more checks done. Lane looked at her with concern. *You canceled that last MRI appointment.*

'I was busy.' Karen didn't want to admit to being scared. At times, her head felt as though something was growing inside, increasing the pressure, and she didn't want to find out she was right. She knew it was stupid, and she would have the MRI, just not in the immediate future.

Let's get you home.

They approached their horses and unhooked the reins from the tree branches. With practiced ease, they tightened the girths, led the horses a few steps, and swung aboard. They both patted their mounts' necks as soon as they settled into the saddles. Communication with horses came naturally to them, and they understood the desire to head home and have a feed.

'Not so fast.' Karen checked the reins of her gelding as he sidled towards the drop-off and gave a couple of excited bunny-hops. 'We're taking the easy route, not plunging head-first down a cliff.'

He'd get you down safe.

'Ten years ago, I'd have given him his head and told him to go for it, and I'd have stuck like a leech to the saddle. Now I prefer the easy path to the one that could kill me. Maybe that's an analogy for life.'

Her words, uttered in jest, prompted a connection of thoughts in Lane's mind. Was he taking the easy path? Staying on the station while his friends investigated the deaths of horses and people seemed like he had chosen the safe option. Were they in danger? Several crows cawed loudly in response to his question. He shivered at the implication of their cries and told himself not to be superstitious.

If something happened to them while he enjoyed the security of hiding in the outback, he would never forgive himself. As his worries began to climb, he shook his head to clear them away. As he'd told Karen, worrying didn't change anything. He trusted them to work through this without him at their sides. It wasn't as though they needed him there – they were all skilled and capable. He wasn't their boss; they were all equal in the team they'd built to tackle the small part of the world that involved horses.

He watched Karen's back as she led the way down the Ellamanga hills, part of his mind still on his friends. Perhaps he could find out from Joe what sort of a storm was raging out there while he and Karen enjoyed the calm. If an unknown adversary was manipulating the crimes and profits with the rescue horses, perhaps it was time to step up and show them the might of horse people united in the desire to protect the lost horses.

***

Dibby and Rev

Once all the Australian horses were loaded onto the trucks, the drivers waited for the signal to move. Dibby continued to call to Rev, who answered his desperate cries with reassurance.

The horses shuffled to find a place to stand in the crowded conditions. All fighting was forgotten as they bonded in shared fear of what was happening.

After several hours, the sun set, and the engines started. One by one, the trucks moved onto the roads of Caracas, taking the horses to a remote location.

CHAPTER NINETEEN

You cannot change the past – it is gone. You live now, in this moment. You can change the future – it starts today. Right now is the best time to start changing your future.

A Facebook post by Lane Dimity. Over ten million shares.

Emails and Messages

To the Goulburn branch of REE from Mel Grant.

Hi,

I hope you'll be able to help me.

Four months ago, I went through a nasty breakup, and my ex took my two horses, Dibby and Rev. I thought he kept them on his farm, but I recently found out that he gave them to the REE branch at Goulbourn. I am trying to find out where they are so I can reclaim them. I am seeking to have my ex charged with horse theft but would like to resolve this amicably because if I go down that path, it means REE received stolen goods, and I don't want to cause trouble for the charity. You do wonderful work for horses, and I simply want to find my two horses and get them back.

The Stock Squad advised me to approach you before taking the matter up with them. I have enclosed photos of both horses (they're both palomino geldings), copies of their AQHA registration papers, their microchip numbers, and diagrams of their brands. I am happy to pay agistment and other costs for the time they have been with you. I am desperate to find them and get them back.

I appreciate any help you can give in this matter.

Regards,

Mel Grant.

***

From the Goulburn branch of REE to Mel Grant.

Hi, Mel,

Thank you for your email. Sorry to take a few days getting back to you. I've looked into the matter of your two horses and regret to inform you that there is no record of either of them here at REE. We keep detailed records of all horses that come here, and none match yours.

Perhaps your ex was not being truthful with you, and the horses were given away to someone else. Unfortunately, that is often the way with these things.

Please accept our sincere wishes that you find your horses alive and well.

Yours sincerely,

Patrice Smith (Goulburn REE)

P.S. If you care to make a tax-deductible donation to REE, it will help save other horses because we truly believe we are Rescuing Equines Everywhere.

***

To the Goulburn branch of REE from Mel Grant.

Hi Patrice,

Would you mind checking your records again? If it was just my ex saying that he gave them to you, I could believe that he was lying, but I've spoken to the truck driver from the transport company who picked them up, and he said that he dropped them off at your facility. I also found a photo on your website with my horses in it (I've attached a copy). The photo has the caption, 'The new arrivals are getting ready to live in horse heaven here at REE – no more worrying about ill-treatment or going hungry.' If you look at the two palominos in the right of the photo, you can see their brands – they are my horses.

Please find where you've put my horses.

Thank you.

Mel Grant.

***

From the Goulburn Branch of REE to Mel Grant.

Dear Mel,

I have rechecked our records and can confirm that neither of your horses has been here. Sadly, it has been our experience that some truck drivers who are supposed to deliver horses here, sell them rather than bring them here. If they think the previous owners are unlikely to check on their whereabouts, like with your ex, they will make some extra money by disposing of the horses themselves.

As for the photo, that is a stock photo provided by our advertising company. It was not taken here at REE. It could have been taken many years ago or recently, and it is just a coincidence that your horse is in it.

Neither of your horses has ever been part of any REE program.

Yours sincerely,

Patrice Smith.

***

To the Goulburn Branch of REE from Mel Grant.

Dear Patrice,

I spoke to the truck driver. He brought up his logbooks and electronic tracking for the day he picked up my horses. They clearly show he went from the place where my ex lived to your facility, and he was there for half an hour before driving back to Sydney. He also signed an affidavit stating he dropped the horses off there. Attached is a copy of the waybill that was signed by someone at Goulbourn REE on the arrival of the horses.

Since I have no doubt that my horses went there, but you claim to have no knowledge of them, I will contact the Stock Squad and proceed from there.

Mel Grant.

***

To Lane Dimity from Mel Grant.

Dear Lane,

I don't know who else to turn to. My name is Mel Grant. I met you two years ago at a clinic in Scone, and I follow you on all social media platforms. I'm hoping you might be able to help me or know someone who can.

Six months ago, I broke up with my ex. It was unpleasant, and I feel that I was lucky to get out alive. I had to leave my two horses, Dibby and Rev, behind. He gave them to REE at Goulbourn. I have proof from the truck driver that they were delivered there. I have contacted them several times over the past two months, and they claim my horses have never been at REE, but I know they were. I can't understand why they'd lie about that. I am happy to pay all their expenses in order to get them back, but REE no longer answer my emails, texts, or calls.

I eventually contacted the Stock Squad because, in effect, my horses are stolen. At first, it looked like they would be helpful, but then they agreed with REE and said that the horses hadn't been there and the truck driver may have dropped them off somewhere between where he picked them up and REE. I know that's not true.

I asked around some of the Facebook horse groups and learned of eleven other people whose horses went to REE for various reasons, but when they tried to find out how they were going, REE claimed the horses weren't there or had died of natural causes. Dozens more said the old or unsound horses they'd given to REE were being well looked after, and they had complete faith in the organization, but what about the horses that seem to have disappeared? I know some might have died, but when I can find eleven people with dead or missing horses, how many more are there?

I've included all the relevant information about my horses, as well as the details from the eleven people who say their horses that went to REE disappeared or died. This whole thing has a really bad vibe to it. I know it's crazy, but I started worrying that those dead horses that turned up in the Hunter region were from REE. They wouldn't do that, would they?

I'm desperate to find my horses. I don't know where they are, but I feel they need to be rescued. I keep dreaming that they are calling out to me for help, but I don't know what else I can do. I don't know if you can help, but I'll be eternally grateful if you can do something.

Regards,

Mel Grant

***

From Lane Dimity at Ellamanga Station

Dear Mel,

Your email arrived today, about five days after you sent it. Emails sent to me go to a team of workers who sort through them before forwarding important ones to me. Your email is important, and I just wanted to explain why I didn't reply immediately. You'll note that this email address is different – it's my direct one, so any replies will come straight to me (but I would appreciate it if you didn't give it out to people - some days, I can get several thousand emails to my public address, and I really don't want that hitting my private email.)

Please be very careful when making any inquiries surrounding those dead horses in the Hunter, as we have reason to believe that two or more people have died after asking about them. I don't know if they are related to REE in any way, but please err on the side of caution. I am passing the details of your horses along to some friends who are currently investigating missing horses, and they will look for them.

If you hear any more information about REE, other rescues, any business related to horses, or missing or dead horses that seems at all relevant to this situation, please send it to me. Do not start asking around as that may not be safe.

At the moment, Karen and I are staying on our property in outback Queensland. I'll be back in NSW next week. Pass on any more information you discover, but – I stress this – keep a low profile. Don't make any public posts about the dead horses, REE, your missing horses, or anything else that might draw attention to you.

Your friend,

Lane Dimity.

***

To Lane Dimity from Mel Grant

Dear Lane,

Thank you so so SO much for replying. It means the world to me. I have found some more information, but I only asked in private and secret horse groups on Facebook, and I trust the other people in the groups.

First up, one of my friends in a small private group of horsewomen has a cousin who was friends with Binky Laurie, the Thoroughbred groom who was murdered in the Hunter. She said the family is sure that it had nothing to do with drugs like the news claimed, and that she was asking about those dead horses found there. So, point taken about being careful.

Secondly, we're now up to twenty horses that supposedly went to REE and are missing or dead. When you look at the small sample of people I'm dealing with and then extend that over the whole horse industry, that could be a lot of horses. A couple of the women were going to the Hunter to try and find the bodies of those horses because they had a bad feeling that the old horses they gave to REE had been killed, but I contacted them after hearing from you and told them not to do that. They said the REE people they spoke to claim one was never given to REE (it was), and the other died peacefully in his sleep, but my friend reckons they were lying.

We understand that any snooping needs to be done so quietly that no one notices. We will be covert. Some of us are going to REE farms taking photos of all the horses we can see. We aren't going on their land; we just point our telephoto lens in their direction. We joined Bird Watchers NSW and have bird field guides, so we are genuine card-carrying bird watchers (or 'twitchers') photographing birds. We're hoping to match some of those horses with ones that REE claim they never received.

If there's anything we can do, let us know. The fact that you are taking an interest in this gives me hope that our horses will be rescued from the rescuers. The night I received your email was the first night I've slept properly in years – the last six months, I've been worried sick about my lost horses and, before that, I was worried about what my husband would do while I was sleeping. I can't begin to tell you what a relief it's been knowing that you care. You are the angel of the horse world.

God bless, and thank you,

Mel Grant.

***

From Lane Dimity at Ellamanga Station.

Dear Mel,

I hope your birdwatching cover works. It would be safer to stay right away from everything until we know more, but I appreciate the information you've gathered.

Yes, twenty horses from a small group of horse people indicate that there may be hundreds of horses missing. The advertising from the rescue is persuasive as they promise to give the old and infirm horses a retirement haven in their final years. I don't blame anyone for giving horses to them.

I imagine you are desperate to find what happened to Dibby and Rev. Perhaps they'll turn up in one of the photos. If so, it makes you wonder why they would deny knowledge of them.

Regards,

Lane D.

P.S. I'm really not 'the angel of the horse world', but I appreciate your faith in me and hope I can live up to it.

***

To Lane Dimity from Mel Grant.

Dear Lane,

I think it's too late for my horses and many of the ones that my new friends gave to REE. We have someone at Sydney airport who helped load eighty-six horses from REE onto two Horse Air Transport Company planes three days ago. They managed to take photos of every horse – I've attached all the images. I recognized my two, Dibby and Rev. There were four others that belonged to friends that REE claimed had already died. The horses are headed to South America.

Why would they lie about this? If the horses are simply doing what REE claims they do with so many of their horses, that is, going to riding centers to help disadvantaged children, why the cover-up? I heard that there were also dead horses found outside Caracas, like the ones in the Hunter. Is there any chance the charity is taking money to care for these horses, and they are just killing them and continuing to collect the money for them?

I am devastated beyond words. I hoped to find my horses somewhere in Australia – I'll never see them again.

My heart aches and it breaks.

Mel Grant.

***

Email from Lane to Matthew, Tom, Vicki, and Joe.

Hi, all,

Karen and I are leaving Ellamanga tomorrow. We were planning on staying the entire week, and we appreciate that you protected us from bad news so we could have this break, but it's time to return from the wilderness and start overturning tables to see what comes of it.

Do we have enough evidence about what is happening with these horses to start taking action? I've learned that REE have been lying about horses in their possession, including some stolen horses, and eighty-six are bound for where you are, Matt – keep an eye out.

They should be nearly ready to come out of quarantine. I've attached photos of them – the two palominos are called Dibby and Rev, and their owner is desperate to find them after her ex gave them to REE. If we are sure that REE and partner companies are behind the dead horses, I want to step up the pressure and see what happens. I want to know that you're behind me on this before I do anything.

Lane.

***

Email from Joe Kaiphas to Lane, Karen, Matthew, Tom, and Vicki.

Greetings, everyone.

I have someone following the money. At least a dozen companies in Australia give donations in the millions to REE and receive business worth ten times that amount back from them – air and road transport, feed companies, agistment companies, advertising, and consulting. We think REE are claiming full care allowances for thousands of horses that are no longer alive, which amounts to fraud in the tens of millions annually. There appear to be hundreds of millions of dollars in REE coffers from overseas donations, and we are still investigating these. There are likely to be crime syndicate connections with that amount of money.

Tom and Vicki are currently in the Hunter. The enemy, whoever that may be, believes they are dead - they are not. Matthew and Grace appear to have run into some trouble in Caracas, and I have a security team on the ground there now. It may be related to REE, but we can't be sure.

I can't predict the consequences of putting pressure on REE at this time, but they are aware of us, so, yes, perhaps it's time to flex some muscle.

Joe.

***

Email from Tom Claw to Lane, Karen, Matthew, and Joe.

Hi, everyone.

Vicki and I are in the Hunter quietly speaking to people who have some contact with REE, Menningala, and the transport companies who move the horses. We've found links between one of the other leading charities, Equines In Need Of Funds and REE. Also, the latest corporate-style equine charity to start up, Caring About Horses And Ponies (CAHAP), has ties, almost as though they are backup organizations if anything should happen to the main one. It just keeps getting bigger.

I think this is a case of using the charity system to make immense profits for those running it, and the horses are the ultimate victims. I don't know if we can bring the organisation down, but I hope we can at least help some of the horses.

Tom and Vicki

***

Post from Lane Dimity on all social media platforms and shared several million times.

I have a favor to ask. I am trying to find two palominos that were placed with the charity Rescuing Equines Everywhere, but REE don't appear to have any record of them. The attached photos show these two horses as they are loaded onto a plane with other charity-owned horses going to South America. I've put images of all the horses on this flight on my website and blog if you want to look at the rescue horses heading to Venezuela. If you have any interesting information about the charity or associated companies, employees, or management, please forward it to me. We're here for the horses, and we want to keep them safe.

***

Text message to several of the REE Directors.

Have you seen what Lane Dimity posted? I want them stopped. See to it before they cause any real damage to what we've built. Alpha.

***

Dibby and Rev

The stock trucks bumped over the rough road in the dark, making it difficult for the horses to keep their balance. Now and then, Dibby called to Rev, who was in the truck ahead and felt comforted by the reply.

Sweating with fear, Dusty remained pressed against Dibby's side. He knew from experience that truck rides rarely led to an improvement in life. Several times, trucks had taken him from sale yards to unpleasant homes, and he dreaded what lay ahead. The presence of the big palomino brought some relief from the fear that tore at him.

The lights of other vehicles and dwellings were left behind as the trucks snaked up the mountain road into a sparsely populated area. The smell of the country replaced the city odors, and the horses raised their heads to sniff the air. Apart from the occasional scent of cattle or sheep drifting on the warm night breeze, nothing else smelled familiar. The Venezuelan jungle was a strange place.

The trucks stopped at a farm that smelled of horses. When Dibby called out, at least a dozen new voices answered.

The first truck backed up to the ramp.

CHAPTER TWENTY

You will make mistakes, and that's OK - just don't let the mistakes make you.

'Top 20 Lane Dimity Quotes', Australian Equestrian Magazine; April 2021.

Deo

When Matthew opened his eyes, he saw dimly lit stone walls, a dirt floor, and a low timber ceiling with light shining between the boards. It took him a moment to realize Grace was nearby, sitting against the wall with her arms tied behind her back. A sinking feeling settled in his chest as he saw a cut on her temple with dried blood forming black streaks down her face. He hated himself for getting her into this. She should be home on her farm feeding horses, not tied up in a basement somewhere in Venezuela.

'I'm so sorry,' he whispered.

'It's about time you woke up,' she replied, her voice managing to sound businesslike and brisk even with the volume low. 'I've been trying to work out how we can escape, but it seems too difficult if I have to carry you out.'

'You wouldn't be here if it weren't for me,' he lamented.

'Stop feeling sorry for yourself, cowboy,' Grace told him in sharp tones. 'I once spent the better part of a day lying with a broken back next to my dying horse with no idea if I'd walk again or even live. Every day since then has been a bonus, so don't ruin this day with apologies and regret. We're alive. Let's take it from there.'

'You scare me,' he managed a wan smile as he moved his head from side to side, trying to ease the stiffness in his neck. 'I thought you were a quiet farm girl from Gatton, and here you are talking like a freedom fighter.'

'Horses for courses,' she said matter-of-factly. 'What works at home needs a whole new level of fierce to keep us alive here. Can you tell if you have any broken bones?'

Matthew took a few seconds to wriggle and move his arms, legs, and torso before coughing and shaking his head. 'Nothing grating and no ribs are hurting when I cough.'

'What about shoulder pain? One of them gave you a fairly hefty kick to the stomach. If they damaged your spleen, you could have referred pain in your shoulder.'

Focusing on his shoulders, Matthew rotated them slightly. 'It all seems in order. My wrists are hurting from these zip-ties, though. I don't suppose there's something lying around that can cut plastic?'

'My teeth.' Grace tapped them together a couple of times. 'If you roll over here, I'll chew through them.'

'What if someone comes in to check on us?'

'Then we're huddled together consoling each other as we fear for our lives.' Grace surprised herself with her calmness. 'The more scared and helpless we seem, the more likely they'll be to let their guard down.'

As Matthew wriggled and dragged himself across the dirt, he made a thorough examination of the room. There was no furniture and not as much as a stick of wood that could form a weapon. 'Have you been awake for long?'

'Longer than you but not long enough to know how far we are from where they grabbed us.'

'I don't remember anything after one of them put a rag over my face with some sweet-smelling stuff in it.'

'Chloroform,' said Grace. 'At least, that's my guess. At school, one of my classmates made it by mixing bleach and acetone and accidentally knocked himself out. I remember the smell and held my breath for ages when they put it over my face. It's why I woke up before you, I guess.'

Reaching her, Matthew shuffled around and bent over so that his wrists were raised as high as possible. 'Can you reach?'

Instead of replying, Grace lowered her head to his wrists, turning slightly so that her canine teeth came in contact with the plastic. With a series of snips, she quickly bit through the fastener, and Matthew's hands were free.

'I'll do yours.' He motioned for her to turn around.

Grace shook her head. 'I'll cut the one on your feet first. One of us completely free is worth more than two of us hobbled.'

Despite the danger they were in, Matthew found himself thinking of other things entirely as Grace's ponytail brushed against the skin of his ankles, and her warm breath sent shivers up his legs. It wasn't the time to notice the curve of her shoulders or wonder what it would be like to trace the line of her spine through the yellow fabric of her shirt. For a moment, one of his hands hovered above her back, his fingers twitching to touch the contours that beckoned like sirens. He lowered his hand to the dirt where it did not risk rejection.

When his legs were free, he moved behind Grace to bite through her wrist ties. The feel of her skin against his face as he pushed against her so that he could reach the plastic was very distracting. He wondered if she'd notice if he rested his lips on her skin once her wrists were released then mentally kicked himself for stupid thoughts.

'Do you think we're still in the city?' he asked as he moved to free her legs.

'No. I was awake for the last ten minutes in the boot of their car. It was a dirt road and no traffic. When they carried us into the house, I saw lots of trees and some run-down buildings. And horses. Lots of horses.'

'Really?' Matthew raised his head to look at her before returning his attention to cutting the plastic with his teeth. He reminded himself to avoid doing anything she might consider creepy while his mouth was against her skin, like kiss her. 'Interesting.'

'It makes me think this abduction is related to REE.'

'Or Menningala,' said Matthew as he broke through the last bit of the zip tie and released Grace's legs. 'I know we haven't visited them yet, but they may have known we were here and went for the pre-emptive strike.'

'Why are we alive, then? Why not kill us like Carolina?'

'There's still the possibility her death was an unrelated accident.' Matthew rubbed his temples and winced at the lingering headache from the chloroform. 'Maybe they made the mistake of hiring killers who want to make some extra money from a ransom.'

'Good point.' Grace walked around the small room, examining the walls and ceiling. 'We're alive now, and we need to get out of here. Even if they expect a ransom, they're probably not going to let us live. This looks to be the only way out.'

She stopped underneath a trapdoor and ran her hands around it, pushing to see if it moved. 'There are hinges on the right,' she touched one edge, 'and what looks to be a barrel-bolt latch on the left, but I can't get my fingers through to move it.'

'The perfect place to keep some prisoners.' Matthew performed some stretches and squats.

His activity amused Grace. 'I'm glad to see you keeping up your fitness regime.'

'It has purpose.' He winked at her. 'Do you think there's anyone in the room above?'

Grace shook her head. 'They left the cabin about ten minutes ago. I heard them talking about more truckloads of horses arriving – some of them spoke English.'

On cue, they heard the revving of truck engines in the distance.

'Can you describe what you saw outside and where it was?'

'Some of it. I was pretending to be unconscious, so I couldn't look around much.'

'If I can get this door open,' Matthew put a hand on the ceiling to measure the height, 'it would be good to know where we can hide.'

It took Grace less than a minute to draw a rough map in the dirt showing the cabin with a road leading to the front and stockyards with horses behind. She added swirls to indicate trees closing in on most sides.

'It's like a small clearing in a jungle,' she whispered her conclusion, mindful of keeping their voices low, 'but I only had a couple of seconds with my eyes almost shut. I could have missed things.'

'Do you think we could make a run for the jungle if we get out of here?'

Grace squinted at the trapdoor. It seemed impossible to open from below. The gap beneath the barrel bolt was too narrow for their fingers, and they didn't have any tools. 'If that truck is bringing horses, I guess it might keep them distracted for a while, but how can we open that?'

'I think I can kick it open.' Matthew moved a few steps back, his eyes on the door. He bounced lightly on the balls of his feet and took a deep breath.

Looking from Matthew's boots to the door in the ceiling, Grace twisted her mouth skeptically. He was tall and athletic, she conceded, but kicking open the trapdoor was the task for a martial arts expert in a Hollywood film, not a horse rider from the outback.

Matthew took two springing steps and launched into the air, twisting as he rose so that his right boot slammed into the precise spot beneath the lock. The power in his kick exploded the door open and pushed him downwards. Like a cat, he continued to twist in mid-air and landed on his feet, dropping to a crouch.

'What the…?' Grace stared open-mouthed at the opening in the ceiling.

'Muay Thai.' Matthew stood under the open door, listening for approaching footsteps or voices. 'I learned it in my teens and did stunt work in some martial arts movies. You'll see that move in *Red Dragon Number Five*. Ready?'

'Not really, but I don't want to stay here. I kind of want to get out and watch that movie.'

Matthew grinned at her, then jumped and grabbed the edges of the opening. He pulled himself up and took a quick look around the room before climbing out onto the wooden floor. It seemed everyone was at the pens unloading the trucks; he could hear shouts and the clattering of hooves. Reaching down, he took Grace's hands and hauled her up. Once she was on the floor beside him, he shut the trapdoor and tried to make the bent latch look as though it was still holding. If they glanced in quickly, it would look as though they remained in the cellar.

The room had a door and two windows. One of the windows gave a view of dust clouds stirred up by the horses and lit by headlights and torches. The glass in the adjacent wall showed a thicket of trees close to the house, barely visible in the faint light. Matthew pointed at the trees, and Grace nodded. That seemed the safest place to run.

'If you can open that window,' Matthew took a step towards the door, 'I'll see if they've left our phones lying about.'

He peered around the door, but the house seemed empty. Quickly and quietly, he went through the three other rooms, finding their wallets on a bed but no phones. There was nothing to indicate if the men worked for REE, and he didn't want to waste time looking through every drawer in the dilapidated dwelling. Taking the wallets, he joined Grace as she climbed out the window, shutting it behind them.

They kept their backs pressed against the cabin as they looked around for any witnesses, but it seemed everyone was preoccupied with the delivery of horses. Side by side, they ran to the nearest trees and slipped into the welcoming shadows. They continued as fast as possible down the slope through heavy undergrowth until they could no longer hear any noise from the farm.

'That was easier than expected.' Grace puffed her words as she bent over to regain her breath. 'Now we just have to get through a South American jungle and find help.'

'Well,' Matthew drawled out the word to indicate he had something else in mind, 'I wouldn't mind getting a look at those horses.'

'That's a good idea,' Grace gave him a flat look. 'We escape from men who probably want to kill us, and instead of getting right away, we go back to look at their horses. What is wrong with you?'

'Lots of things, but in this case, I just want to see if we can recognize any Australian brands. Lots of the REE horses are ex-racehorses, so we might see a brand that proves this is tied in with the charity and not some random kidnapping.'

'It doesn't matter which one it is,' Grace folded her arms over her chest and looked combative. 'What matters is that they have guns, and they will try and catch us again, so we need to get as far away as possible as fast as we can. Right now, I don't care if they work for REE or Santa Claus – I want to get away from here.'

'All good points,' Matthew looked back from where they had come, his mind ticking over. He needed to know if the kidnapping occurred because of the REE horses.

'Stop thinking of going back to look at the horses. We're heading downhill because that's the best way to get out of the mountains. We'll find a creek or a road and follow it until we reach a settlement, and we'll phone for help.'

'What if we run into more kidnappers?'

Grace started walking, pushing between branches and undergrowth as she went down the slope and shuddering at the thought of what lay hidden in the darkness. 'You can kick them. In fact, why didn't you kick those men when they grabbed us?'

'Guns kick harder.'

Glancing back over her shoulder, Grace flashed him a smile. Her teeth, lit by the moon, appeared out of the gloom like the grin of the Cheshire Cat. 'Then you should be happy that we're trying to avoid the men with the guns.'

They fought through the jungle for an hour, barely able to see their outstretched hands as they felt their way through the undergrowth. Matthew led, and the fear of falling off a cliff or into a hole had him placing each foot carefully before putting weight on it. When they stumbled into a small clearing next to a house-sized pile of rocks, they decided to stop for the night. It was too dangerous trying to navigate down a mountain in the dark.

'At least we can have our backs to the rocks,' said Matthew, eyeing what may have been the remains of an ancient temple.

'Basically,' Grace wiped an insect from her cheek and squinted at it in the faint moonlight, wondering if it was dangerous, 'we'll be between the rocks and a hard place.'

Matthew snorted. He appreciated that she kept her humor despite everything thrown at them in the last few hours. 'I haven't seen anything edible, so I'm afraid we'll be going to bed hungry.'

'And thirsty,' she added before tilting her head to the side. 'Although, hang on. Listen.'

Coming from within the tumble of boulders was the faint sound of water trickling. Matthew walked around the rocks until he found a path worn by animals leading into them. There wasn't enough space to walk upright, so he got down on his hands and knees and crawled until he reached a small pool with water flowing from a crack in the rocks on one side and disappearing back into the ground on the other. He scooped some into his hand and tested it.

'Fresh water,' he confirmed before drinking his fill and backing out. 'Sorry, I don't have any way of bringing some out for you.'

'I'll survive,' she muttered as she crawled in to get a drink.

After satisfying her thirst, Grace helped Matthew scrape some leaf litter together and covered it with fresh leaves to make a bed. After some final patting it into shape, they lay side-by-side in unspoken agreement that being close together was safer than sleeping apart.

'You know Ernie will be frantic by now.' Grace lay on her back, looking up at the stars in the small patch of sky overhead. Tree branches crowded around the clearing, and she could see them nodding against the starry background, the light silvering their shiny surfaces.

'I know.' Matthew sighed. He didn't like worrying people. 'The Pilatos team are probably in Caracas, and maybe they've teamed up with Alejandro's people. Someone will have told Joe about it. I hope they don't bother Lane and Karen, though. It's not like they can do anything apart from worry.'

'They should guess we're still alive. If the aim were to kill us, they wouldn't have taken us from our car. It would have been bang, bang, and goodnight to us.'

'Maybe they didn't want it to look like an assassination. If they'd done that, then the first thing anyone investigating the crime would do is check our activity. We'd just visited someone who'd bought a horse from REE and visited the charity riding center, so that might link them to the killing.'

'I think you're onto something.' Grace rolled onto her side facing him and propped herself up on one elbow. 'By staging a kidnapping, it's just another couple of tourists taken for a ransom.'

'And if the hired killers can get a bit of extra money from a ransom before killing us, then it's win-win for them.'

Grace sank back on the leafy bed and closed her eyes. 'I'm glad you kicked the way out of that cellar. I didn't want to die there. I noticed stains on the wall that could have been blood, so I wonder if others died there.'

'Nah,' Matthew rustled the leaves by shaking his head. 'It was probably just mold.'

'Mold forming in a distinct blood-spray pattern.'

Matthew chuckled. 'You shouldn't watch so much of the crime channel.'

'I'm hoping we get out of this alive and we don't end up *featured* in a show on the crime channel.'

'We'll be fine,' Matthew promised without much belief in his words. He almost reached over to pat her hand but thought better of it – she might think it was inappropriate while they were lying together in the dark. 'Think of this like one night roughing it in the wilderness. Tomorrow we'll be back in civilization, and we'll tell the gang it's time to stop pussy-footing around. We need to stop REE.'

'Are you're sure it's them?'

'I don't know if they are the ones who killed Carolina and Luis and grabbed us off the street, but I'm sure they are misappropriating tens of millions of dollars in donations that are meant to go towards looking after horses that they are selling, maybe killing. Right now, as we camp out in Venezuela, there are horses in Australia that REE are going to dispose of, one way or another. Maybe some go to the vaccine place, maybe others get shipped around the world and are sold off like Image, while some starve in forgotten paddocks. That's what I want to stop.'

'I never liked them.'

'It looks like your instinct was right.'

Their conversation continued for almost an hour before they fell silent and drifted off to sleep. Both were experienced campers, so sleeping outdoors didn't concern them; however, Matthew remained alert for as long as possible, listening to the unfamiliar sounds of the Venezuelan night and hoping no jaguars hunted nearby.

They were sleeping soundly at midnight when footsteps approached. A dog pressed its nose against Matthew's face, and he jumped into wakefulness to find the barrel of a gun pointed at his chest. In the faint light, he could see a dark-haired teen holding the gun as well as a leash attached to the brown and white hound.

'I will shoot,' the boy threatened in accented English.

Matthew raised both his hands and saw Grace do the same.

'We're lost,' said Matthew in a soft voice. 'I'm sorry if we are on your land. We're trying…'

'Shut up,' the Venezuelan ordered, waving the gun. 'I know who you are. You escaped from us, but I have found you.'

'We can pay you well if you take us to safety.' Matthew spoke in conciliatory tones. He did not want to excite the boy into pulling the trigger. 'We are not wealthy, but we have friends who will pay for our safety.'

The boy, Deo, laughed. The men at the main house had told him about this couple – criminals who made their wealth from exploiting others. Wealthy foreigners like these ruined the country, making millions while indigenous families starved. They deserved whatever befell them. 'They will pay, but you won't get safety. Both of you – roll over on your faces and put your hands behind you. Do not try anything, or you will die now.'

They did as instructed, and he produced zip ties to fasten their wrists together.

'Get up. If one of you tries something, both of you will die. Understand?'

They both nodded. The boy looked sixteen or seventeen, but his words marked him as someone experienced in delivering violence.

Deo tied the end of the dog's leash to Matthew's belt using one hand, all the while keeping the gun pointed at Grace.'It is not far to my farm,' he told them. 'Follow my dog. I walk behind the woman ready to shoot, so just walk. OK? Bruno – *hogar*.'

Hearing the command to go home, the dog tugged at the lead, his tail wagging as he led Matthew through the jungle. The first ten minutes were difficult as the undergrowth was thick, and it was hard pushing through with their hands tied behind their backs. The dog guided them onto a well-used trail, and Matthew noted with dismay that it seemed parallel to the route they'd been battling to make through the jungle. If they had found the path, they could have run downhill and been far from this place.

'Is everyone out looking for us?' Grace asked as they padded downhill. She was glad they weren't heading back up to the house with the cellar – this was the easier direction on her legs.

'Everyone, yes. And Bruno found you.' There was pride in Deo's voice. He had beaten all the experienced men to the prize, and he was pleased with himself.

Matthew glared at Bruno, who wagged his tail as he pulled on the lead in his eagerness to get home.

'I'm Grace. That's Matthew.' She hoped he might start talking so they could form some sort of relationship with him.

'I don't care,' he snapped. 'Silence, or I shoot.'

Grace grimaced. It looked like relationships were off the table.

Walking was easier and faster on the track, and they followed it for half an hour before Bruno swerved to the right and stopped at a roughly made gate hidden in the overgrowth. On the other side, almost invisible in the night, was a small dwelling made of rock, wood, and old iron sheets. Some chickens clucked nervously at their arrival, and a goat bleated a plaintive hello. Nearby, a horse nickered, and the boy replied in Spanish, his voice soft and filled with care.

'Is that your horse?' asked Matthew, only to be told to shut up. At least he knew that the teen liked horses – that was a foundation he could build on given the opportunity.

They went through the gate, and after Bruno was released, Deo made them sit next to a lean-to at the side of the dwelling. The teen lit a kerosene lantern that hung from a beam, shedding light on two horses standing in their stalls, their ears pricked and their eyes expectant.

In Spanish, the boy apologized to the horses for being late and promised them some extra feed for being patient. He looked around and asked the horses where Mayly was hiding because she was close to foaling, and he was worried about her. Matthew looked at Grace, an eyebrow raised, and she nodded. They might be able to deal with a horse lover.

'Mayly!' Deo left the stalls and stood in front of his captives, calling out to the darkness. 'Mayly!'

A faint whickering and groaning came from nearby.

'Do not move,' he waved his pistol and scowled at them before looking over his shoulder as his horse groaned again. 'If you run, Bruno will find you, and I will shoot your knees. Understand? I have to see my horse, but I will watch you.'

'We understand,' said Matthew, his voice soft. 'I hope Mayly is alright.'

'I think she's foaling,' whispered Grace once the boy merged into the night.

'I think you're right. And he's going to be one worried young man if he hasn't helped with a lot of foalings before.'

Seeing where he was going with this, Grace nodded. 'It doesn't seem like anyone else is home, so it's lucky for him and his mare that he happens to have two very experienced horse people tied up in his yard.'

Matthew gave her shoulder a light bump with his and smiled. 'Lane is right when he says that life is made of patterns, and once you enter into one, you keep finding the quantum connections.'

They could hear the mumbled sounds of their captor talking to the horse, followed by groans as the mare strained.

'Perhaps you could ask him if he needs our help,' suggested Grace.

'I think he's had enough time alone to realize he needs assistance.' Matthew inclined his head at her then raised his voice to call out. 'We've both worked with foaling mares if you need our help.'

There was no response.

After thirty seconds, Matthew tried again. 'If your mare is in trouble, we should be able to help her.'

The figure of the teen emerged from the dark to stand over them. An expression of fear and worry replaced the earlier cold look. He still pointed his gun at them, wiping at his face with his other hand.

Noticing his tears, Grace spoke in a soothing voice. 'We've helped a lot of mares have their foals. We would never try to escape while a horse needed our help. It's what we both do – help horses. Almost everything we do is about helping horses.'

Deo sniffed. 'You lie. You are killers here to trick us and take our land.'

Matthew pulled a face at the description. No wonder the boy was wary of them. 'I promise you, we're not. Do you have a phone? You can look us up.'

Deo shook his head, glancing over his shoulder to where his mare lay. 'No phone. I'm not wealthy like you. Can you help my horse?'

'I hope so.' The concern in Matthew's voice was genuine. 'Is she lying down, and are there hooves – two hooves – poking out?'

'Mayly is on her side.' The teen lowered his gun and watched his captives closely. The fact that they seemed to know something about foaling was reassuring. 'There are no hooves, but I can see the nose.'

'We need to push the foal back in,' Matthew ran through similar births in his memory, 'and bring the legs forward. With the legs back, the foal's shoulders are jamming, and your mare can't push him out. His head needs to be lying along his front legs.'

'And you know how to do this?' The dark eyes regarded him suspiciously. The men at the top farm where the horses were sent did not say anything about these killers being horse people. They were in Venezuela to cause trouble, and they should get a large ransom for them.

'We both do.' Grace assured him. 'You can keep the gun on us if you are worried, and we'll try to help your mare. After the foal is out, you can tie us back up. It's important to save your mare and foal.'

Although he suspected a trap, the teen was more concerned about losing his mare than playing safe with his prisoners. He motioned to them to turn around, then produced a small knife and sliced through the plastic ties. Stepping away from them, he aimed the gun at Matthew's knees.

'I will shoot if you try anything. I think you will try to trick me.'

'That's fine,' Matthew held up his hands in a gesture of peace, 'we're not going to cause trouble. Can we take the lantern so we can see?'

They followed a path through the grass that led to an orchard at the back of the cabin. A big bay mare lay on her side, exhausted. After Grace made a quick assessment of the situation, she went to her head and knelt.

'Hello, beautiful.' She leaned over to examine the mare's shoulder. 'I know your brand. I've had a gelding from your stud at my rescue – he could have been your brother.'

'Small world,' commented Matthew, hanging the lantern on an overhead branch. 'An Australian Thoroughbred having a foal here in the jungle. What are the chances?'

'Pretty good, if all those horses arriving in that truck came from REE.' Grace rubbed the mare around her eyes. She looked up at their gun-toting guard. 'How did you end up with her?'

The boy watched as Matthew knelt at the tail of the mare and struggled to push the foal's muzzle back inside before reaching in to find the front legs.

'They gave me the horses,' Deo told her. 'I work up at the farm. Mostly, they pay me money, but I liked these horses, so they paid me with horses.'

The mare strained with a contraction, and Matthew's face contorted in pain as vice-like muscles gripped his arm.

'We've been looking for these horses,' said Grace, deciding that the boy might listen to the truth now that they were helping him. 'We think someone in Australia gets paid a lot of money to look after them, but they are getting rid of them. Sometimes they kill them. We want to help the horses.'

'Would you take my horses?' A note of fear crept into his voice. His horses and Bruno were his family, and the thought of losing them was unbearable.

Matthew shook his head and wrapped his hand around one of the foal's front pasterns to pull it forward, then repeated with the other leg. 'They're your horses. We'd help you look after them if you needed money to feed them, though.'

'No, you wouldn't,' Deo scoffed. He knew about the lies foreigners invented. 'It's not like you are Lane Dimity.'

Matthew and Grace looked at each other with surprise, and hope quickly followed.

'You've heard of Lane?' Matthew asked, trying to work out how to approach this new twist.

'Of course, everyone has. I have two of his books, and I read them many times.'

Closing his eyes, Matthew offered up a silent prayer of thanks to the universe. 'Can you pass me Bruno's lead? I'll tie it around the legs so we can pull.'

The boy kept the gun trained on Matthew as he tossed him the rope. 'Do you think the foal is alive?'

The anxious look on the teen's face reminded Matthew how young he was. Where was his family? It looked as though he lived alone with his horses and dog.

While he fastened the rope around the foal's pasterns, he continued talking. 'He's alive. He tried to pull his leg back from me. So, Lane Dimity – do you know who his friends are?'

'I do,' Deo replied, pleased to showcase his knowledge. 'There are the McLeay brother and sister, and Tom Claw, and now the American woman, too.' Although he didn't have a phone, when he was at the main farm, he used one of their devices to keep up to date with the news about his idols, including some of the leading Venezuelan riders, Lane Dimity, and Lane's friends. 'I will meet them one day. They will come to Caracas, and I will meet them – in my heart, I know this.'

'I can guarantee that…' began Matthew, then the mare had another contraction, and he pulled on the rope, explaining his actions. 'To start with, I'm pulling the foal out, but once his front legs and nose are out, I'll pull down towards her legs. I need to try and keep one leg slightly in front of the other, too, so that the shoulders can offset.'

'I see the feet!' Deo exclaimed excitedly when two tiny hooves protruded. 'And his nose.'

'While I'm doing this,' Matthew waited for the mare's next contraction before he pulled again, 'why don't you get my wallet out of my back pocket? I took it off a bed up there when we got out of the cellar. Have a look at my driver's license.'

'Why?' There was suspicion in his voice.

'Because I'm Matthew McLeay. Lane Dimity is one of my best friends.'

Deo made a sound of disbelief and disgust at the lie.

'He is,' Grace assured him. 'Lane, Tom, and Matthew are trying to find out about the horses that were killed and buried here and in Australia. We think they came from the same place as your mare. Maybe those horses that arrived tonight in the trucks came from there, too.'

'They come from Australia,' Deo spoke cautiously. He didn't trust them and was sure they were trying to fool him.

'You know that for sure?' Matthew looked back at him, his face shiny from sweat as he worked hard to help the mare birth the foal.

'That's what they say. They stay here for a while, and then they go to…' he stopped, realizing he was saying too much.

'Get my wallet,' Matthew repeated. He needed the boy to know his identity. 'You'll even find a handwritten note from Lane in it. I never go anywhere without it.'

Watching the two Australians with distrust, the teen carefully withdrew the wallet from Matthew's back pocket before backing away to examine the contents.

With a massive heave from the mare and pulling from Matthew, the foal slid further out, revealing the shoulders.

'I'm going to pause for a bit,' Matthew told him as he wiped fluids away from the foal's nostrils, 'so there's time for the placenta to separate properly. The foal's doing fine.'

The foal opened its eyes, and its nostrils quivered.

'Welcome to the world, little one.' Matthew rubbed the foal's neck.

Removing the folded note from the wallet, Deo held it up to the lamplight and silently read Lane's words. *Horses: if we have souls, so do they, and if I meet them in heaven, I want them to know I did what I could to make their lives better in my time here. Lane D.*

Deo looked at the photo on the driver's license, his brows pinching together as he doubted his eyes. 'You really are Matthew McLeay?'

'That's me. Lane Dimity's friend and – hopefully – your friend. If you want to meet Lane, I can make that happen.'

With one more contraction, the mare pushed the foal out, and Matthew crawled away from her. 'We should probably leave them and see if Mayly can handle it from here. They'll rest for a bit before getting up, and it might be best to avoid interfering unless they need us.'

'Is Lane here?' Deo placed the note back in the wallet and closed it.

'No, he's home on Ellamanga, his ranch in Australia. If you had a phone, we could call him and you could talk to him.'

At last, the gun began to lower, but the teen still needed convincing. 'Stand under the light.'

Matthew stood and moved behind the lantern so that it shone on his face. Deo studied him closely.

'What is your sister's name?'

'Andrea, but we usually call her Andy. She's a photographer. If either of your Lane books has photos in them, they were probably taken by Andy.'

Deo nodded and looked at Grace. 'Why is this woman with you?'

'Grace runs a horse rescue in Australia. We're working together to find out what happens to the Australian horses that are going missing.'

'And you want to help the horses?'

'That's what we do. After reading any of Lane's books, you should know that. We've seen the REE horses at the Wellness Center, and that looks to be a fantastic place, but it doesn't account for the thousands of horses that seem to be missing.'

Deo dropped his eyes to the ground. This was the point where the road he traveled divided, and he needed to choose his future. Did he stay on the track selected for him by the men at the top house who welcomed him into their fold? Or did he walk a different path? He looked at the newborn foal, a colt, now struggling to his feet when it was easier to lie still and do nothing. It was time for him to stand.

Switching the gun to his left hand and aiming the muzzle at the ground, Deo stepped forward and offered his right hand to Matthew. 'My name is Deo Escalona Garcia. I am honored to meet you, Matthew McLeay and Grace. I want to help the horses, too, and we do not have much time before they die.'

***

Dibby and Rev

As soon as Dibby's hooves hit the dust in the crowded yard, he called frantically to Rev, who replied with enthusiasm. The two palominos pushed their way past the other horses until they reached each other. Putting their noses together, they shared breath and relaxed, relieved to be reunited. The much smaller Dusty broke into their reunion, adding his nose to the greeting.

The enormous yard they found themselves in held all eighty-five horses that had flown together from Australia. Other pens held more horses, but Rev was interested in checking on the horses that had traveled with him from Australia, not meeting new horses. He moved around the corral with his two offsiders in tow, making the brief nose-to-nose greeting that formed bonds in horse groups.

After so many days near Rev, the horses knew him and stretched their noses to say hello. His presence helped keep them calm when there was much to fear. There were no laid-back ears or threats as the two palominos and their solid little friend made their way around the horses. They acknowledged Rev as the leader of their herd without needing to fight over the position.

CHAPTER TWENTY-ONE

If we have souls, so do they. Like us, they have friendships and fears. They enjoy moments of play and having their backs rubbed. They love their offspring, and will fight to defend them. Horses have the same emotions as we do, only they don't express them in a human language: they don't write about them or sing about them, but that doesn't make their emotions any less real or valuable than ours. They understand forgiveness. I have seen horses recover from horrific abuse and learn to trust people again – that is forgiveness beyond what most people are capable. They remember their loved ones. I have seen horses reunited with friends after a decade apart, and it was clear they recognized each other. They remember, just like we remember. They know fear, care, loss, and love. If we have souls, they, too, have them, and heaven will only be worth visiting if all the horses, dogs, cats, and other animals are there with us.

'They, Too, Have Souls' by Lane Dimity, p. 4

Security

'How will they die?' Grace asked as they waited for the foal to stand and take his first drink.

Deo looked into the shadows, fearing the men might sneak up and see him with the Australians. A glance at Bruno's relaxed posture assured him that no one hid in the bushes nearby. 'I don't know what happens inside the factory.'

'Factory?' Matthew interrupted; his brow creased as he tried to work out what Deo meant. 'Do you mean Menningala, the vaccine laboratories?'

'Yes, that place,' Deo nodded. 'Many horses go in alive, and many times they take out truckloads of bodies to bury somewhere.'

The information supported their suspicions that Menningala and

REE worked together and that the vaccine company was side-stepping animal welfare legislation by using an unmonitored supply of test subjects. While REE gave them an almost endless supply of horses, they could fast-track drugs and vaccines by unethical testing.

Grace shook her head sadly. 'We knew there were a couple of sites around Caracas where dead horses were buried. Are there more?'

'Much more. There are always farmers who need money and won't ask questions about having animals or rubbish buried on their land.'

'So, those horses that arrived up at the farm,' Matthew tilted his chin towards the house they escaped, 'they go to Menningala after here, and how long before they die?'

Deo shrugged. He didn't know how it worked, and he didn't want to know. 'It is best not to be curious. They come here from the airport, but not all – some go straight to the factory. We look after them until trucks arrive to take them there. Other trucks take the bodies away, but they don't all die. Most horses leave alive.'

'How can that be?' Matthew looked at Grace in confusion. It didn't make sense. 'They're a Level Four biocontainment area. They deal with zoonotic viruses like Hendra, West Nile, Equine Encephalitis, coronaviruses, and others that are a risk to horses and humans. Horses shouldn't be coming out at all, but at least the dead ones are getting buried. What happens to the live ones?'

'Do they come back here?' Grace asked Deo.

'No. I heard a driver say he takes them to a farm on the other side of Caracas, but I don't know where or what happens there.'

Matthew rubbed both his hands through his hair, trying to work through the puzzle. 'How long before the horses up at the farm are taken to Menningala?'

'The drivers say they'll be back in two days.'

'That doesn't give us much time.' Matthew watched the foal nuzzle along the mare's side as she stood resting a hind leg. 'We're going to have to do something fast if we want to save them. Once they go into the Menningala compound, we'll have Buckley's of getting them out.'

'Buckley's?' Deo enquired.

'An Australian saying,' explained Grace. 'It means not much of a chance, but since the man known as Buckley lived, it's still a chance.'

The slurping sound of the foal finding the udder caught their attention, and they observed the colt taking his first drink. The mare turned her head to touch the newborn as he pressed against her side.

'That foal's a winner.' Matthew smiled and patted Deo on the arm. 'Some take ages to get their first drink, but he's straight into it. You've got yourself a good one there, Deo.'

'That is my first foal.' Deo's voice filled with pride. 'My dream is to breed show jumpers.'

'Most great horses start with a dream,' said Matthew.

Leaving the mare and foal in peace, they headed to the cabin, taking the lantern with them. Deo gave Bruno the order to stay on guard outside and, once inside, he closed the patched curtains so no one could see in. His home consisted of one large room with a basic kitchen on one side and a table and chairs in the center where he motioned for his visitors to sit. Tired curtains divided a sleeping area from the main room. Pictures of horses cut from magazines colored the drab walls.

'You live here alone?' asked Matthew, unable to see any sign of other people.

'My parents died two years ago,' replied Deo in a matter-of-fact voice as he collected cheese, tomatoes, and bread from a cupboard. 'They were murdered, along with my sister. They worked up at the main farm, and the boss let me work there so I could stay here. I don't like what happens to the horses, but the men there, they are good to me.'

'I'm glad of that,' said Grace. Her heart twisted at the thought of this boy losing his entire family and living here by himself. 'After we've had something to eat, we'll get going so you don't get into trouble. It would be best if they never found out that you helped us.'

'I will show you the way to town,' Deo placed the food down on the table so they could help themselves, 'then come back here because I need to be with my horses and go to work tomorrow. I can tell you everything I know about what happens with these horses. If you can save them without hurting the people at the farm, that would be good. They are not as bad as you think.'

Matthew tried not to grimace as he thought of those men kidnapping them and leaving them in a cellar. It was hard to equate that with good men. On the other hand, what would have happened to Deo if they had not offered him work? They weren't the ones organizing the deaths of the horses; they were merely looking after them along the way.

'They are not the men we want to catch,' Matthew took a drink of water from the cup Deo offered. 'The ones who are paying them Are the men we want to stop. We'll try to find a way to save the horses and not have too much collateral damage. Do you have a pen and paper?'

For the next half hour, Matthew and Grace questioned Deo about everything he knew relating to the horses: how long they stayed, where they went, and which people and companies were associated with them. It gave them a picture of what happened in Venezuela with the

REE horses, and they wondered if the setup was similar in other countries.

After telling them what he knew, Deo led them down a narrow path between the trees to the more populated farmland below. It was almost dawn when they stumbled out of the shadows of the jungle to find themselves on a narrow dirt road. They walked past several farms before Deo chose one with a white security fence and a well-maintained driveway. Bruno whined at his side and occasionally growled at unfamiliar noises but quieted when Deo scolded him.

'He doesn't like coming near the town,' Deo patted his dog and hushed him again. 'There are too many people down here for him.'

'Poor Bruno,' Grace understood the dog's preference for the wilderness. 'Are you going home now?'

Deo nodded. 'You are safe here. These people have nothing to do with us. They breed and show Peruvian Pasos, and I've heard they are honest.' For a moment, he looked longingly down the landscaped driveway as though imagining a life where he lived on such a farm rather than struggling in poverty to keep his dream alive. 'I think they will know of Lane and will help you.'

Deo stretched out a hand to Matthew, but the Australian took him in a hug. 'You're one of us, now, OK?' He patted Deo on the back and ignored Bruno's protective growl. 'I know you need to be with your horses and want to go to work as though this hasn't happened, but it has happened. As soon as this is over, we'll find you work wherever you want, and you can have Bruno and the horses there, too. Lane makes things like that happen. So, hang in there…'

'Get down on the ground NOW!' A man roared the order from the shadows on the other side of the road.

'Get down!' Two more voices yelled from different directions as beams of light sliced through the shadows to illuminate Grace, Matthew, and Deo. 'Face down. Arms out.'

They followed the commands and dropped to the grass. Deo kept a hand on Bruno's leash as the dog continued whining and growling, keen to defend his owner.

'These are not my people,' Deo hissed between his teeth.

'Identify yourselves,' a voice with a Texas drawl ordered.

'Who's asking?' Matthew turned his head to the side and squinted at the blast of light in his eyes.

'I know him,' the Texan told his comrades. 'That's Matthew McLeay. I'm assuming you're Grace Walker.'

'And I'm hoping you're someone from the Flintstones,' replied Grace, remembering the code names of Alejandro's team.

'No, Ma'am. I'm Kayne Pennazza, from Pilatos.' Amusement crept into his voice. 'I think you'll find Fred, Barney, and their friends are surrounding a house up that mountain somewhere.'

A sharp intake of breath from Deo prompted Matthew to sit up and look in Kayne's direction. 'Any chance you can call them off? Our young friend here works for those men, and he doesn't want them hurt.'

'Our intel suggests they are responsible for your kidnapping yesterday,' drawled Kayne. 'And there's a parcel of horses up there that your friend Lane is mighty interested in.'

'I know,' Matthew rose to his feet and offered a hand to Grace, but she stood without accepting his help. He wondered if she was angry at him for the situation they were in, or perhaps she disliked the feeling of being helped. He withdrew his hand and continued. 'It's just that we're going to have to figure out a way to save those horses without hurting anyone up there, and, for now, that means calling the Bedrock crew off. Can you do that?'

'Sure thing.' Kayne instructed one of his men to contact Alejandro's team and have them stand down.

'How'd you find us?' Matthew looked around at the five men and a woman dressed in black and armed like special forces.

Kayne pointed up at the sky.

'Satellites?' Matthew looked up.

'Drones.' Kayne's teeth flashed in the dark as he grinned. 'The local team had information about truckloads of horses going from quarantine to the farm up there, so that was their target. Joe advised us that you'd probably escape and head downhill to the nearest town, and we've had drones with thermal imaging patrolling this region for the last few hours. There's not a whole lot of people who get around in the dark out here.'

'Bruno and I should head home.' Deo looked to the east where the light was beginning to push back the night. 'I start work in a few hours.'

'No,' Matthew shook his head and placed a restraining hand on Deo's arm. 'Having the Pilatos team here changes things. Before, you had to turn up at work so they wouldn't suspect you of helping us and come looking for you or your horses. Now it doesn't matter what they think. We'll send some of the team to your house to collect your horses and lead them down to safety. The foal will be fine to walk that far. We can organize a truck to take them further away. You're with us, now, and we're not sending you back into danger.'

'But Bruno isn't happy here, and you might need me up there with the horses.'

'The horses are important,' Matthew told him gently, 'but we never forget that our lives are important, too. We need to have you out of danger, and Bruno will just have to put up with being away from the farm.' His face split into one of his warm smiles. 'And, this way, you are guaranteed to meet Lane. We'll find somewhere safe for you and your horses – at our expense – and we'll take it from here. And I'll do all I can to keep the people on that farm safe.'

One of the Pilatos men approached, holding a phone in his hand. 'I reported in, and Mr. Dimity wants to speak to you, sir.'

'Thanks, uh…thanks.' Matthew never grew used to being called *sir* by others. He wasn't sure if he should address them in the same manner, and he tended to fumble over his words. He turned to Kayne before taking the call. 'Can you get directions from Deo and organize to bring his horses down? And anything else he wants - I don't want him going back there, OK?'

Kayne gave him a thumbs up and took Deo aside.

Putting the phone to his ear, Matthew closed his eyes to find mental focus before speaking. 'G'day there, Lane. Matt here, mate.'

'Good to hear you,' the text-to-speech voice with a Russell Crowe accent replied. Lane often selected that voice for his phone calls, though Matthew was sure Lane's voice was nothing like that gruff Aussie drawl. 'It seems like you've had the full Venezuelan tourist experience.'

Matthew snorted, amused by the oblique reference to the kidnapping. 'You could say that. We're safe now, we made a new friend, and we know what is happening to a lot of the horses that end up here. So, one step back and two forward. We don't know everything, but we've filled a lot of the gaps.'

'I wanted to speak to you about them. I have some people here desperately looking for their horses that ended up with REE. It seems some were on a recent shipment to Venezuela.'

'Horses were arriving by trucks yesterday at the farm where we were held. Our contact here – who happens to be a big fan of yours – said we only have a few days before they're sent to Menningala, and that'll be the end of them.'

'Are you sure Menningala is involved?'

'Yes. I trust what Deo says. Horses are going in and out of there like flies through stable doors; only some are coming out dead.'

'Then it's time I did more than sit around enjoying my days with Karen.'

'Do you have a plan?'

'I have a cunning plan.'

Matthew smiled at the Blackadder reference. 'Care to let me in on what it is?'

'Be ready to Zoom in about two hours, and we can brainstorm it.'

'If I can find a phone. The kidnappers kept ours.'

'On the bright side, if they didn't cut off your thumb, they won't be able to use it. One of the Pilatos people will have a spare in their bag. They carry everything.'

Matthew looked over at Kayne. 'Do you have a spare phone?'

Kayne gave him a thumbs up.

'Great. Can you tell the others that Grace and I are OK? It'll take me a bit to set up the phone and download my contacts.'

'Karen texted them as soon as we started talking. I'm glad you're OK - we were worried. How is Grace handling it?'

'Like a champion.' Matthew's eyes wandered to where she was standing. She must have been tired, but she managed to look fresh and bright as she watched the layers of color unfolding in the eastern sky. His gaze lingered on her profile as her face caught the light of the sunrise, and he felt warmed by the vision.

'Is she one of us?' asked Lane.

Matthew thought of her courage, humor, resilience, and her desire to help the horses. 'I hope so.'

'Then make sure she's part of the meeting. Take care.'

'Will do.'

While Matthew and Grace said goodbye to Deo and promised to see him soon, Kayne organized a vehicle to take them to Ernie's house with three of his team. On the trip back to Caracas, Matthew downloaded his phone information from the cloud and began making calls. His first was to a very relieved Ernie. He called Alejandro to thank him for sending his men and asked to pay for their services. Alejandro told him that his company had picked up a lucrative Pilatos contract because of the incident, so no money was owed.

As they hit the city's outskirts, Matthew wrote notes on what they learned about the horses, his fingers flying over the phone's keypad. He was aware of Grace sitting next to him, their legs touching as they shared the back seat of the car with a bear of a man who took up more than his fair share of space. Kayne had given her a spare phone, too, and she clasped it in her lap, unused. She didn't call anyone.

The car swept around a corner, and Grace's head tilted sideways and came to rest on Matthew's shoulder. He stopped writing and saw she was fast asleep, her phone slipping from her fingers. With care, he adjusted his shoulder so she could remain asleep. He lowered his mouth to her tangled mess of hair and gently pressed his lips against the top of her head, safe in the knowledge that she wasn't aware of his declaration of affection.

The bear of a man on the other side of her looked away to give them privacy, but Matthew had no intention of doing anything after the stolen kiss. For now, it was enough to have her head on his shoulder.

***

Dibby and Rev

The men shouted in anger as they ran around looking for something. Rev watched with interest as they tried to find tracks on the ground, trotted into the jungle, and came back out again, yelling at each other. The horses settled into eating hay and watching the torch beams that flashed everywhere.

The night was half over before the men turned off the lights and went to bed.

In the morning, the horses snorted in alarm as a dawn chorus of howler monkeys announced their territory to any other troops within hearing. The cacophony of whoops reverberated through the trees and set the horses on edge. It was a sound unlike any they'd heard before.

As the sun rose, the howling ended, leaving the horses watching the jungle with alert eyes. It seemed a place of danger. Dibby stayed close to Rev for reassurance in the strange place.

The men who threw hay to them chatted to each other in Spanish as they wondered why Deo was late to work. They knew his mare was close to foaling, so they assumed he was busy with her. They intended to check on him on their way home that afternoon.

The Australian who walked with death on his shoulders visited when the sun was at its highest. Rev and his friends moved away when his eyes passed over them. He inspected the horses from the fence and nodded, pleased with their condition.

'We're nearly ready for them,' he drawled, slapping his hand against the wooden rail. 'Another couple of days. Three at the most.'

'They'll be safe here until you need them, boss.'

Watching some men walk around in circles near the edge of the jungle, the Australian asked, 'What the heck are they doing?'

Not wanting to admit to losing the Australians who they were supposed to kill, the man shrugged. 'Someone saw the tracks of a jaguar earlier.'

'I wouldn't mind shooting one if you spot him.'

'I'll let you know if they see him.'

'And you took care of our two nosy Australians?'

'Yes. Taken care of. They are gone.' The Venezuelan drew a line across his throat and stared grimly at the forest.

'Good. Keep up the feed for these horses. We want them in the best shape for their final journey.' He laughed, amused at his words. Rev shivered.

CHAPTER TWENTY-TWO

You know right from wrong. Do not stand in silence and allow others to do what is wrong. Speak up. We all need to speak up.

Social media post by Lane Dimity. Over twenty million shares.

Protest

Using Ernie's laptop, Matthew and Grace joined a conference call with Karen and Lane at Ellamanga, Vicki and Tom in the Hunter Valley, Joe in Sydney, and Andrea in New Zealand. Although Andrea was busy with photographic assignments, she kept up with the news about the rescue horses and remained an integral part of the team during decision making.

We thought we'd have another week or two of gathering information, Lane typed the words which appeared on the screen under his and Karen's faces, *but we have to do something to stop the next load of horses going to Menningala.*

'The ones in Venezuela?' asked Joe from his rectangle in the screen.

'There, and here as well,' Karen looked at Lane, who nodded to continue. 'It seems wherever the REE riding centers are located, there is also a Menningala facility nearby. In Venezuela, Myanmar, and Senegal, horses supposedly sent to the riding centers are diverted to Menningala. The company has produced two vaccines in the past year ahead of the competition, which, in part, could be explained by the fact that they're by-passing animal welfare regulations and using an unending supply of disposable horses while the others are limiting testing and following all standard protocols.'

'How are they getting away with it?' Anger heated Vicki's voice. 'Why hasn't this been picked up?'

'They pay the right people,' said Joe, his voice low. 'There are always those who can be bought, and with billion-dollar industries, as we well know, there is money to buy their silence. Plus, look at where they're operating. Apart from their branches in Australia and America, they're choosing countries where animal welfare is not a high priority.'

Grace frowned. She couldn't see what they could do to change the situation. 'They seem to have paid everyone to ignore what's going on. The police over here aren't going to worry about some horses destined for pet food in Australia but got rescued, sent to a laboratory here, and died. To us, the horses are important – we know they have names, we know there are people who loved them and others who want to see them happy. In countries where human life seems cheap, they're not going to place much value on some horses.'

'Lane thinks we can pressure the people behind it all,' said Karen, speaking for Lane as he signed so Grace didn't miss anything. 'So far, we've only been gathering information because we didn't know what we were dealing with. Now, I think we can be certain that REE is misusing donations and working with companies like Derek Anderson's HATCO and several others that show funds moving between themselves and the charity. It's also clear that they are lying about the fate of the horses and sending them to Menningala. People who showed interest in what was going on died or disappeared, and it looks as though they intended to kill Tom, Vicki, Grace, and Matthew for asking questions.'

'I hope that means we're going to hit back,' muttered Tom. 'They think we're an annoyance to be swatted away. I want them to know we can stop them.'

'We agree.' Karen shuffled some papers in front of her. 'Lane has written a series of posts he's going to release on social media. I doubt they realize how much power seventy million followers give us when it comes to horse welfare. Horse people are outraged by things like a charity misappropriating funds and letting the horses die. It won't matter where Menningala operate – there will be an army of horse people to make things right.'

Grace saw an issue with the plan. 'Won't they sue for defamation as soon as you start mentioning their names?'

'Luckily,' Karen grinned into the camera, 'Lane has an excellent lawyer checking everything he writes before release. He is asking questions based on the facts we know, and nothing will constitute libel. Why have so many thousands of REE horses gone to Venezuela when there are only a few hundred in their riding facility? Why have horses that were guaranteed a safe home for life ended up in auctions in

Venezuela? Does anyone know why REE trucks are delivering horses to Menningala facilities at night? Does anyone know why truckloads of dead horses are being buried? Note: we're not saying it's the Menningala horses in those graves, but people may make the link.'

Tom chimed in. 'You'd better ask if anyone knows why REE is claiming that some of the horses buried here in the Hunter are still alive and in their care. I spent last night with two of Joe's men digging up dead horses to photograph them. Some had brands cut off, but not all.'

'Weren't they guarding the sites?' asked Matthew.

A slight twist of amusement touched Tom's mouth. 'Yeah, well - there were guards, but you know what Joe's men are like. The next shift will find them safely tied up.'

'We looked up the brands,' Vicki held up some print-outs from the Australian Stud Book's registry of Thoroughbreds, 'and contacted the last known owners who were happy to phone REE and ask about the horses. Apparently, these horses,' Vicki showed photos of brands on decomposing shoulders, 'are in happy retirement on one of REE's properties and doing well.'

Thank you for that, signed Lane, giving a lopsided grin intended for Vicki and Tom. *I made the assumption that those horses came from REE, and I'm glad you have proof.*

'In light of what Lane is about to tell the world,' said Karen, 'it's just as well you have those documents.' She tapped a finger against her chin as she thought about the web of lies, fraud, and death they needed to unravel. 'Joe, any luck in finding the names of everyone behind this?'

Joe shook his head and flicked through a stack of paper. 'It's a tangled mess of companies working together. On the surface, it looks like the justifiable use of donations. They pay for feed, agistment, vet fees, transport, training, farrier work, horse dentistry, advertising, fencing, printing, and other equine-related costs. Look a little deeper, and you realize they are paying all those costs for thousands of horses that are no longer alive. Menningala, like other associated companies, donates tens of millions to REE, and it appears they receive off-the-record horses in return, which allows them to fast-track equine vaccines. If an official investigation uncovers proof of that, it will be the end of the company. In fact, it'll be the end of a lot of companies.'

Murmurs of agreement came from everyone.

'From what we can work out,' continued Joe, 'one of the companies that is a chief shareholder in Menningala also owns agistment centers that receive millions from REE for horses supposedly boarding there. I sent people to check, and most of the paddocks are empty. The wife of our transport mogul, Derek Anderson, also owns farms that collect millions in agistment for horses that aren't there.'

'How have they got away with it?' Vicki grimaced at the enormity of the crime they were facing. 'People keep donating money – hundreds of millions of dollars – and it's certainly not going to the horses.'

'You need to understand the mindset of the people donating,' put in Grace. She had seen it many times with smaller charities that misused funds. 'As long as the contributors can see some horses getting helped, they feel that they are the ones helping those horses. If you tell them that the charity is wasting money, they'll attack you because they care about the horses they see receiving help, and they don't want that to stop. To be honest, I understand that mindset. After seeing the riding center here in Caracas and all the good it's doing, I'd be happy for some of the fraud to continue as long as they stopped killing horses. Sure, REE has become a money tree for some, but maybe it's worth it to ensure the riding centers continue. The charity has changed the world for these horses and riders in Caracas – in a good way.'

Good points, Lane signed.

As he continued signing, Karen relayed his words. 'We're aware that by bringing REE down, on the one hand, it will save those horses going to Menningala, and on the other hand, it means the horses that did have a good life under REE will be in trouble. Any chance some other charities, like yours Grace, can step in and help them?'

'I can take on some horses, probably a few dozen at the most, spread over my rescues. Kat and Kaz can probably take ten unless they expand. There are others I know and trust, but we'd still be looking at four hundred horses, maybe five. A lot of the rescues that depend on donations have been missing out because REE grabbed the lion's share of everything, so they don't have the funds to take on more horses. Plus, once the public finds out about REE, their confidence in any horse rescue will be shaken, so the good ones will struggle for money.'

Karen nodded her understanding of the problems. 'That leaves a lot of horses - -thousands - that are caught in REE's web with no place to go, and thousands more next year, and the year after that. It was the first charity big enough to pick up almost all the horses going to the pet food market. If they shut down, the unwanted horses will be going back there.'

'Sometimes,' sadness softened Matthew's features, 'death isn't the worst option. If it's humane, perhaps it's better than what happens inside the vaccine laboratories. REE saved them from the pet food trade and assigned many to a worse fate.'

Tapping her chin thoughtfully, Vicki looked at the faces of her friends on the screen. 'Is it possible to rein in REE so that they stop the worst of their actions while they continue to support their riding centers and rescue horses?'

Everyone considered this for a few seconds before Joe's soft voice broke the silence. 'I don't think that's possible. We can't even find out all the people behind this. They've been draining hundreds of millions of dollars from this charity to the network of companies around it – if we cut off their money, they won't have any reason to keep it running. They're not in it for the horses or even the children - they are merely the bait that lures the donations.'

'True,' Karen agreed. 'I think, for now, we'll have to stop looking at the big picture because it is too much to take in – we can't solve everything. We need to focus on one part where we can make a difference. Our immediate problem is how to save the horses currently in the process of going to Menningala in Venezuela. We only have a few days to save them, but I believe that's something we can achieve. Let's play that hand now and see where the other cards fall after that.'

'We're Johnny-on-the-spot over here,' said Matthew, looking sideways at Grace for her approval. She nodded. 'We know where they have the horses, and we have some Pilatos security here to help. What can we do?'

Karen raised a hand to stop that train of thought. 'You and Grace have already been taken once, and next time they might not risk you escaping. It was likely that the men at the top wanted you dead, but the workers decided to make a bit extra on the side without the bosses knowing. You've had your narrow escape so let's not risk a repeat of that. You both sit tight at Ernie's place because when we get moving, they'll go all out to stop us, and I don't want you in their line of fire.'

'With this sort of money at stake,' Joe tapped the papers in front of him, 'they have a strong motivation to get rid of any threat.'

'They do,' Karen exhaled heavily as she considered their options, 'and if we choose to forget the horses that need us today, we could play safe. We could quietly continue to gather enough information to force official action. They might be able to buy off people in local authorities, but they won't be able to influence the big guns like the Australian Tax Office, the Securities and Investment Commission, the Charities and Not-for-profits Commission, the Federal Police, and even the Department of Foreign Affairs and Trade.'

Matthew smiled in appreciation of her knowledge. It was good having a lawyer on the team. 'But we don't have time.'

'No, we don't.' Karen held up some papers. 'These are messages from people trying to find the horses that we believe are a part of the shipment you witnessed arrive, Matt. We spoke to one of the grooms at HATCO, Chloe, and she identified two of them and thought she recognized another couple. If we want to save them, we have to act now.'

'We do have evidence, though, don't we?' asked Andrea. 'Those photos of the brands, the empty paddocks, the payments for feed and care on horses that aren't there.'

Karen rocked a hand back and forth. 'Some, but too much of what we have is hearsay, suspicion, and deduction rather than hard evidence. There's not enough of the right type of documentation to bring the ATO and others into the game, and, even if it were, their actions wouldn't be fast enough to save this shipment of horses. It might save future ones, but we are the only hope for those horses there now.'

'But even if we bring REE down, will it really save horses in the future?' Grace tried to envisage the entire horse industry in Australia, from backyard breeders right through to large Thoroughbred studs. 'We still breed too many horses. If we take REE out of the equation, the horses stop going to Menningala and mass burials, but they start going back to the pet food industry. It's a damned if we do and damned if we don't scenario.'

'It is,' Karen agreed, 'which is why Lane and I decided to do what we can to save the horses that we can save now. They're not a nameless mob of unwanted animals – they have names, they have friends, some have owners looking for them. As we speak, messages from Lane are hitting all social media platforms to raise an army of horse lovers from all sectors of the community in Venezuela so we can keep those Australian horses safe.'

A bark of laughter came from Tom as he recognized the tactic. 'Just like we did when we wanted to stop what was happening in the Pilatos laboratories. It worked.'

Karen offered a good-humored grimace at the memory of the tens of thousands who rallied to support Lane when he called on his followers to picket her family's pharmaceutical company. 'Repeating it seems the safest and fastest option to save those horses and to send a message to whoever runs this cesspit. We know they've killed to keep their secrets, but we're hoping there's safety in numbers.'

'What's in the posts?' Andrea leaned closer to her camera, keen to learn how Lane intended to rally his followers.

'There are about fifty segments timed to go out across all platforms as well as Lane's blog and our main website. I'll send you copies of everything. Without naming any company, we're confident people will talk to each other and work out who they are. He says it's worrying that, to date, several hundred horses have been found in mass graves in countries where the vaccine company and the charity are located in proximity to each other. Some brands on the deceased horses match horses that the charity claims are still alive.'

Tom gave another short laugh. 'No wonder you were relieved about our brand evidence.'

It was timely to have proof of my assumption, Lane signed and offered a lopsided grin.

'We've included details about some of the horses,' said Karen. 'While people are thinking of truckloads of nameless animals, they can justify doing nothing because they're not emotionally involved. When we're looking for Dibby and Rev, two palomino geldings owned by Mel Grant until her ex-husband gave them to a horse rescue to spite her, it engages our feelings. We want an emotional reaction to these horses because that is what will motivate people to step up and help.'

Matthew remembered how the images of the Friesians in the Pilatos laboratories stirred horse lovers to stand up for them. 'What should we do while we're waiting for the protesters to gather?'

'Nothing.' Karen's voice was firm and her grey eyes solemn as she looked into the camera. She needed Matthew and Grace to understand the danger and remain hidden. 'They'll try and stop us, so we all need to stay out of sight. They won't be able to stop the viral spreading of the social media posts.' She paused to look down at her phone, where she was monitoring some of the releases. 'Three minutes in, and we're already looking at thousands of shares. It will grow exponentially in the next few hours and, hopefully, every person who cares about horses will be aware of those horses in Venezuela about to make that final drive to Menningala.'

'There's more to this than what we suspected,' warned Joe, his eyes troubled. 'We need facts about what is happening in the vaccine facility with these horses. We need to know all the people involved and what they get out of it.'

'I agree,' Karen turned her attention back to the camera and raised her hands in a *what can you do?* gesture, 'but if we take the time for that, it will be too late for these horses. We know REE send horses to them when they shouldn't, and we know many of those horses die, so we're going to run with what we have. Perhaps some will argue that the deaths are justifiable if they help produce safe vaccines that save the lives of tens of thousands of horses around the world, but they are breaching all sorts of regulations with their actions.'

'I understand,' Joe's face held disapproval, 'but if you don't mind, I'm going to continue to follow up leads with the vaccine company.'

'We have no issue with that,' Karen glanced at Lane to ensure he agreed. 'We're going to need more evidence than what we have to give to the authorities before they start an official investigation into all of this.'

'For now,' said Tom, 'I guess we ensure that Lane's posts get spread so that awareness grows. Once the spotlight is firmly on REE, Menningala, and these other companies, I'm sure there'll be a flood of stories coming from people who were afraid to speak up before.'

'That's what we're hoping.' Karen told them about some of the emails and messages they'd started receiving that detailed negative aspects of REE.

After a few more minutes of conversation, they ended the call. In Caracas, Matthew sat staring at the screen saver, his eyes glazing over as he thought about the horses on the farm in the mountains. He clicked open some of the files Karen sent him and looked at the photos of the palominos. They were beautiful horses. He could see it in their eyes. He felt a distinct tug on his heart - they needed him.

'Let me guess,' Grace nudged his knee with her own, 'we're not going to remain in safety – we're going to do something really stupid like go back and see those horses.'

Matthew flashed her one of his disarming grins. 'Only if a lot of people start turning up to protest. They won't know where the farm is, of course, but I'm fairly sure we have enough contacts in the horse community here to ensure they get an address. If we have a few thousand people along the roads between the farm and Menningala, we should be able to sneak back to check the horses.'

'We don't need to go back.' A grim tone flattened Grace's voice.

'Of course, we don't *need* to,' Matthew's voice danced with adventure, 'but look at these photos of Dibby and Rev. Great looking horses. They were probably on those trucks that arrived when we broke out. It would be awful if the men at the farm decided to shoot them if they couldn't move them to Menningala.'

One side of Grace's mouth twisted in disapproval at his plan.

'You need to stay here,' he continued, 'while I go back to that farm and do what I can to keep those horses safe.'

'You need to get one thing straight,' Grace crossed her arms over her chest and glared at him, 'you do not get to tell me what to do. If you're going back to help those horses, I'm going with you.'

Without thinking, Matthew leaned sideways and grabbed her in a hug. Used to his tactile friends who accepted physical contact with amiable ease, he was surprised to feel her stiffen in his arms and draw back from him. She rose to her feet and regarded him with a measure of alarm.

'Sorry.' He smiled up at her, hoping she saw his action as a harmless gesture rather than something predatory. The last thing he wanted was to damage the friendship that he hoped was growing. 'I'm just one of those huggy-bear sort of people. You're allowed to slap me if I overstep the mark.'

'No, I'm sorry.' Grace tried to cover her response to his touch. The explosion of emotions through her mind stunned her, and her reaction had been to escape. When he quickly withdrew his arms, she felt disappointed for ruining the moment.

With a racing heart and blood rushing to her cheeks, she turned away from him and mumbled, 'I got a surprise, that's all. Hugs are acceptable. I'll try not to jump next time.'

The fact that she expected a next time was a relief to Matthew. He made a mental note to give her notice and wait for her approval before he invaded her personal space again. 'I'll give you an advance warning of any hugging.'

With emotions running high, she approached the door and then stopped, wanting to explain. 'No need. Honestly. I was just, you know, not expecting...' She gave up on her garbled clarification and changed the subject. 'I don't think Deo should come with us, but perhaps we could speak to him about the farm before we return.'

'Good idea. I'm going to ask Kayne for any video footage from the drones or satellite photos. The Google Earth ones don't show much detail in this region, and I'd like to know where the tracks and fences are.'

'That would have been handy yesterday,' she screwed up her nose as she tried to get an idea of time in her sleep-deprived mind, 'or was it the day before? Whenever it was that we were struggling to make our way through a jungle while a perfectly good track was a stone's throw away from us.'

'That was last night.'

She uttered a *harrumph* and shook her head. 'Really? It feels like ages ago.' A yawn forced her mouth open. 'I need sleep.'

'Go and knock out some zeds while I chase up a few leads. I'd like to tell you to sleep for the rest of today and tonight, but those horses only have limited time, so we're going to have to act fast if we want to help them.'

'And just how do we help them? Cut the fences and let them loose in the jungle? Drive a heap of horse trucks in and try and load a hundred horses while Deo's employers shoot at us? Or will you run them single-handed down that mountain like The Man from Snowy River?'

Matthew clapped his hands together and sprang to his feet, successfully fighting the urge to hug her again. 'And that, right there,' he pointed at her in delight, 'is a perfect example of my belief that women are smarter than men. I had no idea what we could do, and you gave three possible solutions in the space of seconds.'

'I'm not seeing solutions,' Grace closed one eye as she ran her words back through her mind, 'just stupidly crazy ideas that are doomed to failure.'

'Of course, they're insane,' conceded Matthew, his eyes bright with exhilaration as he started planning how they'd save the horses. 'That's why I love one of them in particular.'

'Crazy idea for a crazy man.' She gave him a dry look. 'They do say that like attracts like.'

'Absolutely,' he grinned and shooed her away with one hand. 'Go and have a snooze. I'm all adrenalined up now, so I won't be sleeping. I'm going to organize something totally insane.'

'I'm going to organize a re-think of wanting to join you.'

Matthew pointed a finger at her and winked. 'That would be wise.'

Rolling her eyes, she grumbled, 'I flew to Venezuela with a man I just met, got kidnapped, and ran through a jungle with him. Just how wise do you think I am?'

She left him laughing and headed to her bedroom.

Once alone, Matthew found a notepad and started jotting down ideas, names, and phone numbers, and listing the things he wanted to achieve before going back to the farm in the jungle to save the horses.

'Ernie!' Matthew called out the back door. 'I'm going to need your help.'

***

Dibby and Rev

As the light faded, the howler monkeys started their piercing cries. The sounds made the horses uneasy, but they remembered that no harm accompanied the noise that morning and settled.

Rev looked up at the trees silhouetted against the dying light, trying to find the source of the noise. Dibby, Dusty, and several other horses moved closer to him, studying his actions to guide their behavior. While Rev remained calm, so did they, and the mood spread through the other horses.

When the monkeys fell silent, Rev exhaled a sigh of relief and returned to eating. All the horses copied him.

In the house, men argued loudly, their voices carrying to the horses on the warm air. Rev did not understand the words about the missing Australians, Deo, the viral social media posts about saving the horses, or anything else, but he did recognize the emotions that colored the words. Fear. Anger. Concern. Aggression.

His ears flicked back and forth as he caught the feelings of the men. It reminded him of everything he sensed when Mel and Connor argued - she was fear and concern; he was anger and aggression. Rev shook his head at the memories. They made him uncomfortable. He longed to break through these fences and find a way home to Mel. For a moment, he looked into the darkness, trying to sense where home lay, but there was nothing.

CHAPTER TWENTY-THREE

We all have the power to change the world. Some of us change the entire world. Some of us change the world for one person or one animal. Just make sure you change it for the better.
Social media post by Lane Dimity

Social Media
A social media post by Lane Dimity - over one million shares in the first twelve hours.

A horse rescue should give horses a chance at a better life - they should not prolong suffering, and they should not use their charity status as a means to make huge profits from donations. Do you agree? Yes? Then stay tuned and share what's coming. There are horses who need you.

***

A blog post by Lane Dimity - shared on social media several million times in the first twelve hours.

Do you support a horse charity if they save a hundred horses but condemn a thousand? What if the charity saves horses from a quick death at the abattoir only to send them to a laboratory before killing them, cutting them open, removing their brands, and burying them in mass graves? What is being tested in this laboratory? What are they hiding? Why does the charity continue to collect donations for horses they claim are alive when they've been identified in those mass burials?

***

An update on the main page of Lane Dimity's website - shared to social media several million times in the first twelve hours.

Why does a company that develops equine medicine have a facility in every country near a particular horse charity? Why are horses that are given or sold to this charity being sent to the laboratories? Why are so many horses coming out of Level Four biocontainment areas and being buried without them notifying authorities? Why are the people who work with the horses at this charity unknown in the horse world? Who are they? Who owns the charity?

Why are there companies donating tens of millions of dollars to the charity? Is it because, after the donations, they make a much larger income *from* the charity? Why are good people sponsoring thousands of horses that don't appear to be alive anymore? Why are agistment centers taking tens of millions of dollars in agistment for dead horses? Why is a feed company earning tens of millions of dollars for horse feed for all those dead horses? Why does an advertising company make tens of millions of dollars promoting an equine charity that kills horses? And why the silence?

Where are all the horses? I know there are close to one hundred Australian horses on a farm in the mountains east of Caracas in Venezuela right now waiting to be transported to the laboratories there – and what then? What happens in the Level Four containment area that has some horses coming out alive and some coming out dead when no animals should be coming out at all? What is going on?

How can we save the horses near Caracas? Can we find enough people who care about horses to stop them from going to the laboratory? Can we stop them from being put down on the farm if the charity orders it? Next update soon.

***

A blog post by Lane Dimity - shared more than five million times.

We met Binky Laurie earlier this month – an inspiring young horsewoman concerned about the horses buried in the Hunter region. She went there and asked questions. She was murdered. A machinery driver allegedly paid to bury the horses is missing. Two workers who looked after the horses at the laboratory in the Hunter are missing. A Venezuelan woman who found horses buried in a similar mass grave was questioned by men from the Venezuelan branch of those laboratories – she and her brother were run down by a truck and killed.

Grace Walker from one of our preferred horse rescues, Horse

Helpers, and our own Matthew McLeay are in Caracas asking questions about the charity and the laboratory. They were kidnapped and held at the farm where the Australian horses were sent – luckily, they escaped and are safe. Hundreds of millions of dollars, thousands of missing horses, people who ask questions get killed or go missing, and a whole lot of unanswered questions.

I don't know what we can do about the big picture, but I know I want to save those horses on the farm east of Caracas. I don't want them going into that Level Four containment area. Together, we can save them.

***

A social media post by Lane Dimity - shared millions of times.

To all who want to help the horses outside Caracas – we are hoping if enough people turn up and hold a peaceful protest on the roads between the farm where they are being held and the laboratory where they are going, we can keep them alive. If you can help or know someone who can, please contact us for more information and the location, or ask around – someone will have the information from us. We don't want to put anyone in danger – we do want the charity to know we are aware of what is happening.

***

In the hours following Lane's messages to his followers, lawyers representing REE and Menningala began retaliating with cease-and-desist letters as well as notices of intent to commence litigation against Lane and anyone sharing his messages. Karen read them, yawned, and said her lawyers would take care of everything.

She continued helping Lane release facts about the charity and its associates. It made her smile to imagine the puppeteers who stayed in the shadows having conniptions as the eyes of Lane's seventy million social media followers turned in their direction.

Around the world, people began searching for the names of Australian horse charities and laboratories that specialized in equine medicines and vaccines. Although Lane omitted the names of the companies, they were soon among the most popular searched items of the week.

The team who answered emails and messages directed to Lane reported tens of thousands of communications asking about the horses in Caracas. They replied with the stock message about location, times, and possible dangers. Lane was unsure of his fanbase in Venezuela, but thousands of horse lovers there wanted to help the Australian horses. With the zeal of believers on a mission, horse people around Caracas and beyond began contacting friends, rounding up supporters, and sharing the information about where to gather. Even those who struggled against poverty and hardship found a reason to head east of Caracas because this was a battle where they could make a difference.

Armed guards at the farm gates prevented anyone from entering the property and going up the steep winding track to the horses. Instead, people began taking up positions along the roads between the farm and Menningala. At dawn, a few hundred arrived in cars, on foot, horseback, and bikes. By mid-morning, thousands lined the roads. They continued to come from the local area, from Caracas, and from around the country.

Horse people gathered and spoke of others on their way from Columbia and Brazil. They shared stories of the rumors they'd heard of buried horses and truckloads of animals going in and out of Menningala. And they waited. No one could leave the farm via the road, and the mountains at the back blocked any rear escape. The Australian horses were trapped on the farm.

When the *policia* arrived, three riders on Andalusian horses forced them to stop before reaching the crowds. The sister of the Director-General of the National Police and her two daughters sat proudly on their mounts as an officer called headquarters to check on what action to take. An unequivocal command to leave the demonstrators alone and protect any horse riders came from the top of the police force. The Director-General understood the passion of the horsewomen in his family and knew which side to take – the side defended by his wife and daughters.

Whenever someone took a photo and posted it to social media, others shared it, which caused more to upload pictures and post updates hoping for viral shares. The world hungered for information about what was taking place in Venezuela. They watched and wondered what would happen to the horses. They looked at the images of Dibby, Rev, and the other horses photographed before they left Australia. People who recognized the horses from studs, racing, competitions, or previous homes wrote about what they knew. The horses stopped being a group of unknown animals and became individuals with names, personalities, histories, and stories.

Lane didn't know if this was the way to save the horses, but he knew the power of the crowds helped him free the stallions from the Pilatos laboratories the year before, and he hoped they would help again. The horses wouldn't disappear into the night, forgotten and invisible – there were millions of people around the world wanting them to live.

***

A coded message to the CEO of Menningala Vaccines in Venezuela
Do not attempt to move the horses. Have them killed and burned. We will cease moving REE horses until this is over. Purchase local horses to replace them and proceed. Alpha.

***

Reply from the CEO of Menningala Vaccines in Venezuela.
Understood. Issuing termination orders now.

***

Dibby and Rev
Although the trees surrounding the farmhouse formed an almost impenetrable barrier, faint sounds drifted up the hill across the tops of the branches. The howler monkeys remained silent against the onslaught of voices. Down the mountain, past the security guards and front fence, people kept arriving. The faint chatter of the crowd and the occasional calls from their horses drifted up to the Australian horses. By lunchtime, Rev spent most of his time with his head raised, staring in the direction of the indistinct sounds, his ears flicking back and forth.

Next to him, Dibby stood in a similar pose, his head held higher than all those around. Dusty watched them, unsure of what to do. Rev's level of alertness had all the horses on edge. Like Dusty, they watched the palominos and waited.

Shortly after lunch, two men carrying guns stepped off the veranda of the house. They approached the horses, shook their heads, and their shoulders slumped. Rev recognized the body language – there was something they didn't want to do. He could sense it on them like the jibbing shoulders of a horse that refuses to step into water.

A third man emerged from the house, gesturing wildly with his arms as he pointed at the horses and motioned for the gunmen to go to them. An argument ensued, and Rev watched with interest, curious about their anger. The words meant nothing to him, but he recognized the tones.

'Shoot them. We have our orders,' commanded the man at the house in Spanish.

'They will hear,' one of the gunmen pointed down the mountain at the unseen crowds.

'They have drones,' said the other, looking up. 'We need to wait.'

'We were told to do it immediately. Do it.'

'We need to wait until sundown. The monkeys will start calling.'

'Idiot. They will stop calling at the first gunshot. There is no point waiting.'

'We can make silencers for the guns so they don't hear.'

'We don't need silencers - we need to do the job and do it now. Keep them together so they'll be easier to burn.'

'We should wait for the cover of night.'

'Now. Do it, or I will, and the last bullets will be for you.'

The two gunmen looked at each other before walking towards the horses, their feet dragging.

CHAPTER TWENTY-FOUR

The answer to a lot of life's problems is to get on the horse and ride.
T-shirt with a photo of Lane Dimity.

Crowds Gather

'How well do you ride?' Matthew raised an eyebrow at Deo.

The teen shrugged and wobbled a hand back and forth. 'I am no expert, but I can hang on.'

Matthew, Grace, and Deo sat in the Pilatos security car outside the farm where they'd left Deo's horses. Kayne sat in the driver's seat, his dark eyes continually scanning the surroundings for danger, while Matthew, next to him, twisted in his seat to talk to the two in the back. A second Pilatos vehicle behind them held more guards who, like Kayne, scanned continually for any threat.

'You are not seriously considering going in on horseback?' Grace cast an incredulous look at Matthew. 'There are guards with guns at the main gate. You'll be shot for trespassing the moment you try to pass through.'

'That would be stupid,' agreed Matthew cheerfully. 'I don't plan on riding a horse up there. I'm not insane. I'm going to walk up and ride a horse down.'

Grace's lips pressed together in disapproval. 'Ride a horse?'

'Well, ride one and drive the other hundred or so.'

A snort of astonishment escaped Grace as she realized what he planned. 'You are not the man from Snowy River. You can't singlehandedly drive them down the mountain, and alone and unassisted, bring them back.'

Her paraphrasing of the poem's lines caused his lips to twitch. 'No, of course, that would be madness. I'm going to take Deo with me. We'll do it together, won't we, Deo?'

The teen bounced with excitement for a moment before the enormity of what Matthew was planning hit him. The enthusiasm evaporated, and he frowned. 'You think we can bring all the horses down the mountain. Just the two of us? They have guns. They will use them. I know this.'

'Which is why we'll sneak up there past your home and not on the main road. We'll make a distraction, grab a couple of horses, and head back down. We only have to reach the people down here, and we'll be safe. There's safety in numbers – Lane knows that, which is why he organized all these people to be here.'

'Kayne,' Grace tapped their driver on the shoulder, 'tell Matthew that he'll get himself killed doing that.'

'You'll get yourself killed doing that, Matthew,' Kayne told him in a flat voice.

'And tell him why,' Grace urged.

'Because they'll shoot you.'

Matthew grinned at Kayne. 'Now tell me what you really think rather than what Grace wants you to say.'

Kayne gave Grace an apologetic grimace in the mirror. She reminded him of his younger sister, and he didn't want to hurt her feelings. 'I think it doesn't matter what I say; you are going to do something stupid and risky. I know Lane and Miss Lawford expect two things of us – keep you two safe and save those horses. I don't think we can achieve both by keeping Matthew locked up, so we'd better hear his plan to save the horses and try to make it as safe as possible.'

'Without shooting the men up there,' put in Deo. 'To you, they are criminals, but they have families. They took care of me when my parents died. They take good care of the horses that are sent here. They are not all bad and don't deserve to die because they work for the wrong people.'

'They did kidnap us,' pointed out Grace dryly.

'But they did not kill you,' he insisted. 'If they were paid to release you, I believe they would have let you go unharmed.'

Although he had sincere doubts about that, Matthew did not argue. 'Good men occasionally do bad things and don't deserve to die for that. We'll try to extract the horses without harming your friends, alright?'

Deo nodded. 'Good.'

'Now, you say they take good care of the horses. Do they actually *like* horses?'

'They do, and some want to leave because they are,' he paused to think of a suitable word in English, 'unwell – sick – about what happens.'

'Have they told you what happens to the horses after they leave the farm?' Matthew wondered if Deo held important information.

'I suspect some die.' Deo's voice grew small, as though he'd returned to childhood and spoke of dangerous things that roamed the night without understanding what they were. 'They go to the factory - Menningala Vaccines. Some come out alive. Others don't. The men up there seemed frightened to talk of what happens. We are one part of the engine, and we don't understand the other parts. We care for thc horses when they arrive, and then they leave. Do you think they all die?'

His eyes were large and sad as he asked the question, as though he knew the answer but could hide from the truth as long as he didn't hear it stated. The men at the farm protected him from many things, he knew that, and perhaps they hadn't shared what they knew about the horses because they understood he loved them.

Grace gave his shoulder a comforting pat. 'We're not sure what happens, Deo, but we think the horses up there at the moment may die if we don't save them. We're going to work out a way to sneak up there and bring them down without hurting your friends.'

'What's this *we*?' Matthew quizzed her. 'You can't ride.'

'I beg to differ,' Grace arched a brow at him. 'I competed successfully for Australia in junior eventing and expected to ride at Burghley, Badminton, Kentucky, and the other big three-day events until my accident. I can ride perfectly well.'

'You know what I mean.' Worry creased his brow as he thought of the last time she rode, ending up with a broken back and the prospect of never walking again. 'You haven't ridden since that accident, and this isn't the time to get back on the horse.'

'It's the best of times to do so.' Her chin lifted to a defiant angle. 'I've devoted my life to saving horses, and there are horses up that mountain that need saving today. It's not like you ever forget how to ride a horse – I'll be fine.'

'We don't know the horses there. We don't know if the ones we pick to ride are going to be OK about it, and you can't afford to have a fall.'

'So, I won't fall.' His level of worry touched Grace, but the more he tried to dissuade her, the more she dug her toes in. She recognized the stubborn streak in herself and knew there was nothing Matthew could do to stop her from joining him. 'I read what the owner of those two palominos wrote about them – give me one of them, and I'll be fine.'

'I had them picked for Deo and me,' said Matthew, mulishly.

He didn't want Grace to put herself in danger. He also knew that the set to her chin indicated he couldn't stop her. A cold shadow swept through his mind as he imagined her coming off a horse and hurting her back. If that happened, he would leave the horses behind and carry her down in his arms.

'Then find another horse. I'll take Dibby. Mel wrote that he was unflappable and good on his feet, so he'll be the perfect mount for me. She said Rev is the leader in any situation, and other horses follow him, so he should suit you. I'm sure we'll find something suitable for Deo.'

'There's no need for you to come.' Matthew looked to Kayne for help, but he kept his attention outside the car. 'If Kayne and his men can provide a distraction, Deo can take me in and help bring the horses down.'

'You might be able to do it with two, but three improves the chances.' Grace held up a finger as Matthew began to open his mouth to object. 'If I were a man, you'd be fine with it. You're roping in a teenager because he's a boy - so stop protesting and accept that I'm coming with you. If the people behind this realize that they can't get those horses to Menningala, you know they're likely to put them down. These aren't the sort of people who lose graciously.'

Matthew rubbed a hand across his eyes. She was right. If she were male, he wouldn't have this desire to protect her. The thought of anything happening to her terrified him. He believed in equality of the sexes, but he couldn't shake the instinct to keep Grace away from danger.

'Alright,' he inclined his head to accept her terms. 'Kayne – three of us are going to try and bring the horses down. Can you organize something to keep the men busy without endangering anyone – them or you? Once we're ready, I'll call you or, if the phones don't have reception there, perhaps we'll just...'

'Use these,' Kayne interrupted, holding out a couple of black watches. 'We all have them. They're directly linked within a ten-mile radius, so we don't need a carrier service – think of it as a single channel walkie-talkie network. They come with earbuds, and there are texting and voice-to-text options if you want them. There's also internet and phone capability, GPS tracking, camera, video, voice recording, health tracking, and an EPIRB in case everything goes wrong, and you need us to find you.'

Matthew strapped the watch on his wrist. 'But does it tell the time?'

'Idiot,' muttered Grace as she snapped hers in place. The time was clearly displayed on the dial.

'I don't have one for you, sorry, Deo, but you're probably better off without anything that indicates you're working with us. If they catch you, you're the same person you were yesterday – you just took your horses away from home because your mare needed a vet. OK?'

Deo nodded his agreement.

Over the next hour, Kayne showed them how to operate the devices, ran through their plan with his fellow Pilatos employees, and relayed reports back to Joe. He had intended to take his team up to seize control of the farm and bring in trucks to collect the horses, but since they were acting in a foreign country against local citizens, their actions could be seen as terrorist activity. The case of two unarmed Australians going in to steal Australian horses was legally and politically less incendiary than an armed U.S. security team attacking Venezuelan farmers.

As they looked at images of the gathering crowds relayed to them by drones, Matthew asked Deo if the men at the farm were likely to kill the horses if they couldn't get them to Menningala.

It took a full minute for Deo to process an answer. He knew these people had never known the fear of starving to death or watching their families die in front of them because of drug cartel violence or preventable diseases. It would be difficult for them to understand that, even though the men liked horses, if they had to choose between the lives of the horses and the lives of their families, the horses would lose.

'They would not *want* to kill them,' he said with some sadness, 'but if they were ordered to do so, they would follow orders.'

'Then we'd better get moving.' Matthew turned to Kayne. 'Is there a drone that can check on them?'

'They shot one down, but this one appears to be out of range.' Kayne enlarged one of the drone windows on his laptop screen to show the farmhouse and the horses.

'Good.' Matthew examined the layout, committing it to memory. 'Can you zoom out?'

Once Kayne adjusted the drone camera, Matthew placed his finger over a small cluster of rooftops visible in the jungle below the main farm. He could see a faint path linking them and, further over, the main driveway wound up the mountain. The gate to the property was easy to make out because of the thousands of people lining the road outside it.

'That's Deo's place, isn't it?' Grace looked at the buildings under Matthew's finger. 'We'll make our way there and take Deo's walking track to the horses.'

'I think so,' Matthew nodded. He wanted to tell her to stay with the Pilatos team, but he understood her determination to be a part of the rescue. At least Kayne had sourced a sturdy back protector that Grace agreed to wear.

Kayne started the car. 'Joe said you're magic with horses, so I'll leave that part up to you. If you run into trouble, let us know and we'll get you out. Don't risk dying for some horses.' He paused to smack himself on the forehead. 'What am I saying? That's exactly what you are doing.'

'We'll be fine.' Matthew wasn't sure what lay ahead but knew it was better to display confidence than doubt. 'We're just going for a ride down a hill. What could go wrong?'

With a grunt of disapproval, Kayne steered the car onto the road and followed Deo's directions to get as close to his farm as possible while avoiding the roads lined with people.

The news channels had crews on-site, broadcasting the phenomena of tens of thousands of horse people turning up to protest the fate of a few Australian horses. Matthew and Grace flicked through coverage on their phones, smiling at how Lane's call to action had prompted the mass turnout. Social media was flooding with photos and videos from those standing at the roadsides, hoping to help the horses.

'I wasn't sure his influence would reach here.' Matthew turned his phone to show Deo images of the roads lined with people.

Deo looked at them, a sad expression in his eyes. 'They turn out like this to save some horses.' He shook his head at the broader meaning. 'My family was murdered, and the police said it was part of the drug gang violence. No one cared except for the men on the farm. More than three hundred people are murdered in my country every week, many by the government forces who are supposed to protect the people, and the world ignores what happens to us. And yet they turn out like this to help some horses.'

The three adults remained silent. The enormity of his words affected them deeply. How could anyone adequately explain to a teenager why so many cared for the fate of the horses when the killing of his family went unnoticed? Most of the people responding to Lane's words came from the wealthier sections of the community – the network of people who owned horses and cars and who could afford to take a day to stand at the side of the road because an influencer asked them to go there.

Deo knew many like himself who struggled at the survival point of life: farmers whose crops failed, children who left school at a young age to work, and women who remained at home with their children while their husbands tried to find work elsewhere. The poor grew poorer while the wealthy turned out to save the lives of some horses from the other side of the world. Lane might say that they were speaking for the horses who had no voice, but what voice did his family have? Who spoke up for them?

'I'm sorry, Deo,' murmured Grace, placing a gentle hand on his arm. 'We'll make sure we do more to help you and others like you after we help the horses. I promise. Perhaps these people,' she pointed at the crowds pictured on the screen, 'feel overwhelmed by the immensity of what is wrong in a world where so many are murdered and so many families are hungry, but this one small act is something they feel they can achieve. They're not here because they don't care about what is wrong with all those hurt by poverty and crime – they're here because they see they can make a difference to something today. They can't fix everything that is wrong, but Lane has given them a small achievable task that makes them feel like they are making the world a better place.'

Regarding her with soft eyes, Deo nodded. Her words made sense and provided solace.

'Beautifully said,' put in Matthew, 'and Grace is right. We will do more to help when this is over. I'm not sure how, but we'll find a way.'

Grace gave him a disheartened look. 'Maybe if we find a charity that puts more than five percent of its donations towards the people it's meant to help. One thing that REE has taught me is that too many charities are a way to make the wealthy wealthier.'

'Preaching to the converted, sister.' Matthew winked at her before holding his phone up for Deo and clicking through some photos. They showed armed guards standing at the entrance to the farm and a security fence with cameras in the jungle. 'We didn't see anything like this on our walk out of there.'

'The fences are only along the front and part of the sides,' Deo explained. 'They don't expect anyone to fight through the jungle to see some horses. We're not drug cartel workers, so we don't have their level of security. My home is well past the point where the fence ends, and who would go that way?'

He was right. When Kayne dropped them off at the end of an overgrown track, they entered the forest far from the front gate. No one would think to come here if they wanted to reach the farm. The path that disappeared into the jungle shadows bore the hoofprints of Deo's horses from the previous day. They followed it, jogging between the trees.

It took extreme effort from Grace to move without showing signs of the pain that hammered her spine with every step. Even with the painkillers that she took when no one was looking, she battled to contain the grunts and groans that threatened to escape as she ran. She didn't want Matthew to know that the kidnapping and escape had strained her back because he would call Kayne and insist that she go back to safety.

She wanted to be here, jogging through the jungle on the way to rescue the horses. It was dangerous and it was probably unwise, but she felt more alive and exhilarated than any day since the accident. Despite the aching of her back, she looked forward to climbing on board a horse for the first time in years. Of course, she should never ride again, and she understood the risks, but the excitement that bubbled inside at the prospect of a wild bareback ride down a mountain made her toss all caution aside.

It was easy for the doctors to order her not to ride, and she knew it was a sensible directive. As she walked through the pain barrier, she decided that riding for her was like flying for a bird – it was something she was born to do. Even if she ended up in a wheelchair, she would have someone strap her to a horse so she could ride again. The years of remaining wisely on the ground ended today. She grinned to herself: she was a horsewoman, so she was crazy by nature.

When the steep climb forced them to walk, relief flooded her. There was no way that she would ask them to slow down, but the gradient was taking its toll on her muscles.

'Not far to my home,' Deo informed them. 'We are making good time.'

'When we are near the horses,' Matthew's breath puffed between words, 'maybe you can sneak in close and see what's happening. Make sure the horses are all OK and see how many pens they have them in.'

'I can go in and speak to the men,' he offered. 'They will believe me if I say I had to take my horses down the mountain to a farmer who can doctor them. They will not know we are together.'

Matthew admired the teen's courage, but he was determined to keep him safe. If there was a chance the men suspected Deo of changing teams, he feared they might harm him. 'The three of us will stick together, OK? No going in on your own.' He turned to look at Grace. 'How are you traveling?'

'All good with me.' She tried to sound less out of breath than him and smothered a chuckle at her competitiveness. 'Though, I would prefer it if the horses were in a valley and we had to walk down to them and ride back up.'

'Maybe next time.'

'Next time?'

'There's sure to be more horse adventures if we get out of this one.'

'Could you revise the *if we get out of this one* part? That kind of sounds like there's a good possibility that we aren't going to get out of it.'

A grin split Matthew's face as he turned his attention back to the path. The fact that Grace didn't immediately declare that she was never going on another horse adventure with him implied that maybe she would, and that made him happy. 'Sorry. In future horse escapades, we'll try to make the rescues a little more convenient than this.'

'Good,' Grace smiled at the back of his head before her eyes dropped to his shapely posterior, and she lost track of her words for a moment. The old *Wrangler butts* bumper sticker flashed through her mind, and she felt her cheeks grow hot. Dragging her gaze away, she continued, 'Don't forget – we walk downhill and ride uphill.'

Matthew held up a hand and ticked the air. 'Mental note of that has been made.'

Their conversation bewildered Deo, and he looked back at them, a comical expression on his face. They chatted and bickered as though they were sitting safely at home and not walking up a mountain to clash with dangerous men. Very dangerous. He imagined that they would avoid shooting him even though he betrayed them, but he remembered the anger in their voices when they talked about the two kidnap victims who escaped. His new friends were walking into a potentially deadly showdown, and they joked with each other.

Deo shook his head and pushed through some leafy branches that bent across the path. He had heard Australians were crazy.

***

Dibby and Rev

Twice, the men with guns entered the corral and aimed at the horses before lowering their hands and walking away. Rev watched them closely and wondered about their actions. They started to do something they did not want to do and stopped – that he understood. They talked in hushed voices, and Rev understood the worry and stress in their tones.

'You know we have to do this.' The shorter of the two men waved his gun at the horses from the other side of the gate.

'I know, I know,' the taller man wiped a hand across his brow, 'but we can wait a little longer. The boss has walked up the mountain to check on his mother. He won't be back before dark.'

'And they should all be dead by then and ready to burn.'

The tall one looked at Rev. 'You know Deo would want those two golden horses. He's a good boy. It would mean much to him.'

'If he would turn up to work instead of spending the day with his horses, perhaps he might get them, but he's not here.'

'Wait a little longer.'

The smaller man shrugged and headed back to the house, speaking over his shoulder as he walked. 'It has to be done. If those people break through the gate and come up here, the boss will want our heads for not killing the horses.'

'How much could it hurt to let them live? Why kill them?'

'Because that is how they are, these people. If they can't have them, no one will. They will see it as a lesson to those people,' he pointed down the mountain where the crowds continued to gather along the roads, 'so that they don't try this again. It is their way of saying that they own these horses and they will do what they want with them.'

A look of disgust crossed the taller man's face as he considered the unknown men in the chain of command above them. 'They make me sick. They are filth.'

'Their money feeds our families and buys our clothes. Being with them gives us protection from the drug gangs. It could be worse.'

'It could… but those horses,' he cast a regretful look back at them, 'they only want to live.'

'They die either way, my friend. At least we can make it quick.'

CHAPTER TWENTY-FIVE

When I ride a good horse, our souls fly together.
A bumper sticker of a Lane Dimity quote.

Ride Boldly

By the time Matthew, Grace, and Deo reached the trees around the farmhouse, the sun was close to the western horizon. Knowing that twilight was almost non-existent in these latitudes, Matthew wanted to move quickly. They crouched out of sight while Matthew instructed Kayne to start the diversion.

On the other side of the house and slightly further up the mountain, drones operated by Kayne's team dropped flashbangs that were triggered remotely. Speakers on the drones relayed voices to give the impression that the intruders were calling to each other.

Six armed men left the house at a run and headed towards the disturbance.

'There should be another three or four here,' whispered Deo, pointing at the house. 'They might be inside or in the shed on the other side of the horses.'

'Hopefully, they'll be watching Kayne's diversion and won't notice us until it's too late to stop us.'

Bent over, they left the trees and crossed the stretch of short grass to the railed fence. They slipped between the rough-hewn timber and approached the horses. Frightened by the sounds of the flashbangs, the horses crowded together against the rails, their heads raised in apprehension.

'That's a lot of horses,' said Grace, looking at the large mob.

'There should be eighty-five that came in from Australia a few days ago,' said Matthew as he laid a hand on the horse nearest him. The white shapes of the neck brand identified it as a Standardbred, and he expected the horse to be quiet. 'Lane said eighty-six left Australia, but one had to be put down on the plane.'

'Forty-two horses were already here.' Deo indicated the next corral where the smaller group of horses also stared up the hill. 'That is not counting the horses belonging to the men here. They are not with these. They are in a small field further over.'

'We're not taking them,' Matthew assured him. 'It's bad enough that we're stealing horses in order to save their lives without stealing horses that have homes.'

'How are you?' Grace crooned to a Thoroughbred who stretched his nose out to her. At the sound of her Australian voice, the horse took a step closer, his eyes shining with memories of others who sounded like her.

'I'm going to get the palominos.' Matthew pulled some lightweight rope halters from his pockets and moved between the horses, talking to them and stroking them as he passed. There were a few palominos, but he recognized Dibby and Rev from their photos when they turned to face him. His presence calmed and reassured them, and even Dusty's sad expression grew hopeful.

'Well, hello big yellows,' Matthew smiled at the horses and offered the back of his hand for them to sniff. Rev checked him first, his ears forward as he saw friendliness and understanding in Matthew's body language. 'Your owner wants you back, and we're going to take you, OK? She says we should be able to ride you bareback even if you haven't been ridden for ages, so how do you feel about that?'

He passed one of the halters to Grace.

'The big one for me?' Grace looked at the two palominos, assessing their intelligence in their inquisitive eyes. They looked to be everything that Mel described. 'I haven't ridden in few years,' she confided to Dibby as she placed the lead around his neck, 'so I'd appreciate a calm ride if you don't mind. A small pig-root shouldn't be a problem, but if we can skip a full-blown bucking session, that would be great, and I've never been a fan of the shy and suck-back move, if you could make a note of that.'

Dibby snorted happily. Her voice reminded him of Mel and he enjoyed the flow of soft words.

Once they had the halters on the palominos, Matthew looked around for a mount that Deo could ride. The taller, athletic horses appeared too skittish for a teen who, by his own admission, was still mastering the basics. The mud-colored Dusty pushed his way between

Dibby and Rev and looked at the two Australians, his wise eyes telling Matthew all he needed to know.

'I know this one is only short,' Matthew began putting the third halter on Dusty, 'but it's my bet he's as smart as they come, and if we need speed, I bet his pony legs will have no trouble moving twice as fast as the longer ones to keep up. He has some white hairs from saddle rubs, so he's spent plenty of time under saddle, and he seems to like these two big fellas. Do you think he'll do you, Deo?'

Taking the lead rope from Matthew, Deo patted the solid neck of the pony, admiring his tank-like proportions. 'His back looks more comfortable than some.'

Matthew smiled. The pony's broad back looked more of an armchair than some of the narrower ex-racehorses. 'Do you want a leg up before we get this show on the road?'

In reply, Deo quickly tied the other end of the lead to Dusty's halter to make a set of reins and vaulted on board. Matthew was not at all surprised to see the pony calmly accept his rider as Deo turned him in a circle left and right.

'Can you stay low on his back and open the gate between this yard and the next?' Matthew put a loop of baling twine around Dusty's neck and tied it off at the correct length for Deo to pull it while his hands remained in a good position for his reins. 'This will work better than a bit in his mouth, OK?' He gave the rope a light pull, and Dusty backed a step. 'If he doesn't want to stop when you pull on the reins, pull this instead. Release as soon as he responds. To him, it will be like having his neck over the top wire of a fence – he's going to stop going forward and, if he tries bucking, it will stop him doing that, too.'

Deo nodded. 'I understand. I'll get the gates. What then?'

Casting a questioning look at Grace, Matthew waited for her to speak. He didn't want to call all the shots when they were working together.

'Rev's owner said he's a natural leader,' Grace looked at the confident stance and noble eye of Matthew's chosen mount, 'so he needs to lead the way because the others should follow him. You and I, Deo, will drive the horses from behind.'

'That sounds like the best plan,' agreed Matthew, 'but be prepared to change if it all goes to rot. If they don't follow me, I'll come and join you two. We have to get them moving and – hopefully – moving at speed so that nothing stops them.'

'The gates at the bottom of the road will stop them,' pointed out Deo, thinking of the security fence and guards there.

Matthew tapped his temple. 'I may have thought ahead and put something in place for that.'

Flashing him a smile, Deo tapped his heels against Dusty's side and guided the pony through the crowd of horses towards the gate that separated the yards. He lay along Dusty's neck, but the pony was shorter than most of the horses, so no one would spot him among the raised heads even if he sat upright.

Eyeing the considerable height of Dibby and feeling her back twinge at the thought of trying to vault on board, Grace asked Matthew for a leg up.

'Of course,' Matthew put his hands under her bent knee and raised her onto the horse's back, where she lay along his neck in an effort to remain hidden. 'Don't fall.'

Perhaps it was the tension of the situation, or maybe it was the look of concern on his face, but Grace found his advice so ridiculous that she smothered a hoot of laughter. Once it escaped, she clapped a hand over her mouth, but the damage was done, and she followed up with several wheezing gasps. It took an effort to stop her asthmatic-goose outburst, and the twinkling in Matthew's eyes didn't help.

'A stupid time to laugh, I know.' She bit at her lower lip so the pain would kill her untimely amusement.

'Maybe it's the best time.'

'It's not,' she disagreed, 'but telling me not to fall seems pretty silly. Does anyone *want* to fall off their horse? It's a bit like saying *don't stop breathing* or *don't jump off the cliff.*'

'Both perfectly reasonable suggestions.' Matthew tied the baling twine neck-rope around Dibby's neck and wished he could hear her laugh again. The crazy sound was one of the best things he'd ever heard. Some nights he woke with a smile because he dreamed of her laugh. He pulled on the neck rope. 'Will you be right with this?'

Her eyes narrowed in a *really?* expression. 'I can ride, you know.'

Matthew held up his hands in surrender and turned his attention to Rev. Running his hands along the golden neck, he spoke to the horse through touch. It was a language Rev understood: this man would look after him, and they would work together.

With an athletic spring, Matthew landed on Rev's back. Like Grace, he remained bent along the horse's neck to avoid being seen. He hoped the horses were as reliable as their owner stated - he could ride a buck bareback but not if he was already leaning forward. He gave a light tug on the neck rope, and Rev immediately backed up a step.

'Good boy, Rev. Are you ready for an insane ride? If we don't get you away from here, you may not have long to live, and I know your

Mel wants to see you again.'

The horse had no comprehension of the meaning of the words, but he understood the tone of friendship. He would carry this rider through fire or storm because together they were greater than him alone.

Seeing that Deo had opened the main gate onto the driveway and returned to chase the other horses through to join the two mobs together, Matthew urged Rev forward. 'It's time to go, big fella. They trust you, so you lead the way, and they'll follow.'

Grace turned Dibby to help Deo. For a moment, the big horse balked, not wanting to leave Rev. Understanding his separation anxiety, Grace patted him, crooned some words, and gave him clear directions with her legs, seat, eyes, and thoughts to move on, and he did as she instructed.

Riding behind the horses, Deo and Grace clicked softly to start them moving. They glanced frequently at the house, but no one emerged. All attention remained on the diversion.

The horses began bunching up, and when a couple saw the open gate to the other yard, they trotted through. Across the soft haze of dust rising from the hooves, Grace could see Matthew steering Rev out onto the driveway. As they'd hoped, the horses, once pushed from behind, followed Rev, and one hundred and twenty-seven horses started making their way out of the yards.

Knowing they were likely to spread out if they kept walking, Matthew squeezed Rev into a jog, quietly chanting, 'Trot, trot-ting, trot-ting,' over his shoulder to encourage any horses who knew the command to increase their speed. Many of the horses knew the words and broke into a trot, their hooves clattering loudly on the gravel driveway as they passed the house.

Clenching his teeth, Matthew prayed for luck to favor them and clicked Rev into a canter. With his head low in the waving white mane, he was thankful for Rev's comfortable gait that was easy to sit.

Holding the aerial map of the driveway in his mind, Matthew guided Rev at an increasingly fast canter past the house and between the trees. Once they were on the driveway and enclosed by the jungle, the horses had no choice but to follow, although even in the open area past the house, they showed no inclination to deviate, their eyes and ears fixed firmly on the palomino that led them.

Behind, the last of the horses passed through the gateway with Deo and Grace clapping their hands lightly to urge them on. The sound of the hooves on the gravel drowned out most other noises, but the horses nearest them responded and picked up their pace.

A yell from the house reached Grace, and she looked to the right to see two men on the veranda, both with guns pointed at her. She lay as low as she could along Dibby's neck, leaning over to the near side so that she provided a minimal target.

Seeing them aiming at Grace, Deo urged Dusty into a gallop and rode between her and the men. He sat upright and stared at them so they could see him. Their guns moved to target him. He knew they were excellent shots, so he remained in line between them and Grace - she was not going to die while he could protect her.

The two men had procrastinated all afternoon about shooting the horses, and they had argued about waiting for Deo to return in case he wanted the palominos. They helped look after him when his parents were murdered, and now they looked down the sights at the teenager.

They both fired.

They fired again.

They hit their targets.

At the sound of the gunfire, Matthew looked back, a look of horror on his face. He was over one hundred meters in front of Deo and Grace and could barely see through the rising dust. There was no sign of either of them - just horses. He began to check Rev so he could go back when he saw Grace.

She rose from the tall horse's neck and sat upright. In that instant, he saw her riding ability – she wasn't sitting on the horse; she rode as part of him.

The gunmen had not missed their targets. Four bullets struck the ground behind the horses, accelerating them into a gallop and leaving the riders safe.

Deo grinned and saluted the men. They fired a few more bullets so the others might believe they tried to stop the horse thieves, and they smiled back at the boy who loved horses.

With almost one hundred and thirty horses reaching full gallop on the narrow driveway, Matthew knew he had to stay on Rev. A fall under that many hooves meant death, and he had no intention of dying. He rested a hand on Rev's neck for a moment, and the gelding flicked an ear back to show he was listening to his rider.

'Fly, Rev. Fly,' Matthew urged.

Rev flew. His iron-hard hooves flashed over the gravel and dirt. His nostrils widened as he sucked in the warm mountain air. Horses crowded him, keen to pass in this mad downhill race, but Rev found more speed, and more again. Like most Quarter Horses, his ancestors were Thoroughbreds, and their racing DNA remained strong in him. He was born to win, and no horse would pass him in this flight down the mountain.

Matthew's body melted into Rev's movement. He threw back his head and laughed with the exhilarating madness of the ride. There were few things more glorious than to ride a sure-footed horse at full gallop.

In a straight section, he looked back to see the two riders at the rear. He raised an arm, and both responded in kind. They had this. They were saving the horses. There were the security gates to get through, and then they'd be in the midst of thousands of horse people who wanted to help. Nothing could stop them now.

Glancing up, Matthew could see the Pilatos drone keeping an eye on them. He knew there were only another few turns before the fence and gates, and the sound of five hundred hooves behind him was a constant reminder to stay on Rev no matter what.

He rounded the last corner and grinned as he saw one of the Pilatos vehicles ram the gates, knocking them off their hinges before reversing back down the road, leaving the way clear for the horses. For a moment, he wondered why the men who were supposed to be guarding the road didn't appear. He assumed they were called away because of the earlier diversion.

With only a hundred meters to go, he was so focused on the road ahead that he didn't notice the men in army greens standing in the trees to his right, arguing. When they first heard the commotion up the mountain, they started walking up, but the sound of the approaching horses sent them into the trees. One, aware of possible witnesses, wanted to remain hidden and let them pass while the other wanted to do his job.

As Matthew rode past, a single rifle was raised. The shooter held him in his sights for less than a second before squeezing the trigger. He had the satisfaction of seeing the bullet strike the Australian in the center of his back, his body jerking forward before pitching sideways off his horse. There was no chance to fire a second bullet because his co-worker punched him hard in the temple, knocking him out.

Even though the sound of the rifle didn't reach her until Matthew was falling, Grace knew he'd been shot the instant she saw him lurch. A cold panic seized her. The horses would avoid him if they could see him, but in their mad downhill flight, they wouldn't see him. They would trample him unless he could roll out of their way. *Move, Matthew*, she clenched her teeth and tried to throw the thoughts at him, *get out of their way.*

Matthew hit the ground hard and rolled. Rev dropped his hindquarters into the dirt and started sliding to a halt when he felt Matthew leave his back. The horses immediately behind him swerved to avoid the palomino and, in doing so, missed Matthew as well.

Aware of the stampede coming at him, Matthew bounced to his feet as the first horses ducked around him. He looked for Rev, but it took the horse another ten meters to stop, and he couldn't reach him. He had to move out of the way of the equine tsunami. Ignoring the pain in his back, he jumped to the left side of the driveway, narrowly missing being flattened by horses that twisted mid-stride to avoid him.

When Grace saw him stand, relief burned through her. She watched him move out of the horses' path and could see him looking for Rev, but the flow of animals had forced the gelding to move further down the track. Matthew turned to look at her, his expression a mixture of pain and worry. She put her left hand on her hip and used her right hand to point to it then to him, and hoped he understood.

Fearful of being shot at again and worried about the men who might be pursuing them down the mountain, Grace knew she had to get Matthew to safety. As she drew closer, she checked Dibby and was relieved that he responded to the lightweight rope halter and slowed.

'How well can you turn, big fella?' she asked her horse.

Judging from his willingness to drop back from the others and the way he kept his feet under him, she believed he could give her a good barrel racing turn. She called to Deo to keep going, and as the last of the horses flashed past Matthew, she angled Dibby so that Matthew was on her left. With her left arm acting as a catch, she swung the horse in a small turn around Matthew. Dibby slowed to a balanced canter and executed a small circle. Reaching his left arm up, Matthew hooked her arm and used the momentum of the turn to swing himself up behind her. By the time Dibby had completed the three-sixty, Matthew was sitting securely behind Grace, his arms around her, and they bounded back into a gallop.

'Thanks,' Matthew spoke next to her ear. 'Nice pick-up.'

'I'm glad you knew what I meant.'

'I figured you were either signaling about a rescue relay pick-up or were starting to sing *I'm a little teapot*.'

She snorted. 'My favorite song in life-threatening situations.'

'Mine too,' he laughed, his relief at being alive making his spirits soar. Although, he admitted to himself, perhaps riding behind this woman who rode like a warrior was responsible for some of his winged emotions.

They passed through the gates and caught up to Deo, who had slowed Dusty to wait for them, his face pinched with concern as he looked at Matthew.

'Kevlar,' Matthew took one arm from Grace's waist to tap his side.

Kayne had fitted the three of them with bullet-proof vests, which they wore under their shirts. Grace's vest had extra back support for which she was thankful as it allowed her to undertake the twist and pull of Matthew's mount without collapsing in pain.

Once well past the farm gates, they slowed to a canter and watched the rest of the herd gallop between the lines of people. Some of the Pilatos team and Alejandro Mendez's men kept the crowds a safe distance from the farm gates, but thousands of people lined the road beyond them. Tens of thousands.

They stood back from the road, giving the horses a clear path through their midst and a safe passage down the rest of the mountain. In the valley below, hundreds of riders waited for their arrival, ready to herd them into paddocks where others would catch them and ferry them away in the fleet of horse trucks.

'We've done it.' Deo's voice held astonishment as they cantered past the security teams who closed ranks behind them, cutting them off from danger. They were safe.

'Let's hope we don't get charged with horse theft,' said Grace as they dropped back to a walk.

Matthew shook his head. 'The Pilatos lawyers are all over it. Keep in mind, those Venezuelan farmers back there don't own the horses – we didn't steal their animals. These are owned by an Australian-based charity that is illegally sending them to an Australian-owned Level Four Containment laboratory that endangers the local people by illegally releasing animals – both dead and alive – from their facility. I'm fairly sure they don't want the publicity of taking us to court.'

'Look!' Grace pointed ahead.

Rev cantered towards them with pricked ears and a happy expression. Both Dibby and Deo's pony called out, pleased to see their friend. Matthew slid down from behind Grace and stepped forward to take the reins of Rev's rope halter.

'Good to see you, boy.' He patted the golden neck. 'Thanks for the ride.'

Rev's soft dark eyes regarded Matthew with friendliness.

From one of the Pilatos vehicles, Kayne called to them. 'We have people here to lead those horses down. We'll drive you.'

Looking at Grace's shining eyes as she caressed Dibby's white mane, Matthew replied, 'We'll stay with them, mate. Ernie and others are down there to gather up the horses, but we'll stay with these ones.'

'Thanks,' Grace smiled at him. 'It's been so long since I rode, and I really don't want to get off him yet. He's a good horse.'

'What about you, Deo? Grace and I can take your horse if you want to go in one of the cars.'

Deo patted his chest and pointed at both the Australians. 'We are in this together. I am staying with you. And this horse,' he patted the brown neck, 'I stay with him. He has the heart of a lion.'

'They all do,' Matthew walked, leading Rev and leaning an arm over his neck. 'They certainly didn't deserve to be used to test vaccines.'

'It has to be more than that,' said Grace, her mind going over some of the things that came to her in dreams the previous night. Locations. Horses moving in and out of countries. Travel. Her brow pinched as she grabbed at fleeting memories of ideas that danced through her sleeping mind. 'There's more to it.'

***

Dibby and Rev

With nostrils flaring to allow a massive airflow into their lungs, Dibby and Rev walked proudly, their ears pricked and their eyes shining. Adrenalin still coursed through them from the exhilarating gallop down the mountain, and they felt more energized than they had for months. Their riders had merged with their bodies and souls, and together they had been greater than their parts.

As Rev's respiration slowed, he briefly touched nostrils with Dibby, sharing the joy of being with riders who understood them. The Australian voices were like the most beautiful birdsong in their ears, and their hands spoke the language understood by horses. If these riders asked them to gallop through fire or cross flooded rivers, they would do so willingly.

With a pat to his wither, Rev's person told him that he was about to mount again, and with a light spring, he left the ground and landed on his back. The two palominos glanced at each other – these riders would make everything right.

Dusty tossed his head and shook his mane. Carrying his human made him feel like a noble steed carrying a young king. It was how he felt when he taught a new child to ride and took them from a nervous worrier to a little champion ready for a more advanced horse. He didn't want this ride to end. Once more, he was a king's horse, and he walked with pride. Occasionally, he had to jog with pride to keep up with the longer legs of the palominos.

The horses did not fully understand why they had fled down the mountain, but the sense of freedom was an elixir in their blood, and they walked without fear between the growing crowds of people. When a few hands clapped, they arched their necks and snorted but did not change their tempo. As the applause grew thunderously with tens of thousands of people joining in, the three horses raised their heads slightly, not in alarm but with the knowledge that this vast herd of humans showed respect for them and their riders.

CHAPTER TWENTY-SIX

Like humans, horses have different personalities. Unlike humans, they don't seek to hide their nature or pretend to be anything other than their true selves. Sweet-natured, honest horses are just that – they don't pretend to be something they're not to trick you. Their honesty is one reason I like spending so much time with horses – I've never known one that lied to me.

'Horses Think, Learn, and Remember' by Lane Dimity, p. 54

Quest

There's more to it, Lane signed to Karen as they sat at the Wunya breakfast table watching the news.

His frown deepened as he studied the live footage from Venezuela. A few days earlier, REE's reputation as a horse rescue pulled in more donations than all the other equine charities put together, but the reporters were bringing an end to that. For years, REE had managed to keep their secret activities well-hidden, but every horse-loving person involved in the news business was shining the spotlight on them and asking questions.

'Isn't that enough?' asked Henry, waving a hand at the screen as the headline declared *REE Rescue-horses Rescued.* Changing the channel showed other views of the same incident in South America.

We're missing something. Lane narrowed his lips as he concentrated.

They watched the drone footage showing tens of thousands of people lining the rural roads outside Caracas as one hundred and twenty-four horses careened between them, directed to paddocks in the farmland below. Far behind, the final three horses walked with their riders. The reporter informed viewers that Matthew McLeay and two friends were responsible for saving the horses.

'There's Ernie!' Sheree sat up in her chair and pointed at the screen.

A camera panned around the paddock where horse trucks and trailers waited to collect the horses. Ernie stood next to his show jumping truck, talking on the phone and directing others to park.

'No wonder you can't get him on the phone,' noted Henry with a look of relief, 'he's there organizing everything like it's a horse show in Gatton. Look at him!' He laughed as Ernie tapped the door of a large horse truck and indicated a parking spot.

Sheree hushed him as the television switched to a close-up of an attractive middle-aged reporter who smiled at the camera.

'We've all heard of The Man from Snowy River,' she spoke in an Australian accent that had overtones from her years of living in South America, 'and today we've seen that spirit of horse-loving Australia come alive here in the mountains outside Caracas. Australian horses rescued by the international charity Rescuing Equines Everywhere arrived recently from Australia. They were allegedly consigned to the Menningala Vaccine company in a move that has outraged horse people around the world. Officials have yet to answer questions about the legalities of animals moving in and out of Menningala. However, we have been informed there should be no animals leaving a Level Four Containment facility, which contradicts some of the information we've obtained from witnesses who stated horses left there in considerable numbers – dead and alive.'

'When you break the code of silence,' Karen looked at Lane, who gazed back at her with a distracted expression, 'lots of voices start speaking up. I think there will be some interesting witnesses come forward after this.'

Lane nodded, his thoughts on the missing pieces that beckoned from the edges of his mind.

'At least with the entire world looking on,' Karen continued, 'it should offer a bit of protection for Matthew and Grace. And Ernie, of course.' She smiled as Ernie appeared on the television, smiling at the camera.

'Ernie Lomond, an Australian living in Caracas,' a male reporter held a microphone up to Ernie, 'is here organizing people to catch and collect the horses. How did you get involved with this?'

Ernie grinned. 'The same as everyone else. If Lane Dimity asks for help with some horses, that's what we do.'

'Are you saying that Lane Dimity is behind all of this?'

'No – the actions of REE are behind all this…allegedly. I hope the Australian Tax Office, the Australian Charities and Not-for-profit Commission, the Australian Securities and Investment Commission, and other regulatory bodies examine the people and companies associated with REE and what has been happening with the donations and these horses.'

'It seems you have a lot of information about it. Can you give us some specifics?'

'I think you'll find that Vicki Marshall will have an exposé in U.S. newspapers tomorrow.'

At Wunya, Sheree turned to Karen. 'Is that correct?'

'Apparently. Vicki, Tom, and Joe have been busy gathering information, and they know a lot about the funds and where they are going, including lists of most of the companies involved and what they are providing.'

'It sounds complicated,' said Sheree.

'It's a tangled web.' Karen spoke while trying to watch the images of the horses galloping between the ranks of people. 'There's a lot more to discover. There are tens of millions, maybe hundreds, unaccounted for, but it's enough to ensure all those offices and commissions that Ernie listed will turn their attention to REE.'

Henry interrupted to point at the television. 'The horses are turning into the paddock. How on earth will they catch them?'

'From what we've been able to find out,' said Karen, 'they're mostly quiet, well handled, and educated horses. They were careful to choose horses that would transport calmly and accept whatever they had in mind at Menningala. They'll be easy to catch.'

'What happens now?' asked Sheree. 'What about all the other REE horses? And their riding centers?'

It's a work in progress, Lane signed, a crooked smile indicating that he was aware of the long road ahead. *We still have other things to do. Tom and I will bring your two stallions here from quarantine, and I want to go and see Quest run.*

'And hope he loses by a mile,' Karen smiled, knowing how much he liked the Thoroughbred. 'Quest's owner has promised Lane he can have the gelding once he retires from racing. If he's slow, he might retire sooner.'

'Matthew and Grace!' shouted Jasper, jumping up and down excitedly when he saw his neighbor and friend riding side by side on the palomino horses.

'She should not be on a horse.' Sheree spoke with firm disapproval at the risky behavior of her neighbor. She knew Grace was never to ride again. Then, her voice softened, 'But it sure is good to see her there. Look at her smiling!'

'That must be Deo.' Karen admired the way the teenager sat on the pony, his hand patting his mount in reassurance as the crowds closed in around them and television crews jostled to reach them.

'Ernie was talking to us about him last night.' Sheree kept her eyes on the television, hoping to see her son again. 'He's quite the horseman considering the tough upbringing he's had. His dream is to meet you, Lane.'

'Lane is planning a trip over there in a few weeks.' Karen squeezed Lane's hand as she spoke. They didn't like time away from each other, but she wanted to avoid South America while pregnant because of the Zika virus. 'He'll meet Deo and see what we can do about keeping the REE riding center open. Matthew said they do brilliant work there with the local kids.'

'Ernie will be pleased to see you.' Sheree flashed him a smile. 'You can catch up with Cameron O'Shea while you're there. Ernie called on him to help out, and he's taking four horses back to his place.'

Lane's phone rang. It was Matthew with an update about their ride. Switching his phone to text-to-speech mode, Lane took the call and told Matthew that they could see them on the news. The live broadcast had a slight satellite delay, so it was a few seconds before Matthew grinned at the camera and waved.

Lane convinced Matthew that he, Grace, and Deo should hand their mounts over to Ernie and leave the area as soon as possible under the protection of the Pilatos team. If REE or Menningala demanded retribution, their faces would be the ones on the hit-list, so they needed to disappear. As reporters jostled to speak to the riders, Lane was pleased to see them melt away with the Pilatos people, leaving others holding their horses while the news crews looked for them.

Over the next few days, Karen and Lane stayed at Wunya while gathering information on the rescue horses, the charity, and the related companies. The Federal Police and several government departments contacted them for any evidence they held concerning REE, and they gladly turned it over.

'Do you think it's over?' Karen asked as she and Lane flew to Melbourne. They were meeting Tom and Vicki and collecting the Wunya stallions from quarantine.

A slight crease between Lane's brows indicated he remained troubled. *We should watch our backs for a while. They're not going to be happy about their charity empire disappearing because of us.*

'They seemed happy to kill people to protect their operation.' Her thoughts wandered to the methods used to silence people. 'I can't help wondering what they might do to punish us.'

The men at the top might be too busy trying to destroy any evidence that leads to them. There's still a lot to be uncovered.

'Hopefully, we won't have to do any of it now that they're exposed and the big guns can see them. It's a shame that the reputable charities and rescues might suffer because of what REE has done - and Equines In Need Of Funds as well as Caring About Horses And Ponies.'

In his investigations, Joe had uncovered links between the three charities. They were correct when they guessed that EINOF and CAHAP were established as backups if anything happened to the main charity. Karen wasn't quite sure how Joe had managed to find the connections, and she didn't want to know as she guessed he might have crossed the line of legality in his search. She knew there were hackers on his payroll whose public role was to check Pilatos cybersecurity, and she suspected they were skilled enough to break into other systems to undertake cyber espionage.

So many horses. Lane looked out the vast dry landscape below the jet, his thoughts turning to the horses that had suffered in the hands of REE. He wasn't sure if they would ever know the numbers.

'They did save some. Think of all the ones used as the pin-up horses for the charity. They are well cared for. And the ones in the riding centers have great lives.'

I can't stop thinking of what happens to the ones that went to Menningala. What went on there?

'We can't change what happened in the past, but we can work to make sure that those horses in Venezuela have a good life.'

Looking into her eyes, Lane felt her strength flow into him. He was thankful for everything about her, not least her ability to understand a thousand unspoken words that passed between them in a glance. They had righted a wrong on behalf of many: the horses, the honest people who donated money to support them, and the owners who believed they gave their horses a better life with REE. And, hopefully, there would be justice for a groom called Binky who asked questions about some horses that died.

After landing at Tullamarine Airport near Melbourne, they took a hire car to the nearby Mickleham quarantine facility. Tom was there with a horse truck to collect the Warmblood stallions. Sheree and Henry had organized for the stallions to have a few days at a farm near Werribee on the other side of Melbourne before flying to Queensland. That allowed Lane and Tom to ride the horses before they settled into their new home. It also gave Lane the time to watch Quest run at Flemington.

When they retired to the apartment they'd rented for a few days, they sat on the veranda overlooking the waters of Port Phillip Bay. The intensity of previous days was offset by sharing some laughs at the posts on their favorite social media group about eventers uniting to share funny stories, videos, and photos. It was a chance to clear their minds of everything connected to REE as they scrolled, laughed, and chuckled.

After an hour of laughter, they turned their attention to more serious matters.

'Can I speak to Brian Farley-Wells, please?' Tom winked at Lane as he spoke. He knew how his friend looked forward to seeing the horse with the question mark on his forehead. 'It's Tom Claw speaking; I'm with Lane Dimity.'

'One moment,' replied the efficient female voice.

'Tom! Good to hear you.' Brian's affable voice boomed out of the phone. 'Are you getting those big Warmbloods out of quarantine?'

'Yes. They're spending a couple of days here at Werribee before heading to Queensland. We received the entry tickets to the Members' area at Flemington and wanted to thank you for them. Lane is looking forward to watching Putin The Question run, as you can imagine.'

Brian laughed loudly. 'He really took to that horse, didn't he? You might say love at first sight. Can't say that I blame him, though. A fine horse.'

'How's his quarantine training gone? Is he likely to be a first start winner, or will it be a run to get him ready for the next race?'

'I only run them to win. It's all about the winning. His times have been great, but I have a bit of bad news.'

Lane looked up sharply. Even without the phone on speaker, Brian's words were easy to hear.

'The gelding developed signs of colic a few days ago. We scanned him yesterday, and he has an inoperable tumor in his gut. There's nothing we can do for him. If Lane wants to say goodbye to him, he's scheduled to be put down tomorrow at about three at our Lancefield farm. That's not too far from Werribee.'

'That is bad news,' murmured Tom, his eyes filled with compassion as he regarded his friend.

'It'd make me feel better to know Lane was there as I know he and the horse had a real connection in the short time they knew each other. I can send a car for you if you like. I'm at the farm this week, and I'd be honored to show you around and get your opinion on some of the youngstock here.'

When Lane nodded agreement, Tom made arrangements to drive to Lancefield the next day.

'I'm sorry,' Karen laid a hand on Lane's arm when Tom finished the call.

You'd think after a lifetime of loving and losing horses, I'd be used to it by now. I didn't even know the horse. It was just a feeling that he was important.

'I've learned to trust your feelings,' said Karen, hurting for the man she loved. On the one hand, he was the toughest and most resilient person she knew; on the other, his empathy knew no bounds. He would grieve for a horse he barely knew because it was in his nature to love. 'You don't have to go, you know. We can stay here.'

I want to go.

The following day, after giving the two stallions another workout, they drove north for an hour to Mount Macedon, where Lane gave his American friends a tour of the picturesque region. They walked around the Forest Glade Gardens, admired the views, and decided it was one of the prettiest places they'd seen in Australia.

It was a short drive from there to Brian's Thoroughbred facility at Lancefield. White railed fences and a substantial wrought-iron gate with rearing horses marked the property. At the end of the tree-lined driveway sat a bluestone mansion, and its magnificence befitted the self-proclaimed billionaire.

'I'm not saying it's as impressive as Bisente,' Tom eyed the stables and other outbuildings along with the irrigated pastures, 'but it's one heck of a property.'

Karen agreed. Growing up at Bisente in Kentucky made her qualified to compare the two, and this ranked on a par with her family's home.

'From what I read about it last night,' said Karen, 'he's spent a fortune doing the place up. He spends more on horses than my mother does - I don't think she would pay twenty million for a horse.' She referred to Sucre Noir, the stallion that accompanied Quest on the flight into Australia.

Are you sure? Lane gave her a wry look thinking of Isabella's extravagance when acquiring the best show jumping lines for Bisente.

She laughed and tapped her fingers as though counting. 'What's the exchange rate? That's about fifteen million in our money, a bit over eleven million pounds, and close to thirteen million euro. OK. Maybe she would.'

They parked in the visitor's car park, and the stud manager, Ross O'Brien, met them and led them to the main house where Brian Farley-Wells was finishing some paperwork in his office. The impeccable finish of the house's interior with its polished wood floors, expensive artworks, leadlight windows, and period furniture matched everything else they'd come to associate with Brian. No expense had been spared to create an impression of wealth.

Ross knocked on the office door and opened it when Brian called to them to enter. The powerfully-built horseman looked up from his desk and smiled at his visitors, his brown eyes creasing with pleasure. His jeans, checked shirt, and suede jacket lent him the air of a man on the land, although few farmers could afford his designer brand outfit.

'Welcome, welcome,' he stood and strode forward, offering his hand. 'I am sorry we are meeting in such circumstances, but,' he shrugged, 'you know what it's like with horses – they all die in the end. Just as well I have him insured, eh?'

The comment jarred Lane's mind, although he could see the sense of it. He tended to see horses for their emotional value, like a friend or family member, but he accepted that the worth of racehorses lay more in their sale price and what they could win or make at stud.

'I imagine he'll leave a hole in your racing plans for this year,' said Karen, knowing that racing experts favored Quest as a likely contender for some of the country's major Group 1 races.

'I'm already shopping for a replacement,' Brian assured her, casting a smile at Lane. 'I'll keep the next one away from your boyfriend so we don't break his heart again.'

'It is certainly the mark of a superior man,' Karen narrowed her eyes slightly as she regarded the Australian businessman, 'to have the ability to love animals. Don't you think?'

Brian guffawed at that and led the way out of the house, saying over his shoulder, 'You women might think that way, but it's not natural for men to love animals.'

Lane and Tom glanced at each other; their brows raised. Was Brian making a joke, or was he unaware of his audience's attitude towards animals?

Maybe he's been drinking, Lane signed to Tom as they followed their host, *he seemed to care for the horses when we met him at the airport.*

Something's off about him, Tom signed back.

'Would you like some refreshments before we go out to farewell your horse?' Brian asked as he paused under a wisteria arbor behind the house.

'We haven't long eaten,' Karen told him. 'We stopped while we were looking around Mt Macedon. Beautiful area.'

'It is.' Brian made his way across the lawns to the large bluestone stables built to match the house. He talked over his shoulder as he walked. 'I saw your friend - Matthew, is it? He was on the news with those horses in South America. Interestingly, the reporters are taking the angle that he saved the horses but, the way I see it, he stole them.'

His voice lost its warmth, and he threw a challenging look their way. 'It looks like he trespassed onto a farm and stole the horses. Having the support of all those people doesn't make it any less theft.'

'It's a matter of perspective,' Karen spoke coolly, sensing his hostility. 'If they were, say, inanimate objects like handbags, then it's open and shut. When they are horses about to be used in a cruel and illegal manner, then rescuing them may not be viewed in the same light.'

'They are objects,' Brian stopped and looked her straight in the eyes, his force of intelligence hitting her like a punch, 'owned like any other object can be legally owned. I may not have much sympathy with that horse charity, but I can't support theft.'

She wanted to argue but was uncomfortably aware that he had a valid point. Far too many people viewed animals as chattels owned by humans. They were more than possessions to her, but if someone stole one of her horses, she'd see it as a crime. 'I doubt that either REE or Menningala will seek to have charges laid against Matthew. I imagine they have far more pressing issues to contend with at present.'

'Do you think one publicity stunt in Venezuela will stop them?' Brian's mouth twisted into a sneer. 'Have you any idea how big they are?'

'Do you?' asked Tom, curious about Brian's interest.

'As a matter of fact, I think I do. After offering to donate to an equine charity a few weeks ago, I did some investigations of my own.'

Brian continued to the yards at the back of the stables. The first held Quest, and the next contained the stud's teaser stallion, a pinto pony that pinned his ears at the big bay and threatened to attack if he stood too close to the fence. Beyond him, Thoroughbreds stood, one to a pen, enjoying the sun.

Quest held Lane's attention. To the casual observer, the horse looked in peak fitness apart from a slight hollowness in his flanks. He stood on the far side of the small yard, watching them, his head held high and his ears twitching. The stance immediately told Lane that something was wrong: the horse wasn't happy. He remembered Quest as a calm horse with a kind nature that liked being with people. That impression was very different from this nervous and wary animal.

When they reached the gate, Quest fixed his gaze on Brian. There was apprehension in his eyes and tension in his muscles as he watched his owner. Lane knew he saw the surface of something that ran far deeper. He looked from the horse to Brian and sensed something sinister. He strained to understand what it was, but it eluded him.

'He's a beautiful horse.' Karen's voice held sadness as she looked at the bay with the question mark on his face. 'Are you sure there's no treatment for the tumor?'

'There is surgery,' Brian admitted, 'but he isn't likely to win a race for at least two years, so this is the best option financially. Killing him gives me the insurance payout.'

The harshness of his words surprised Lane. He thought Brian cared about horses, but this was at odds with that notion. He looked at Tom and began signing, *Can I buy him? I'll pay for the surgery. I don't care that he won't race.*

'Lane wants to know,' said Tom, 'if he can buy him. If there's a chance he can be saved, he'll take it.'

Brian laughed. 'Do you know how much this horse cost?'

'Yes, we do,' Karen replied, not hesitating for a second to support Lane's desire to own Quest, 'and it isn't an issue. If you organize the paperwork, we can arrange to transfer the money.'

A wolfish smile spread across Brian's face as he looked at Lane. 'You'd pay that for a broken-down horse? Just as well I'm the owner, then, isn't it? I can save you a lot of money by making sure he dies.'

Tom frowned, disturbed by the animosity leeching from the man. 'The money isn't important.'

'It's always important.' Brian opened the gate to the yard. 'Go and say goodbye to your horse, Lane.'

The way he spoke the words caused Tom to look at Vicki. She arched one speculative brow at him, and he mouthed *Joe* to her. Nodding, Vicki took her phone out, tapped it to silent, and sent a text.

Does Brian's name come up anywhere?

Almost immediately, Joe replied, *Farley-Wells? I haven't seen it. Checking now.*

Vicki knew he would be running a search of all their documents for Brian's name, though she guessed it wouldn't be there.

Can you work backward from him? She texted as she glanced around at the lavish display of wealth with his farm and racehorses. *Where did he get his money?*

Setting the team on that now.

Stepping through the gate, Lane went to Quest and laid a hand on his neck. The horse breathed in the essence of the man next to him and relaxed. He remembered Lane's help on the plane, and the energy that flowed through his hand was calming and protective. Quest turned his head to rest his muzzle on Lane's shoulder.

Lane closed his eyes and stilled his mind. He understood the horse's feelings of concern, fear, worry, and the desire for protection. In the presence of his owner, Quest responded like a horse watching a large predator. There was no sense of illness under his hand, and Lane wondered what that meant. He always found that gravely sick horses had a waning of the life force, perhaps not discernible to most, but a subtle change that a wolf pack might sense when picking out the weakest in the herd.

Based on the strength pulsating under his hand, he believed Quest was healthy. He could hear normal gut noises, there was no temperature, sweating, or elevated heart rate that might accompany colic, and a quick rub down both sides of his neck revealed a lack of injection sites. The manure he could see was normal, lacking the oily consistency of a paraffin drench or any sign of an unhealthy gut. His coat was sleek and shiny, and there was no odor of medication. There was neither feed nor water in the yard, which could explain the hollow flanks. He knew the horse was not dying from an inoperable gut tumor.

What he could see and feel were faint welt marks. A whip had landed on him repeatedly.

Lane turned to face Brian, his eyes hard as his hands moved small and fast to tell the others, *He's not sick.*

'I read about you,' began Brian, moving into the yard with Lane and shutting the gate behind him. The businessman's affability morphed into contempt. 'It must have been awful when your father shot your horses in front of you when you were a kid.'

Patterns and thoughts twirled and clicked into place in Lane's mind as Brian spoke. When they first met, the businessman was genuinely grateful for the help with his Thoroughbreds. What had changed? Lane could think of one reason and, as bizarre as it was at first, within seconds, a thousand jigsaw pieces rearranged themselves in his mind, and it made sense.

He could see Vicki texting while Karen and Tom watched Lane for more messages. *Let him talk.* Lane kept his hand movements as small as possible so Brian might not notice.

'I hope seeing this horse die in front of you doesn't cause any flashbacks.'

'Is your vet doing this now?' asked Tom, looking around but seeing no one else nearby.

'We don't need the vet,' Brian studied Lane's expression as he reached into his jacket and drew out a Glock 43.

'You need the vet for the insurance,' Tom pointed out, forcing his voice to remain calm. He could see that Brian was finding sadistic pleasure in recreating a scene that traumatized Lane in childhood.

Brian chuckled, keeping the handgun aimed at the ground. 'My vet will sign off on this so that we meet the requirements of the insurance company.'

Desperate to protect Lane from seeing the horse shot in front of him, Karen spoke in commanding tones. 'We'll sign an affidavit claiming you needlessly killed a healthy horse to commit insurance fraud.'

'That's easily fixed,' Brian dismissed her words and raised the Glock. 'I won't claim the insurance. It'll be worth it to see what you bleeding hearts do when the horse dies in front of you. It's just a horse.'

'Binky Laurie wasn't a horse.' Tom could see the texts flying back and forth between Vicki and Joe. Without any confirmation of Brian's connection to the charity, he made a quantum leap in assumptions based on the man's behavior. 'Did she die in front of you, or do you only kill horses and send other men to kill people?'

Shaking his head, Brian lowered the gun slightly. 'I don't know what drugs you are on - I have nothing to do with her death.'

'What about the missing machinery operator and the attempt on Vicki and me?'

Brian's eyes glittered dangerously. 'I have no idea what you are on about.'

'We thought there had to be one person behind it all,' said Karen, her expression grim as she attempted to join the dots. 'Someone who understood how to rort the charity system to create the sort of money-spinner that bleeding hearts like us throw money at. Someone who probably had an involvement in the racing industry because that was the source of so many rescue horses. A man like you who knew which companies you could entice to join the web you were weaving.'

The confidence in Brian's cold smile indicated that either he was innocent and knew the accusations were nonsense, or it showed his complete faith that no one could connect him to REE. If he were involved, Lane imagined that from the moment he conceived the idea of making money from a charity, he ensured that he remained well hidden to avoid anything that might incriminate him. It was possible – no, probable, he thought as he remembered them meeting at the airport - that the other men involved in the fraud, like Derek Anderson, didn't know of Brian's role. If everything came crashing down, he expected to step away unharmed and anonymous while they took the fall.

Perhaps, he could escape undetected, except he needed to punish Lane for his part in switching off the flow of money to the charity. The rescue in Venezuela was not an isolated incident that he could overcome – it heralded the end of REE, and he knew it. Lane imagined the rage of the puppet master when he realized the turnout near

Caracas and the articles written by Vicki would bring the charity and its associated companies to the attention of the government agencies that had the power to stop them. Bribing and threatening individuals at the lower levels of government and enforcement worked for years, but bribes would not influence the combined forces that were about to descend on them.

In Lane's mind, the puzzle was almost complete. The story of Quest's tumor was a fabrication designed to hurt him. Brian intended to shoot the horse in front of him, hoping it would trigger the childhood memories of his father shooting all their horses and ponies during the drought. He wanted to see Lane suffer. He still might pay someone to kill Lane, but he needed to witness his pain, and he was willing to sacrifice this horse to achieve it.

'The horse isn't even sick, is he, Brian?' Tom wanted to give Joe more time to find something on the man, so he continued to talk. 'It makes me wonder what would have happened if we hadn't come along. What if he was injured on the plane or turned out to be slow? What would have happened to him then? Another REE horse sent to Menningala for their experiments?'

A flash of disbelief crossed Brian's face, quickly followed by a mix of disdain and amusement. After a lifetime studying the non-verbal language of horses, the fleeting emotions that barely touched his expression were clear to Lane. Brian had thought they knew something else about the Menningala horses, and it amused him that they thought it was about using horses in the laboratory.

Once more, the pieces of the puzzle shifted in his mind, and then he saw it – the key to everything. It was why Brian ensured he remained so far in the background. It explained why they set up the REE riding centers in developing countries. The cover story of using the horses to help disadvantaged children was so admirable that it worked like a mask to conceal the monster beneath.

A physical pain hit Lane as he thought of the horses, and he felt his blood pressure drop as the full horror of REE, Menningala, the dead horses, and this man's empire washed over him. His hand on Quest's neck turned to a fist clutching at the mane to help him stay upright as dizziness and sickness weakened him.

'Why are you all so worried about those horses?' Brian's voice mocked them. 'No one wants them. They are thrown away like rubbish. They're just horses – nameless horses that aren't even useful anymore. No one cares about them.'

'Lane does,' declared Tom. 'We all do. People cared enough to breed them. They each have a story, and somewhere in their lives are people who cared about them. It's not their fault they ended up with REE, but we care.'

'And look where that got you.' Brian scoffed. 'Standing on my farm about to witness me shoot my horse because I can. And when you're done, everything will start over again with another charity.'

He started to raise the gun, the barrel pointing at Quest. Lane stepped in front of the horse.

'Lane!' Karen saw him stand between Brian and the horse and tried to slide the latch of the gate so she could enter the yard.

The gun swung towards her.

'No!'

The word erupted from Lane's mouth, shocking everyone present, but no one more than Brian, who expected silence behind him, not a loud voice. Startled, he pulled the trigger, and the gun fired. Karen took a sudden step back from the gate, a surprised look in her eyes as she looked at the weapon in Brian's hand.

If Brian had shot Quest in front of Lane, it might have reminded him of his childhood when his horses died, but he had long since accepted that horses did not live forever. No matter how much he loved them, he understood that if life ran its natural course, all of the horses he cared about would die before it was his turn. The emotional punishment that Brian planned was always doomed to failure.

The thought of losing Karen to a bullet as he'd lost his father that day cleaved his mind like an ax. In a blind rage, he lunged at Brian.

Quest sprang forward ahead of him, shoving him to the side. The gunshot was similar to the crack of a whip, and for the two days since leaving quarantine, the horse had suffered as Brian unleashed his anger at Lane, terrifying Quest with a stock whip. Horses with a broken spirit might not retaliate when beaten, but Quest was far from that. Brian did not give him the opportunity to strike back when he held the whip, but now his back was turned.

The lethal speed of Quest's front hooves smashed into the back of Brian's legs, sending him to the ground. The gun fired a second time, spurring the horse to strike again. His hooves crashed down on Brian's back, and the gelding sank to his knees on his owner, grabbing at the back of his neck with his teeth.

The gun fell loose on the ground, and Lane kicked it through the fence as he grabbed the rails, his eyes on Karen. She looked back at him and raised both her hands to show she was safe. The bullets had missed. Relief surged through him, and he turned his attention to Quest as he held Brian on the ground.

Placing a hand on the horse's forehead, he conveyed a sense of protection and calm to the gelding. The wild brown eyes grew soft, and Quest released Brian and stood up, stepping back from the prone man. Lane shot a glance at Brian to see he was breathing before patting the horse and opening the door to his stall so he could escape the scene.

'Is he alive?' asked Vicki as Lane locked the horse away.

Yes, Lane signed as he faced them. *Call the police. He'll need to be arrested.*

'Why will the police arrest him?' Vicki checked her phone for the last message from Joe and called him so he could listen in. 'Joe says he can't find anything on Brian - yet. He only comes up as a minor donor to the charity.'

'You've got nothing,' gasped Brian, trying to ignore the pain in his back and legs so he could sit up. He glared at Lane, pointing a finger at him. 'Nothing. That horse will die, and you have nothing.'

It's all been smoke and mirrors, Lane met the furious gaze with calm assuredness. The jigsaw was complete. He saw the whole picture, and it sickened him. *We've been looking at the charity as the crime, but it's covering and enabling the bigger crime. Tell him we're not calling the local police - we're calling the Federal Police. The ones who will arrest and prosecute on charges of international drug smuggling.*

Vicki stared. Tom uttered a swear word before passing on Lane's words to Brian, who tried to stand but collapsed in agony as his left leg crumpled from the damage inflicted by Quest. He pulled up the leg of his jeans and saw the white end of a bone poking through the skin, and promptly passed out. Lane regarded him dispassionately. At least he wouldn't try to run from them.

Karen saw the clues jump from her mind and gather together. Her eyes opened wide. 'Menningala weren't performing autopsies on horses that died during drug testing,' she stated, seeing the confirmation in Lane's nod. 'They've been shuttling drugs around the world *inside* the horses. Matthew said that the Caracas woman who died thought the horses had been through colic surgery.'

Vicki saw more of the signs that supported Lane's revelation. 'The developing countries where REE have their riding centers – not all of them, but most are known for their drug connections.'

I'm sure some have nothing to do with drugs. Lane was confident that the intricate web included REE facilities that would hold up under any scrutiny.

'But any that have a Level Four biosecurity facility nearby,' Tom took up the train of thought, 'are the ones that are the cover for moving horses in and out of that country. Australian rescue horses go into the animal labs where they have what? Five kilos? Ten? Maybe twenty kilos of drugs placed in their gut and are then doped to the eyeballs to keep them alive as they fly to the next country, where the drugs are removed at a Menningala lab and distributed. The horses are disposable containers to them, so they are dumped after use – the dead bodies that Binky wanted to investigate.'

Vicki heard her name coming faintly from her phone. 'Sorry, Joe,' she clicked him onto speaker so everyone could hear him. 'Did you get all that?'

'I did. I've forwarded a quick summary – very quick – to my contact at the Federal Police as you've been talking. He'll have someone there within the hour. Can you hold Brian?'

Vicki wrinkled her nose up at the barely conscious man on the ground. 'I think his horse has taken care of that – he's not going anywhere.'

'Do you think we're right, Joe?' Karen wondered about the enormity of the crime they suspected. Greedy people using a charity as their means to more wealth was one thing, but jumping from that to international drug smuggling took it to a whole new level. 'We're not grabbing the bit and bolting with our ideas?'

'I think the evidence will be there,' he replied with certainty. 'It's not something we were looking for, so we didn't see the signs. Maybe those involved with the charity rort aren't involved in the drugs, but he needed their companies to enable the movement of horses. With HATCO and other international transporters moving the horses and receiving so much money from REE, they will keep quiet about horses going in and out of countries. The money they were taking from REE meant they wouldn't speak up even if they suspected something.'

'He doesn't look like a drug lord.' Tom scowled at the businessman groaning on the ground and clutching at his leg.

'He lives like one,' Joe pointed out. 'I'm accessing more information about him now. The racehorses, the properties, private jets - it's like he suddenly appeared on the Australian scene as a self-made billionaire who kept spending more money than his legitimate businesses made. A quick tally of horses he's bought in recent years comes several hundred million, and not all were winners on the track or the breeding barn.'

'Kat and Kaz thought he was above board,' recalled Vicki, wondering for a moment if the sisters had any involvement. They didn't live anywhere near the extravagant level of Brian Farley-Wells, so she doubted they had anything to do with it. They'd been fooled, like everyone else.

'They also said that he was a sexual predator.' Tom gave Lane a knowing look. 'You always say that bad behavior is rarely an isolated event; it's a pattern. If this man had a reputation for hitting on stablehands and objectifying women, then that should have told us there were other problems. No respect for women. No respect for the lives ruined by the drugs. No respect for the horses that died.'

The vet and his assistant walked around the corner of the barn and stopped when they saw their employer on the ground. The vet quickly pulled out his phone to raise the alarm, but Karen stepped forward and laid a hand on his arm.

'I wouldn't if I were you.'

She saw the relief in the young assistant's eyes as she looked at Brian in the dirt. Perhaps she had been a target of his predatory behavior.

'We have it on record,' Karen spoke to the vet and raised her phone to indicate she'd been recording, 'that you were going to work with Brian to commit fraud and kill a healthy horse in order to collect the insurance.'

The color drained from the vet's face. It wasn't the first illegal action he'd done for Brian, and he saw his career vanishing in front of him.

'I assume you're an excellent vet,' Karen continued, casting a hand around at the stables and fields. 'Brian would only employ the best. So, I'm going to give you a second chance. You're going to sign those forms that you'd agreed to, claiming that Putin on the Quest was put down because of illness, and use the fake results Brian requested. Then, you're going to organize transport to take the very healthy and alive Quest to Werribee, where we're currently staying. I don't care if the insurance is claimed or not, but I do want copies of the horse's death certificate and your falsified health reports, so there's no chance of anyone ever trying to claim him back from Lane.'

Lane's eyes creased in admiration at her words. She knew he'd never want to use Quest's registered name for racing or showing, and with the horse officially recorded as deceased, he could live out his days in the outback as a riding horse, and no one would come looking for him.

Thank you, he signed when she looked his way.

Karen smiled at him, her eyes shining with warmth. There was a lot to finalize about REE, the Venezuela horses, and the drugs, but this started when Lane fell in love with a bay horse on a plane, and now the horse was his. In the midst of so much that was wrong, that felt right.

CHAPTER TWENTY-SEVEN

I like a horse of any color,
Some are bright, others duller.
I like them plain like a sleek black cat
And I rather like a patchytwat.
A doodled poem by Lane in one of his notebooks.

Together

'This has been one of the best days ever.' Grace leaned against the rails of the catamaran as they sped back to Isla de Margarita. They spent the day exploring the archipelago of Islas Los Frailes off the Venezuelan coast, and it was everything Matthew promised.

'I'm glad you had a good time. Relieved, even.' Matthew stood next to her, gazing out at the infinite blue of ocean and sky. It was a day filled with laughter and wonder with scores of moments worth storing in his memory so he could bring them out and enjoy them again. Lane was right when he claimed that life's greatest treasures were the special moments, not the money.

'Relieved?' Grace chortled, and shoulder bumped him. 'Am I such a cow of a person that you thought I'd be cranky and sullen about this glorious day?'

'No, I didn't mean that. I didn't know if you'd enjoy doing something like this, that's all. I'd have felt bad if you hated scuba diving and spent the day being seasick.'

Grace moved to pat his hand and assure him that she'd loved every part of the experience. When her fingers touched the back of his hand, tingling shot up her arm, and she froze. Physical contact was something they'd avoided in the three days since rescuing the horses.

For two days, they worked hard to place the horses in temporary homes, keeping Dibby, Rev, and Dusty together at Ernie's stables. They set up accounts for Darby to access so he could continue running the *Equine Learning and Wellness Center for Children.* They knew the funds from REE would cease, and Matthew wanted to ensure the center continued to operate, so he financed it. Darby understood that the equipment and property might be sold, and he was looking for another property if Matthew was unable to secure the current one.

The National Anti-Drug Office, the law enforcement agency that dealt with drug-related crimes in Venezuela, seized the Menningala facility. They learned that horses went into the facility and had a small incision made in the abdomen where the veterinary staff inserted packages containing the drugs. The non-reactive covering did not trigger any response within the horses, and, once stitched up, the entry point was not noticeable. With heavy doses of painkillers, anti-inflammatories, and antibiotics to ensure the horses would remain well for the quarantine period at the end of their trip, they moved around the world with the drugs.

At their destination, the horses went to Menningala or one of the other secure laboratories at the heart of the operation. They were euthanized, cut open, and the drugs removed. Most facilities had on-site crematoriums or well-hidden mass graves, but laxness in Australia and Venezuela led to people discovering the dumping sites.

Once the officials at local and international organizations took over investigations, Joe ceased his involvement. He passed on his suspicions that drugs weren't the only things smuggled using the horses. It seemed likely that the Botswana arrangement of a REE riding center and nearby Menningala laboratory used the horses to smuggle diamonds out of the country.

The complicated layers of crime lay hidden beneath the work of the horse charity. The public saw the carefully crafted business that persuaded them to donate money. Under the surface were the men and women whose businesses fed off the charity, and it was in their interests to convince everyone that REE was above suspicion. Hiding unseen beneath them was the main crime of drug smuggling orchestrated by Brian Farley-Wells for several large drug syndicates. They provided the men responsible for bribes, blackmail, and murder to keep everything flying below the radar of federal and international regulatory agencies.

Lane felt that the REE was already close to collapsing because of the number of horse people concerned about missing horses supposedly in their care. The final push came when he and his friends became curious about the links between the charity, the buried horses, and a groom called Binky. The criminal core of REE underestimated the voices of horse people when they joined together to save the animals they loved.

For Grace and Matthew, their time in Venezuela was coming to an end. They expected Lane to arrive in the morning, and this was their last day to spend together. Everything they'd shared since meeting in the house at Wunya seemed to come down to this moment. They both looked at her hand hovering above his, testament to the fact that they did not know how to proceed with their relationship. They were friends. They enjoyed being together, bouncing ideas off each other, and laughing. Could it be any more than that?

Grace withdrew her hand. 'No seasickness and a whole lot of love for scuba diving. I'll do it again.'

'How's your back?' He knew she'd strained it when riding, especially with her slick pick-up of him after he fell.

'It's there,' she rolled her shoulders and arched her back, imagining the bones and metal pins straining, 'but not too bad until I think about it. I'm glad I did it, though.' She flashed him a grin. 'I haven't felt so alive since doing cross country. I know it's sensible to follow the doctors' advice and never ride again, but when we were full charge down that driveway…'

Her voice faded as she relived the exhilaration of the downhill gallop.

'Will you keep riding?'

'I think I'll have to. It's like a drug, isn't it? I was forced to quit cold turkey when I had my accident, and I was getting by without it, but after having this hit, I'm craving it again. What do you think?'

She looked at him with trust in her eyes, and he felt surprisingly moved to know that his opinion was important.

'I think you should do what you want to do. It's safest to avoid riding, but walking down the street can be dangerous. If you lived to be ninety-nine and looked back over your life, how much would you regret not riding?'

'A lot,' she said without thinking, then paused to consider the question more deeply. 'You know, it really would be a huge regret.'

'I think we have enough regrets without the big ones like never riding again. You rode like a champion, by the way.'

'I was good,' she laughed, but not hard enough to activate the asthmatic geese sounds that amused him so much.

Matthew watched a pod of dolphins racing the boat, his mind-twisting over what he wanted to say. *So much to say, so much not to say.*

Matthew suffered the sting of those words as he struggled to find a way to tell Grace how he felt about her. He risked ruining their friendship if he revealed his feelings and she didn't return them, but he risked losing more by remaining silent.

'I'm happy to come and strap for you if you ever go back eventing.' He hoped she could read between those lines. He wasn't sure of her feelings towards him, so he didn't want to scare her away by attempting to take their friendship further than she wanted, but he didn't want her to think that he didn't care for her. It was a difficult balance.

'Could those Hollywood beauties stand to be without you while you tightened my girths?'

Matthew raised his eyebrows suggestively, causing her to splutter and snort.

'Sorry,' she grinned, amused at his expression, 'that sounded like a euphemism for something more personal than helping with my saddlery.'

'Hey, look, either way – I'm happy to help. I'm here for you whatever girths you want tightened. Or loosened. Or removed altogether.'

Grace narrowed her eyes and regarded him closely. She hoped he was telling her what she wanted to hear, but his vagueness made it hard to guess. *Oh, heck,* she berated herself for overthinking, *life's too short for this. It's time to put the foot in the stirrup and get on this horse.*

She smiled at him. 'Do you know, it's been two years since anyone kissed me?'

'Two years?' Matthew's lips twisted to the side as he thought about that surprising fact and where he could go with it. Was it an invitation? He wasn't sure. 'I could probably fix that for you if you wanted.'

'I think it needs fixing.' Grace tilted her head so she could look into his eyes before dropping her gaze to his lips.

'I don't want to do something that will cause you to hit me,' he whispered as his head lowered slightly towards hers. 'I mean, you do want me to kiss you, don't you?'

Grace nodded in the final moment before their lips touched. The world and all it contained spun away from them as they lost - and found - each other in that kiss.

An hour later, they disembarked at Palomar, holding hands and joking about taking too long to change the nature of their relationship.

'You scared me,' Matthew admitted as they took a taxi back to the *Sunsol Isla Caribe* resort in the northern part of the island.

'I'm not scary,' she scoffed.

'You are small and feisty and very intimidating.'

'You're a fool,' she chuckled at his comic display of fear.

'Is that why it took you this long to admit you wanted me to kiss you? You think I'm a bit of a clown?'

'Well, of course, I think you're a clown,' she teased, 'but that's not why I held back. It didn't seem right to have to tell you that I wanted to be kissed.'

'I'm not in the habit of doing the lip-to-lip with people unless I know that's what they want. If you don't tell me, how can I know whether or not it should happen? By using my famous male psychic abilities?' He snorted lightly at his lack of intuition when it came to understanding women. 'I'm the sort who needs to wait until I have it spelled out in large letters that permission is granted.'

'That's one of the reasons I like you so much.' She rested a couple of fingers on his cheek, and he leaned into them. 'You aren't pushy. You're patient, and you have manners.'

He gave her a droll look. 'Maybe we should end this today while I'm ahead. I'm worried if I give you enough time, I'll ruin that good impression.'

Grace chuckled. 'I think I know you a little by now. We've flown across the world and ridden like lunatics down a mountain together. That counts for something.'

'So, you're willing to take a gamble on me?'

'For a few days, at least.'

'That should get us through the rest of our time here and the flight home.' She looked down at his hand covering hers, their fingers entwined. His life seemed so much larger than hers. Would he be content with a girlfriend from Gatton when he mixed with the rich and famous? Her voice grew small as she added, 'I don't know what happens then.'

'We could go shopping for an eventer together. If you want to, that is. Or I could help you with your rescue horses. If you think you can stand being around me for much longer, we could see what Lane has lined up. We seem to have done OK with this adventure - maybe we should saddle up for another one.'

'I'm down for that,' she smiled. She saw a new life ahead and felt excited about the changes. 'For all of it – the eventer, the help at home, and another go at some craziness like this.'

'Good. And I'm going to need a hand in Caracas helping Darby transition to a new employer without upsetting his riders. Plus, Deo will want you to see how he's going once he starts riding there.'

'He'll be competing for his country in no time.'

Thinking of how their young friend enjoyed his first show jumping lesson with Ernie, Matthew had to agree. 'I can't wait to see his face when he meets Lane tomorrow.'

'He'll be glad he didn't shoot us that first night.'

He gave her hand a light squeeze. 'I'm glad of that, too.'

***

Dibby and Rev

The three geldings ate their hay muzzle-to-muzzle. Since arriving at Ernie's stables, Dibby, Rev, and Dusty shared a yard and enjoyed watching the activity. Ernie and his riders fussed over them, and though they felt far from home, they found the Australian accents comforting.

'There they are,' said Ernie as he led a small group from the house.

Used to his voice, the palominos merely flicked an ear to acknowledge his presence. They knew and trusted him and didn't stop eating when he approached.

'I can't believe it. Dibby! Rev!' Mel's voice shook as she saw her two horses.

At the sound of her voice, both geldings froze mid-chew before turning their heads, their ears pricked. Their nostrils quivered in excitement when they saw Mel approaching, and they whinnied as they swung to face her. Leaning over the top rail of the fence, they called loudly to her.

Matthew, Grace, Lane, Ernie, and Carla, Mel's cousin, stood back as she ran to her horses. The two palomino heads stretched over the fence to greet her, and when she reached them, they pressed their faces to her, breathing her in. Mel cried as she hugged them, overwhelmed with joy at being able to hold them again. The geldings made soft *whuffling* noises against her shirt, leaving no doubt that their emotions were every bit as strong as hers.

Lane elbowed Matthew and waggled his eyebrows at him. *You rode them. Did they greet you like that?*

'I can't say that they were that happy to see me.' Matthew smiled as Dibby and Rev continued to push their noses against Mel.

She probably smells better than you.

Matthew laughed, causing Grace to look at him with a curious pinch between her eyes.

'Lane is saying nice things about me,' lied Matthew.

Lane shook his head at her.

'Clearly not,' replied Grace dryly.

'What happens now?' asked Ernie. 'Will they go home to Australia?

What about the pony?'

'We're sorting it,' said Matthew. 'We'll pay to have Dibby and Rev sent home for Mel unless she wants to move to here, of course.'

'Not as crazy as you might think.' Carla smiled at her cousin, who was burying her face into Dibby's neck. 'She has some bad memories at home, and this is a good safe distance from her ex.'

'We can look into that for her,' said Matthew. 'On the one hand, the country has a bit of a bad rep; on the other, we've met a lot of people who have a good life here, and it is beautiful.'

'What about the pony?' Ernie looked to Matthew.

'He's going to Deo. Two previous owners in Australia recognized him from the tv footage and gave us his history - a great pony that ended up with REE. They are more than happy to think of him with Deo and have offered to sponsor his upkeep.'

Lane frowned as he thought of the horses that had nearly ended their lives smuggling drugs out of Menningala. So much for Brian saying that no one cared for them. Here were three already guaranteed safe futures, and he knew other people had identified their horses from the televised rescue.

Will you take some for the riding center once that's sorted?

'There's no way I'll let the riding center shut down,' declared Matthew. 'They do amazing work, and Darby has been brilliant. We're hoping to transition from REE ownership to mine without too much disturbance to the riders. He's organized safe lodging for all of the horses until they can enter the program. When they picked the sort of horses that were quiet enough to travel and accept the handling at Menningala, they also selected horses that are ideal for the riding center.'

'Some of the horses will be going home,' said Grace. 'Kat and Kaz have started a fund to help send them back. There are a few people who are so disturbed by what happened to their horses when they thought they were giving them a good retirement with REE that they are desperate to get them home. Horse people in the other countries where REE had horses are working to identify them and make sure they are all safe.'

'What about all the ones still in Australia?' Matthew asked her. 'REE had thousands of them.'

'Some of the more reputable horse rescues are offering permanent homes for as many as possible. I'm taking in a few dozen. Kat and Kaz have leased some extra land and are taking on thirty that are young and fit enough to do well out on grass. Jody at Horsley Horse Rescues can take on twenty. There's a whole network of us trying to save them.'

'You won't be able to rescue them all.' Ernie's voice overflowed with sadness as he watched Mel's reunion with her horses and thought of all the horses that would never find someone to care for them.

'I know,' agreed Grace, 'but it doesn't stop us from trying.'

***

Remembered Forever.

Lane ran a campaign to find the history of the one hundred and twenty-seven horses that came down the mountain. Together, they were merely a number and easily forgotten. Individually, they had stories and people who loved them. Sixty returned home after Australian horse people raised the funds to cover transport costs. The remaining horses found good homes in Venezuela.

The 127

Dibby - QH gelding, loved by his owner
Rev - QH gelding, loved by his owner
Dusty - pony, helped many learn to ride
Salty - 15.3 Cremello gelding, gentle
Melly - Salty's dam, Cremello mare, pretty
Quit - 14, 15.2 QH mare. Brave.
Lucky and Ophelia – bay and cremello. Friends.
Digga - liked digging at the beach.
Romulus - big gelding. Sweet nature.
Amelie - grey QH mare. Good mover.
Randy - 15hh bay mare. Standardbred. Sweet and kind.
Valentine - black. Beautiful.
Derringer - a little pistol of a horse.
Dan, Wilbur, and Sprinkles – always together.
Tuscan – small burnt-buckskin, three socks & star.
Rifle - palomino. Loved.
Denver -16 hh Paint gelding. A look-at-me horse.
Cyrus - enjoyed show jumping
Shorty - 14.2 chestnut QH. Loved children.
Luca - Chestnut TB mare.
Takota - Chestnut. Friendly.
Xena's Silver Lining - Grey mare.
Toby - TB. Gentle giant
Ichabod - Black QH gelding.
Drum - Andalusian gelding. Great nature.
Inez - grey QH gelding
Lass -16h sorrel QH mare. Great heart.
Cherrystone - Bay TB. Dream horse.

Lightning - QH X Paint. Mischievous and gentle.
Chico - Bay roan pinto. Tough and smart.
Mojo – palomino QH. Kind.
Leelu and Kahlua - Cremello QH and her buckskin Paint daughter.
Prukamzan - Arabian. Feisty and brave.
Theodora - A filly known as Teddie.
Cabriolo - 18hh dark bay. Sporting.
Preacher Man - TWH stallion. Gentle and brave.
Renaldo - best friend.
Justice and Bramble - black. Big horses. Friends.
Federico - grey PRE.
Riot - QH gelding. Kind.
Bux - chestnut Arabian gelding. Loyal.
Sway Big Lover - wrecks rugs and buckets.
Chipper - QH 15.2H. Chestnut. Personality plus.
Star - she shines.
Roanin - buckskin gelding. Surefooted and loyal.
Banjo - huge and kind.
Echo - Appaloosa gelding. Loves children.
Sid - blue roan varnish Appaloosa gelding.
Mush-Mush - kind and loving.
Gallant Little Bandit - black. Brave.
Tanna - smart and brave.
Ladybug - Clydesdale mare.
Cooper - chestnut gelding. Loves children.
Jack and Almira - friends.
Phenomenal – he was friends with Gunther, the dog.
Denver - QH paint. Sweet and brave.
Moon Dance - grey Anglo mare. Sweet.
Rhaya - mare. Friesian X Arabian X Paint. Kind.
Chance - brave and intelligent.
Iolanthe - bay Welsh. Good jumper.
Tmaya - Morab mare. Smart.
Ryver - gentle and kind.
Dan - 16.2hh, Black TB. Showjumper.
Wilbur - 15hh Chestnut Stock horse x QH. Smart.
Sprinkles - Palouse. Quiet. Loves children.
Kick Back Jack - 15.2 QH. Likes young riders.
Eclipse, Captain Jack, Churro, 4WD Willie, River, and Rhinestone
Alpha - 16.2 TB gelding. Brown. Showjumper.
Hector -brown TB gelding. Show horse.
Frieda - Clydesdale x QH. Great nature.

Rare Diamond - 15.3 bay QH. Courageous.
Mike and Ike - Clydesdales. Always together.
Spin - chestnut. Likes children.
Abby - brown Trakehner. Eventer.
Toffee - buckskin Gypsy Cob mare.
Billy the Kid - Palomino Gypsy Cob.
Phoenix - 16hh Brown QH. Gentle and playful.
Selena - black pinto. Barrel racer.
Mystic - Palomino. Smart. Enjoys attention.
Rio - Paint. Smart.
Baronov - Bay Arabian. Good trail horse.
Trooper - Medicine hat. Fast learner.
Punch – a showjumper
Badden - Black. 17.3hh. Mischievous.
Zavidovici - gentle giant. Cavalry horse.
Caesar - brown Saddlebred gelding.
Shiloh - QH X. Sweet nature.
Just Racey - champion show horse.
Riverdance - Leopard Appaloosa. Smart.
Peppseelon and Justalon - bay and chestnut. Friends.
Pippin - Fjord gelding. Playful
Preacher - QH buckskin. Sweet and smart.
Bossman - 14.2 QH. Willing child's horse.
Arloh and Angel – friends.
Maximus - bay with a spanner blaze
Blue, Teewee, Casey, and Aussie – always together.
Eemaiaj - mare. Kind and intelligent.
Hardy, Sassy, and Zero - three friends.

Ten more horses were never identified, but someone, somewhere, once cared about them, and Lane, his friends, and a network of horse rescues made sure they lived out their days with respect.

A message from Lane.

There are times when you can't change the big picture, but you can make a difference to a part of it. Always choose to improve the piece that you can change, no matter how small. I can't save humanity, I can't stop greed, and I can't make life better for all the horses, but together we changed the world for these one hundred and twenty-seven horses. Never forget that every person and every horse has a story worth telling – including you.

Lane Dimity in a social media post. Over twenty million shares.

THE END.

ABOUT THE AUTHOR

Leanne Owens has spent her life around horses – riding, training, breeding, competing, judging, and writing about them. She has won dozens of national titles with her horses, has done freelance writing for horse magazines for decades, and also wrote and reported for Horse Talk TV. Leanne is an English teacher with a Master's in Education who loves the art of story telling and hopes her readers will enjoy the range of novels she produces, most of which are horse themed. She and her husband live on their 100 acre farm in Queensland's picturesque Lockyer Valley.